BLESSED
GENNARO MARIA
SARNELLI

THE CONSCIENCE OF A NATION

His Life and Letters

Readings in Redemptorist Spirituality, English Edition: Vol. 6

Gennaro Maria Sarnelli by Lomuscio G. A.,
Sketch of portrait of the tapestry for the beatification.
Ciorani, Missionari Redentoristi
(*photo by Giorgio Vasari*)

BLESSED GENNARO MARIA SARNELLI

THE CONSCIENCE OF A NATION

His Life and Letters
Edited and Translated by

J. ROBERT FENILI, CSsR

Liguori

Imprimi Potest:
Stephen T. Rehrauer, CSsR, Provincial
Denver Province, the Redemptorists

Published by Liguori Publications
Liguori, Missouri 63057

To order, visit Liguori.org or call 800-325-9521.

Library of Congress Cataloging-in-Publication Data

Names: Sarnelli, Gennaro Maria, 1702-1744. | Fenili, J. Robert, editor.
Title: Blessed Gennaro Maria Sarnelli : the conscience of a nation : his life
and letters / edited and translated by J. Robert Fenili, CSsR.
Description: First Edition. | Liguori : Liguori Publications, 2015. | Series:
Readings in Redemptorist spirituality, English edition ; Vol. 6 | Includes
bibliographical references.
Identifiers: LCCN 2015038785 | ISBN 9780764825484
Subjects: LCSH: Sarnelli, Gennaro Maria, 1702-1744. | Redemptorists--History.
Classification: LCC BX4700.S33 A25 2015 | DDC 271/.6402--dc23
LC record available at http://lccn.loc.gov/2015038785

p ISBN 9780764825484
e ISBN 9780764871221

Cover art of Blessed Gennaro by Lomuscio, G. A., Gennaro Maria Sarnelli, Sketch of portrait for beatification tapestry. Ciorani, Missionari Redentoristi (photo by Giorgio Vasari).

Liguori Publications, a nonprofit corporation, is an apostolate of the Redemptorists. To learn more about the Redemptorists, visit Redemptorists.com.

Printed in the United States of America
19 18 17 16 15 / 5 4 3 2 1
First Edition

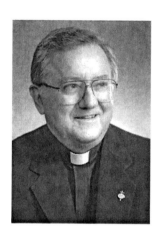

*This book is dedicated to the memory of
the man who initiated its publication:*

Rev. Raymond Corriveau, CSsR, 1936–2010,
*Priest, Scholar, Leader, Spiritual Guide,
and Redemptorist Confrere*

CONTENTS

Introduction ix

Acknowledgments xiii

Abbreviations and Citations.................................... xv

Original Portrait of Gennaro Maria Sarnelli xviii

Biographical Chronology of Gennaro Maria Sarnelli xix

Part One: Life and Spirit

Chapter One: A Summary of the Life of the Servant of God,
Gennaro Maria Sarnelli of the Congregation of the Most
Holy Redeemer *(St. Alphonsus Maria de Liguori, CSsR)* 1

Chapter Two: The Moral Work of Gennaro Sarnelli:
An Outsider Among Outsiders
(Bishop Noel Londoño Buitrago, CSsR) 21

Chapter Three: Blessed Gennaro Maria Sarnelli,
Redemptorist Missionary, Apostle of Naples
(Rev. Fabriciano Ferrero, CSsR)............................. 45

Chapter Four: Sarnelli and the Redemptorists
(Rev. Domenico Capone, CSsR).............................. 95

Part Two: Writings

Chapter Five: Letters of Gennaro Maria Sarnelli 135

Chapter Six: Affections and Prayers to the Most Holy Trinity 257

Chapter Seven: Meditations on the Holy Eucharist 347

Chapter Eight: Union With God 387

Chapter Nine: Lessons on Prayer 397

Chapter Ten: Some Aspects of Priestly Ministry 427

Bibliography of Works of Gennaro Maria Sarnelli 445

INTRODUCTION

Blessed Gennaro Maria Sarnelli (1702–1743) was an eighteenth-century priest in the kingdom of Naples who combined sanctity with an activist role in the social and political life of his time. He was a force in the founding of Congregation of the Most Holy Redeemer (Redemptorists), with its purpose of bringing the Gospel message to the poor of the countryside who were virtually abandoned of any spiritual care. At the same time, he was a tireless advocate to find solutions for the social evils of prostitution in the great port city of Naples, probably the most populous city in Europe at the time. His concern with this problem was not solely because of its sinfulness but largely because of the huge number of poor women and children forced into the trade by pimps and madams. He campaigned tirelessly for establishing safe alternatives for those who were at risk. By means of his extensive writings in the areas of spirituality, spiritual direction and social and political practice, *he acted as a moral conscience to hundreds of thousands of his contemporaries.*

This translation was initiated by Father Raymond Corriveau, CSsR, when he was the chair of the North American Redemptorist Spirituality Commission in 2008. He assisted in locating editions of Sarnelli's texts and in editing the first three chapters of this book before his untimely death in 2010. Since his loss also suspended the work of the Commission, it was only in 2012 when a new Commission was established by the North American Conference of the Redemptorist Congregation that I was again able to take up the work of translating and editing.

This work is patterned after a book published in Colombia by a fellow Redemptorist, Rev. (now Bishop) Noel Londoño, CSsR, *La vida y la espiritualidad del beato Jenaro Sarnelli, Espiritualidad Redentorista,* vol. 14, Bogotá: Ediciones Scala, 2007. While most of the chapters of this present text are from the same sources as those used by

Bishop Londoño, the chapter by Father Fabriciano Ferrero, CSsR, has been substituted for one in the bishop's work. All of the translations of material in the present text have been made directly from the original language of the letter, book, or article.

The first part of this work presents four essays on the life, spirituality, and significance of Blessed Gennaro Maria Sarnelli. Chapter One contains the first biography of Sarnelli, written by his dear friend and confrere, St. Alphonsus Liguori. Later biographies are generally based on the information this contemporary account contains. As was the custom in writing about the lives of holy people at the time, it concentrates heavily on his virtues and piety. The second chapter, by Father Fabriciano Ferrero, contains sections of his booklet published as one of the projects for the 1996 celebration of Sarnelli's beatification. It synthesizes Sarnelli's spirituality and provides contemporary insights into many of its aspects. The third chapter, by Bishop Londoño, presents an extensive treatment of the social and political work of Gennaro Maria. The fourth chapter discusses the relationship of Sarnelli to the Redemptorist Congregation, a matter which formed a serious issue in the process of his beatification.

The second part of our book contains writings of Gennaro Maria Sarnelli himself. Chapter Five consists of a selection of forty-eight of his letters that provides us with a view into his heart and mind. The first group of letters deals with the founding of the Congregation and Sarnelli's role in it. Next, we witness his spiritual direction in relationship to the Nuns of the Order of the Most Holy Redeemer (Redemptoristines); in these, he often unburdens his own interior suffering. Then appear two letters to his confreres among the Redemptorists. The remainder deals with his work as a writer, especially treating his approach to the issues of prostitution.

The sixth chapter contains the last work Sarnelli composed shortly before his death. It is probably the best expression of his unique spirituality, which centers on the Holy Trinity.

The last four chapters are selections from other works he wrote that exhibit further elements of his spiritual life: (seven) the Eucharist, (eight) the spiritual journey, (nine) prayer, and (ten) the ministry of preaching.

It is my hope that this first English translation of material from and about Blessed Gennaro Sarnelli will introduce more Redemptorists and others who seek to be inspired by the example and advice of the saints to a deeper appreciation of this important man. In his time, he was one of the most influential voices of his day for both Church and state. He was a groundbreaker in establishing the ministry of the Redemptorists in the publication of books as a tool of Christian and civil morality. May the hope be fulfilled that Blessed Gennaro Maria proclaimed when asked on his deathbed about his endless efforts of writing and publishing: "I wish to preach right up to Judgment Day."

Blessed Gennaro Maria Sarnelli, pray for us!

J. Robert Fenili, CSsR
Feast of Blessed Gennaro Maria Sarnelli,
June 27, 2015

ACKNOWLEDGMENTS

My first and foremost thanks go to Father Raymond Corriveau, CSsR, without whom this book would not exist. In addition to his initiative in seeing to the presentation of an English work on the life of Blessed Gennaro Maria Sarnelli, he diligently worked with me in finding a suitable edition of Sarnelli's Italian texts, especially in the collection maintained by the Edmonton-Toronto Province of the Redemptorists located at St. Patrick's Church in Toronto, Ontario, Canada. He also edited the text of the opening chapters of the book.

Other Redemptorists who helped locate materials were Father Carl Hoegerl, CSsR, of the Baltimore Province, who provided me with items in his province's archives. Father Gilbert Enderle, CSsR, a member of the Redemptorist Historical Institute in Rome, also generously researched and provided materials that were available only in the Institute and the General Historical Archives of the Redemptorist Congregation at Collegio Sant'Alfonso in Rome. One of the most competent historians of the early days of the Redemptorists, Father Giuseppe Orlandi, CSsR (recently deceased), answered several questions regarding the context and idioms of the period that were important in properly translating certain texts. Rev. Juventus Andrade, CSsR, Director of the Congregation's Commission on Spirituality, is also to be remembered for his gracious assistance in obtaining materials.

I also thank the North American Commission on Redemptorist Spirituality and its liaison, Rev. Richard Boever, CSsR, for agreeing to continue to sponsor the project and to Rev. John Kingsbury, the coordinator of the North American Conference of the Redemptorists to see to its publication through Liguori Publications. Liguori staff members Mark Bernard, Bill Townsend, and John Krus were considerate and attentive in the detailed tasks of preparing the printed edition.

Of course, I cannot overlook the men who provided earlier translations of two articles that were adapted for use in this book: Father Ruskin Piedra, CSsR, and Norman Simmons.

In thanking these people, I alone remain responsible for any errors or limitations that appear in this work; may they not prove misleading in making our Blessed Sarnelli better appreciated in the English-speaking world.

JRF, CSsR

ABBREVIATIONS
AND CITATIONS

Two decisions about this translation are worth mentioning in order for the reader to better understand some peculiarities of the text.

The first is in the matter of the English version of Scripture citations. Unless otherwise indicated, all these English texts are taken from the *New Revised Standard Version (NRSV)* of the Bible. Obviously, Sarnelli used one of the versions of the Latin Vulgate that was approved in his era. The accepted English translation of the Vulgate in our age was the *Douay-Rheims (DR)* version. Because of the changes in translation accepted into modern English versions based on the original Hebrew and Greek texts, *DR* many times differs greatly from modern-day versions. The decision to use the *NRSV* was made to aid readers who want to find the context of the text cited. In several passages where the *DR* differs so greatly from the *NRSV* that Sarnelli's comments would not make sense, the *DR* is used; this is indicated by the insertion of the abbreviation *"DR"* after the text. Also, in the case of the Psalms, the numbering of psalms and verses differs between the *DR* and the *NRSV;* where this is the case, the difference of numbering is mentioned in the footnote.

Second, there are two types of footnotes: those that are part of the original work and those that are inserted by the translator for this English version. These are differentiated by using regular type for notes that are in the original text while employing italic typeface for footnotes inserted by the translator. The same difference is found in the body of the text when parentheses or brackets appear.

Aggiunta   G. M. Sarnelli, *Aggiunta delle maniere particolari da racchiudere, e rattener perpetuamente a freno le meretrici, da ricapitare le ravvedute, da conservar le fanciulle pericolanti, e manetener sempre purgata la repubblica dalle dissolutezze carnali. Colle risposte alle opposizioni.* Naples, 1739.

AGHR   Archivium Generale Historicum Redemptoristarum, Rome.

Alphonsus,   Alfonso de Liguori, *Opera Omnia Italiane: Testo completo e*
Opera Omnia   *concordanze delle opere in lingua italiana e delle lettere a cura della Provincia napoletana della Congregazione del SS.mo Redentore.* Direzione: P. Salvatore Brugnano, CSsR, edizione elettronica: Biblioteca Digitale IntraText, I edizione, maggio 2003. (intratext.com/TXT/ITASA0000.)

Analecta   Analecta CSsR, Rome, Vol. 1–present.

Anima illumiata   G. M. Sarnelli, *L'anima illuminata, nella considerazione de'beneficii di Dio, generali, e particolar, nell'ordine della natura, e della grazia. Con varii tratti illuminativi, utilissimi, ed acconci ad ogni stato di anime, per accendersi nell'amore del sommo Benefattore.* Naples, 1740.

APGR   Archivio della Postulazione Generale dei Redentoristi, Rome.

Autobiografia   Maria Crostarosa, *Autobiografia*, ed. by Sabatino Majorano and A. Simeoni, Materdomini (AV): Valsele Tipografica, 1998.

Bibliografie   Maurice de Muelemeester, CSsR, *Bibliografie générale des écrivains rédemptoristes*, 2 Vol., Louvain: Imprimerie S. Alphonse, 1935.

Carteggio   Giuseppe Orlandi, CSsR, *Carteggio di S. Alfonso Maria de Liguori,* Vol. I: 1724–1743, Rome: Edizioni di Storia e Letteratura, 2004.

Compendio   Alfonso de Liguori, "Compendio della vita del Servo di Dio D. Gennaro Maria Sarnelli, Sacerdote Missionario della Congregazione del SS. Redentore e della Congregazione delle Apostoliche Missioni eretta nell'Arcivescovato di Napoli." Published in G. M. Sarnelli, *Il mondo santificato,* Naples 1753, 326–352.

Divozioni   G. M. Sarnelli, *Divozioni pratiche per onorare la SS. Trinità e Maria SS. Operetta nuova, impressa ad istanza d'un'idegno secolare.* Naples, 1736.

ESAed   Archivium Generale Historicum Redemptoristarum, Rome: Editiones Epistolarum S. Alfonsi.

FS   Archivium enerale Historicum Redemptoristarum, Rome: Fondo Sarnelli (Copies of the letters of Gennaro Maria Sarnelli).

Il mondo santificato	G. M. Sarnelli, Il *mondo santificato dove si tratta della meditazione e della preghiera. Opera istruttiva ed illuminativa utilissima ai secolari, ecclesiastici, e religiosi, per facilitare a ciascuno stato di anime l'esercizio della vita divota, e per introdurre nella Chiesa Comunitá e famiglie l'uso dell'orazione in commune.* Naples, 1738.
Il quatro Maggio	G. M. Sarnelli, Il *quatro maggio 1738, Napoli, a futura memoria dei posteri e per esempio di ogni cattolica nazione*, Napoli 1738
Lettere	(Unless another author is named) Gennaro M. Sarnelli, Letters 1–5, *The History of the Congregation of the Most Holy Redeemer,* Vol. I/ii, ed. by Francisco Chiovaro and J. Robert Fenili, translated into English by J. Robert Fenili, Liguori: Liguori Publications, 2010, "Appendix 1: Selected Documents, A. The Protagonists of Scala," 174–191. Footnotes to letters 1–10, *Carteggio.* Letters 11 to 40, Lettere spirituali di Ven. Gennaro M. Sarnelli, Naples: 1851. Letters 41 to 48, *Lettere spirituali del Venerabile Servo di Dio P. Gennaro Mᵃ Sarnelli, Opera Omnia,* Naples: Tipografica e Libreria di A. E. S. Festa, 1888, Vol. 14.
Lettere, Falcoia	Tommaso Falcoia, *Lettere ad. Alfonso de Liguori, Ripa, Sportelli, Crostarosa,* edited by Oreste Gregorio, Rome: 1963.
Origines	Maurice de Muelemeester, CSsR, *Origines de la Congrégation du Très Saint-Rédempteur: Etudes et Documents,* 2 Vol., Louvain: Imprimerie S. Alphonse, 1953, 1957.
Positio super Virtutibus	Sacrum Rituum Congregatio: *Neapolitana Beatificationis et canonizationis Servi Dei Ianuarii Mariae Sarnelli, sacerdos e Congregatione SS.mi Redemptoris: Positio super Virtutibus (1889); Nova Positio super Virtutibus (1906).*
Ragioni legali	G. M. Sarnelli, *Ragioni legali, cattoliche, e politiche in difesa delle repubbliche rovinate dall'insolentito meretricio.* Naples, 1736.
Ristretto della Ragioni	G. M. Sarnelli, *Ristretto delle ragioni cattoliche elegali e politiche in difesa delle repubbliche rovinate dall'insolentito meretricio...,* Napoli 1739.
Spicilegium	*Spicilegium Historicum Congregationis SS.mi Redemptoris.*
Tannoia	Antonio M. Tannoia, *Della Vita ed Istituto del Ven. Servo di Dio Alfonso Maria Liguori, Vescovo di S. Agata de'Goti e Fondatore della Congregazione de' Preti Missionari del SS. Redentore,* Naples, 1798– 1802, 3 Vol.
Tellería	Raymondo Tellería, *San Alfonso Maria de Ligorio, fundador, obispo y doctor,* Madrid, 1950–1951, 2 Vol.

Original portrait of Sarnelli

Anonymous, July 1, 1744, *Gennaro Maria Sarnelli*.
Portrait based on corpse. Ciorani, Missionari Redentoristi
(*photo by Giorgio Vasari*).

Most portraits of the early Redemptorists were made when they were on their deathbeds or had just died.
As religious who were to avoid vanities, they did not have portraits made during their lifetime. St. Alphonsus,
though, wanted a visual memory of the confreres kept for posterity and so he adopted this practice at their deaths.

CHRONOLOGY OF THE LIFE OF BLESSED GENNARO SARNELLI

1702: September 12, Naples: birth of Gennaro Maria Sarnelli. September 14, Church of St. Anna de Palazzo, Naples: baptism.

1716: Sought admittance to Society of Jesus, but he was too young.

1722: Completed degrees in canon and civil law.

1728: September: Ended law practice; entered seminary.

1729: June 4: Moved into residence of Holy Family (Chinese College).

1730: June 5 to May 28, 1731: Novitiate with Congregation of the Apostolic Missions.

1731: December 22: Ordination to the diaconate.

1732: June 8: Ordination to the priesthood.

1733: June: Joined Alphonsus Liguori at Scala.

1734: January 15: admitted to Congregation of the Most Holy Savior (Redemptorists).

1736: Returned to Naples for medical care because of sickness.

1741–1744: Planned and participated with Alphonsus in the mission to the villages, a vast preaching program throughout the area of Naples.

1744: April: became too sick to continue preaching, returned to Naples. June 30, Naples: died at age 41 years, 9 months, and 18 days.

1861: Cause for canonization introduced.

1906: December 2: Declared "Venerable" by Pope St. Pius X.

1996: May 12: Beatified by St. John Paul II. June 27: Annual Optional Memorial of Blessed Gennaro Sarnelli, CSsR

CHAPTER ONE

A Summary of the Life of the Servant of God

GENNARO MARIA SARNELLI

of the Congregation of the Most Holy Redeemer

By Alphonsus Maria de Liguori, CSsR [1]

HIS BIRTH, INFANCY, AND YOUTH

[Trans. note: Section headings were not in the original.] Father Don Gennaro Maria Sarnelli was born in Naples on September 12, 1702. His parents were Signor Don Angelo Sarnelli, the Baron of the Land of Ciorani, and Lady Donna Caterina Scoppa. They had eight children, six boys and two girls; of these, Don Gennaro Maria was the fourth son. The fifth son was Signor Don Andrea, a secular priest who is still alive and who, with great edification and public service, used his income to establish on his estate of the aforementioned Ciorani, a house of missionary priests who go about the diocese of Salerno and other areas helping the impoverished people of the Campagna *[Trans. note: That is, the group that was to become the Congregation of the Most Holy Redeemer (Redemptorists).]*

From his earliest days, Gennaro Maria tended toward piety and the Christian virtues to such an extent that even then his modesty was so outstanding that he kept his eyes cast down even in the presence of his sisters and his own mother as well. His obedience and reverence toward his parents was so thorough that if it happened they became annoyed at him, he immediately sought their pardon, kissing their hand and at times even kneeling to calm them. Likewise, his mortifications were numerous from his very childhood, since even then he would deprive himself of fresh fruit. If he was at his home, which faced [the Church of] St. Francis Xavier, when some great festivities were being held he would

---

[1] S. Alfonso Maria de Liguori, Compendio. Alphonsus wrote this work shortly after Sarnelli's death to be published for the Congregation of the Apostolic Missions; but it was not published until 1752, in the fourth edition of Sarnelli's *Il Mondo santificato*.

leave the house in order to avoid gaping at the carriages and cavalcades and attending the receptions. So from all this, we can easily deduce that, right from his youth and throughout his entire life, as we shall narrate, he preserved his baptismal innocence.

At the age of fourteen, he ardently begged his father to allow him to leave secular life and to join the Company of Jesus in order to give himself entirely to God, but he was not permitted to do so because he was not yet old enough for this type of decision. But this did not interfere with his seeking to be more devout, more solitary, and more fervent in his prayers. He would not spend his time with schoolmates of his own age and interests, but because he loved solitude he would hurry from his classes to enter a church and there pass a great deal of time before the Blessed Sacrament, begging the Lord to reveal to him what status he wanted him to choose. Then he would go home, where he lived such an exemplary life with his whole family that there was no evidence he bore any grudges.

FROM LAW CAREER TO CHURCH VOCATION

At his father's insistence, he entered the law profession, and he advanced even as a young man, becoming the counsel for the [*Agency for the*] Provisioning of Salt as well as for His Lordship, the Duke of Cirifalco. But even amid all these occupations, he did not omit his attendance at Mass, visits to the Blessed Sacrament, or his dedication to mental prayer, which he so loved that when he was not busy elsewhere he would go to spend long periods of time in the Church of St. Francis Xavier. This practice was such that when someone came looking for him and he was not at home, the servants, aware of his customary behavior, [*would say*], "Go over to St. Francis Xavier; you will find him there." When he went to relax on his father's estate, he would spend the day in the parish church, and there he would pass a long time in solitary prayer.

Also at this time, several days a week, he would go to care for the sick at the Hospital of the Incurables. He said that it was there that he found himself surrounded by all of God's lights, to the point that, as he said, the hospital served as a continuous meditation and he left there completely at peace with himself and filled with God. Here it was that he finally was called by the Lord to give up the secular world. In effect, it was then that, with his spiritual director's advice, he decided to give up the practice of law and to become a priest so he could dedicate himself totally to God's service. Thus he put on clerical attire, took himself completely away from secular matters, and donated whatever money he had in reserve as alms to the poor along with all his secular clothing. He dedicated his whole life to God, spending his days in prayer and in the studies necessary to become a priest, as well as in charitable works for the good of his neighbor.

Then, to live a quieter life further from secular disturbances, he retired to the Residence of the Venerable Congregation of the Holy Family in Naples, called the Chinese Residence, where some pious priests lived an exemplary life to the great edification of the whole city. While he stayed there, he spent his time only in prayer or study or in teaching catechism in the neighborhood, as well as frequenting several times a week the Hospital where he would spend as long as six hours at a time consoling, attending to and instructing the impoverished sick there.

During this period, he joined the Venerable Congregation of the Apostolic Missions established in the Archdiocese of Naples to participate in the Holy Missions. Later, when he was ordained, he conducted these with great inspiration and public success, as we shall see.

ENTERING THE REDEMPTORIST CONGREGATION

After some years, he heard of the Congregation of the Most Holy Redeemer, founded a few years earlier, in the city of Scala in 1732 under the direction of Monsignor Falcoia, the Bishop of Castellammare. Learning that the purpose of this Congregation was to devote itself to the care of the abandoned people of the Campagna by means of missions and other spiritual exercises, and that in this Institute life was lived with strict regular observance obligated by the simple vows of poverty, obedience, and chastity together with a vow of perseverance, out of a desire for greater perfection he decided to dedicate and to consecrate himself exclusively to God. After consulting Father Manulio, the Jesuit who died a few years ago with a reputation of great sanctity, Gennaro Maria joined this above-mentioned Congregation and moved from Naples to Scala without, however, resigning from the above-mentioned Congregation of the Apostolic Mission. He continued to be a member and to assist in all of its zealous works. He lived there for a few years, giving to all an excellent example in the practice of the virtues, especially by his mortification, charity to his neighbor and obedience. (His response to the bell [*for community activities*] was such that if he was writing, he would immediately rise from the table even leaving a word unfinished.)

APOSTOLATE IN NAPLES

Then due to his failing health, since the climate did not agree with him and also because he had to care for the extraordinary work he was directing, especially that of removing the prostitutes from the center of the City of Naples, a work in which he had long been involved and which demanded his continual attention, it was necessary for his superiors to give him permission to return to Naples, where he later died. However, even though he lived in Naples, he did not hesitate every so often to come help his confreres in the Congregation with their missions.

In Naples, in addition to his work among the prostitutes, he involved himself in helping people so zealously that His Eminence, Cardinal Spinelli, currently Archbishop of Naples, insisted that Don Gennaro Maria be one of the confreres to accompany Father Don Alphonsus de Liguori, the Rector Major of the above-mentioned Congregation, in a missionary campaign in the environs of the city that the Cardinal had appointed [*Alphonsus to head.*] For this reason, the Cardinal had assigned them a permanent lodging in the vicinity of the village of S. Jorio, in the area called St. Agnello, so that they could move around the other villages near Naples giving missions at the expense of the Eminent Archbishop. When Father Don Alphonsus had to leave the Diocese of Naples because of the business of his Congregation, the Lord Cardinal left the task of directing all the missions in the villages to Father Don Gennaro Maria. He continued the work, at first, with the help of Signor Don Matteo Testa, an excellent missionary, as is well known, and who is today a most worthy Canon of the Archbishopric of Naples. Don Gennaro Maria continued to carry out these missions to the immense profit of the people right up to his death that occurred in Naples a few years later [*His death caused*] great sorrow not only for the very zealous Pastor but for the whole city, who wept over the death of such a great worker in the Vineyard of the Lord. It was said, as is still repeated, that by himself he was worth more than ten missionaries.

SARNELLI'S LOVE OF PRAYER

Before moving on to tell of his remarkable death, it is valuable to convey in a few words some of the rather special aspects of his virtues that are worth noting. He was such a lover of prayer that even as he lived a secular life and was employed in the law profession, whenever he found himself free of business, he would leave his home and go to pray in some church, as we said above. But once he took up the ecclesiastical career, he dedicated himself wholly to that holy practice. During the day, he especially frequented the Church of the Cross near the plaza, where he sat with closed door in a little room behind the sacristy, remaining in prayer from after the midday meal until early evening. He did this almost every day before he moved into the Chinese Residence, except when he went to the Hospital. In prayer he found such great light and heavenly fervor along with an abundance of tears, that, as he later personally confessed, at the beginning of his spiritual life he feared these constant tears would make him lose his sight. The reading from which he gained the greatest light and consolation was that of the Holy Gospels. He used to say that after reading even one verse, he received such an illumination of Divine goodness that he would break into a flood of tears and that, as he would later say, in comparison to this experience, the world was like a handful of chaff.

He was often seen in the cloister of the Church of the Cross and in that of the Holy Spirit walking along, almost beside himself, with open arms and eyes fixed on heaven, breathing forth deep sighs. This was such that some came to consider him out of his mind. When he was once told that because of this he was thought to be crazy, he answered: "That is true; I am crazy because whoever does not love God is crazy and I do not love him." One day he was questioned by a priest as to why he did these things and went around like that. At these words he blushed and replied to his friend that in such moments he was overcome and he sighed without realizing that he did so. From then on, as long as he lived, he would not speak or listen to talk unless it had to do with God and the good of others, and I who am writing bear testimony to this. When he heard idle talk, it pained him, and so he would then try to introduce some spiritual topic or find a polite way to leave the conversation.

His Principal Devotions

Our Father Gennaro Maria was very devoted to the mystery of the Most Holy Trinity and recommended this devotion to everyone. He celebrated its votive Mass whenever he could, and he published a very devout book on the subject.

He also had a special devotion to the Passion of Jesus Christ and so his room was full of images of Jesus' sufferings and of the Cross. He had a large number of such images produced to dispense to others, asking them to display them in their homes and in public. He was also very attentive to the Holy Sacrifice of the Mass, as one can gather from his written works. He never omitted celebrating Mass every day to the end of his life, even though, due to the weakness brought on by his poor health, he sometimes almost fainted at the altar. In fact, once he really did faint during Mass, but he forced himself to complete it, practically bringing himself to the brink of death in doing so. He protested that in Mass he rekindled all his hope. He was so convinced of the love that Jesus Christ deserved that he would say nothing should be preached to others except "Love Jesus Christ, love Jesus Christ."

He also had a very great devotion to the Most Holy Mary, especially under her title of the Immaculate Conception. To encourage everyone in this devotion, he would go everywhere, handing out holy cards and also a great number of scapulars and rosaries. Therefore, in the years he was among the members of the Congregation, during their periods of recreation after lunch and dinner, he would string rosaries and cut out cards and scapulars as a pastime.

A particular devotion he had was to the Name of Mary. Once he heard a sermon about the Blessed Sacrament by a preacher who spoke with a great deal of zeal, and he was touched by the sermon. However, he was troubled as he reflected back on it that the preacher had not, even once, mentioned the beloved name of Mary. Therefore he humbly asked him not to leave out mention of the name of Mary in his sermons because, if he had mentioned it, his sermon would have had much greater results.

It gave him great joy to have the name Gennaro Maria, and if someone called him only Gennaro, he would kindly take exception to the fact that the name of Mary had not been included. In the month of September he used to ask his friends to thank the Mother of God in his name because in that month he said he had received from her all the graces he had requested. At night when he went to bed, in order to remember his beloved queen, he always wound the rosary around his arm and so fell asleep. He confided to a friend that, in his greatest sufferings and battles with hell, he sensed a great comfort in having the rosary in his hand. He preached the glories of Mary everywhere and in every sermon he gave he included devotion to her. In different places he would have novenas in honor of the Mother of God celebrated at his expense. He also composed a booklet of her praises titled [*Considerations on the...*] *Greatness of Mary* that can be found among his spiritual works. At his death he said that it bothered him a great deal that he would die without having left behind a large book that he had planned to produce on the glories of the Most Holy Mary and for which he had already gathered material.

HIS INTERIOR TRIALS

It should be noted here that, after the great abundance of heavenly consolation that the Lord made him feel for many years as we stated above, from the time that he fervently made a novena on the vigil of a certain feast, on that very feast day, he began to experience a dryness of heart. This desolation was very strong, and he endured it right up to the last hours of his life when the Lord finally favored him with a sensible fervor which allowed him to die, burning with a great desire to see his God, as we shall narrate. Aside from that, at other times of his life, whether at prayer or in his work in favor of others, he always acted in such an aridity of spirit that it seemed to him that he was abandoned by God, and he found no relief whatever in all the spiritual activities he undertook. This is the way it was even in the most sacred times of the year, such as Christmas, Holy Week, and so forth.

At those times he suffered the same terrible temptations, especially to unbelief, to gluttony, and to despair. These were such that he used to say that he was left as if incapable of everything divine, and it seemed to him that he constantly heard in his ear words like those of the psalm: *Many say to my soul: There is no salvation for him in his God.*[2] As soon as this happened, he could catch his breath again only by repeating "my God, my God." Even in the course of the apostolic works for his neighbor into which he poured his life (thereby certainly shortening it)

---

[2] Psalm 3:3 *[DR]*.

and in the commitment he had out of a great desire for the divine glory in all his works, he never felt any sensible consolation but only great suffering and weariness. He admitted he had to do it all by sheer force of will. But in reality, through it all, he maintained a spiritual effort and zeal to spread the glory of God and to fulfill his divine will. Throughout his life, in all the words he always kept in his heart, in his mouth and on the tip of his pen (as can be seen in all his books) he was never heard to speak of anything except the glory and the will of God. Thus when he worked he did it all solely for God. And sometimes, when he felt a certain hidden pleasure at the sight of some good result from what he undertook for the glory of the Lord, he would pray to God and make others pray as well that even that pleasure be taken away.

But in the midst of such lack of divine consolations, he kept up his trust in God, putting all his confidence in the power of prayer. He would say that amid the storms of temptations and darkness, his comfort was in the words of Christ: *If you ask the Father anything in my name, he will give it to you.*[3] He swore that if God had not given him any other grace except solely that of prayer, this was enough to make him very happy: the promises made by the Lord to the one who prays. In fact from this confidence in prayer, he obtained all the graces that could be received from God, and so he overcame the great difficulties in the magnificent works that he undertook for the divine glory. In his greatest needs and difficulties, he always resorted to prayer and to the prayers of others. For that purpose he celebrated many Masses, made novenas several times each year, and attended Exposition of the Blessed Sacrament. So he would say that he was indebted to God for always obtaining more that what he asked.

SPIRIT OF MORTIFICATION AND HUMILITY

To prayer he added mortification. Even as a layman, it is said, he never tasted fresh fruit, and from the beginning of his entrance into the ecclesiastical state he fasted on bread and water three times a week. He was later forced to give up this practice because of his poor health. But throughout his whole life he never partook of fresh fruit; and if sometimes he was forced to taste it, it was out of obedience to his superiors. His mother stated to one of her confessors that when he lived at home and some

---

[3] John 16:23

tasty food, like pastries and pies, was served at table, he never ate them. He measured the portions of his food so that it was just enough to sustain him and he never went beyond the limits he set. Whenever he could, even when he was worn down in his health, he took the discipline, striking not flesh, but only bones covered by skin, since whoever saw him could only see a skeleton just made up of skin and bones. When there was nothing else to suffer, he would simply put up with not shooing away the pesky mites whose bites were a harder torment than a hairshirt or discipline.

He always fostered a great desire to be despised out of love for Jesus Christ. He therefore resolved firmly not to ever excuse himself with explanations whenever he was accused of some defect. Therefore in all his Masses, he begged God to give him a love of being despised; for that reason, whenever he could, he would say the oration "to beg for humility" at Mass. He confided to one of the Brothers in his Congregation that shortly after he had begun to say that prayer, the Lord granted it and sent him many occasions of contradiction. He then confessed that God had not only granted him the grace to suffer these patiently, but even to do so happily, immediately and wholeheartedly thanking His Divine Majesty. Likewise he confided to the same Brother that the slanders brought him no temptations, but rather that he felt a fervent desire to see himself dragged through the mud right in the middle of Naples.

In order to invite contempt, he always wore used and torn clothes bought in the Jewish Quarter, saying he wanted nothing to do with this world. It got to the point that he was scolded by his relatives who said that going around looking so bedraggled brought shame on their family; his response was that they should not be upset by this because whenever he was asked who he was, he had never indicated that he was the son of the Baron Sarnelli. Instead, he told everyone to call him Gennaro Maria as if his surname was Maria and his given name, Gennaro. He once went to say Mass in the Church of S. Maria dell'Ajuto in Naples, but the cleric there threw him out very nastily and would not let him say Mass when he saw him so ragged. He was able to avenge himself on this man in the way that saints get even with those who abuse them. He sought to do favors for this person who was so discourteous to him by helping him to obtain [the funds for] priestly ordination. In summary, he lived and died so poor that, when he passed away, the same priest he had helped donated the clothing for Gennaro Maria's burial since his own were so torn and threadbare.

His Charity Toward His Neighbor

In treating of his charity toward others, it can be said that our Don Gennaro Maria possessed this virtue to an extraordinary degree. When he resided outside the houses of the Congregation, he lived in the utmost poverty, ate little, and dressed poorly, not just so he could be despised, as we have said, but also in order to have something he could give as alms to the poor from what he would save on food and clothing. He sometimes went so far as to take the clothes he was wearing, the shoes on his feet, and the food set before him while he was eating so that he could give them to the needy. He would go around gathering the poor of Naples and bring them all together into his house to wash them top to bottom and feed them, waiting on them himself. This was the reason he took a room in his father's house right by the stairs, a room so dark and uncomfortable that a friend who visited him could see the mice jumping on his bed. He did this so he could welcome the many poor people who came to see him without the servants trying to shoo them away. He did not, however, want women to visit him there. When they wished to speak with him, he went to meet them in some church. When he entered the Congregation, he ardently requested permission, and obtained it from the superior, to be able to dispense to the poor alms that he obtained in the best way he could.

The love he had for the sick in the hospital was incredible. He wore himself out to relieve their suffering, in body as well as in spirit. Even as a secular he went begging what he could for food from his family members, packed it and sent it to the Hospital [*of the Incurables*]. When he became a cleric, as often as he went there, he always carried under his cloak some treats of candy or fruit for the poor sufferers that he had bought for them or he would deprive himself of some of his own servings of food. It is further known that for this purpose he had some long clay containers made into which he put cooked food so he could carry them [*on his shoulders*] and bring them to the poor. He made many packets of tobacco to give to these people. He made their beds, washed them, and left nothing charitable undone that could give them relief.

HIS ZEAL FOR THE GOOD OF OTHERS

As far as his spiritual works of mercy and his zeal for souls, we can say Father Gennaro Maria Sarnelli was absolutely heroic. From the time he left secular life and gave himself to serve the Lord in the ecclesiastical state, this was his continuous and sole thought. In his studies he busied himself with nothing other than finding out how he could best help souls. Even during recreation in the time for small talk he always thought and spoke about this.

At times, while others were diverting themselves elsewhere, he looked totally preoccupied and lost in thought. When asked what he was thinking, he answered "I am thinking about what I can do to help the souls that belong to Jesus Christ."

Especially when he spoke about the great need the poor have for spiritual help and for workers to do this, you could see his face light up out of zeal, and at times he was seen shedding tears of compassion. He would say that he felt specially called by God to help the poor, and the abandoned, repeating to that effect the statement of Isaiah: *Evangelizare pauperibus misit me.*[4] He asserted that he would consider himself damned if he did not attend to this task, feeling himself spurred on by the words of St. Paul, *Woe to me if I do not proclaim the gospel!*[5]

While he was at Naples before he entered the Congregation, he was determined, with two other priests, to go to preach missions throughout the Provinces of Calabria and Abruzzo, these being the places most destitute of spiritual help. His favorite patron was St. John Francis Regis, who was the saintly minister who was most enamored of the poor. With this in mind, as it is has been passed down, he entered the Congregation of the Most Holy Redeemer because he knew that this was its principal purpose: to aid the poor abandoned people of the Campagna.

As long as his health permitted, he was a tireless preacher and confessor. During missions, after having worked hard all morning, just stopping to take a bit of food (usually a slice of bread and some raisins) that he ate in the sacristy of the church, he spent the rest of the day preaching or hearing confessions. It is especially remembered that, during a mission given in neighborhood of Bracigliano, he worked alone for two months straight. He went morning to night hearing

---

[4] Luke 4:18 [*"He has anointed me to bring good news to the poor."*]

[5] 1 Corinthians 9:16.

confessions. As soon as he had refreshed himself with a cup of chocolate at a late hour, he applied himself to preaching and then went back to the confessional until he had heard the confessions of about two thousand people there. Similarly it is stated that, in another mission given in Villa de' Schiavi in the Diocese of Cajazzo, during his stay for a total of forty days, he heard confessions every day until around 4:00 PM and then, right after taking a little food, he immediately went up into the pulpit to preach. When that was finished, he again went to the confessional until 10:00 or 11:00 PM. Moreover, it is known that while taking care of some people, he ended up going two days without food.

We should note that the great efforts he put forth for the good of others, working or writing, he did while he was almost always sick. To anyone who told him he ought to take care of his health first and then go back to work, he responded: "If I had decided or wanted to work only when I felt well, I would have done little or nothing until now. And I would never do anything since I see that the Lord wishes to forge me continually through infirmities." If the person responded that this way his life would not last long, he replied: "And what better way is there to consume one's life than for God?" This was a continual miracle: to see someone so sick and frail still laboring continually for the good of others without losing a moment of time. When he was engaged at night in the writing of outstanding spiritual works, which he later published, he would continue to work until after midnight. He would only stop writing when fatigue overcame him. So when anyone asked what Don Gennaro Maria was doing, the Brother who worked with him used to say: "He is either writing or suffering." Sarnelli himself testified that on the day before he was to undertake some special work for the good of others, his health usually worsened. However when the day came that he was to actually do the work, he found himself filled with new strength. Sometimes he would begin to preach, feeling he would rather be in bed than in the pulpit, but when he finished preaching he felt much better.

When he preached, so great was his fervor and so strong the emotions that his sermons produced that at times people began banging their heads against the walls in sorrow, anxious to get to confession. When people went to his missions, they used to say: "Let's go to hear the saint; the saint is preaching." When he was in Naples, he often went to St. Gennaro outside the Walls, despite its distance from his house, to preach to the poor old invalids who were housed there. When he moved to the room provided for him by the Congregation in Scala, he would tell how great was the pain and sorrow he experienced in giving up this work.

He also had a great desire to help poor children. This led him to say that he found his greatest happiness during missions when he had the task of teaching catechism to the youngsters. In Naples he went to meet with the children suffering in the hospital from ringworm, in order to teach them, to exhort them to go to confession, and also to provide them with amusement. He did this with such kindness that they called him their father. He used to go through the plazas of Naples gathering the children or the poor youngsters, who made a living as porters. Since they were generally ignorant of matters of faith, he would bring them to his house where he taught them catechism, prepared them to make their confessions, and afterward gave them something to eat. So as not to inconvenience the people who lived there, he himself helped to serve the food and he would go to the kitchen to wash the dishes the children had used.

One could say that our Don Gennaro Maria was enamored of the sick people in hospitals, since he constantly went there and remained there for long periods of time. When he went in the mornings he would stay until noon and if he went after supper, he would remain until late at night, and he would leave wishing he could do more. It is not possible to express the love he gave them, encouraging them to bear their sufferings, teaching them about the divine precepts, and helping them make a good confession. When he could no longer hear their confessions, he would get other good priests to do so. It is known that he considered going to live permanently in the Hospital of the Incurables in order to more easily assist the poor especially at the hour of death. He had already taken steps to procure a room there, but some problems got in the way of his realizing his plan. It is also reported that at the hospital of the prison—where he also went to help poor, condemned men regain their spiritual health—he once almost lost his life because of this kind of zeal.

His Work Among the Prostitutes

It is well known throughout Naples what this zealous worker did to rescue prostitutes from this state of sin. Every feast day he went to the parish of St. Matthew to preach in order to bring these pitiable women to repentance. For this purpose, he was the one who induced the Congregation of the Archbishopric to sponsor annual spiritual exercises in that parish. Then in order to help these poor lost women to maintain themselves, he did not hold back anything that he had in his house, even to the point of going through the city in rags, as we have mentioned. He maintained several women at his own expense, giving each a monthly subsidy so they could stop selling their honor and their souls. He not only managed to help these who came to him but went about searching all through Naples where there might be some to be saved from sin. Among these, he placed sixteen in conservatories and for many he managed to find a husband. In particular, there were two that he supported for two years, and then found a place for them to live, providing them with a bed and household goods. Because the costs being incurred were enormous, he could not cover them by his own personal means. In a few years of his work on this project he had spent from five to six hundred ducats.[6] So he went about seeking alms throughout Naples, not just in religious houses but going to individual homes as well. He felt such repugnance in doing this that he later said he felt he would die of shame, since in this work he not only had to suffer the great awkwardness in making repeated visits, but also the bearing of contempt and insults. He confided to a friend that some people, who at first esteemed and were pleased with him, later would avoid him when they saw him or dismiss him with vile language.

He also suffered indescribable weariness and persecutions in the great undertaking that he began of reducing the prevalence of prostitutes by moving them to a secluded place outside the City of Naples. It was our Don Gennaro Maria's thought that if these notorious women remained spread throughout the quarters of the city as they had, first above the Toledo, at the Duchesse and in other quarters where they were very numerous, there was immense scandal given both to those who

---

[6] [At the time, this sum would equal a skilled craftsman's earnings for four or five years. See *The History of the Congregation of the Most Holy Redeemer*, ed. by Francisco Chiovaro, Liguori, MO: Liguori Publications, 1996, Vol. I/₁, 61].

lived nearby as well as those who passed on the streets. So he decided that there was no other way to remedy this immense evil except by forcing them to live together outside the city. To accomplish this project, God and all Naples know the great amount of trouble it caused him, as well as the large expenses he incurred in having several books printed on the topic of the abuses of prostitution. This undertaking drew down on him the opposition and abuse not only of his enemies but even of friends who judged that he could not succeed in the venture. They tried to dissuade him or laughed at him. But he still remained strong with confidence in God alone and not in human support. He made every effort to convince the principal ministers of the King, our patron, so that he finally experienced the joy of seeing his desire fulfilled. This occurred with the issuance of a nine-section decree sent to the Lord Duke of Giovenazzo, then Regent of the Court of the Vicariate on May 4, 1738. This decree promulgated the banishment of prostitutes who were to leave the city to live in the places designated for them. The royal order was executed with such vigor that those prostitutes who resisted leaving their house had their possessions tossed out the windows. In this way, the City of Naples was relieved of some thirty to forty thousand prostitutes. Some of these found husbands, some were housed in conservatories, and the rest retired to the designated places or simply moved away. But because of this affair, our Don Gennaro Maria suffered many threats to his life and deadly assaults from the lovers of these forlorn women. For this reason his family did not stop trying to impede his efforts out of fear of the harm that could come to him, and because of him to the whole family. Still, he replied that he was ready to suffer any danger and that it would be a blessing if he would even lose his own life because of this work, which gave such glory to God.

His Books

This same zeal for the salvation of others induced him to go to great lengths of suffering in publishing his books. In the material he chose to treat in these books and the spirit in which he wrote them, one can discern his one great desire: to sanctify the whole world if that would be possible. In addition to the above-mentioned book for the City of Naples on the abuses of prostitution, he also wrote another for all the cities and territories of the Kingdom. In this book he demonstrated that in these lands and in the small cities permission for prostitution was in fact prohibited. This work he sent to all the bishops in the Kingdom. After this, he had published the book titled *Il mondo santificato* (*The Sanctified World*). One could say that, in its own way, it did sanctify the world, since it produced good results in those who got a copy of it in their hands. This is not just a few people, because the book circulated throughout the Kingdom of Naples, and even in other Kingdoms.

Furthermore, he published an entire book against the vice of blasphemy from his desire to see it stamped out, especially in the Kingdom of Naples, where this cursed vice was entrenched. He wrote a treatise, gathered into another book titled *Il mondo riformato* (*The Reformed World*), on respect for the Church, which was something that was also very much lacking in this Kingdom. He also produced a pamphlet on the obligation of parents to educate their children. Another book, meant to give spiritual guidance for pious persons, was titled *la Discrezione de' Spiriti* (*The Discernment of Spirits*). Also, another was for priests with the title *Il ecclesiastico santificato* (*The Sanctified Clergyman*). Another one offered an easy method for all the activities of missions, very useful for priest missionaries. Another work he had printed at the cost of much effort, as he mentions himself, since he composed it while he was suffering and in pain under the burden of the disease of tuberculosis, that finally took his life. It was titled *l'Anima desolata* (*The Desolate Soul*) and was meant to serve persons in spiritual aridity. Another contained very devout meditations and was titled *l'Anima illuminata* (*The Illuminated Soul*). He published other works as well that could be mentioned. He plotted out further works, some of which he had already begun to have printed, such as a treatise on compassion for the souls in purgatory, another on appeasing God at the time of plagues, and finally, one of selected devout reflections for each day of the year. These were left incomplete because his death intervened.

There were still others planned that he had not yet put down on paper: sermons on the Blessed Virgin Mary for every Saturday and all her Novenas and a textbook on morals and the truths of Faith. In short, all the books that he wrote or planned to write were composed or designed out of the desire to help people, as he said, even after his death. When he was dying, it was precisely this that he expressed to the Lord Canon Sersale, who had come to visit him: "Lord Canon," he said, "I wish to preach right up to Judgment Day."

HIS FINAL ILLNESS AND DEATH

But we have now finally come to his last sickness and holy death. Our Don Gennaro Maria labored while he endured sickness and even fever for many years, as we have said. He gave his last mission at Posilipo, half dead and consumed by hardships and sickness. On returning from the mission at S. Agnello in Posilipo, Sarnelli's pains so increased that he had to give up his usual activities and was no longer able to celebrate Mass. This was a sure sign to everyone that he was near death, because he had never before left it out, as we said above. One day he wanted to force himself to offer it, but he fainted while he was at the altar. As the sickness progressed, he moved into his brother's house in Naples where he remained sick for a month and a few days. Even with all the pain and weakness increasing, he did not stop praying. Since his spiritual desolation continued, he sought comfort in the devout people who came to visit him.

His doctors recommended he be taken to a healthier climate, but because of his extreme weakness he could not be moved. For about fifteen days before he died, he was unable to get out of bed. During this time, the Lord willed to lighten his cross of abandonment, since he began to enjoy a great peace. Every other thought left his mind except for a great desire to be one with God in the Holy Fatherland. This was so great that when one of his father's servants expressed his hope that God would make him well and let him get up and about, Gennaro Maria responded: "Oh, if I could shout, I would shout that at this moment my one consolation is to think of embracing death. And you want to talk about getting well?"

At this very time, he showed how great was his patience and love because, while enduring insufferable pain and in need of continual assistance, he thought mainly about those who were caring for him. When he needed something he would say to the Brother of the Congregation whom the superior had sent to care for him: "Brother, be patient out of love of Jesus Christ, because in a little while you will be able to rest." During these last days, he made provision for the final disposition of his goods. The few sweets that remained he sent to the hospital to be given to the sick. He still had a little tobacco, and from this he wanted some small packages made to distribute to the poor. He gave all his possessions for the benefit of his Congregation of the Most Holy Redeemer so that they could be used for alms and other good works. Before he died, he gave out many donations. In particular, we are aware that his brother had given him a certain amount of money for his funeral and for Masses to be said for him after his death. When the confessor from the Conservatory at Castellammare came to visit him, he gave him twenty ducats for the conservatory, saying that what remained would be enough for the costs of the final rites. To his oldest brother, who helped him greatly in life and in death, he said: "My brother, the time is drawing near when I hope I can repay you for all you have done for me."

During this time the devil appeared to him as a man dressed like an abbot and tempted him to pride, saying: "O Don Gennaro, all Naples weeps for your illness since they see it as the loss of a great man." But he called on the Most Holy Names of Jesus and Mary, and the devil disappeared and did not return. One day when Canon Sersale came to visit and wished him to get well, he responded in these words: "Sir Canon, I have been troubled for some time by scruples, but by the grace of Jesus Christ I have been freed of them. I now die in peace and without scruples. All that I have done, I have done purely out of the intention of pleasing God. The sacrifice is now consumed. Don't talk to me about life any more. I want my God."

During these final days of his life, he did not stop making short prayers to the Holy Trinity, often repeating these words:

"Blessed be the Holy Trinity and Undivided Unity, let us confess this to him because he shows us his mercy." From one moment to the next, he embraced and kissed the images of Jesus Christ and of Mary. As death drew near, the Lay Brother who assisted him noted these loving words that he whispered to God: "My Father, see me here. Now the creature returns to his Creator, the son comes back to his Father. Lord, if it pleases you, I long to come and see you face to face. But I neither hope to die nor hope to live. I want only what you want. You know that whatever I have done, whatever I have thought was all through your grace." These words spoken by a dying man in the moment of truth makes it apparent that he truly did all things as he stated. The morning of the day he died, he said to the Brother at his side: "Brother, go lay out the oldest clothes you can find so that when I am dead, you waste nothing on me."

The doctor visited him that morning at around 8 AM and, as the doctor was leaving, he said, "I'll be seeing you later today," to which Gennaro Maria responded: "Today I want to give myself over to a quiet last breath." He had urged the serving Brother to make sure that he reminded him to say the rosary every day, because he told him he wanted to die reciting the rosary. And in fact, that is what happened because he began saying the rosary that morning and, at about the third decade, he was assailed by great anguish and broke out in a sweat. He said to the Brother, "I know this is the sweat of death." Since the Brother saw that the hour was quickly approaching, he immediately sent for a priest and began to say some consoling things about the goodness of God, but Sarnelli interrupted him saying, "Leave the talking to me." Then he began to talk tenderly with the Lord, but soon he was not understandable because he lost the strength of his voice.

When he entered into his agony, two Brothers of the Congregation who were assisting during these last hours asked for his blessing and, raising his hand, he gently gave it. His agony did not last more than about half an hour, without much disquiet. During this time, with his rosary wrapped around his arm and holding the crucifix in his hands, he kept kissing it every so often. After receiving absolution from the priest, he reached the final moment and peacefully gave up his spirit at the sixteenth hour of the morning [10:00 AM] of Tuesday, June 30, 1744, at the age of 42. His happy death occurred two days before the feast of Mary's Visitation, fulfilling his constant hope that he would die during a novena before the feast of the Most Holy Virgin.

Though he was dead, his face became beautiful and gracious, composed with a smile on his lips as those who were present attest. And his body began to give out a sweet fragrance that was sensed in the room where he died for a long time, not only by those who were there at his death but also by others who came there after his death. His brother, Don Domenico Sarnelli, said that he did not know how to break away from that room after his death since he found such great spiritual consolation there. The next morning the body was brought to the Church of St. Maria dell'Ajuto, called degli Coltrari, accompanied by his confreres of the Congregation of the Apostolic Missions of the Archdiocese of Naples as was their pious custom. They followed right up to the church, filled with very great sorrow over his death. Upon arrival there, more people came, crying and saying, "The saint is dead." It was the same throughout the whole area. They began ripping off pieces of clothing, each one trying to get what they could, to the point that the body had to be covered so it would not end up naked. The body remained two days before burial, when many priests and other people came, and it remained supple and did not give off a bad odor. When it was cut on the arm and head, fresh blood flowed from both places. From all over there were requests for his relics. Everywhere the news was passed along, as it still is, that a saint had died. Out of devotion, people came to the house where he died, where they cried, exclaiming: "Oh, the holy one of Jesus Christ who was not appreciated." Many people there, who recommended themselves to God through the merits of Father Don Gennaro Maria, have received outstanding graces. Desiring not to fail in my purpose of providing a short synthesis of his life, I will not recount all these other things. But I stop with the hope that in good time someone will not fail to report them by writing at greater length about the life of this great Servant of the Lord.

CHAPTER TWO

The Moral Work of

GENNARO SARNELLI

An Outsider Among Outsiders

By Bishop Noel Londoño Buitrago, CSsR[7]

Gennaro Sarnelli was born and died in Naples during the eighteenth century. He dedicated his whole life to the service of the most destitute, especially the potential victims of prostitution. He died at the age of forty-two, in 1744, practically from burnout. When he died, the people said: "An unknown saint has died." With the exception of some specialized publications, Sarnelli is even today an unknown person.

In these pages, after a brief note about his life and his writings, we will present the manner in which he perceived the problem of prostitution, the moral evaluation he attached to it, and the social and pastoral solutions he offered in its regards. We conclude with a look at the concepts he had of prostitution and of women in general.

LAWYER, PRIEST, MISSIONARY

In the past, Naples was one of the most populous cities of Europe: "The richest and the most vice-ridden city in the world," said Cervantes in *El Quixote*. In the 1700s, it was overloaded with nobles, lawyers, ecclesiastics, and prostitutes. And there was Sarnelli, in the epicenter of that reality.

He was the fourth of eight children of Baron Sarnelli and was born in 1702. At age twenty he received a doctorate in law from the University of Naples. At age thirty he became a diocesan priest. He was also a member of the missionary association called the Apostolic Missions. He began to work in the rural missions and to collaborate in

---

[7] Father (now Bishop) Londoño originally wrote this article for Sarnelli's beatification and published it in the provincial bulletin of the Redemptorist Province of Bogotá, Colombia [*A shorter English translation from the Spanish by Rev. Ruskin Piedra, CSsR, was originally published in* Spiritus Patris 23 *(March, 1997): 19–28; it did not contain footnotes and other critical apparatus. In this chapter, citations from Sarnelli are those used by Londoño from the 1851 edition of the* Opera Omnia *of Sarnelli, published in Naples.]*

the parish of Saints Francis and Matthew in the city. Right from the start, he was concerned about abandoned children, especially poor girls, victims of misery, and easy bait for prostitution. This fact and his manner of living, so foreign to the nobility of his origins, was a cause of shame to his family, which did not welcome the fact that he walked through the streets followed by a troop of miserable urchins. Gennaro was content to tell them "that they should not be upset by this because whenever he was asked who he was, he had never indicated that he was the son of the Baron Sarnelli. Instead, he told everyone to call him Gennaro Maria as if his surname was Maria and his given name, Gennaro."[8]

Some contemporaries who were not very friendly toward him considered him an idealist in his projects, independent in his activities, and sickly in health.[9] Deep down, he was a man of personality and decision who got excited about large and apparently impossible projects and gave himself over completely to their accomplishment, even to the point of exhausting his energy and health. We would almost call him obsessive-compulsive, in the best sense of that term. When he was told to take care of his health first, he would respond: "If I had decided or wanted to work only when I felt well, I would have done little or nothing until now. And I would never do anything since I see that the Lord wishes to forge me continually through infirmity."[10]

He had known Alphonsus de Liguori for a number of years, both in the courtroom and in pastoral ministry; they were good friends. When he became aware that Alphonsus intended to found a new institute, he wanted to get a closer look. "Learning that the purpose of this Congregation was to devote itself to the care of the abandoned people of the Campagna by means of missions and other spiritual exercises and that in this Institute life was lived with strict regular observance obligated by the simple vows of poverty, obedience, and chastity together with a vow of perseverance, out of a desire for greater

---

[8] Alphonsus de Liguori, Compendio.

[9] This is reflected in the correspondence of Tommaso Falcoia and of Matteo Ripa. See *Carteggio*, I, #167, pp. 416–418; #171, p. 425–428. See also O. Gregorio, "Il ven. P. Gennaro Sarnelli e l'abate Matteo Ripa", *Spic. Hist.* 11 (1963): 245–251. On differences between Falcoia and Sarnelli, see D. Capone - S. Majorano, *I redentoristi e le redentoriste. Le radici*, Materdomini [1985], 232–235, 249–250, 269–271. Not to be forgotten, however, is that the same Falcoia praised the pastoral work of Sarnelli among the prostitutes and invited all the Redemptorists to follow his example and support his work; *Carteggio*, I, #221, pp. 506–507.

[10] Alphonsus, Compendio, 490.

perfection he decided to dedicate and to consecrate himself exclusively to God. After consulting Father Manulio,...Gennaro Maria joined this above-mentioned Congregation and moved from Naples to Scala."[11]

He was beginning a new stage in his life or, better, a new dimension, because externally he continued to do what he was already doing: missions and the care of abandoned children. For that very reason, he hesitated at the moment of taking the decisive step:

> Since I am already one foot into that holy Institute and have the desire that, after I get in, I may live with blind obedience to the indications of whoever is in charge, it seems right that I first briefly explain the difficulties involved in coming to the Institute that cross my mind along with other things.

> First was the fear I have that if I am required to teach school, it would seem that I would not be able to pursue my ardent desires to lead many souls to God, while on the missions I would be able to teach countless children...The other difficulty was that, finding myself committed here to rescue the girls who are at risk and to write in their defense to reveal the endless damages done them because of which they sell their honor while still children, it appears that by entering this Institute, gaining this great good, at least by my [current] writing, could be impeded.[12]

Sarnelli was in the primitive Redemptorist community of Scala from the end of August 1733 until April 1736. "Then, due to his failing health, since the climate did not agree with him and also because he had to care for the extraordinary work he was directing, especially that of removing the prostitutes from the center of the City of Naples...it was necessary for his superiors to give him permission to return to Naples, where he later died."[13]

---

[11] *Ibid.*, 482.

[12] Letter of Sarnelli to Alphonsus July 17, 1733, *Carteggio*, I, #87, p. 258. See De Meulemeester, *Origines*, II, Louvain 1957, 273.

[13] Alphonsus, Compendio, 483. Capone has reason to say: "I think that in the founding of the Redemptorist Congregation, little or no consideration has been given to the presence and the work of the Neapolitan priest Gennaro Sarnelli (which was without a doubt decisive), because its founding is looked at only as a juridical-liturgical action that took place only on the morning of November 9, 1733, rather than as a "gestation" considered, prolonged, suffered that lasted several years up to the death of Falcoia. It has as its focus directed fixedly on Alphonsus as Founder, with his faith in the journey just

That made him, in the history of the Redemptorists, something of an anomaly, almost one who was considered outside of the Congregation. This history accents only his friendship with Alphonsus while his physical distance from the community was exaggerated; forgotten was the total harmony between his work and the charism of the Congregation. He loved the Congregation above all things, Alphonsus himself insists, and wished "to see it spread throughout the whole world and to promote it at the cost of his own blood.""However, even though he lived in Naples, he did not hesitate every so often to come to help his confreres in the Congregation with their missions." "He entered the Congregation of the Most Holy Redeemer because he knew that this was its principal purpose: to aid the poor abandoned people of the Campagna."[14]

Sarnelli felt he lived in special circumstances but not outside the Institute of St. Alphonsus, in which he saw an excellent way of serving the marginalized poor.[15] As a Redemptorist, he continued to live his charism in the city, not only on the missions in the surrounding areas (1741–1743), but also in the pastoral care of prisoners, those condemned to the galleys who were sick in the hospital of the Darsena, the dying in the hospital of the Incurables, the elderly of St. Gennaro Outside the Walls and orphaned children, especially, poor girls in danger of becoming prostitutes.

There are two elements which make Sarnelli authentically creative within the first Redemptorist community: on the one hand, the relationship between pastoral work and moral discourse; and on the other, the use of the means of communication in pastoral work, in this case, written publications. In both areas, he was the one who introduced Alphonsus Liguori into these areas; also not to be forgotten are Sarnelli's influence in catechetics and the way he conceived the post-mission and the "devout life."[16]

---

like that of Abraham. But if one considers the foundation-gestation, Gennaro Sarnelli immediately appears as the first priest who, with a truly Redemptorist spirit, effectively helped Alphonsus, especially in regard to the wider dimensions of the missionary charism of the Congregation"; Capone - Majorano, *I redentoristi*, 176.

[14] Alphonsus, Compendio, 483 and 493.

[15] He says himself: "It is necessary to know that my preference above every other good work for the charity involved in rescuing girls in danger is not meant as a desire to belittle the very important and divine work of the holy missions. Indeed, truthfully, these [missions] are the support of the Christian faith, the honor of the Church, and like the pupil of the eye, they are to be preferred to every other pastoral endeavor"; *Aggiunta*, 289.

[16] He constantly insists on saying that the missions are not meant to offer a passing benefit but to instill a new way of living and, in a special way, to learn a method of mental prayer.

SARNELLI THE WRITER

A year after his ordination, Sarnelli published his first work, *La via facile e sicura del Paradiso* (*The Easy and Sure Way to Paradise*). In ten years he published more than twenty books, with a total of more than five thousand pages, an equivalent of producing forty pages each month. When he died he had planned at least three more works: a selection of pious thoughts for every day, sermons on the Blessed Mother for Saturdays of the year, and instructions on Faith and morals.

It is not easy to make a catalogue of his writings, in part because Sarnelli wrote them on the go and saw them all as prolonged preaching.[17] Some are devotional works with a theological foundation, for example, *Santissima Trinita e Maria Santissima* (*Practical Devotions to Honor the Most Holy Trinity and Most Holy Mary*); others are meditations, such as *Il Cristiano santificato* (*The Sanctified Christian*); others are certainly more of a spiritual theology, for instance, *Il Cristiano illuminato* (*The Enlightened Christian*) or *Della discrezione degli spiriti* (*On Discernment of Spirits*); some are works of pastoral practice, as for example, *Il mondo reformato* (*The Reformed World*). Another series of works has to do with public morality, especially with prostitution and blasphemy. Then we must not forget his sermons and letters.[18]

Here we are especially interested in the writings on prostitution, which Sarnelli himself describes as "writings in defense of girls in danger": *Ragioni, legali, cattoliche e politiche* (*Legal, Catholic, and Political Reasons*), published anonymously in 1736, which presents the various motives for regulating the phenomenon of prostitution. *Il quatro maggio in Napoli* (*The Fourth of May in Naples*) underlines the legislation which established May 8, 1738, as a definitive date for expelling the prostitutes; this is where he comments on the effects of these new laws. In 1739, he published the *Ristretto delle ragioni* (*Synthesis of the Reasons*), in defense of

---

See the Introduction to *Il mondo santificato*, Naples 1740, 19–23, 28–53, and the letter to Alphonsus during the mission in the neighborhoods around Naples, *Carteggio*, I, #268, pp. 593–596.

[17] "All the books that he wrote or planned to write were composed or designed out of the desire to help people, as he said, even after his death. When he was dying, it was precisely this that he expressed to the Lord Canon Sersale who had come to visit him: "Lord Canon, I wish to preach right up to Judgment Day." Compendio, 501.

[18] A "rehearsal" for preparing a list of Sarnelli's publications is available in *Bibliographie*, II, Louvain 1935, 373–377. His list shows 24 titles, some with several editions during Sarnelli's lifetime.

the cities ruined by prostitution, together with the *Aggiunta* (*Supplement*) showing concrete ways of permanently controlling prostitutes, of rescuing the ones who are penitent, of preserving girls in danger, and of maintaining the Kingdom of Naples purified of sexual licentiousness.

In these four books, Sarnelli shows some of his personal characteristics. First, there is the enthusiasm he brings to what he does: he writes with passion, convinced of his reasons and ready to convince others. This fire comes from his pastoral charity, from his apostolic zeal, but also from his own observations. He does not speak from hearsay or from what he has read in books; he expresses what he has personally experienced. He likes to repeat: "Trust someone [*namely, himself*] who has the experience of many years."[19] He is more an expert on the problem than a "specialist on the subject," a moralist of the streets and of the confessional rather than a theorist. In other words, his moral discourse is born of the ethical indignation lived in the first person and of dialogue with other experts.[20]

The method he uses, more than simply social analysis, is rather historical, legal, theological. He appeals to the authorities of the Kingdom with political reasons, to the magistrates with historical and legal arguments, to bishops and priests with theological reflections, and to the faithful with spiritual and pedagogical reasons. It is a moral discourse open to all social levels and is very different from the books of moral theology of St. Alphonsus, which are oriented more toward confessors.

Another important aspect of these works is their literary genre. They appear to be texts close to traditional apologetics; perhaps they give evidence of his former profession as orator and lawyer. He gives the impression of having a negative view of the social reality and of the means of protection from prostitution, as if what made him uncomfortable was the immoral scene ("social esthetics") and not the human problem ("social ethics"). Let us not forget, however, that he lived in the eighteenth century, in a thoroughly "Christian" ambient and amid a lifestyle that was lavishly baroque, where public perceptions had a decisive influence on moral values.

---

[19] *Ragioni legali*, Naples 1851, 20, 47; *Aggiunta*, 249–250.

[20] "As to the author of the work, it is sufficient to know that he did not produce it on his own without being sure that it agrees with the considered understanding of many learned people"; *Ragioni legali*, 7. Sarnelli was convinced of the seriousness of his reflections: "[This text] is not to be taken as an excess of zeal because it is serious doctrine, founded in theology and without exaggeration"; *Aggiunta*, ed. 1739, 2.

The criticism made about his work in Naples, both by his contemporaries as well as by his biographers, usually stresses his zeal "against prostitutes." As a matter of fact, this expression is rarely found in Sarnelli. He speaks of measures "against insolent prostitution"; [writing of himself in the third person], he asserted: "Let it be seen very clearly that in attacking vice, he did not intend to show spite toward poor sinners, whose eternal salvation he so much values."[21] It is clear that his point of departure and the prime objective of his pastoral labor and his publications about prostitution have to do with girls in danger.

THE PHENOMENON OF PROSTITUTION IN NAPLES

Speaking of female prostitution in the eighteenth century, Sarnelli says:

> There are three disorders of prostitution in this Kingdom which make one weep today. The mixing of indecent women with honorable families, the overflowing number of them and their brazen_liberty...And the origin of such disorders is due, in the first place, to having tolerated prostitutes within the city; second, to not having safeguarded the decency of girls who are poor and in danger; third, to not having punished the transgressions and the evil activities of prostitutes.[22]

How many prostitutes were there in Naples? St. Alphonsus speaks of thirty to forty thousand,[23] that is, almost ten percent of the population. Sarnelli alludes to the area of the city which he knows best: "In the neighborhood of the parish of Sts. Francis and Matthew on Toledo Street, lived sixteen thousand people, among whom two or three thousand are prostitutes mixed in with the people." But he clarifies: "At this time the exact number of publicly indecent women in the city is not known except by hearsay. And because the author wishes to remain truthful in everything he expresses, he does not offer a number; all the more because hearsay tends to exaggerate. What is certain is that we are dealing with an immense number of scandalous women and that they are found in every corner and at every hour."[24]

---

[21] *Ragioni legali*, 7; *Aggiunta*, ed. 1739, 41.

[22] *Ragioni legali*, 144.

[23] Compendio, 345.

[24] *Ragioni legali*, 20, 157. He also says, however, "There is no doubt that more harm is done to piety by forty or sixty thousand scandalous women taking a stroll than by years and years of instructions, sermons, and confessions"; *Ibid.*, 122.

"They are so numerous that they have taken over almost the whole city": the squares, the bars, the alleyways, and the vestibules of the churches; so much so that "in order to visit the churches one has to pass through brothels. Left at liberty, they go out in groups at night, driven more by hunger than by lasciviousness; they wander around the city and circulate throughout all districts and even go right up to decent homes; they park themselves in restaurants and gambling halls, and are the first to go to all the processions and feasts in the square."[25] What most worried Sarnelli was the influence of such an ambient upon decent families; and, in a special way, upon girls in need, because if prostitution ceases to be an occasional phenomenon and becomes a pervading influence, the consequence is a contagion (immorality) and the relativizing of its gravity (amorality).

The causes of this proliferation of prostitutes, affirms Sarnelli, in a long section of his *Ragioni*, are seven:

1. Indifference in the face of the reality of girls who have to beg and the scant protection offered them.

2. The presence in the brothels of so many innocent girls, relatives of the prostitutes themselves.

3. Conservatories that could preserve indigent girls and rescue repentant prostitutes are not fulfilling these purposes.

4. The violators and deceivers of young girls are not punished who, most of the time, have seduced them with promises of marriage.

5. The adultery and concubinage of so many men and the absence of any punishment to serve as an example.

6. The seductive pimps, who go seeking defenseless girls to condemn them to such an occupation.

7. The presence of prostitutes throughout the city.[26]

---

[25] *Ibid.*, 31, 32 and 44. See *Ibid.*, 36, 40–41, 45, 65, 121. Do not let this sad list make us forget that at the same time Naples was also a city full of good Christians and even saints; see R. De Maio, *Società e vita religiosa a Napoli nell'età moderna*, Naples 1971.

[26] *Ragioni legali*, 157–175; *Ristretto delle ragioni*, Naples 1739, 31–34. He also says that another cause of this overwhelming increase of prostitution was inefficiency in the application of existing laws; *Ragioni legali*,180. "Sarnelli's 'memorial' of the world's oldest profession in Naples can find a place among other sociocultural studies of the period for its profound and wide observation, for its frequent references to the political and

This is a clear and honest appraisal, without exaggeration or dissimulation, which clarifies the principal aspects and the causes of the phenomenon. Although public immorality is the tip of the iceberg, Sarnelli does not limit all the problems of prostitution to it; nor does he emphasize the theme in terms exclusively religious or moral. For him all the causes of the proliferation of prostitutes have to do with the lack of protection of poor girls who walk the streets begging for a piece of bread. And because political, economic, social, legal, and religious concerns are all mixed together indiscriminately, he directs his efforts to the different strata of the city and of the Kingdom.

After we have seen the actual situation of prostitutes in Naples and the freedom with which they operated, it does not seem possible to speak of them as "outcasts." The prostitutes were rather the pushy ones and were even in high places. For that reason, Sarnelli's proposals about dealing with the professional harlots were measures of segregation and "ghettoization." But the title of "outcasts" is indeed valid for the unprotected girls who were the point of departure for Sarnelli. They are excluded from families who, because of poverty, abandoned them; excluded from social welfare and forced to ask for alms and to sell themselves for a piece of bread; excluded from the institutions intended to help them, since the administrators had given the preference to other girls who did not need it; excluded from the benefits of pastoral care and ecclesiastical financial help.

From this analysis of the reality follows the analysis of the legislation and of the teaching about the phenomenon of prostitution, which is perhaps the most complicated and the weakest part of the works of Sarnelli. He uses criteria of the eighteenth century, a time when it was fashionable to cite the anthologies of traditional teaching. And it is there that he lets himself be carried away by the weight of tradition and by fiery oratory to use expressions that today sound inappropriate and show a narrow view of sexuality. More interesting are the concrete proposals he makes to overcome the problem and to which we dedicate the following section.

economic environment and for its accurate analysis of the distance between existing laws and their concrete application"; A. De Spirito, "La prostituzione feminile a Napoli nel XVIII secolo," *Ricerche di storia sociale e religiosa* 7 (1978): 33.

Moral and Social-Pastoral Strategies

It is worth repeating that Sarnelli's moral reflection arose from a felt pastoral experience.

Then in order to help these poor lost women to maintain themselves, he did not hold back anything that he had in his house, even to the point of going through the city in rags, as we have mentioned. He maintained several at his own expense, giving each of them a monthly subsidy so that they could stop selling their honor and their souls. He not only managed to help these who came to him but went about searching all through Naples where there might be some to be saved from sin. Among these, he placed sixteen in conservatories and for many he managed to find a husband. In particular, there were two that he supported for two years, and then found a place for them to live, providing them with a bed and household goods. Because the costs being incurred were enormous, he could not cover them by his own personal means…And since the expenses were large and were above his abilities, he went about seeking alms throughout Naples, not just in religious houses but going to individual homes as well. He felt such repugnance in doing this that he later said he felt he would die of shame.[27]

But he was very quickly convinced that an individual undertaking was not enough. Returning from Scala in 1736, he already had a concrete plan of action, which he would continue to clarify and complete in his various writings. Comprehensive social action, which would face the problem from all angles, was indispensable. Sarnelli had this intuition in the eighteenth century, so we cannot expect him to make a precise social analysis that would individuate the economic and political inequities which were at the heart of the situation. Let us not forget that the great teachers of sociology would be born only a century later. What Sarnelli did grasp in this matter was that the primary cause of prostitution was destitution and that charity had an indispensable social-political dimension.

---

[27] Compendio, 499. "On seeing that there is little chance of success with the women hardened in sin, I dedicated all my energies toward those that had most recently begun and were pushed into it because of their poverty even though they were ashamed of this life and carried it out without wanting to do so"; R. Giovine, *Vita del gran servo di Dio D. Gennaro Maria Sarnelli*, 2 vol., Naples 1858, I, 166.

Then he began to meet with priests, magistrates, politicians, and ministers, and he interested them in a plan of city improvement and of restoring the conservatories to their true purpose. His biographers say that this project unleashed against him the criticism of politicians, the animosity of the professional prostitutes and of their protectors, the distrust of the administrators of the conservatories for girls, the sarcasm of people of goodwill. The famous Father Gregorio Rocco, OP, commented: "Father Gennaro wishes to remove all sin from the world!" Meanwhile his relatives feared even for his physical safety. He, however, insisted so much with the high officials of the court that he had the satisfaction of seeing the promulgation of the decrees of May 8, 1738.[28] We can understand, then, why Sarnelli wrote:

It is sad to listen to those who say we cannot cure every evil; that there is no cure for all the disorders; that we have to leave the world as it is and just keep on living; that it does more harm than good to seek a remedy and that fads should not be encouraged. Oh God! This implies wanting to be guilty and negligent, to sin by omission and with no hope of repentance and to give free rein to the abuses... Today we live with so much discretion, we act with so much hesitance and circumspection, with so much precaution, and so much worldly caution in seeking to end an abuse and to promote the works of God that no sooner does an initiative arise than it is drowned in a thousand prejudices, which are called foresight, prudence, reflection, vigilance, caution while, in reality, we are dealing with pettiness of spirit before God, vain fears, human respect.[29]

---

[28] It was a triumph for Sarnelli that, strangely enough, he had to defend the result of many years of work, reflection, and prayer: "Esteemed Mother, I recommend to your charity and to that of your sisters, fervent prayer and intercession before God and Most Holy Mary for this old matter that is now being carried out in Naples with good results, although they are few"; Letter of March 7, 1737 in *Lettere spirituali*, "Opere Complete," vol. XIV, Naples 1851, 17. It is also important to realize that in this legislation, "a good part of the praise belongs to Tanucci. It probably entered into his calculations, as well as that of his consulters, that this cleaning out could be presented as homage to the gentile young princess, the promised spouse, Maria Amalia, who was about to arrive and bring to the royal marriage bed an innocence like that of the monarch"; R. Telleria, *San Alfonso María de Ligorio, fundador, obispo y doctor*, I, Madrid 1950, 282–283.

[29] *Il mondo riformato*, in *Opere complete*, vol. IV, Naples 1849, 19, 21.

Legal, Public-Safety, and Hygienic Proposals

He was convinced that the spread of prostitution did not avert greater evils but rather fomented them and that, with so much license allowed the prostitutes, it would be best to stop them completely. In the event they must be tolerated, some legal norms of separation of "professional prostitutes" should be established in an area outside the city, where a census could be taken of them and they could be constantly supervised, and from which they could leave only for medical attention or to go to a nearby church.

The old moral question then arises: Is prostitution necessary? The "tolerant" tradition of St. Augustine and St. Thomas presents prostitution as a lesser evil, like a building's drain for waste water: to remove the drain would be to convert the entire house into a dirty and foul-smelling place. Sarnelli, for his part, feels that prostitution does not serve to avoid other evils. But he is not naive and knows that prostitution is a reality which you have to deal with, given the corruption of morals. That is why he concludes: It may be tolerated in large cities, if it is controlled; but it should not be allowed in small towns.

Some bring up [*the argument*] that, according to the opinion of the learned, prostitutes are necessary in large cities. And who denies it, when youth are already corrupt? But, in what way are they necessary? The same learned men say: [they are] like toilets on ships or sewers in buildings. But toilets are not placed up on the stern or the prow of ships, nor are sewers placed prominently in parlors or in the main corridors of noble mansions; on the contrary, the least possible number are constructed and are placed in the most discreet and hidden places. What we are seeking, then, is not to do away with prostitutes, but rather to displace, contain, and diminish their number.[30]

---

[30] *Aggiunta,* 245. Further on, he says: "Many cities, very wisely, have forbidden organized tolerance of a large number of prostitutes. And if our city would like to know what I really think, I will state it frankly before God. Given the fact that our youth are so unprincipled and that there is such a huge number of prostitutes, they may be tolerated, but only if they are isolated into ghettos inside or outside the city. But those who are witches, usurers, pimps, minors, adulterers, or concubines should not be accepted. The degree to which the number of present prostitutes is reduced and new generations of more chaste young people arise in the city, to the same degree will the population of prostitutes be reduced to a small number who could be set apart in a few closed sectors

It is not sufficient simply to banish the prostitutes from the center of the city. Sarnelli proposes making a record of each woman (name, state in life, age, condition) in order to discover the causes...why she chooses to prostitute herself and perhaps she can be helped. A determination can be made whether she is being forced by her parents, as constantly happens now or it will become evident whether she has already lost her virginity and who was the cause. Thus the guilty will come to light and be punished...because today many of these women, violated with the promise of marriage and then left abandoned, do not know to whom they might turn and so they drown themselves in prostitution.[31]

Sarnelli proposes, moreover, that care be taken that the law does not quickly become a dead letter: the norms for new places to live, conditions of rent, weekly medical exam, punishment of protectors, and of the unruly ones, and so forth, should be concrete, clearly explained, severe and urgent, applied as resolutely as possible and using the most efficacious remedies.[32]

PASTORAL PROPOSAL: EVANGELIZATION OF PROSTITUTES

Sarnelli's first biographer says: "It is well known throughout Naples what this zealous worker did to rescue prostitutes from this state of sin. Every feast day he went to the parish of St. Matthew to preach in order to bring these pitiable women to repentance. For this purpose, he was the one who induced the Congregation of the Archbishopric to sponsor annual spiritual exercises in that parish."[33]

Sarnelli proposed to subdivide the city into areas and to establish in each zone a group of upright persons who would take care to visit and counsel the prostitutes. The pastors would be the spiritual force behind

outside the city"; *Ibid.*, 255. See *Ragioni legali*, 119, 148, 169; *Il quatro maggio*, 219. Alphonsus also assumes this is "less permissable"; *Theologia Moralis*, lib. III, tract. IV, 434 (Gaudé edition, vol. I, Rome 1905, 678–679). "And since Alphonsus explicitly cites Sarnelli, one can say that thanks to the latter's work, he arrived at a moral answer to this problem"; G. Wiggerman, *Der ehrwürdige Diener Gottes P. Januarius Maria Sarnelli*, Regensburg 1888, 248.

[31] *Ristretto*, 10; *Aggiunta*, 230.

[32] *Ragioni legali*, 10–12; *Aggiunta*, 1739 edition, 26; *Il quatro maggio*, 217–218.

[33] *Compendio*, 496.

this work and would be obliged to know personally, or through a priest delegate, the human and spiritual condition of those wayward sheep. The pastors themselves were to take care to give them the yearly retreat and the solemn preaching for the feast of St. Mary Magdalene.[34]

Social Proposal: Rehabilitation of Penitent Prostitutes

One of the most honored activities of Neapolitans of the eighteenth century, similar to convents that received abandoned children, was the rehabilitation of prostitutes. To this end there were confraternities, funds, convents, and celebrations that made Mary Magdalene the Penitent a very popular saint. It was a show of the baroque religiosity of the era which was filled with emotion and guilt.

We must situate the work of Sarnelli within this context, with the exception that he did not limit himself to housing those who were repentant in the appropriate monasteries and conservatories, of which there were several in the city.[35] In his pastoral practice and in his writings, what emerges clearly is his concern to understanding the motives for which a woman prostitutes herself, his generosity in providing them support while removing them from vice, his interest in giving them a dowry for marriage or, in some cases, to take them to a convent for reformed prostitutes. Sometimes it was not easy to find an available place.

In order to rescue repentant prostitutes and girls in danger, it is necessary that the authorities analyze rigorously the rights of those women in regard to those conservatories and convents which have been diverted totally or in good part to other uses [They must] decide either to reorganize them for their primary purpose or to have them give priority to repentant women or, at least, to restore the funds meant for this purpose produced by the rent from these buildings.[36]

---

[34] *Ragioni legali*, 236–237.

[35] In 1588, the conservatory named "Rifiuto" was created for women who had lost their virginity; in 1602, the one named "Soccorso" for those who wished to give up prostitution; in 1613, "Santa Maria Sucorre Miseris sucurre miseris"; in 1631, "Le Pentite"; in 1674, "Pontecorvo" for younger girls; in 1712, "Vergine dei Dolori" for virtuous young women under 21 who were in danger. In addition, there were numerous monasteries for the repentant, such as the one established near the Hospital for Incurables. A discussion of these appears in G. M. Galanti, *Descrizione geografica e politica delle Sicilie*, vol. II, Naples 1789, 137–138.

[36] *Aggiunta*, 262–263.

ADMINISTRATIVE PROPOSAL: TO RESTORE THE CONSERVATORIES

Here belongs the struggle waged by Sarnelli to restore to their original purpose the institutions which existed in Naples for repentant prostitutes and women in danger of falling [*into prostitution*], as well as for orphan boys and girls, and children of prostitutes. In the conservatories for daughters of prostitutes, the maintenance and the dowry at the time of marriage were so ample that many mothers endeavored to prove that they were prostitutes in order to obtain a place in them for one of their daughters. Sarnelli considered this giving of preference to less needy individuals the gravest of injustices, for it left in the streets the prostitutes who wished to change their lives or the indigent girls in danger; to him, it was "taking advantage of the blood of the poor."[37]

The conservatories should be administered with the greatest justice and vigilance, preventing a few privileged individuals from embezzling the pious legacies destined for orphans and needy girls. By civil and divine law, these funds should be restored completely [*to their intended purpose*], with compensation for all the physical and moral harm to those for whom they were legally intended. Nor does he show himself favorable toward a tendency at the time of converting conservatories of repentant women, which were temporary arrangements [*for those who sought to be married*], into monasteries of penitents [*planning to*] remain [*as nuns*], for all the subsidies spent in providing for the few who remain for life depleted what could be used for the marriage of many young women.

PEDAGOGICAL PROPOSAL: PROTECTION OF GIRLS IN DANGER

In order to give permanent help to many girls in danger, there is little use in constructing one or two conservatories and keeping the women there permanently as nuns, for in a

---

[37] *Ibid*, 273; it is found in a longer form in the edition of 1739, 52–55: "The third cause of the increase of prostitution is that the works and instruction provided for poor girls are not used for the purpose intended. In order to be able to enjoy success in such institutions, good influences are needed and these poor children have practically no one to offer it. Meanwhile, the few who recognize their needs and dangers and who are willing to address them are neither to be listened to nor believed"; *Ragioni legali*, 159. He suggests this by saying that it would be less unjust if these helps at least ended up in the hands of people who need them, even if they do not deal with young girls in danger. However, what is worse is that they benefit people who do not need them"; see *Ibid.*, 160–165; Giovine, *Vita*, I, 232–235.

short time the available places would be taken up. A greater help to the civic morale and to these girls in danger is that they not waste away in those conservatories, but rather that at the right time they receive help to prepare for marriage… Be wise enough to realize this very obvious truth: many young girls would lead better Christian lives in marriage than in the convent, since the Lord does not call all of them to a celibate life.[38]

No commentary is necessary on his words. The same holds for these other remarks of his: "It is better to rescue girls in danger than prostitutes." "To preserve one girl from prostitution is worth more than a thousand holocausts…more than constructing new churches, lavish altars, or extravagant decorations." "It is more meritorious to preserve a girl in danger than to rescue a Christian in captivity."[39]

Girls in danger of becoming prostitutes were "the headache" for Sarnelli, his holy obsession. For this reason he "abandoned" the community at Scala and "wasted" all his goods and his health. It would cause him anguish to see them begging for a piece of bread and to know, if no one intervened, in a few months they would become prostitutes.

His proposal begins with these practical ideas. The first thing is to ask the girls about their family, their town, the reason for their vagrancy, and see whether they can be returned to their homes. If they cannot return to them, then establish a welcoming home and teach them various occupations; later it will be easier to position them socially. Where this second option is not possible, take them to a conservatory or recommend them to an upright family. The ideal would be that, little by little, the *Maestre Romane* (a religious community dedicated to the education of girls) could establish a school and the girls could be confided to them.[40]

Poor girls, Sarnelli clearly says, are prostitutes in the making. If they are not helped and educated now, later efforts to rescue them from vice will prove useless. He also laments that there are more donations for other pious works of greater outward appearance but of much less usefulness:

[38] *Aggiunta,* 270, 272.

[39] *Aggiunta,* 284–286.

[40] *Il mondo riformato,* 30–33; see *Ragioni legali,* 78; *Aggiunta,* 270; Giovine, *Vita,* I, 162–163.

In order to rescue [active] prostitutes, O God, how much effort, how many sacrifices, how many expenses, all with so little certainty about their perseverance. Yet, all that is needed to save [poor] girls is a place to house them, since these poor unfortunate ones are happy to have a mouthful of bread. *Poor girls are prostitutes in the making; those who are saved are so many prostitutes rescued. In fact, today's prostitutes were, a few years back, almost all poor girls in danger. If they had been freed from danger at that time, they would not have lost their virginity, nor insulted the Most High, nor scandalized the towns, nor adversely affected good morals, nor harmed the Church, nor ruined the republic, nor peopled hell.* But pious Christians choose to collaborate with other pious works because they are more glamorous.[41]

For this reason, alluding to the noble ladies who dress up statues for processions, he says:

Our holy patron saints would be more honored if, instead of being clothed with gems and gold, they would see their beloved city preserved from so much vice. The saints in heaven would gladly give up, in favor of girls in danger, all the silver, precious stones, gold, and other decorations which adorn their churches and altars, provided they could preserve even one girl from prostitution.[42]

ECONOMIC PROPOSAL: FINANCING THE WORK OF PROTECTION

The general cause of prostitution is the indifference to girls who survive by begging. Such is the background at play in the writings of Sarnelli regarding prostitution. It is logical for him to say, moreover, that many prostitutes cannot change their lives because they do not find an economic alternative or a place in the institutions for the repentant. In other words, the problem of prostitution is, in great part, a reflection of social injustice. "Poor families, driven by hunger, are the closest to prostitution."[43]

---

[41] *Aggiunta*, 285; ed. 1739, 67. The text in italics was not included in the nineteenth-century edition.

[42] *Aggiunta*, ed. 1739, 45. Another censored text.

[43] *Ragioni legali*, 155. "The first cause of *[the increase of prostitution]* is the indifference of pious people toward giving alms for orphaned or abandoned girls who wander begging

Sarnelli's proposal to break out of this vicious circle of poverty and prostitution is not a social revolution, nor a redistribution of interests, nor anything of the sort. It is consistent with the climate of the eighteenth century, but with a disconcerting clarity. He appeals, in the first place, to the conscience of the rich:

"Let the rich know that on account of poverty, parents and children, brothers and sisters, sleep in the same bed... that many prostitutes remain in the brothels because there is no one to help them change their lives; and that the virtue of poor girls is exchanged for a few crumbs of bread. Consequently, even from their childhood they live off of prostitution."[44]

He denounces the superfluous expenditures of "well-to-do families" and invites them to dedicate their wealth to more humanitarian ends by taking a girl into their household.

It would greatly help to purge the city and to diminish the number of prostitutes if each well-to-do family would accept into their home and take on as a servant one of those poor homeless and abandoned girls in order to educate her in a Christian fashion. Pay attention to someone who has the experience [i.e., Sarnelli]...These docile and obedient girls, not yet inured to vice, usually outdo themselves marvelously with a good education and are content with a slice of bread. What a great thing it would be to give those poor creatures the leftovers from the table, a minimal part of the abundant riches the wealthy receive from divine Providence and something they often waste in feeding dogs and horses, or in promoting luxuries and vanities.[45]

He proposes the creation of a fund whose interest would be dedicated exclusively to the work of rescuing and sheltering those endangered:

in the plazas so they would be able to marry or to be cared for in a conservatory or by an upright family. These youngsters, realizing they are deprived of all human help, pressured by basic needs and starving, end up despairing and make the deplorable exchange of holy chastity for a piece of bread. Virtue gone, pleasure tasted, shame reined in, they take up the life of a prostitute"; *Ibid.*, 157.

[44] *Aggiunta*, 283. See *Ibid.*, 275, 282.

[45] *Ibid.*, 266.

It would be very useful for the effective and continuing preservation of the morality of the citizens if a special fund was established or the best assets dedicated to help repentant prostitutes and their children, and to protect helpless youths and orphan girls who wander asking for alms and sleeping anywhere. And, in a special way, they would give protection to those poor girls who have lost their virtue *and are the most prone to fall into prostitution. Many girls seven and eight years of age already live as prostitutes. A reality difficult to believe for one who has not had the experience, but it is the absolute truth* [The administrators of those funds] would be continually concerned to put an end to everything that encourages prostitution."[46]

The last proposal is even bolder. At the zenith of the baroque era, the things Sarnelli proposes in the last chapter of the *Supplement* about concrete means would have been shocking, to say the least, and incomprehensible: "It is undeniable that to dedicate so much wealth to the construction of churches and luxurious decorations while one's neighbor suffers so many severe needs is not a sacrifice pleasing to God!" This chapter, filled with citations from the Church fathers, was "logically" suppressed in the edition of 1851.[47]

"With a small portion of those church riches spent on feasts, edifices, or paintings, how many thousands of girls in danger could be sheltered each year in a conservatory or helped toward marriage? How many prostitutes rescued in order to live in repentance?"[48] But Sarnelli was not dealing only with humanitarian motivation. For Sarnelli there is a very clear theological conviction in the background, which helps discern the authenticity of religion: those poor girls are the true Temple of God. "Let whoever wants to, continue constructing churches, but the true lovers of the Crucified cannot remain at ease while...so many poor girls, living temples of the Holy Spirit, precious members of holy Church, preferred souls of the Creator, made in the image of the Most Holy Trinity, redeemed by divine Blood, are now infected with so many vices."[49]

---

[46] *Ibid.*, 269–270. The italicized portions were censored from the 1851 edition but are found in the one of 1739, 48.

[47] *Aggiunta*, ed. 1739, 73–80.

[48] *Ibid.*, 75.

[49] *Ibid.*, 77. "Wall-hangings, silver, gold do not give glory to saints, but instead, faithful souls do. These give to the Lord thousands of women who, preserved from brothels and rescued from sin, dedicate their affections and that of their children to God, something that is equal to thousands of pious devotions"; *Ibid.*, 79.

SARNELLI'S IMAGE OF WOMEN

This topic would require a fuller study that would need to take into account the other writings of Sarnelli. We limit ourselves to some general observations.

The first observation is of a hermeneutic nature: How to understand the differences of language? Sarnelli expresses himself in one way when he refers to professional prostitutes and in another when he alludes to the potential victims of prostitution. In the first case, he speaks as a fiery, prophetic, and moralizing orator who condemns the vices of a corrupt city. When he speaks of the girls in danger, he criticizes luxury and begs and intercedes. They are like two faces of the same prophet.

As far as female prostitutes are concerned, he suggests they fall into various classes. Some are victims: obliged to become prostitutes on account of poverty; pressured or sold by their own family; violated and/ or abandoned by their lovers or husbands; already used to that lifestyle and with no other alternative because they are old, deformed, or sickly.[50] The majority of them fell into that way of life because of the lack of timely help. And some, if helped economically, could repent and change their lives. Another class of prostitutes is the "professionals": the ones who voluntarily and for pleasure have assumed this lifestyle. To them he dedicates his worse epithets. They are not victims but tormentors. They are a pack of ferocious wolves who take advantage of the darkness of night to devour the sheep. They are treacherous souls who have wickedness as their profession, sin as their occupation, scandalizing and bringing the innocent to the precipice as their artistry. In their caves the worst heresies are born.

Sarnelli is not, therefore, a naive person who condemns all prostitutes or who justifies them all. He knows that many are in that life for love of vice and as a business and a life choice. Some have added witchcraft to prostitution and have "an open relationship with the devil." The worst are the procurers, those who make a business of them and of others. Especially those who draw into vice indigent girls, buying them for a little money. "They go through all areas destroying poor innocent girls. And they even travel to the farthest reaches of the

---

[50] *Ibid.*, 230. "What a horror it is to see so many publicly violated little girls of 7 or 8 go for care to hospitals, emaciated, destroyed, and then leave with no safe place to stay and, losing all shame, become prostitutes; and they are only little girls"; *Ragioni legali,* 123. See *Ibid.*, 20, 88, 183.

Kingdom, buying girls to sell them in the city to the highest bidder."[51] Not simply evil, they are saturated with malice: "They know the needs [of their victims] and are always alert; they find out when someone's father or mother dies...and then they go to console her and they begin to describe the great difficulties she will undergo if she lacks money. Thus, under an evil pretense of charity, they offer her an easier life."[52]

But a prostitute can also be a redeemed woman. When Sarnelli points out that "actual prostitutes were at one time themselves poor girls in danger," he is admitting the fact that basically there is a question here of "an occasion of grace that was neglected"; and that we must offer them the means of recovering it. Even the "professional prostitutes," who should be locked up, have the right to a pastoral visit of the parish priest and to the medical attention of doctors, as well as be allowed to go to listen to sermons and make retreats. This redemption of prostitutes is a difficult, slow task, filled with failures.

For this reason, Sarnelli wagers everything on the protection of honest women; especially of poor girls and children related to prostitutes. A protection which begins with bettering the social context. "Would it not be a greater charity to free young girls from the proximate occasion of giving themselves over to prostitution for a trifle than to raise up those who have already become prostitutes from so many faults and from such a great risk of falling again into that hell of vice? Monasteries and conservatories are built with immense expense and great effort to rescue a hundred or two hundred repentant prostitutes...while with the spread [*of prostitutes throughout the city*], there are so many women each year who are in a true and proximate danger."[53]

In summary, Sarnelli's idea of women in general is positive. She is not a demon or an occasion of sin for men. She is fragile and has an immense dignity, for she is a temple of the Holy Spirit and made in the image of the Trinity.[54] Professional prostitutes are perverse persons and tempters; in their presence every precaution must be taken. But in herself, a woman is not a "dangerous Lolita."

---

[51] *Ragioni legali*, 172; *Ristretto*, 32.

[52] *Ragioni legali*, 170.

[53] *Aggiunta*, 268.

[54] In the nineteenth century edition, the texts were censored in which Sarnelli spoke of woman as an image of the Trinity; see *Aggiunta*, ed. 1739, 47 and 77.

It is not true that young women are temptresses of men. On this point, trust someone who has had years of experience [in dealing with them]. If honest women did not have men who tempt them, they would remain chaste and innocent. For the proper piety of that sex, the fear of the men who govern them, the modesty which nature itself has given them, all of this protects them from contamination. But when the unwary are repeatedly attacked and flattered with false promises, cheated by the weakness of their sex and at times even violated, they give up. It is true that women can be very astute and scandalize men, but those are the shameless ones who have lost their faith and their virtue.[55]

Besides being protected, the girl must also be educated. Only in this way will she be truly protected. It seemed normal to him that girls should have access to primary education, although he understood education of women as training in home skills. There does not exist a social class more "adapted" for education; even the girls in the street "usually excel marvelously." Even from the first years of his ministry, he had striven to include girls in the program of Christian education, since public schools were not yet a reality. It was he who proposed to Alphonsus the creation for girls of some sort of "evening chapels," or of oratories like those established by St. Philip Neri which enlisted the help of some women of each neighborhood.[56] And later he was a great promoter of the schools for girls run by the *Maestre Romane*.

---

[55] *Ragioni legali*, 167. How one compares this passage with the "hagiographic" version of the life of Sarnelli is a matter for future biographies to clarify, for example, "According to a manuscript found in the house at Ciorani, we know that the servant of God, after becoming a deacon, made the firm decision not to look at women nor to touch their hands." "He spoke with downcast eyes not only to women in general, but even to his sisters, his sister-in-law, and his mother. Other women, even those he dealt with often, he many times did not recognize on sight"; Giovine, *Vita*, I, 107; II, 129; see Wiggermann, *Der ehrwürdige*, 458.

[56] See Giovine, *Vita*, I, 164–165. Regarding education for women, Sarnelli dedicates long sections in *Il mondo riformato*, 29–34, 120–124. See also A. Illibato, *La donna a Napoli nel Settecento. Aspetti della condizione e dell'istruzione femminile*, Naples 1985; E. Chiosi, "Intellettuali e plebe. Il problema dell'istruzione elementare nel settecento napoletano," *Rivista storica italiana* 100 (1988): 155–175.

CONCLUSION

Sarnelli appears as a moralist who combines experience and creativity, apostolic action and prayer, dialogue with others and personal reflection, exposition and defense of his own ideas. Criticizing those who did nothing because they did not want to complicate their lives, he says: "It is delightful to live in leisure, without worries, without opposition, without obligations, in tranquility, and repose. But this repose and peace are an authentic image of death." [57] He preferred agitation, sleeplessness, contradictions. He suffered when he saw suffering; he could not remain unmoved. He gave his life for a cause that he considered the most noble of all: to save before a fall. It was just such pastoral charity that vitalized all his life. For this reason, it appears to us that the best synthesis of his life can be found in the text of 1 John 3:14: "We know that we have passed from death to life because we love one another. Whoever does not love abides in death."

On the occasion of the 250th anniversary of the death of Sarnelli [*1994*], his mortal remains were transferred to the small town of Ciorani, the place where his family received and supported the community of Redemptorists in its infancy. There he awaits a glorious resurrection. In the meantime we look forward to his anticipated glorification as saint.

BASIC BIBLIOGRAPHY

Sarnelli, Gennaro. See Bibliography of Major Writings on page 445 of this volume under *Ragioni legali* (1736); *Il quatro maggio* (1738); *Ristretto delle ragioni* (1739); *Aggiunta* (1739).

Alfonsus de Liguori. "Compendio," See "Abbreviations." Written shortly after Sarnelli's death, it has formed the basis of later biographies [*Chapter One provides the English translation of this work.*]

Capone, Domenico - S. Majorano. *I redentoristi e le redentoriste.*

Le radici. Materdomini [1985].

---

[57] *Il mondo riformato*, 22.

De Meulemeester, Maurice. *Origines de la Congrégation du Très Saint-Rédempteur. Études et Documents.* 2 vol., Louvain 1953–1957.

De Spirito, A. "La prostituzione feminile a Napoli nel XVIII secolo," in *Ricerche di storia sociale e religiosa* 7 (1978): 31–70.

Dumortier, François. *Le vénérable serviteur de Dieu, le Père Javier Marie Sarnelli de la Congrégation du T.S. Rédempteur.* Paris 1886.

Giovine, Raimondo. *Vita del gran servo di Dio D. Gennaro Maria Sarnelli, padre della Congregazione del SS. Redentore e di quella delle Apostoliche Missioni.* 2 vol., Naples 1858.

Guidi, L. "Un mondo trasformato in monastero: L'utopia sociale di Gennaro Maria Sarnelli e il problema delle fanciulle pericolanti," in *Campania Sacra* 27 (1996): 255–278.

Orlandi, G. *Alfonso de Liguori: Carteggio.* Volume I: 1724–1743. Rome: Edizioni di Storia e Litteratura 2004.

Sampaoli, A. *La prostituzione nel pensiero del Settecento.* Rimini 1973.

Valenzi, L. "Prostitute, pentite, pericolanti, oblate a Napoli tra '700 e '800," in *Campania Sacra* 22 (1991): 307–322.

Valenzi, L. "Sarnelli e le prammatiche *de meretricibus*," in *Campania Sacra* 27 (1996): 279–298.

Wiggermann, Gebhard. *Der ehrwürdige Diener Gottes P. Januarius Maria Sarnelli.* Regensburg 1888.

CHAPTER THREE

BLESSED GENNARO MARIA SARNELLI

Redemptorist Missionary
Apostle of Naples
(1702-1744)

By Rev. Fabriciano Ferrero, CSsR [58]

I. ANOTHER REDEMPTORIST MISSIONARY PROCLAIMED BLESSED

Interest in the "lives" of the saints constitutes a characteristic of Alphonsian spirituality and Redemptorist traditional spirituality. In the community library at Ciorani, quite close to the present tomb of Father Sarnelli, is preserved the library of another Redemptorist Servant of God, Father Manuel Ribera (1811–1874), whose cause for beatification was introduced on May 8, 1912. Among the books in this library are more than 500 volumes containing the lives of saints and books written by them. Among these books are those of Father Sarnelli, on whose re-editing Ribera had participated when he was dedicating himself to spiritual direction, above all with youth, and to the spreading of religious literature.

There is a very simple explanation of why Redemptorist spirituality had an interest in knowing and meditating on the lives of the saints in the form of spiritual reading. The saints, called as every believer is, to continue the mission of the Incarnate Word, made their own the style of life that he wanted them to assume. In this way, the figure of the saint acquires, like that of Christ, a prophetic and paschal meaning.

---

[58] *[Father Ferrero wrote this article on the occasion of the beatification of Blessed Gennaro Maria Sarnelli in 1994; it was translated from the original Spanish by Norman Simmons in 1998. Here it is presented in a reduced and modified form by the present editor.]*

On May 12, 1996, the beatification of Venerable Father Gennaro Maria Sarnelli (1702–1744) was celebrated in Rome.[59] He was one of the first followers of St. Alphonsus in the Congregation, besides being his friend and collaborator in apostolic works during the first years of the Institute.

It was Alphonsus who gave the funeral discourse for his friend (we still preserve the original, handwritten outline) and who, shortly afterward, composed the *Summary [Compendio] of the Life of the Servant of God*, the first biography of Sarnelli. Alphonsus wrote this and other biographies for his friends and confreres, died with the reputation of sanctity, because he discovered in them examples and models of lay, priestly, and religious holiness. Saints, whom he had had the privilege of knowing while they lived and, in some way, had been able to incarnate their own ideal of holiness.

With Sarnelli so little known among us, and to understand him a bit better, we will begin by proposing some keys to read his character (II) and a little biographical data of his life that will help in understanding his spirituality (III).

The "Holy Apostle of Naples" was the title that his contemporaries gave him in the first half of the nineteenth century. To see why this is so, we will examine the genesis of his apostolic vocation (IV and V) and the most significant expressions of that vocation: missionary evangelization, spiritual formation of the people (VI), the social ministry (VII). This allows us to know better the printed works (VIII) and his spirituality based on the mystery of the Most Holy Trinity, of Christ the Redeemer, and of the great Mother of God. Finally, we will show his manner of formulating a way of holiness and of prayer for everyone (IX).

II. KEYS FOR UNDERSTANDING THE CHARACTER OF SARNELLI

Sarnelli is best known by his relationship with the person and work of St. Alphonsus Maria Liguori (1696–1787); so much so that it would be very easy to write a biography of our Blessed from the passages that refer to him in the great biographies of Alphonsus. Moreover, the life of Sarnelli acquired its full historic meaning in the Alphonsian and

---

[59] [*Translator's note: Because Father Ferrero wrote this article in the months prior to Sarnelli's beatification, he spoke in the future tense; for this translation we have changed these verbs into the past tense.*]

Redemptorist universe. Nevertheless, in order to understand what we want to say, it is necessary to keep in mind some key points that let us identify and frame the uniqueness of his character in its origins and in the evolution of the Congregation of the Most Holy Redeemer.

"THE OTHER" NEAPOLITAN LAWYER

Being a lawyer in Naples throughout the course of the eighteenth century was a concrete way of approaching the world of justice, the Palace of the Tribunals, and the middle class of the academic toga. Nobleman, military officer, lawyer, bishop, monk, religious: these were the forms of life emerging in the Neapolitan high society of that time. On the periphery of that baroque and learned society were the artisans, the poor, the vagabonds, and the sick in the hospitals. Farther away still there were the peasants, the migrant herders, the pimps, and the bandits.

One of the ways to have a career in this society was the legal profession. This was also the thought of the parents of Alphonsus. Another detail that should not surprise us is that among the first Redemptorist missionaries, there are many, proportionally speaking, who had a career in law.

Now, 300 years after the birth of Alphonsus, we see also on the altar "another lawyer from Naples" in the eighteenth century: one of his best friends and a Servant of God, whose biography Alphonsus himself wrote in 1744, shortly after the death of our Blessed. The two characters complement and clarify one another, above all, if we keep in mind some other details.[60]

AMONG THE LAITY IN THE RELIGIOUS ASSOCIATIONS IN NAPLES

Just as Alphonsus, so also Sarnelli begins a more intense spiritual life with the association for lawyers and doctors: daily prayer, periodic meetings, spiritual exercises, extraordinary practice of Christian charity, etc. From these associations he makes contact with the world of the poor and the sick. Here he presents us with a basic requirement he offers us as a model of holiness: the sense of the poor and the active dedication to their service.

---

[60] For a study of the context from this point of view, see Giuseppe Orlandi, "The Kingdom of Naples in the Eighteenth Century," in Francisco Chiovaro (ed.) trans. by J. Robert Fenili, *The History of the Congregation of the Most Holy Redeemer*, Vol. I. *The Origins (1732–1793)*, Liguori, MO: Liguori Publications, 1996, 39–96.

On the other hand, his pastoral work, while preparing for the priesthood and as a member of the Apostolic Missions, was such that Sarnelli experienced the social, family, youth, and children's problems of the city; the diverse forms of prostitution; religious ignorance; the vice of blasphemy; and the abandonment of the country people, above all in the periphery of Naples.

This is the context in which the vocational, apostolic, and priestly process was developing for Sarnelli up to his incorporation into the Congregation of the Most Holy Redeemer: member of a fraternity, seminarian, cleric, boarder in the Chinese Residence, member of the Apostolic Missions, priest, Redemptorist Missionary, writer.

THE HISTORICAL ROLE OF SARNELLI IN THE CONGREGATION OF THE MOST HOLY REDEEMER

What we have just explained about Sarnelli reminds us of the life of Alphonsus, up to the point where the "definite calling" of both makes one of them a "founder" and the other, a "member" of the Congregation of the Most Holy Redeemer, even though they remained members also of the Apostolic Missions up to the end of their lives.

The character of the saint and the blessed acquire their proper historical dimensions if we contemplate them from the perspective of the Congregation of the Most Holy Redeemer. We may be surprised by the peculiarity of the influence that Sarnelli had on the Congregation, which was truly significant, even though he followed a completely unique process.

Actually, the character of Sarnelli, wasted and tattered, lost among the books and papers when he was at home, or surrounded by poor and sick people when he dedicated himself to the service of the others, has left a mark on the Redemptorists of all times due to his apostolic zeal, his type of hermitlike and martyrlike holiness, and the books that he wrote. "Father Mautone, at the time, Provincial of the Province of Naples, is the echo of the whole century (1744–1843), affirming that, during his novitiate, the old fathers called Sarnelli a St. Peter of Alcantara for his penances, a St. Louis Gonzaga for his purity, and a new St. Francis Regis for his zeal for souls."[61]

---

[61] F. Dumortier, *Le venerable Serviteur de Dieu le Pere Janvier-Maria Sarnelli de la Congregation du T. S Redempteur,* Paris, 1886, 251.

Let us look at some comments from early documents.

LETTER FROM BISHOP THOMAS FALCOIA (APRIL 19, 1738)

We have, in the first place, a letter from Monsignor Thomas Falcoia to the Redemptorists, dictated to his secretary, Father Caesar Sportelli on April 19, 1738. In it, he recommends the social ministry of Sarnelli to all the members of his Institute. He points out a man who, almost by accident, brings to the evangelizing project of Falcoia and Alphonsus and the missionary mysticism of Venerable Celeste Maria Crostarosa an outstanding apostolic restlessness with a social perspective. Even though he is a "learned" author, he shows a remarkable ability to put words into action. In *Il mondo riformato* and in the "moral works" of Sarnelli, the pastoral problem has sociopolitical roots that cannot be ignored in planning an effective ministry. This is an aspect at our beginnings that today calls for our attention, above all, because we are accustomed to pay attention only to the pastoral issues in the lives of our great early missionaries.

Sarnelli is also the one who began to organize, in an explicit and systematic way in this evangelizing project, a path of holiness and prayer for all people.

The death of Falcoia in 1743 and the premature loss of Sarnelli in 1744 obliged Alphonsus to take charge of the all the inheritance of both of these figures, who are so significant for the beginnings of the Institute. The holy founder will assume, in a paradigmatic way, the apostolate of the missions and of the pen that had begun with Sarnelli. On the other hand, the initiative of a ministry with social issues will acquire its own particular spirit, above all, with St. Clement and with his disciples and imitators. Here is Falcoia's letter:

My Dearest Brothers in the Lord:

Since it has pleased H.D.M [*His Divine Majesty*] to assist one of your brothers and to bless his great works in stopping the intolerable shame of loose women of the world who in the City and Kingdom of Naples together with all its surroundings, were being mixed among respectable families, to the dishonor of the blessed God and with extraordinary detriment to good morals, we have believed it opportune to exhort you and to beg all the temporary superiors of each House, the priests and all the subjects of our blessed Institute, that you be concerned (*zelare*) prudently in the future with such an important service for the Lord and for the peoples, and support the zeal and the hard work of the man who has been called into our own way of life (*sorte*). In this you will bring happiness to the Heart of the Most High, and you will console our spirit, which ardently desires this. It is demanded of you through the depths of the mercy of our Savior. Meanwhile, we remain begging from H. D. M. the fullness of his heavenly blessings.

> From our residence of Castellammare,
> this 19 of April, 1738. (seal)
>
> Tom. Vec. De Castell. etc.

P.S. Preserve this original in the archives of the house in Scala, and make copies for the archives of the other houses.

> D. Cesare Sportelli[62]

COMPENDIUM OF SARNELLI'S LIFE
WRITTEN BY ST. ALPHONSUS (1696–1787)[63]

Alphonsus summarizes the first steps of writing his biography of Sarnelli (which would not be published until 1752) in his letter to Canon Giuseppe Sparano at Santa Restituta in Naples. Later, it would almost always appear in editions of the work of Sarnelli, with some editions of the biography published in the form of an independent booklet.

---

[62] The original Italian text is in the General Redemptorist Archives in Rome. Transcription in: *Positio,, Summarium additionale*, 12–13.

[63] In Gennaro Ma. Sarnelli, *Il mondo santificato*, Naples, 1752, 258–288, where it appears as an appendix of the 4th edition. See Maurice de Meulemeester, *Bibliographie*, vol. I, 77–78 [*This biography appears as Chapter One above*].

Ciorani, June 17, 1744

Praised be the Most Blessed Sacrament and Mary Immaculate!

My Most Learned and Reverend Lord and Most Venerable Father:

The Lord Canon Sersale commanded me to write some notes [*"notizie"*] on the life of Don Gennaro, of happy memory, telling me that he would like to publish them in the Congregation (of the Apostolic Missions) along with those of the Life of Carace. I have already written them and sent them to Father Superior (Canon Rosa of the Apostolic Missions). Sersale told me that it had been Your V. S. Ilma [*Most Illustrious Lordship*] who had the idea; and for this reason, I ask that you arrange the manuscript as it best may appear and, above all, that you correct the errors, for one of our lay brothers has copied it and the mail did not leave me time to correct it.

But, above all, I ask you, that you urge the gentlemen of the Congregation to get it published. I realize that this is our responsibility. But God knows our situation, and D. Gennaro has bequeathed his books to us; but they are burdened with debts and restrictions. I know that V. S. Ilma can do a lot. I ask as much as I can. It will not only serve for the honor of the Congregation, but also for the benefit of many. V. S. Ilma loved Sarnelli in life but must love him more now dead because he has died a saint [*da santo*]. Finally, I ask that you give me a reply and that you commend me to Jesus Christ.

With humble reverence, I remain yours,
Long live Jesus, Mary, Joseph, and Teresa![64]

This biography of 1752 emphasizes the edifying life of Sarnelli as it was seen in the Institute. What interested Alphonsus more than the biographic data was the model of holiness which he incarnated and why the people called him "the holy missionary." This biography had great importance for the cause of beatification of Sarnelli, as also for the image that the Redemptorists formed of our Blessed in later biographies.

---

[64] Alphonsus de Liguori, *Lettere*, I, 94–95.

SARNELLI IN THE HISTORIOGRAPHY OF THE CONGREGATION

1. A significant development of the biography of Sarnelli's life was written by Father G. Landi (1725–1797), in his *Istoria della Congregazione del ss. Redentore*.[65] He wrote this work as *a help in his position* as master of novies in Rome (St. Clement was with him in 1784). The text gives us a portrait of Sarnelli. Clearly what Landi wrote shows the situation on which Father Nicholas Salzano reflected during the cause for beatification: "Every master of novices was presenting V. P. Sarnelli as a model of holiness and of virtue."[66]

Our interest in Father Landi at this point is due, above all, to the influence that he exercised on St. Clement Maria Hofbauer (1751–1820). Without doubt, it is due to Father Landi that Clement knew the life and works of Sarnelli, that some of them would be brought to Warsaw, and that it would be possible to discover a certain parallelism between the apostolic concerns of both men: the education of children and of youth, the fight against the marginalization of women, The Devout Life, the importance of prayer, etc.

2. But there is something more. In a letter, written on June 12, 1800 from Warsaw by Clement to Father Paul Blasucci, Superior General of the Redemptorists, we read:

> We are very happy to know that the Life of our venerable Father (St. Alphonsus., written by Father A. M. Tannoia) is published (1798); I do not doubt that the second volume may already have come out (1800, the third would come out in 1802).

> How we desire to have this biography as soon as possible, if it would be possible, along with the other works of our Father that can be acquired, except the Moral Theology, which we already have, as well as the little works of Sarnelli and any others that refer to our Congregation!...

---

[65] This work was written in 1782 but never published; it exists in manuscript form in the Redemptorist General Archives. The section on Sarnelli appears in the second of the two-volume work, Ms., I, 111–136.

[66] *Positio, Responsio de Animadversiones*, 19.

We also have the following little works of our Father: *La visita al santissimo Sacramento ed a Maria santissima, L'amore dell'anime, Opera dogmatica contro gli eretici,* and nothing more. From Father Sarnelli, *L'anima desolata,* and nothing more.

I also request authentic images of St. Alphonsus. And just as well, if they are available, some copies of the lives and images of other well-known members of our Institute who have stood out due to their virtues. Because, if is pleasing to God, I want, now that my life and that of Father Huebl are declining, to make known perfectly to the confreres all that concerns our Congregation; they already also burn with desire to know in depth the beginnings, the works, the outstanding members that the Institute has had and many more things.[67]

These words of Clement show the importance that he gives to the works of Sarnelli for the deepening of the Redemptorist identity. In fact, the enumeration that he makes for us of the books that he has is of the highest interest for studying the process of his own formation. In these, it speaks to us, in effect:

• Of the biography of the Founder and of the general history of the Congregation (Father Tannoia and, as Sarnelli mentions elsewhere, Father Landi).

• Of the works of St. Alphonsus [Those mentioned above, as well as the *Praxis Confessarii* and *Opere Ascetiche*].

• Of the works of Sarnelli and of other confreres. Actually, at the time, he only possessed *L'anima desolata.*[68]

---

[67] See Commission of Redemptorist Spirituality, *To Be a Redemptorist According to St. Clement Hofbauer,* Readings in Redemptorist Spirituality, vol. 4, Rome. 1994, 201–202. The original text is in *Monumenta Hofbaueriana,* VIII, 75–76.

[68] For a more extended discussion of these contents, see F. Ferrero. *Función histórica de S. Clemente Maria Hofbauer en la Congregación del Smo. Redentor (1785–1820):* SHCSR. 34 (1986) 338–339.

3. The other early historian of the Congregation, Father Antonio Maria Tannoia (1727–1808), also refers expressly to the life of Sarnelli.[69] Among the details that he recalls appear the following:

- The friendship and dealings between Alphonsus and Sarnelli (I, 38) and other priests and companions, "all apostolic men, deceased, as is known, with the reputation of holiness" (I, 43–44).

- The desire of Sarnelli to join Alphonsus when they were in the Chinese Residence (I, 72). "The priest, D. Gennaro Sarnelli (son of D. Angelo Sarnelli, Baron of Ciorani), who lived with Ripa, began to admire the work of Alphonsus and followed him. He also was a great theologian and great lawyer, a man versed in every kind of literature, hungry, as Alphonsus was, for the salvation of souls, full of zeal for the glory of Jesus Christ, as is seen afterwards" (I, 77).

- The absence of Sarnelli in the opening of the Congregation in Scala (II, 82). He was in Naples when the first companions abandoned Alphonsus (II, 93). He was incorporated into the group later to the saint's great joy (II, 98).

- The work of evangelization and preaching at the foundation in Ciorani (II, 103–107).

- Sarnelli involved in preaching in the Archdiocese of Naples with Alphonsus and Father Villani (II, 124–126).

- Speaking of the vows and the oath of perseverance which the Redemptorists made, Tannoia says: "Among others, as I said, who were in the Congregation were the Fathers Sportelli, Mazzini, Sarnelli, Rossi, Villani, and Cafaro. These, who ought to be considered as other pillars of the Congregation for being of special merit, more than being encouraged by Alphonsus, they made each other want to make such a sacrifice and they pushed Alphonsus to keep

---

[69] Tannoia, *Della vita ed Istituto del V. S. D. Alfonso Ma. Liguori, Vescovo di Agata de'Goti e Fondatore della Congregazione de'Preti Missionori del SS. Redentore*, Naples. 1798, 1800, 1802, 3 Vol.

at it. Everyone was willing. But the final push, especially for the vow and oath of stability, was the inconstancy of Father D. Carlos Majorino of the Land of Saragnano, Diocese of Salerno" (II, 134).

- The absence of Sarnelli in solemn expression of the vows and oath of perseverance, in the hands of Monsignor Falcoia, on July 22, 1740 (II, 136).
- The ministry of Father Sarnelli in Naples against the scandal of prostitution (II, 145, 154, and 207).
- The pain of Alphonsus "at the loss in Naples of the excellent D. Gennaro Maria Sarnelli, one of the keystones of his incipient Congregation" (II, 154).

4. Also significant is the influence that Sarnelli has exercised in the Congregation by means of Very Rev. Manuel Ribera (1811– 1874). In the *Responsio ad Animadversiones*[70], he recalls how he heard his family speaking of [Sarnelli] since his childhood, how he found in his family house, from the most tender age, some "works of Servant of God that from then on, they had constituted nourishment of my spirit with great spiritual benefit." His elders, whom he heard speaking of the Servant of God, related to him many things about him, sometimes, at his own insistence, "that, even then, because of the great idea that I myself had formed of the Servant of God by reading his works, I always desired to know even the smallest fact of his life."

He also collaborated with R. Giovine in the writing of his life of Sarnelli, published in 1858. He did the same with Father

A. De Risio when he wrote the resume of another biography of our Blessed (*ibid.*, pp. 29–30).

Finally, Father F. Dumortier adds to the text that we were citing above: "For this period and on the same date, the resume *[of Sarnelli's life]* of Alphonsus was translated into French for the first time. Austria, Germany, and Poland knew of the Servant of God before France and honored his memory, thanks to the concern

---

[70] Pp.14–15 and 29–30.

of Venerable Father Clement Mary Hofbauer, of Father Huebl, and of Father Passerat. Finally in 1848, Italy offered the supreme homage, accepting with enthusiasm a new edition of his complete works prepared by Fathers Ribera and Tortora."[71]

We insist on the importance of Father Ribera due to the influence that he had in the Congregation as master of novices as well as in Naples, from 1846 to 1874, with his spiritual direction and with the apostolate of the press. With his apostolate of writing, he managed to include the complete works of Sarnelli.[72]

From Father Ribera, the influence passed also to Father Victor Loyodice (1834–1916), who left us a biographical sketch of Sarnelli, in his Hijos Ilustres de San Alfonso Maria de Ligorio (1898). When it was reprinted in 1922,[73]6 the new editor remarks: "The life of this Servant of God, the Venerable Father Gennaro Maria Sarnelli, is in first place (pp. 5–27) because he was the first subject of our biographies to receive the immortal reward for his virtues." It begins with the biblical text: Zeal for your house consumes me (Psalm 68:10), because "the Venerable Sarnelli was the Apostle of Naples in the first half of the Eighteenth Century. Zeal for the glory of God consumed his soul as it did that of the Divine Redeemer. Because of the excess of stress that he imposed upon himself in the short lapse of the ten years that his ministry lasted, he came to be the apostle and martyr of charity" (p. 5).

---

[71] F. Dumortier, *Le venerable Serviteur de Dieu le Pere Janvier-Marie Sarnelli de la Congregation du T. S. Redempteur,* Paris, 1886, 250–251.

[72] See F. Ferrero, "Bartolo Longo e i Redentoristi," in F. Volpe (ed.), *Bartolo Longo e il suo tempo,* Vol. I., Rome, 1983, 247–282.

[73] This work was reedited and republished in Montevideo (1922) by an anonymous Redemptorist as *Hijos Ilustres de San Alfonso Maria de Ligorio o sucintas biografias de los Venerables de la Congregación del Santisimo Redentor.*

SARNELLI AND THE REDEMPTORISTINES

Even today, we can become acquainted with the relationship of Sarnelli with the Order of the Most Holy Redeemer by means of his correspondence with Sister Maria Angela del Cielo (Teresa de Vito), Neapolitan Redemptoristine, "who died in the monastery of Scala on May 30, 1783" when she was about 81 years old.[74]

A woman of virtue and of spirit—as Sister Maria Celeste Crostarosa spoke of her—is a figure of the highest stature in the tortured vicissitudes of the Redemptoristine beginnings. She was Director of Novices in 1725, when Crostarosa planned the new religious project (*Institute and Rule of the Most Holy Savior Contained in the Holy Gospels*) and tried without success to put it into practice. Maria Angela was elected superior June 5, 1726 at the instruction of Falcoia. Re-elected on May 22, 1729, again on June 1, 1732, and for a third time, May 27, 1735, she headed the nuns during the difficult beginnings of the two Redemptoristic Institutes. She once more returned as superior from 1751 to 1754, again from 1760 to 1769 and, finally from 1773 to 1779.[75]

Sister Maria Angela del Cielo "maintained her correspondence by letter with Alphonsus and with other Redemptorists of the early period. Bl. Gennaro Sarnelli was her spiritual director for several years. From the letters that he wrote her as director, thirty have been published. They encompass the years 1737 to 1744."[76]

In a quick reading of this correspondence,[77] what catches our attention is the trust between the two involved in the conversation, the exchange of prayers (Sarnelli requests insistently her prayers for his works and for his personal problems), the exchange of concerns and problems, of exhortations and mutual consolations, and a series of basic themes from traditional spirituality, especially the following:

---

[74] S. Majorano, "Il P. Fiocchi Direttore spirituale, II. Corrispondenza con suor Maria Angela del Cielo," SHCSR, 31 (1983), 3.

[75] *Ibid.* 3–4.

[76] *Ibid.* 4.

[77] F. Dumortier F. M. Bozzaotra, *Vita del V. S. D. P. Gennaro M. Sarnelli della Congregazione del SS. Redentore scrita in francese dal P. F. Dumortier e tradotta dal F. M. Bozzaotra, aggiuntovi le Lettere del Venerabile*, Naples, 1889, 207–312.

- Union of the soul with God.
- Tendency toward perfection.
- Imitation of Jesus Christ.
- Love of God and desires to please God always.
- Gratitude toward the greatest Good, correspondence with supernatural grace and in the contradictions.
- Trust in God and fear or lack of trust in oneself in feelings and in contradictions.
- Obedience in accepting community duties.
- Corporal mortifications, spirit of penitence, denial of one's own will, detachment from creatures.
- Humility without faintheartedness and sincerity without scrupulosity.
- Counsels for living the tribulations through which the community passes on the way to obtaining peace and unity.
- Reference to published works and to the use of them for the community.
- Necessity of prayer in order to overcome difficulties and to accomplish the works under way.
- Practices of piety.
- Norms about confession, communion, the vows, temptations, encouragement of the community, cautions, etc.

Sarnelli always showed a certain bias against extraordinary phenomena of the spiritual life. Thus, on April 8, 1743, he wrote the superior of Scala: "I also have always prized the Institute of the priests of the Most Holy Savior as being a work of God, not founded on private revelations, but on the basic reality of things and an Institute guided by the Gospel and tradition of the Church of God, and seeing in it great fruit and real profit for its members and for our neighbors."[78]

But, among the many aspects that could stand out in the spirituality of Sister Angela, due in some way to Sarnelli, we would like to emphasize, with Father Dumortier "the zeal for the salvation of souls":

---

[78] See below, Chapter V, Letter dated April 8, 1743.

Our Lord tells his disciples in the Gospel to raise up their eyes, to look at the various counties of the world, and to contemplate how many souls are ripe for the harvest: *The harvest is great, and the workers few; therefore ask the Lord of the harvest to send out laborers into his harvest* (Matthew 9:37–38).

Therefore, may all of you keep frequently on your lips this prayer for the salvation of souls, supporting it on the merits of the precious Blood of Jesus Christ and uniting it to the zeal that moved the Divine Savior for the glory of his Father: *Lord of the harvest, Lord of the harvest, send workers into your harvest.* God the Father all powerful, Creator of all souls, send numerous laborers who may bring in the harvest. We commend to you the souls that are so dear to you…

Beg help for them with ardent sighs, stretch out your hand to them, snatch them away from the precipice, to the edge of which they find themselves, and place them in the bosom of the immense kindness of God. Hide them in the holy wounds of our Savior; place them under the protective mantle of our Most Holy and most powerful Mother.[79]

Such were the teachings—concludes Father Dumortier—that the Servant of God gave to the superior of the convent of Scala. That the community lived the apostolic zeal of Sarnelli was something that the same author deduced from this paragraph of a letter of his from June 19, 1738 to the same superior: "I ask you and your sisters for the sake of the very loving compassion of Jesus Christ that you unite in acts of thanksgiving to the Most Holy Trinity for the happy result of the works undertaken earlier in Naples. It is entirely due to the powerful efficacy of holy prayer."[80]

All this lets us see the involvement of Sarnelli at the beginning of the Order's existence.

---

[79] Cited from F. Dumortier, *Le Venerable Serviteur de Dieu le Pere Janvier Marie Sarnelli de la Congregation du T. S. Redempteur*, Paris, 1886,135.

[80] *Ibid.*

IV. GENESIS AND DYNAMICS OF SARNELLI'S APOSTOLIC VOCATION [81]

Sarnelli's spiritual dynamic has a very definite development. We will not deal, for the moment, with the influence of the Neapolitan family of that time on the choice of state of life for their children.[82] We also simply recall that Sarnelli's two brothers were a secular priest and a Jesuit, respectively. On the other hand, the biographers bring out the autonomy and independence of Sarnelli's personality. His personal problems begin with obedience and submission to spiritual directors according to the mentality of that time and his difficulties with Falcoia. We learn of them from the commentaries of Alphonsus about the subject, from what he himself said in his writing, and from the *Animadversiones* of the Promoter of the Faith during the cause for beatification.

1. The point of departure of his apostolic vocation seems to be his incorporation into the Congregazione dei Cavalieri Togati e Dottori eretta sotto if titolo della Nativita del'Beata Vergine. From the discipline of this life as a member of this confraternity, he begins to have a system and spiritual practice, marked by the following elements:

   • Prayer, meditation, sacramental practice, practices of piety, etc.

   • Weekly retreat and spiritual exercises.

   • Extraordinary practice of charity: Hospital of the Incurables.

   • Apostolate of children's catechesis, Evening Chapels.

2. He hears his calling to leave the world and become a priest in the midst of his dedication to the world of the poor out of charity. Alphonsus joins him at the Hospital of the Incurables.

---

[81] Due to its length and because it largely repeats material in other chapters of this volume, Section III is omitted.

[82] See M. Vidal, *La familia en la vida y en el pensamiento de Alfonso de Liguori (1696–1787). Proceso a la familia "tradicional,"* Madrid, 1995; A. De Spirito, "La scelta dello stato el 'esperienza familiare di Alfonso de Liguori." SHCSR, 43 (1995), 457–464; and the works of Sarnelli on the theme.

3. After this choice, he begins another step: his preparation for the priesthood. On the way to the priesthood, besides spiritual experience and the previous apostolic experience, it is fitting to highlight:

   • The consecutive applications and examinations related to the conferral of various ministries: minor orders, subdiaconate, diaconate, priesthood.

   • The assignment, as clerical seminarian at home, to a parish in order to exercise his ministry and practice the apostolate of children's catechesis.

   • Friendship with Alphonsus and other priests and youth from Naples.

   • The incorporation into the Apostolic Missions, with everything involved in spiritual, priestly and apostolic formation, in the new ministerial activities of this Congregation and in the parishes to which he had been assigned.

   • Life in the Residence of the Holy Family of Naples, (Father Ripa), called the Chinese Residence.

   • His priestly ordination.

4. The influence of Alphonsus and his work led to his incorporation into the Congregation of the Most Holy Redeemer.

5. The problems of health, his personality, his apostolic zeal, his missionary and priestly experience and his spirituality work together to make him a spiritual master and an extraordinary collaborator with Alphonsus and Cardinal Spinelli in the Archdiocese of Naples on the spiritual, socioreligious, and missionary levels.

6. In his apostolate, Sarnelli incarnates in a very personal way, the same ideals that had moved Alphonsus, before and after founding the Redemptorist Congregation: care of the sick, evangelizing the *lazzari* of Naples, uniting artisans in the *cappelle serotine*, helping abandoned children, marginalized women, people from the countryside, etc. For him there was a concern for:

- The formation of clergy and of priestly academies.
- The formation of laity and Evening Chapels.
- The Devout Life, mental prayer, communion, visits.
- Education of children.
- Fights against blasphemy and against the exploitation of women.

7. The most important contributions to pastoral ministry in Naples, from the time of his choice of a priestly and apostolic life up to his death, are probably found in his formulation of a spiritual way, that is to say, in the outlining of the origin and meaning of traditional and popular practices of piety. He alludes to these, in an abbreviated way, in *Il Cristiano diretto nel cammino della devozione [The Christian on the Way of Devotion]*[83] In this little work, we find precise indication about the following themes:

- The path of the spiritual life.
- The practice of the virtues: theological virtues, religion, conformity to the will of God, brotherly love, apostolic zeal, moral virtues, evangelical counsels.
- Temptations and small faults.
- Penances and mortifications.
- Right intention and holy desires.
- Sacraments of Reconciliation and the Eucharist.
- Practical exercises for a spiritual way: examination of conscience, spiritual retreat, spiritual exercises, spiritual reading, Word of God.
- Prayer, meditation, imitation of Jesus Christ, devotion to the Most Blessed Sacrament, devotion to the Mother of God.
- Practical exercises that dispose one to union with God: presence of God, practice of withdrawal from activities, divine inspirations, silence, and solitude.

---

[83] G. M. Sarnelli, *Il Cristiano diretto nel cammino della devozione. Istruzion spirituale, che contiene in compendio le Regole, gli Avvertimenti, Le Pratiche, per guida, e profitto delle Anime che desiderano introdursi, ed avvanzarsi nella Via della Perfezione*, Naples, 1743.

- Union of the soul with God.
- Advice about growth in the spiritual life; the works of each day; not advancing on the spiritual journey is falling backward; disregard for human respect; recollection for final perseverance.

But, there is another factor, deserving special note: in the vocational dynamics as well as in his apostolate and in all the works of Sarnelli is found the presence of the poor. It is to this that we will now dedicate some pages.

V. SARNELLI AND THE POOR: "WOE TO ME, IF I DO NOT PROCLAIM THE GOSPEL!" [84]

The group founded by Alphonsus for the missionary evangelization of the most abandoned, constituted a form of the concrete option for the poor of his time, above all for those who, like him, were concerned for the spiritually abandoned. For this reason, when he tells of the missionary vocation of his great friend, Sarnelli, he makes us see something similar. In fact, his description of Sarnelli's option for the poor and for their missionary evangelization seems, on more than one occasion, an autobiographical witness to Alphonsus himself.

The saint begins presenting Sarnelli's love for the poor as a revelation of his heroic charity, and he describes it for us in this way:

When he resided outside the houses of the Congregation, he lived in the utmost poverty, ate little, and dressed poorly, not just so he could be despised, as we have said, but also in order to have something he could give as alms to the poor from what he would save on food and clothing. He sometimes went so far as to take the clothes he was wearing, the shoes on his feet and the food set before him while he was eating so that he could give them to the needy. He would go around gathering the poor of Naples and bring them all together into his house to wash them top to bottom and feed them, waiting on them himself.

[84] 1 Corinthians 9:16.

This was the reason he took a room in his father's house right by the stairs, a room so dark and uncomfortable that a friend who visited him could see the mice jumping on his bed. He did this so he could welcome the many poor people who came to see him without the servants trying to shoo them away.[85]

Among all the poor of the city, those who held a special place were the children, above all the children of the neediest families, the victims of prostitution, and the sick:

The love he had for the sick in the hospital was incredible. He wore himself out to relieve their suffering, in body as well as in spirit. Even as a secular he went begging what he could for food from his family members, packed it and sent it to the Hospital. When he became a cleric, as often as he went there, he always carried under his cloak some treats of candy or fruit for the poor sufferers that he had bought for them or he would deprive himself of some of his own servings of food. It is further known that for this purpose he had some long clay containers made into which he put cooked food so he could carry them [on his shoulders] and bring them to the poor. He made many packets of tobacco to give to these people. He made their beds, washed them, and left nothing charitable undone that could give them relief.[86]

The visit to the Most Blessed Sacrament and the visit to the sick poor are emphasized by Alphonsus in the Sarnellian spirituality and in the vocational process for both of them.

Also at this time, several days a week, he would go to care for the sick at the Hospital of the Incurables. He said that it was there that he found himself surrounded by all of God's lights, to the point that, as he said, the hospital served as a continuous meditation and he left there completely at peace with himself and filled with God. Here it was that he finally was called by the Lord to give up the secular world. In effect, it was then that, with his spiritual director's advice, he decided to give up the practice of law and to become a priest so he could dedicate himself totally to God's service. Thus he put

[85] Compendio, 23 [See Chapter One].
[86] Ibid.

on clerical attire, took himself completely away from secular matters, and donated whatever money he had in reserve as alms to the poor along with all his secular clothing. He dedicated his whole life to God, spending his days in prayer and in the studies necessary to become a priest, as well as in charitable works for the good of his neighbor.[87]

It is known that he considered going to live permanently in the Hospital of the Incurables in order to more easily assist the poor, especially at the hour of death. He had already taken steps to procure a room there but some problems got in the way of his realizing his plan. It is also reported that the hospital of the prison, where he also went to help the poor, condemned men regain their spiritual health, was the place where he once almost lost his life because of this kind of zeal.[88]

This love for the poor was being converted for Sarnelli and Liguori into a pastoral and missionary zeal. For Alphonsus, it led him to the foundation of the Congregation of the Most Holy Redeemer; for Sarnelli, it led him to see an effective way to help spiritually the poor and the most abandoned, above all those of the countryside.

Especially when he spoke about the great need the poor have for spiritual help and for workers to do this, you could see his face light up out of zeal and at times he was seen shedding tears of compassion. He would say that he felt specially called by God to help the poor and the abandoned, repeating to that effect the statement of Isaiah: *Evangelizare pauperibus misit me.*[89] He asserted that he would consider himself damned if he did not attend to this task, feeling himself spurred on by the words of St. Paul, *Woe am I if I do not preach the Good News.* While he was at Naples before he entered the Congregation, he was determined, with two other priests, to go to preach missions throughout the Provinces of Calabria and Abruzzo, these being the places most destitute of spiritual help. His favorite patron

[87] *Ibid.*
[88] *Ibid.*
[89] Luke 4:18 *["He has anointed me to bring good news to the poor."]*

was St. John Francis Regis who was the saintly minister who was most enamored of the poor. With this in mind, as it is has been passed down, he entered the Congregation of the Most Holy Redeemer because he knew that this was its principal purpose [*l'intento principale*]: to aid the poor abandoned people of the Campagna.

VI. MISSIONARY EVANGELIZATION AND THE FORMATION OF THE PEOPLE

If popular missions constitute the principal activity of the Redemptorists, the domestic apostolate ought to be "a perpetual and continual mission" for those who live in the neighborhood of the community. With this purpose, they attempt to aid the faithful of the region in the development of an authentically Christian life by offering them a series of pastoral helps. Here they implemented the means of perseverance that they tried to introduce during their missions in the various Christian communities after the missions.

THE "DEVOUT LIFE."

The first of all these means was the "Devout Life." Ordinarily, it supposed a daily meditation on themes related to the liturgical seasons, on the eternal truths, on the Passion of Jesus Christ, on the Sufferings of Mary or on some other theme, suited to the participants. It was developed into a pattern for a daily service:

- Litanies of the Blessed Virgin Mary.
- Reading followed by silent meditation.
- Praying the Christian acts.
- Benediction of the Most Holy Sacrament.
- Hymns.

Bishop Falcoia spoke of it in 1733: "I recommend to you The Devout Life, which produces an immense good and offers the missionaries a little bit of rest." He is referring here to the introduction of this practice in the missions. Nevertheless, with regard to the importance that one concedes to ordinary pastoral ministry, Tellería points out an interesting text for understanding The Devout Life: "The Prelate of Castellammare [Falcoia] introduced it in the episcopal city and reports on it to the Vatican Congregation of the Council in his Relation of October 1, 1733" with these words:

> In order that the flock confided to my care would not lack its daily sustenance, I have introduced in the cathedral, in the parish churches, and in some chapels the daily exercise called "The Devout Life." Every afternoon, one hour before the Angelus, the people arrive at the temple and there, after adoring His Divine Majesty and asking his help, the pastor or another priest leads the litany of the Most Holy Virgin. Then, a point on the Passion is read aloud, and it is meditated upon for the space of a quarter of an hour; the priest then takes the crucifix and leads the formulas of the acts of faith, hope and charity, contrition for sins and the purpose of amendment; the service ends with the blessing of the people. The gathering lasts no more than a half-hour and produces great good, as the whole population and all the confessors attest.

Tellería goes on to say: "For…Alphonsus, these are called *esercizio divoto [The Devout Exercise]*. From the start, the Most Reverend Falcoia had highly recommended it. Alphonsus confessed that this initiative was copied from the Pious Workers."[90] The Redemptorist Constitutions of 1764 present a similar arrangement of the service.

All of this explains for us the attention that Sarnelli gave to the theme in his published works and in the pastoral activity. From this, on the other hand, we can discover the significance of this apostolate in the context of the pastoral renewal of the eighteenth century in Naples, in which the work of the Congregation is incarnated. This paragraph of Sarnelli in *L'ecclesiastico santificato* expresses this idea of the role of "The Devout Life" very well:

> The primary purpose of our ministry and office and the provident plan of our Most Eminent Archbishop do not consist in simply offering the people a transitory and fleeting benefit, as that which is derived from only the mission. Rather,

---

[90] Tellería, I, 204–205 and 687.

it also lies in procuring for these people, in a stable way, all the means useful for them to acquire the perfection of spirit and the kingdom of the heavens by means of final perseverance in the good that they have undertaken. Therefore, in order to attain all this and to confront such a great undertaking, the most adequate and effective means and practices are here recommended, namely, those which missionaries proposed, studied, tested and put into practice among the people.[91]

It was precisely for this reason that, in 1738, he had published *Il mondo santificato*. In a work of a few years later, *Il mondo riformato*, he makes a series of references to most of the exercises involved in The Devout Life and in the apostolate of the Redemptorists in their churches. Finally, in *L'ecclesiastico santificato* (1742), cited above, he deals with the more pastoral perspective, the formation of children and youth, common prayer, preparation for a happy death, novenas and whatever else pertains to the formation of the clergy: confraternities, meetings to study moral cases, academies on moral and dogmatic theology, preaching, celebration of the Eucharist, etc.

This pastoral concern for the poor explains the relationship between the spiritual writings of Sarnelli and Alphonsus and these pious practices: The writings arose from these practices, which constitute the pastoral context in which they were born and to which they are directed. The themes, the style and even the very format of these books are better understood if they are considered in relation to the pastoral activity of the Institute. The book of the Visits is familiar to us, but we could say the same of almost all the works of Sarnelli and of Alphonsus, including the poetical, pictorial and musical works. With the death of Sarnelli (1744), Alphonsus had to take over responsibility personally for the literary activity that the pastoral ministry of the Redemptorists needed and to which Sarnelli contributed.

Within The Devout Life and its activities, one would have to underline: the practice of mental prayer, eucharistic piety, Marian piety and preaching. Tannoia, speaking from Scala, says that Alphonsus...

...immediately established in the cathedral meditation with the people every morning and evening, along with the

---

[91] *L'ecclesiastico santificato*, 4.

visit to Jesus in the Blessed Sacrament and to the Most Holy Mary. Every Thursday there was a sermon with Benediction of the Sacrament and every Saturday a sermon in honor of the Most Holy Mary. On Sundays and feast days, since all the people were at home in the city, he did not refrain from providing instruction through sermons on their duties and giving catechetical instruction.[92]

Speaking of the community at Villa Liberi, Tannoia also adds the Way of the Cross to these.

The Redemptorist Constitutions of 1764 (# 167–173) sum up for us the practical development of these acts, according to the Redemptorist tradition. We find the concrete methods, as well as the spirit and pastoral attitudes instilled by them, in the works of Sarnelli and Alphonsus, since they were actually engaged in them. For this reason, we have insisted on the attention that Sarnelli gives them. Little by little, their influence, in some way, was extended to the whole Church, by means of the practice of the Redemptorists in the various foundations, the popular missions, and the ecclesial teaching of Alphonsus. Nevertheless, in its beginnings, there are found to be "the most adequate and effective means and practices...which missionaries proposed, tested, and put into practice among the people."

If the Constitutions of 1764, which were largely the work of Tannoia, collect the practice of Congregation up to that moment, it would not be an exaggeration to say that they intended to sum up much of the teaching that Alphonsus and Sarnelli had expressed in their works, above all the pastoral ones, when they treat of the themes, which the Redemptorists carried out in their own churches. These would reflect their thoughts about the means of perseverance of the effects of their missions, the importance of confession, the pious associations or confraternities of the laity, meditation—in a word, the apostolate in the locations of their houses would mirror the activities they regarded as essential for the success of their missions.[93]

---

[92] Tannoia, II, 84.

[93] We might also mention here the regular attention that Sarnelli gave to furthering devotion to St. Joseph by means of the pious exercise of *The Seven Dolors and Joys of St. Joseph.*

RELIGIOUS ASSOCIATIONS FOR LAY PEOPLE

Another of the significant activities of the internal apostolate of the Congregation is the formation of "pious associations." We have to seek the antecedents of this apostolate, as in other occasions, in the personal and apostolic experience of Alphonsus and of the first Redemptorists. In effect, he, as much as Sarnelli, belonged to various pious associations and defended the usefulness and even the necessity of these groups for persevering in an authentically Christian life. In the same way, from the first years of their priestly apostolate, they were concerned with implanting these associations where they did not yet exist. Tellería speaks with praise of the establishment of associations on the island of Procida "that still exist today" and where they keep the *Regola ovvero Costituzioni d una minima Congregazione Segreta de' divoti Fathertelli eretta sotto il titolo della Ssma Vergine Addolorata nella Chiesa parrocchiale di S. Michele di Procida. Anno 1732.*[94] "Its members," continues Tellería, "were above all unmarried men. In 1742, it counted twenty-three professed and forty-two novices. Its statutes were approved with the signature of the Kings Carlos and Fernando. Alphonsus had been inspired to make its statutes according to the pattern of the Marian congregations of the Jesuits, from which he had taken a great diversity of pious practices, which today could seem to us to be excessive."[95]

This practice of the Congregation remained formulated in the Constitutions of 1764 (# 999–100). They explain that the purpose of these "congregations" *[confraternities or associations]* is related to the means of perseverance and of renewal of the Christian life involved in The Devout Life. For this reason, they ought to be made available to all the faithful and should follow determined conditions. Among the most important of these are: to be free of charge; to always have a priest as a director; to keep faithfully the rule of the association; to offer an adequate religious formation to its members; to care for their sacramental life; to urge practices of piety and charity, designated for each day and for each group.[96]

---

[94] Rule or Constitutions of a Small Private Confraternity of Devout Brothers Erected under the Title of The Most Holy Sorrowful Virgin in the Parish Church of St. Michael of Procida. Year 1732.

[95] See Tannoia, II, 84.

[96] Constitution 183. See also Alphonsus' *Le glorie di Maria [The Glories of Mary]*, Part II: Sections IV and VII, in *Opere Ascetiche*, VII, 334–348.

VII. THE SOCIAL APOSTOLATE OF SARNELLI

This is another of the outstanding features in the life and apostolic activity of Sarnelli. How could Sarnelli arrive at his unique apostolate? In order to understand it, I believe we must pay attention to the following points:

1. The historical character of prostitution, that is to say, of the context which provokes it and the consequences that it presupposes, such as the attitudes that society, public powers and even the church come to assume in regard to it.[97]

2. The experience of the problem on the part of Sarnelli: the arrogant activity of prostitution in Naples, and more concretely, in the neighborhood of one of the parishes to which he had been assigned as a catechist when still a deacon. The experience of Sarnelli in relation to the social and pastoral problem which will lead him to his apostolate can be understood by anyone who has had to spend time ministering in homes, hospitals, or old and poor tenements of a great city, precisely the kind of neighborhood that, in Naples in the time of Sarnelli, corresponded to the *quartieri Spagnoli [Spanish Quarter]*, where, as he says, "once these were luxurious neighborhoods, now places of sordid corruption."

Working as a deacon, he came into contact with one of those neighborhoods. He points out the reality of prostitution to describe for us the gravity of the phenomenon about which, he insists, he does not want to give numbers so as not to exaggerate. On reading his descriptions, scenes and characters spring up that recall for us the scenes of marginalization so familiar today on television and in movies.[98]

Sarnelli is struck by the inhuman promiscuity of those poor neighborhoods— poor, dirty, overcrowded, clamorous—he especially seems to feel the strident outcry of these poor women who involve themselves

---

[97] Bibliography and interpretations, many times debatable, on this particular subject are found in A. Riviere Gomez, "Caidas, Miserables, Degeneradas: Estudio sobre la prostitución en el siglo XIX" in *Mujeres en Madrid*, Madrid: Horas y Horas, 1994.

[98] Chapter Two, in Section 3, discusses this matter further.

and are employed in the traffic of prostitution. He is
a young lawyer, a pious and modest cleric, who has to
come and go in this world in order to attend to the sick,
to go home or to church, to bring viaticum to the sick, just
as many other priests, religious, and social workers must.
The images which he sees, the shouts and the brawls
that he hears, the songs which he listens to, the most
unashamed provocation to which he is victim, in a single
word, public prostitution: all these are tolerated on the
streets and in the small squares in the poorest and
most squalid neighborhoods of the city of Naples; all
this leaves him stunned and anguished.

Scenes characteristic of that environment are
vivid to Sarnelli the writer, as he makes his legal brief
and demands, and he does not keep quiet about the
experiences that characterize this atmosphere: the
presence of those poor women with their provocative
stance on every street corner; the small degraded
stores and shops selling objects and clothing related
to prostitution and serving as locations to make their
rendezvous and welcome their customers; songs, dances,
provocative festivals in the little public squares; the
exploiters of prostitution, pimps, and madams; brawls
among the customers; boys and girls, youths, and women,
widows, mothers of families, and single women who
have to live in that world where the prostitutes live; the
children of these women. These are some of the images
which appear in Sarnelli's writings on the phenomenon.

3. The causes of this, according to his way of seeing it, and
   that he explains fully in his "moral works," are many.
   Sarnelli enumerates several principal reasons at the root of
   prostitution in a poor, violent, and oppressed society. Without
   going into detail, we recall: promiscuity, social, and political
   permissiveness, poverty, the lack of institutions and means for
   confronting the problem, the provocation of this widespread
   presence of prostitutes, the exploitation of the phenomenon
   by pimps and madams, the political corruption, the lack of
   observance of the established laws.

4. He insisted on the wider repercussions of the phenomenon on the victims and on society, government, the authorities, the family, the Church, the ministry, etc.

5. He centers his concern on the pastoral dimension he sees in the causes and in the remedies necessary to overcome this issue in a positive way. He understands the evils sprouting from it, above all, in the world of children, of youths, women, families; he proclaims the demands it makes on the social, religious, and Christian elements of society.

6. He finds in this work the same pastoral concern that Alphonsus addresses in his apostolate to the poor who are abandoned by the Church's ordinary ministry.

In recalling this historical experience of Sarnelli, in which was incarnated his experience of God and the way of holiness and prayer that he offers us with his works and with his life, we can surely ask: Is it strange that he experienced distress and dryness of spirit, anxiousness in prayer and in retreat, precisely from when he started his preparation for the priesthood? In order to live a life of charity amid the world of the Incurables and the "Spanish Quarter" of that time, the apostolate and the priesthood presumed confronting a reality that was deeply depressing. And, if one's strict noble upbringing and poor health accentuated the problem even more, how much worse would the depression become?

In addressing these ills of prostitution, Sarnelli wrote several works trying to initiate action:

- *Legal, Catholic and Political Reasons in Defense of Republics Ruined by Blatant Prostitution.*

- *The Fourth of May of 1738 in Naples as a Future Memorandum for Those Who Come Later and as an Example to Other Nations* (this was the date on which the royal decrees concerning this problem were promulgated).

- *Synthesis of the Catholic, Legal and Political Reasons in Defense of the Peoples Destroyed by Prostitution.*

- *Supplement to the Legal, Catholic and Political Reasons. On the Concrete Ways of Putting a Perpetual Brake on Prostitution, of Rescuing the Repentant Ones, of Preserving Children in Danger, and of Maintaining the Republic Purified of Carnal Licentiousness.*[99]

---

[99] See Bibliography of Major Works, below, p. 445, for complete titles and dates of publication: Ragioni legali; Il quatro maggio; Ristretto; Aggunta.

VIII. Writer and Spiritual Master: "I Want to Keep on Preaching up to the Day of Judgment."

The above quote is how Alphonsus concludes his comments on Sarnelli's apostolate of writing.[100] Sarnelli is the first Redemptorist who writes for the people and who formulates many of the concerns and pastoral practices that the work of Alphonsus entails. For that reason, it is not surprising that, after Sarnelli's death, it would be Alphonsus himself, who felt called to continue the apostolate of the pen and provide pious literature for the humble people because, after 1744, he had no one else who could do so. It was how Alphonsus was converted into "the teacher of the humble people."

The apostolate of the pen, among the Redemptorists, began with Sarnelli, and once received by Alphonsus it became an "appropriate activity," related to the ecclesial mission of the Institute, and has been continued through all the Redemptorists who have felt themselves called to write in order to continue that apostolic activity at the service of the Congregation and of those they serve.

There is no way to know when the actual writing of a work was done. Nevertheless, the first works actually published by a Redemptorist are those of Sarnelli. In the beginning, the works of the Founder arose from the demands of his first pastoral activity, while those of Sarnelli seem to be the fruit of a specific activity, as would happen later even with Alphonsus. For this reason, it is not surprising that the first works of the founder remain as something inserted in the literary apostolate of Sarnelli.[101]

M. De. Meulemeester, a specialist in the literary activity of the Congregation, worked to clarify "les premieres et discrètes manifestations d'un apostolat literaire."[102] "He refers to the world of missions and

---

[100] Compendio. Other authors have expressed Sarnelli's final saying with this nuance: "I die content because I kept preaching right up to the day of judgment." See *Responsio ad Animadversiones*, 67–68.

[101] We ought not to forget that there are some other Redemptorists of this period who appear as authors of published works and many more that, without having published some book, have left us written testimony of their activity and their life. See *Bibliographie*, II, Louvain, 1935.

[102] *[The first discrete manifestations of a literary apostolate]; Origines*, I, 173– 176.

popular piety in which Alphonsus and Sarnelli lived and in which they began their literary activity with *carte, libretti, novene, corone, orazioni y canzoncine*.[103] The greater part of the works of Sarnelli appeared in these formats. Only later he himself, and in the nineteenth century his editors, tried to group them together to form the volumes that we know today.

"The literary apostolate" of the Redemptorists in the period of their founding was a noted characteristic of Gennaro Maria Sarnelli. We find the *Massime Eterne [Eternal Maxims]* (1728?) usually attributed to Alphonsus, among the works published by Sarnelli in 1737, 1738, and 1743. De Meulemeester notes:

> Doubts have been raised on the authorship of the *Massime Eterne*. The perfect literary and apostolic community between Alphonsus and Sarnelli authorized appropriations that today we would censure as plagiarism, but the question remains: Had Sarnelli taken the text of Alphonsus or had he been the one who took the *Massime Eterne* from the book of Sarnelli? *[After the work appeared under Sarnelli's name]*, it was republished as an appendix to Alphonsus' *Visits*, to his *Dell'amore dell anime* and to other of his short works. Could this have been an occasion of an inexact attribution? Nevertheless, the ideas and the style incline one to award the little work to the holy Doctor."[104]

The literary activity of Sarnelli, as that of Alphonsus, was part of the apostolate in which both found themselves immersed in the Archdiocese of Naples as members of the Confraternity of the Apostolic Missions and of the Congregation of the Most Holy Redeemer. For this reason, Sarnelli published books dealing with spirituality, common meditation, The Devout Life, Christian formation and the missions in the villages. But he had others that were directed to the education of children and youth, to the formation of clergy, and to the moral and religious problems of the city and kingdom of Naples. These problems, against which Sarnelli was fighting with pen and pastoral action, were considered by Falcoia, as much as by Alphonsus, something proper to the Congregation.[105]

---

[103] Letters, booklets, novenas, rosaries, prayers, and songs.

[104] *Origines*, I, 174, note 80.

[105] *Ibid.*, 174–175.

At Sarnelli's death, Alphonsus continued the literary activity of his friend and fellow brother at the service of The Devout Life, priestly pastoral ministry and Marian preaching. In effect, Alphonsus' activity continued that initiated by Sarnelli as a pastoral activity, but Alphonsus sees himself obliged to initiate a different series of works as a ministry of the Congregation, namely, his moral works. Besides this, over the years, a kind of community of literary apostolate was being developed among the confreres up to the point where one could hypothesize that, even if he did not allow his name to be put on publications entirely created by other confreres, works were published under his name, even though the gathering of materials and the basic editing was not done by him personally. This would be the case, above all, for the works composed in the moments of his life, when due to his state of health, it seems impossible that he could have composed them personally. If this is in fact the case, we would be able to say that there were moments in which Alphonsus gave his name to the literary activity of some Redemptorists who had helped him before as simple collaborators.

Whatever may be the situation with this, it does seem clear that many works of his followers were brought about in response to this activity of Alphonsus, above all in the area of moral theology. In one way or another, a time came when the Redemptorists had to take charge of preparing the different editions, to attempt a new synthesis, and defend his doctrine.[106]

The literary activity of Sarnelli, outlined by M. de Meulemeester, comprises twenty-two works and a volume of correspondence. From them, one may deduce that *Il mondo santificato*, published in 1738 by Sarnelli, shows the discovery of a new aspect of their missionary apostolate that explains much of the literary activity of Sarnelli, of Alphonsus, and of the Congregation of the Most Holy Redeemer itself.[107]

---

[106] For more details on the literary activity of the Redemptorists in the time of Sarnelli, See F. Ferrero, "L'attivita letteraria," in F. Chiovaro, (ed.), *The History of the Congregation of the Most Holy Redeemer, I. The Origins (1732-1793)*, I, Liguori, MO: Liguori Publications, 1996, 391-399. See also F. Ferrero - S. J. Boland, "Las obras impresas por S Alfonso Maria Liguori," SHCSR, 36/37 (1988/1989).

[107] From the 1752 edition on, the biography of the Blessed written by Alphonsus is included (first as an appendix, later at the beginning) in *Il mondo riformato* (1739).

He sums it up in the *Advertencia al Reverendo Clero de la Diocesis de Napoles*[108] with which he presents one of his last works, *L'ecclesiastico santificato* (1742), where, before offering it to all "the pastors of souls," he concludes: "Therefore, in order to attain all this and to confront such a great undertaking, the most adequate and effective means and practices are here recommended, namely, those which missionaries proposed, tested, and put into practice among the people."[109]

For this purpose, in this as in his other works, he had tried to describe and order in a detailed way the rules and practices for facilitating the execution of those "works of eternal life and for making more secure those fruitful ministries...for the instruction and salvation of souls...And, for the purpose that each one may have in hand the opportunity of practicing those pious exercises, we have published these copies for universal knowledge and benefit."[110]

This work is directed toward the clergy. In others, however, the ultimate audience about whom he is thinking comprises the whole people of God on their way of conversion, sanctification and prayer, without forgetting the problems that they are called to face from their position in society and in the Church. This makes Sarnelli a spiritual leader proclaiming the principles of the spiritual life through his works the echo of which continues even after his death. We will try to point out the structure contained in his writings by noting the nucleus of teachings found in them.

FOR THE SANCTIFICATION OF THE WORLD

The most significant work of this nucleus is *Il mondo santificato* (1738). Its frontispiece states: "which treats of meditation and prayer—an instructive and illuminating work—very useful for laity, churchmen, and religious. To facilitate in each state of life the practice of The Devout Life, and to introduce into the Catholic Church, community and families the use of common prayer." Explaining the title, its introduction ends: "Chrysostom calls the world conversing with God by means of prayer a world made holy, a world justified, a wise world, a world adorned with all the virtues...Thus our world will be, if people give themselves to the

---

[108] Notice to the Reverend Clergy of the Diocese of Naples

[109] G. M. Sarnelli, *L'ecclesiastico santificato*, *Opera omnia*, Vol. 11, Naples, 1888, 4.

[110] *Ibid.*, 3.

consideration of the eternal maxims and to the exercise of holy prayer. O heavenly Father, through the love of Jesus Christ, you sanctify the world: sanctify it so that your name may be glorified and sanctified in it: *Pater, santificetur nomen tuum.*"[111]

In the following section, an explanation is given of the possible "ways of introducing into the Church, communities, and families the exercise of meditation (*orazione mentale*) and of prayer of petition (*preghiera*), according to the norms of the primitive church."[112]

Also it expounds on "the necessity, efficacy, and gentleness of mental prayer, which all classes of persons, whatever may be their state in life; the malicious tricks and deceits of the demon; and the way of conducting oneself properly during dryness and temptation."[113]

It continues with the following themes: rules and requirements to make prayer fruitful and efficacious; significant examples; exercises of prayer and of common meditation; meditations on the eternal maxims; a short exposition on the ways of carrying out the exercise of prayer in some dioceses.[114]

---

[111] *Il mondo santificato*, I:38 [Ivel Mendanha outlines the work in this way:] "In this two-volume work, Sarnelli shared the best of his ideas. This is the book that most influenced his contemporaries. It was also his longest lasting success—going through another sixteen editions in the eighteenth century and twenty-two more in the nineteenth. It was a theoretical/practical treatise on prayer.

"In the first volume, popular missions and retreats were envisioned as the most suitable means to teach people the practice of mental prayer and the prayer of petition. Sarnelli wanted prayer to be made in common, whether in families or in churches. He then moved on to the necessity of mental prayer and, following that, the necessity and efficacy of the prayer of petition.

"In the second volume, the practical part contained a series of devotional practices and meditations on the eternal maxims and truths of the faith. Here he reprised and amplified themes already treated in his earlier book: *La via facile e sicura del Paradiso.* This book was important because its vision of the Christian life was no longer based on the specific problems of Naples. There was a sudden openness to the world that reached far beyond the limits where Sarnelli's original apostolic activities were shaped. The adjective "Sanctified" in the title indicated Sarnelli's concept—that holiness is available to all people, especially the laity. Perhaps Alphonsus Liguori is in debt to Sarnelli for this discovery. Or perhaps both of them drew out the consequences of what they saw happening among the little people of Naples whom they met in the Evening Chapels."
[*From a Redemptorist conference held at Mt. St. Alphonsus College, Esopus, New York, in October 2006. Father Mendanha was, at the time, a member of the Redemptorist Spirituality Center, an office in the Redemptorist General Curia in Rome.*]

[112] *Ibid.*, 1:39.

[113] *Ibid.*, 1:95.

[114] *Ibid.*, I:191, 235: II:3, 31, 283.

Through this work, one understands better how The Devout Life is a systematization of the ideals Sarnelli sets forth here.

FOR THE RENEWAL AND PERFECTION OF THE CHRISTIAN LIFE

To understand this nucleus, we have to pay attention to *Il mondo riformato* (1739). This book discusses spiritual reading (*sacre lezioni*) and its relation to meditation in order to accentuate, above all, its formative dimension as enlightening the principal and more important requirements for every Christian to be able to live according to their profession of faith and to develop esteem and veneration of its sacred mysteries.[115] "The consideration of the eternal maxims and prayer, which I have recommended to you in *Il mondo santificato*, will prepare the world for the reform of its disorders and abuses, while the instructions and practices that I now propose will try to reform and perfect it

...For this reason, it is not advantageous for you to set aside the practical use of each book, if you want to sanctify your diocese, your family and yourself; and to sanctify it completely with progress in perfection and through perseverance in doing good."[116] The different volumes which the work contains form a whole and "they are directed toward making the world instructed, purified, enlightened, and sanctified."[117]

The principal themes that he presents explicitly are:

- Zeal and the virtues of churchmen in order to reform the world.
- Spiritual reading.
- The world: maxims, prejudices, and consequences.
- The sacrament of confession.
- The sacrament of the Eucharist, and practical exercises for preparing for Holy Communion and thanksgiving after Communion.
- The usefulness, opportunity and obligation of instructing children and youth.
- The religious associations in honor of the Most Holy Virgin Mary.

---

[115] *Il mondo riformato*, I:4, 23–25.

[116] *Ibid.*, I:4.

[117] *Ibid.*, I:5.

- The great sacrifice of the Mass and on the reverence for churches.
- The choice of a state of life and the norms and pious exercises to develop a proper style of life.
- Devotions to the Most Holy Trinity, the Holy Spirit, Jesus Christ, and the angels and saints.
- Pious practices.

For Pastors

In *L'ecclesiastico santificato* (1742), Sarnelli explains how to structure the nucleus of themes found in the two preceding works. This book is directed, above all, "to the clergy of the Archdiocese of Naples for the instruction and sanctification of these peoples. Nevertheless, it is not beyond the intention, plan and desire of the author that it be received and put into practice by all pastors of souls."[118] His motivation and the book's basic structure are found in the frontispiece, which says:

The work is divided into three parts:

First part: Exercises of piety, taken from the instruction of His Eminence Cardinal Spinelli to which are added his new directives that must be followed by all reverend clergy, economes, coadjutors, and priests. Proposed by the missionaries delegated for their execution in order to facilitate the practice of them.

Second part: Doctrinal exercises for the formation of the priests.

Third part: Considerations for each day of the week that are destined for priests in their preparation for the celebration of the Holy Sacrifice of the Mass and for the thanksgiving after Communion. It also deals with the proper celebration of the ceremonies.[119]

---

[118] *L'ecclesiastico santificato*, 4.
[119] *Ibid.*, 3.

The core features of the first part are as follows:

- Formation of children and youth.
- The practice of common prayer, of the "preparation for a happy death," of novenas and catechism for children.

The second part, dealing with the formation of priests considers:

- Moral cases.
- Academies for moral and dogmatic theology.
- Exercises for sacred preaching and doctrinal preparation for different types of preaching.
- Preparation, celebration, and thanksgiving for Eucharist.

Finally, in the third part, we have these themes on the spiritual life:

- Reflections on eternal life for each day of the week for the purgative level.
- Guide for the Christian on the journey.
- Formation of the Christian in the principal mysteries and obligation of their Faith.
- Considerations on the Passion of Jesus Christ.
- Two weeks of meditations on the purgative life and illuminative levels.
- Orientation and accompaniment on the way.

For Orientation and Accompaniment Along the Road of the Spiritual Life

Sarnelli later develops this core of spirituality in another series of works containing outlines and methods, as well as concrete suggestions on The Devout Life, on prayer, and on meditation. These works are:

- *The Christian Enlightened, Directed, Experienced, and Sanctified.*
- *The Enlightened Soul.*
- *The Desolate Soul.*
- *On the Discernment of Spirits.*[120]

---

[120] *See Bibliography of Major Works, below, p. 445 for complete titles and dates of publication:* Il Cristiano illuminato; L'anima illuminata; L'anima desolata; Della discrezione degli spiriti.

For Pastoral and Sociopolitical Action Against Public Immorality

In addition to Sarnelli's moral works dealing with prostitution, mentioned above, there is also his writing that argues against what was considered another rampant public vice, blasphemy:

- *A Work Opposing the Abuse of Blasphemy.*
- *An Instructive and Illuminative Rationale Against the Vice of Blasphemy.*
- *Very Effective Procedures Proposed to Holy Pastors and Bishops of the Church for Banishing the Disgraceful Abuse of Blasphemy.*[121]

General Works for the Practice of Christian Piety

We sum up these works in three major themes: Trinitarian piety

- *Practical devotions to honor the Most Holy Trinity and Mary Most Holy.*[122]
- Christological piety
- *Considerations on the Incarnation of the Divine Word.*
- *Considerations on the Passion of Jesus Christ.*[123]
- Marian piety
- *The glories and greatness of the Divine Mother.*[124]

---

[121] *See Bibliography of Major Works,* below, p. 445 for titles and dates of publication: Opera contro all'abuso della bestemmia; Ragionamenti istruttivi; Maniere efficacissime.

[122] *See Bibliography of Major Works,* below, p. 445 for title and date of publication: Divozioni pratiche.

[123] Both these short works were added to *L'anima illuminata* when it was published in 1740.

[124] *See Bibliography of Major Works,* below, p. 445 for title and date of publication: Considerazione sulle glorie; this was republished with *Il Cristiano santificato* in 1740

IX. THE HOLY UNIVERSE OF BLESSED SARNELLI

REASON FOR THE THEME

What we are going to treat in this section may perhaps be surprising, but I hope that it will be seen as another approach to understand Sarnelli's spirituality. The point of departure is the picture that accompanies the frontispiece of *Il mondo santificato*.[125] The discussion of the engraving is based on the *Dichiarazione dell'immagine*[126] made in the 1863 edition of the work, pages 10 to 14.

The engraving, which is presumed to be commissioned by Sarnelli, and its statement acquire an unsuspected meaning if one compares it to a section of Giambattista Vico's *The New Science*.[127] Vico presents an engraving which is followed by a presentation of the "idea of the work" including an "explanation of the representation of the engraving that serves as the introduction to the work." Giambattista Vico (1668–1744) was a significant influence on modern culture. This "academic thinker and Neapolitan baroque man anticipated by half a century the romantic ideas on history, language and poetry, as illustrated by the interest of Herder and the young Goethe for the work of Vico, as well as the enthusiasm that Michelet shows for it. They recognized him as the precursor of some very diverse figures of philosophy (from Herder to Hegel, from Marx to Dilthey). And Benedetti Croce considered him the authentic founder of esthetics" (G. Solana).[128]

We should recall the relationship of Vico with St. Alphonsus and his influence on the saint as one of his instructors. Alphonsus had to pass the exam before Vico, or before his delegate, in order to validate his private studies for his bachelor's degree and to enroll in the university.[129] Keeping in mind the engravings we have mentioned and the chronological proximity of both men, one question is logical: Could we not see in Sarnelli's engraving (and himself a possible disciple of Vico or at least one exposed to his work) something similar to what Vico sought with his own engravings.

---

[125] *Il Mondo santificato*, I, Naples, 1863.

[126] *Statement of the Image.*

[127] G. Vico, *The New Science*, translated by T. G. Bergin and M. H. Fisch (Ithaca: Cornell University Press, 1948. (pp. 43ff, Spanish edition.)

[128] No reference given.

[129] See R. Tellería, *San Alfonso*, 1, 28.

The annotations of the one responsible for the Spanish edition of *The New Science* did no more than confirm the suspicion. "The use of paintings and images in view of reinforcing memory is tied to this writer of the treatise on the 'artificial memory' which was in vogue in the Renaissance." G. B. Vico expects those representations "to serve the reader for conceiving the idea of the work and for the memory, with the help provided by imagination, to recall more easily after having read it."[130]

Among the symbols used by Vico in his engraving, only two also appear in the Redemptorist iconography with a religious and spiritual meaning: *the globe of the world*, "or, it may be, the world of nature,"[131] and *"the bright triangle with one seeing eye inside of it*, (that) is God under the aspect of his Providence, the aspect under which metaphysics contemplates in the posture of *exstasis* without paying attention to natural things, and under which, up to now, the philosophers have contemplated it." [132]

Because of this use by Vico, we give special attention to the engraving, attributed to Sarnelli, in order to explain what he lives and thinks on prayer and meditation, which is the same as saying his "sacred universe" or his vision of God, of the cosmos, of what is beyond, and of our relationships with what that sacred universe represents. So we look at this engraving and its captions, which we can find in the published works of Sarnelli and can be applied to other engravings used in his works. Please remember that we are only attempting a provisional explanation.

---

[130] *The New Science [Spanish edition, p. 45, note 1]*.

[131] *Ibid., [Spanish edition, note 2]*.

[132] *Ibid., [Spanish edition, note 2, pp. 46–47]*.

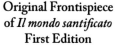

Original Frontispiece
of *Il mondo santificato*
First Edition

Frontispiece of Sarnelli's
Il mondo santificato,
Third Edition (1740)

FOCAL POINTS OF THE ICONOGRAPHY IN *IL MONDO SANTIFICATO* [133]

The focal points of the engraving and of the sacred universe of Sarnelli are: The Most Holy Trinity, the Redeemer with the Cross, the Blessed Virgin, the angels, the saints, the blesseds, and the Church in prayer before these mysteries.

1. *The Most Holy Trinity:* Father (old, majestic, with a scepter in his left hand, and with his right hand, gesturing in dialogue with the Son and with the Blessed Virgin); Son (adult with a robe over the half-naked body, a glorious cross in his right hand, his left hand gesturing toward the Father as a sign of relationship, as he gazes toward the Blessed Virgin as if he would receive a sign from the Mother and transmit it to the Father); Holy Spirit (in the form of a dove which descends toward the hand of the Father).

   The *inscription* in the upper, external part of the engraving says: *"Pater vester de coelo dabit spiritum bonum petentibus se.* » [134]

---

[133] Several parts of this section have been modified and reduced by the English translator.

[134] "Your Father in heaven *[will]* give good things to those who ask him" (Matthew 7:11)

1. *The Most Holy Virgin Mary:* "At the right of the *Trinity,* with the scepter of majesty (equal to that of the eternal Father) as Queen of the *Angels* and of *humans,* and upon a throne of gold, is seated our *heavenly* Mother. She, as the most powerful *Mediatrix* of the *believers,* guarantees the value of our *supplications with* the most *effective* intercession and obtains for us by entreaty the attainment."

2. *St. Joseph:* (Model of the Interior Life),[135] *St. Januarius* (Protector of the City and Kingdom of Naples) and *St. Teresa* (Great Master of Prayer) offer all their merit to *enrich* the prayers which we present to God through their intercession.

3. *The Angels:* found in the lower part of the engraving with censors of smoke in their hands which drifts up to the throne of the Most Holy Trinity. They represent all the *angels* who offer to the Most High our prayers, symbolized by the smoke of incense; the angels are destined for this office, as the Archangel Raphael revealed to Tobias: *when you and Sarah prayed, it was I who brought and read the record of your prayer before the glory of the Lord,*[136] and St. John saw in the Book of Revelation.[137] For this reason, in the rays descending from the figures we find the words: *Dirigatur oratio mea sicut incensum in conspectu tuo*[138]. Also, in the lower, outside margin of the engraving, there is another inscription with these words: *In omnibus operibus tuis memorare novissima tua, etc.*[139]

4. *The temple with the faithful at prayer:* Directly below the angels is pictured prayer in common inside the church, referring to the daily *exercises of the Devout Life in the local church.*

---

[135] For Sarnelli's devotion to St. Joseph, see the work attributed to him: *Exercise of the Seven Dolors and Joys of St. Joseph* [The author only cites a Spanish translation of the work, and not the original text:] *Los siete Domingos y Novena de San José,* Madrid 1944, 3–4.

[136] Tobit 12:12.

[137] Revelation 8:4–8.

[138] "Let my prayer be counted as incense before you" *(Psalm 141:2 [DR 140:2]).*

[139] "In all you do, remember the end of your life" (Sirach 7:36 *[DR Ecclesiasticus 7:40]).*

5. *Family at prayer:* In the bottom right of the engraving, the Devout Life being practiced in the family home *in the city is suggested.*

6. *Prayer in the countryside:* At the bottom left are people at prayer before a country shrine to a saint [or a mission cross)].

INTERPRETING THE FUNDAMENTAL FOCAL POINTS

As one can see, the fundamental focal points in the composition and in the dynamics of the engraving are in the upper part of it. The unity of the ensemble is derived from them. The same has to be said in relation to the sacred universe which they reflect. We are going to explain it on the basis of some works.

As the point of departure, we take this phrase of the instruction in which "he explains the two principal mysteries of the faith," namely, "the unity and trinity of God, the Incarnation and death of our Lord Jesus Christ."[140]

1. For Sarnelli, the *Most Holy Trinity* is the inscrutable mystery of God, One and triune. God is Creator and Providence of the universe, infinite in grandeur and in perfection, all powerful and eternal, without change, without beginning and without end. God is the One who has created, regulates, governs, orders, and conserves all things. "Well then, in this deepest mystery of our faith, that is to say, in the unity and trinity of God, there is contained the beginning and the end of humans, who have originated from the immensity of this God, triune and one, and to this God Creator of theirs ought to return..." Now the marvelous greatness of the mystery of God is hidden from our eyes, "but we hope to be worthy of reaching a day to enjoy God and to see his unspeakable majesty face to face. Then we will comprehend the greatness of the Creator, which we now believe, confess" and "we profoundly adore."[141]

   The source of all good things is the Most Holy Trinity, Father, Son, and Holy Spirit. For this reason, we are obliged to venerate it and worship it above all the saints. And we owe them all honor and all love as

---

[140] *Il Cristiano illuminato,* 235.

[141] *Ibid.,* 242–3.

much for who they are as for the benefits which they have given us. The Trinity, as a matter of fact, is in itself infinite essence, majesty, greatness, power, wisdom, an endless ocean of all perfection, each of them in turn infinitely infinite.[142]

And among the benefits that they have bestowed on us is that of having been revealed to us, by means of the Word made flesh, as Father, Son, and Holy Spirit. Through holy baptism, "we become God's children, living temples of the Trinity and heirs of paradise."[143]

2. The Most Holy Redeemer is God as Son of the Father and is true man by having been incarnated by the work of the Holy Spirit in the most pure womb of the Virgin Mary. He redeemed and saved us with his Incarnation, life, passion, death, and resurrection. With his blood, he paid the price of our ransom and he merited for us all good.[144]

With the sign of the cross of Christ, symbol of redemption, we call upon the Most Holy Trinity by means of the Passion of the Savior ... and we await the victory over evil in the name of the Father, of the Son, and of the Holy Spirit and by virtue of the Passion of Jesus Christ.[145]

But our Lord Jesus Christ, after his glorious resurrection

... ascended triumphant and glorious to heaven by his divine power and is at the right of the Father, that is to say, with equal greatness, dignity, glory and majesty with the heavenly Father and the Holy Spirit and above all the choirs of angels and the blesseds.[146]

The Son of Mary, the glorious Virgin, the most loving Mother, after he had risen,

...is all majesty, all light, all dignity and beauty in his appearance, in his wounds, in his Most Holy

---

[142] *Divozione pratiche*, 3.

[143] *Ibid.*

[144] *Il Cristiano illuminato*, 237.

[145] *Ibid.*, 238.

[146] *Ibid.*, 242–243.

soul, in all his members. He has conquered death, has subdued hell, has destroyed guilt. The heavenly armies, the multitude of the forefathers liberated from Limbo, the most chosen of his followers, the pious women, all creatures, acclaim the God Man and his Mother victorious.[147]

Easter Sunday is a day of great joy and a day for requesting the longed-for grace of "breaking the chains of sin and of the world, overcoming the temptations of the hellish enemy, rising to the spiritual life of the soul and to the love of Jesus and his most sweet Mother."[148] For this reason, we begin, singing with the Church: *Regina Coeli laetare*, alleluia...[149]

Our Redeemer, in so far as he is human:

...gives honor and glory to the Most Holy Trinity with his divine Mother and with all the heavenly court. He is the head, of that heavenly choir, which begins the praise of the Most Holy Trinity. The Mother of God responds and, together with Jesus and Mary, all the angels and saints of heaven, who never cease to proclaim with one single voice, respond without ceasing: *Sanctus, Sanctus, Sanctus, Dominus Deus Sabaoth...*[150]

To this praise of the heavenly choirs is united the honor and glory that rises up to God from all creatures and is due God under countless titles from the Incarnate Word, from the Most Holy Mary and from all the Church, not only those triumphant in heaven, but also militant on earth. With them, we are united with the *Gloria Patri et Filio et Spiritui Sancto...* and we offer God praise, blessing, thanksgiving, and adoration, "which, from the beginning of the world and for all eternity, God has received and will receive from all creatures with his King and his Queen, Jesus and Mary."[151]

---

[147] *L'anima desolata*, 303–305.

[148] *Ibid.*

[149] *[Queen of Heaven, rejoice...]*

[150] *Divozione pratiche*, 8–9.

[151] *Ibid. [The author continues with a practical application found in one of the outlines*

X. THE FINAL WORD

We close with the account of Blessed Sarnelli's death and burial found in *Hijos Ilustres de San Alfonso Maria de Ligorio o sucintas biografías de los Venerables de la Congregación del Santisimo Redentor:*[152]

The last mission in which he could take part was that of Posilipo (April 1744), where he preached the exercises to the clergy. The weakness of the good father kept on increasing day by day. At last, this obliged him to go back to St. Agnello. But, as his state deteriorated more and more, he was transferred to the house of his brother, Domenico...

St. Alphonsus relates that the sick man, in spite of his pains and of the weakness, did not give up on prayer, even though it seemed to him that he could not pray. "Nothing else remains for me," he himself writes with the date of April 21, 1744, "than to breathe out my spirit into a sea of darkness and desolations...My greatest pain is not being able to pray. Ah! If I could pray, my state would not be so lamentable. This trust in prayer is the only thing that remains with me."

From the middle of June, he had to stay in bed. In this period, a great change was worked in his spirit: the darkness, that had clouded him for so long was dissipated and gave place to a great and benevolent peace. From then on, he had no other desire than that of uniting himself with God. His last letter, written three days, before his death, breathes entirely of peace and calm. It starts with the words of the apostle: "I desire to see myself free from the bonds of the body and to be with Christ."

Canon Joseph Sersale, later the Archbishop of Naples, went to see him during these days, and, as he expressed the hope of seeing him recuperated, the sick man answered him:

Sarnelli gives for a mediation service to be held in common: see L'anima illuminata, 1869 Naples edition, Part I, 3–4.]

[152] *[Anonymous]* Redemptorist priest, *Illustrious Sons of St. Alphonsus Maria de Liguori: or Short Biographies of the Venerables of the Congregation of the Most Holy Redeemer,* Montevideo 1922, 24–27.

"Father, for some time, scruples have tormented me; now, by the favor of Jesus Christ, I am free from them and I die at peace; whatever I have done, I have done with the intention of pleasing God; the sacrifice is consumed; do not speak to me of life; the only thing that I long for is to be united with God."

The Redemptorist Brother, sent by St. Alphonsus, to help the sick man, heard him say the following words: "My Father, I am here: the creature already returns to the Creator, the son to the Father. Lord, if it pleases you, I desire to go to see you face to face; but I do not want to die nor to live, I want only what you want. You know that whatever I have done, whatever I have thought, all has been for your glory."

Such words, uttered by a dying man, St. Alphonsus observes, cannot be less than an expression of the truth. The patience of the sick man in those last days was, by all accounts, edifying. If he needed something, he asked for it from the Brother with these humble words: "Be patient, Brother, that I still remain a little time." The very day of his death, in the morning, he said to the Brother: "Brother, prepare the oldest clothes to lay me out in so that the better ones are not lost with me...."

He had requested the Brother to remind him every day to pray the rosary; then he said that he wanted to die praying it. And that is the way it actually happened. After he had begun to pray it that morning, when they reached the third mystery, a great anguish came over him with a heavy sweating. He said to the Brother: "I see that this is already the sweat of death." The Brother ordered for a priest to be called and, meanwhile, he began to suggest some short prayers. But the dying man interrupted him, saying, "Stop it, Brother, so that I may speak." And he continued praying alone right up to when his strength left him. It was referred to in the processes of beatification that, in these last moments, the sovereign kingdom of the heavens appeared to him, then his countenance, pale and wasted away, suddenly was illuminated and these words were heard:

"Welcome, welcome, my sweet Mother!" His agony was tranquil and did not last more than a half hour. With the holy rosary wrapped around his arm, and with the crucifix in his hands, he expired peacefully, after having received a last absolution of the priest, on June 30, 1744, at 10:00 in the morning, at the mere age of forty-two...

In the morning of the following day, the corpse was brought to the neighboring church of Our Lady of Help. An immense crowd accompanied him. Once in the church, a strange commotion took hold of the people and all, as one voice, shouted, "The saint has died." Everyone wanted to take a relic of the Servant of God.

The corpse remained on view up to the following day, on which the funeral was celebrated with the participation of numerous clergy and people. Then he was buried at the foot of the steps of the altar of St. Nicholas.

Later his mortal remains were transferred to the Chapel of St. Alphonsus in the residence of the Redemptorists of St. Anthony of Tarsis in Naples, where they were up to 1994. At that time they were transferred to the Redemptorist Church in Ciorani on the occasion of the 250th anniversary of his death.

The sepulcher was covered with a tombstone of white marble on which one can see the sculptured image of the deceased in priestly garb with the following inscription, which says in Latin:

Gennaro Maria Sarnelli

Neapolitan Priest and Apostolic Man

He renounced riches and honors.

He embraced the Cross with humility.

He fought against the marginalization of women.

By spoken and written word

he was wholly consecrated to renewing the life of the clergy,

of children and of every class of persons.

Worn out by these works, he died June 30, 1744

at 42 years of age.

At the time of Sarnelli's beatification, his shrine was remodeled and the remains placed in a new crypt. The inscription on the coffin in which he lies now reads:

Here in this Bright Urn lies

GENNARO MARIA SARNELLI

A Man of Shining Character Harshly Snatched from this Life,

Outstanding Among the First Followers of St. Alphonsus de Liguori and Now Within the Realm of Light

He is Called Father by

All the Young Women Saved from Desperate Ways, and

the Youth and People of God whom He Led Along the Way of Salvation by Introducing New Guidance.

CHAPTER FOUR

Sarnelli and the Redemptorists

By Domenico Capone, CSsR [153]

The theme of this chapter is not Sarnelli *as a* Redemptorist, but Sarnelli *and the* Redemptorists. It is based on the fact that he, as a priest of the Archdiocese of Naples, was first a member of the Congregation of the Apostolic Missions and then also a member of the Congregation of the Most Holy Redeemer. From the point of view of history, an issue can be raised about the dialectic of such memberships: were they or were they not exclusive of each other? Raising such a question demands a careful consideration of a large portion of Sarnelli's rich and colorful history. In an oral presentation, limited to a very short space of time, I could only briefly touch on a few outstanding and decisive factors. But here what I offer the reader is something longer and more documented, but still not something exhaustive due to the vastness, variety and importance of the work of this great eighteenth century man and priest. [154]

---

[153] This chapter first appeared as an article in *Campania Sacra* 27 (1996): 73–108.

[154] As the main reference points for my research I chose Sarnelli's *Corrispondenza epistolare* in the edition prepared by Antonio Marrazzo, who graciously allowed me to consult it. Also, *Le lettere T. Falcoia*, Rome 1963 and the *Epistolae R. P. Cesare Sportelli*, Rome 1933. Also of importance are the *Novissima positio super virtutibus*, Rome, 1906 from the apostolic process for Sarnelli's beatification and the work of A. Tannoia, *Della vita de istituto del ven. Servo di Dio Alfonso M. Liguori*, in three volumes, Naples 1798, 1800, 1802. Neapolitan scholars of the eighteenth century, such as Benedetto Croce, highly esteemed these latter works because in them not only did facts emerge but also his human personality as well. Today not a few people find in these works an overly appreciative attitude that they censure for somewhat obscuring the facts in order to promote the cause of a saint's beatification. Today we prefer to consider even a saint's negative side in order to round out the person's image and bring him or her closer to our experience. For example, Alphonsus' letters truly reveal the man [In Tannoia's use of these,] I indeed do believe that he exaggerates; just take as an instance, his silence about the episodes of the famous *Regolamento* of 1780. Here his silence was not simply to avoid spreading a negative idea about the saint; it exists just as much in order to avoid upsetting the sensibilities of participants in the affair who were still alive. It is also true that Tannoia had his own ideas about spirituality; many aspects of the saint that, for example, are evident in his correspondence, are not brought out. Still, it is certain that without Tannoia we would know very little about St. Alphonsus during a century of profound cultural changes that often were viewed very critically.

FROM ONE CONGREGATION TO ANOTHER

Sarnelli enrolled in the Congregation of the Apostolic Missions as a novice on June 5, 1730 at the age of twenty-eight; he was already a cleric in minor orders, and he began to participate in their Monday meetings. He was received as a brother on May 28, 1731. On June 7, 1732, the Saturday after Pentecost, he was ordained a presbyter by the Archbishop of Naples, Francisco Cardinal Pignatelli. On June 2, 1733, he participated in the presbyteral ordination of his brother Andrea and decided to meet Alphonsus in Scala and probably planned to participate in the Redemptorist mission at Ravello, which he did in fact from June 14 to 28.

When he returned to Rome, he wrote Alphonsus on July 9, 1733: "Today, Thursday, I spoke with Father Manuilo [Sarnelli's spiritual director] about my situation. He listened to me very attentively, and then he gave me the good news that it is the will of God that I join the Institute...I hope that this resolution of mine, made with the approval of such a man as Father Manuilo, will shut the mouths of many and stimulate others to come to you," that is, into the Congregation of the Most Holy Redeemer then involved in a great crisis.[155] He adds: "They

---

Permit me (and excuse me) for referring to another work of mine that offers this kind of reintegration, *I redentoristi, le redentoriste: le radici*, D. Capone e S. Majorano, Materdomini 1985.

Because the research in this chapter is meant to be a simple contribution to the historical question it treats, I do not cite a number of histories that deal with it. It is true that in 1906 it was thought that the decree of the Congregation of Rites, which clearly indicated that the venerable Sarnelli was "a priest of the Congregation of the Most Holy Redeemer," resolved the question forever; but doubts of historical facts, unless they are on dogmatic issues, are not solved by authority but by authentic documents and good reasoning. It can be maintained that the decree considered the favorable documents as preemptory; it is, however, precisely because these documents are historical that a historian can always restudy them, either to confirm them or to present them again for discussion, either because new documentation is found or because the documents, already known, were not properly integrated into the context.

[155] In Naples, the cause of the crisis was placed on what was presumed to be Alphonsus' naiveté in believing Sr. Celeste Crostarosa, who had told him that God had called him to found an Institute. As early as 1725, this nun had been branded a "visionary" in Naples. She was expelled from her monastery at the command of Bishop Falcoia on May 25, 1733. Her leaving came shortly after the departure from the Redemptorists of the first three companions of St. Alphonsus, and this was thought to indicate the ruin of the Institute. It is from this perspective that Sarnelli is writing in a letter to the saint after July 9: "I assure you that this Celeste (May God make her a saint!) has struck a great blow to the Institute;" (Rome, Archivio Postulazione Generale Redentorista *[APGR]*, Lettera 5). If we analyze the events by reconstructing how they happened day-by-day from February 12 to May 25, 1733, the evidence suggests that the one directly responsible for the sister's departure was actually Falcoia, even if he had been deceived

say that the mission we gave was heard about, and that Carace[156] said that the superior had written me a strong letter for me to quit and come back down there."[157]

Sarnelli then feared that, upon his return to Scala, he would be assigned to teach elementary school to a few children of the neighborhood and so be constrained to spend the major part of his time with them. This would mean he could never get away from Scala even for a few days, and so he wrote Alphonsus:

I find myself committed here to rescue the girls who are at risk and to write in their defense to reveal the endless damages done them because of which they sell their honor while still children. It appears that by entering this Institute, succeeding in this great good, at least by my [*current*] writing, could be impeded. Coming there [*to Scala*], I would be hard pressed to have the time and place to finish it so as to be able to give help to so many poor little souls. This would be something that I could not in fact do if I was stuck in school.[158]

He also mentions that

I am laboring on another work on Christian doctrine that Borgia asked from me in order to give it to the Secretary General of Doctrine here. This work would also help those who come to the Institute to realize the great necessity and the powerful effectiveness of Christian doctrine and the means to insure its fruitfulness.[159]

by some of the sisters hostile toward Celeste. But at the time Falcoia was not viewed as culpable, but rather as a saint, even though the Bishop of Scala had reproved his great error in protecting Silvestro Tosquez against Alphonsus' advice; it was Tosquez who was behind the whole sad affair. Yet, Falcoia called his action "an innocent mistake"; (Falcoia, *Lettere*, 144). Unfortunately, in June–July 1733, Alphonsus and Sarnelli believed him unquestionably. This was a fatal unquestioning for the true history of the facts. Without Falcoia, however, the Institute was completely collapsing.

[156] Tommaso Carace was a celebrated preacher who guided Alphonsus in his first missions. See De Meulemeester, *Origines*, II, 100; Alphonsus de Liguori, *Lettere*, I, 94, 107–108; Tellería, *San Alfonso*, i, 108, 302, 381; ii, 222.

[157] S. Alfonso de Liguori, *Carteggio*, Vol. I, ed. by Giuseppe Orlandi, as quoted in *The History of the Congregation of the Most Holy Redeemer*, ed. by Francisco Chiovaro and J. Robert Fenili, trans. by J. Robert Fenili, vol. I/ii, 169.

[158] *History*, I/ii, 177.

[159] *Ibid.*

Sarnelli Attracted by the Redemptorist Charism

A question arises (Father Manulio must have raised the problem). Here was Sarnelli, burdened by a very important social program of evangelization and a no less important one of composing a catechism for the Archdiocese of Naples and for missionaries. How could he, I ask, decide to move to Scala for a missionary endeavor so strongly criticized by the Neapolitan clergy, and one that was in the middle of a crisis as well? Merely the great personal friendship he had with Alphonsus could not have been enough to justify such a decision. Why then did he make this choice?

In a later undated letter to Alphonsus, right after the election of the superior of the Congregation of the Apostolic Missions, perhaps written on July 22, 1733, he writes this:

When I think how it is possible that the Lord wishes to make use of me in some way for this magnificent work *[Alphonsus' Institute]* and to join with the first [members] as well as promote it here even amid so much hesitancy and so many doubts, I comfort myself by remembering what St. Paul wrote: *Quae infirma sunt mundi, quae stulta, quae contemptibilia sunt mundi elegit Deus ut confundat fortia,*[160] and that the Lord called to his apostolate even the tax collectors.[161]

Therefore, the apostolic missionary charism that moved Alphonsus to found the Congregation showed itself to Sarnelli to be of higher grandeur, even in the moment it was on the brink of failure. Alphonsus himself, precisely when he was tested by being left alone, abandoned by all, said: "he felt he would die of consolation" when he realized "that God had certainly called him to this great work."[162] So it is clear that the same apostolic charism that was given to Alphonsus so he could become the founder of the new Congregation was now revealed to Sarnelli in all its greatness, despite the negative judgment

---

[160] 1 Corinthians 1:27-28 [*"God has chosen what is weak in the world, what is foolish, what is contemptible so that he may confound the wise."*] *[The Vulgate text actually reads:* "quae stulta sunt mundi elegit Deus, ut confundat sapientes: et infirma mundi elegit Deus, ut confundat fortia": *"But God has chosen the foolish of the world, so that he may confound the strong. And God has chosen the weak of the world, so that he may confound the strong."]*

[161] *History,* i/ii, 181.

[162] O. Gregorio, "Corrispondenza epistolare inedita o edita di sant'Alfonso," in *Spicilegium Historicum Congregationis SS.mi Redemptoris* 19 (1971): 243.

spread throughout Naples. So Gennaro Maria was confused and yet stirred when he heard from his spiritual director that he was called by God to be one of the first to promote this work. By the will of God, one of the first promoters! The apostolic charism of the foundation thus reached out to Sarnelli as well because in that moment God saw and wanted him to be the strongest support for his troubled friend, Alphonsus de Liguori.

REDEMPTORIST MISSIONARY WITH ALPHONSUS

On August 17, 1733, Sarnelli, who always felt himself to be a member of the Congregation of the Apostolic Missions, took part in that group's regular Monday meeting, but by September 4, he was already at the cathedral in Scala to preach the novena in preparation for the feast of the Exultation of the Holy Cross on September 14. That was the week that the Redemptorist Congregation left the place where it was born, that is, the nun's guesthouse, and moved to a larger house that by the end of the century would be named *"Casa Anastasio."*[163] That will be the house where Sarnelli remained the longest, until 1736, while he attended to his literary work.[164]

Falcoia informs us that on September 28, 1733, Alphonsus and Sarnelli, already living at the *Casa Anastasio*, began a mission campaign in Cilento.[165] This town is right at the horizon of the panorama which the two of them could see, either seated or walking on the large terrace of the house now restored and still in use today.[166]

In the fall and winter, Sarnelli was a missionary with Alphonsus along the Amalfi Coast and its neighborhood. But at times during this same period, Gennaro Maria went to Naples, and there he attended the Monday reunions of the Congregation of the Apostolic Missions. In the meantime, he also applied himself to his social apostolate to defeat

---

[163] Falcoia, *Lettere*, 177.

[164] It is important that in the first listing [*Catologo*] of Redemptorists, now found in Rome at the Archivium Generale Historicum Redentoristi (AGHR), Sarnelli's name appears as entering the Congregation of the Most Holy Redeemer on January 15, 1734. This listing began to be compiled in 1744, the year of Sarnelli's death. The compiler has obviously made a mistake [in the date].

[165] Falcoia, *Lettere*, 179.

[166] *The Casa was remodeled at the end of the twentieth century into a retreat center and no longer has the same appearance it had at the time of Alphonsus and Sarnelli. See History, I/II, "Illustrations: Places," Figure 28*

the disturbances caused by prostitution in Naples and to obtain from the government authorities the royal program of June 23, 1734, that limited the movements of prostitutes in the city. In July, he was at Santa Maria dei Monti in the hills over Scala, both for relaxation as well as to work on his writings. In April 1736, he left Scala definitively and made his home in Naples. Alphonsus, in his *"Appunti per Sarnelli"* writes: "Notice: [for the sake of] change of climate."[167] This is meant to say that Sarnelli left Scala, not because he was leaving the Congregation, but because his health was failing seriously at Scala. He had need of medical care and Scala, a small and isolated town, did not offer the means for a successful cure. Besides, *Casa Anastasio*, despite the assiduous care of the heroic and holy Brother Vito Curzio, was both cold in the long winter and tight living even for only four or five people.

RETURN TO NAPLES

In Naples, Gennaro Maria lived in his family home and worked on preaching and composing his publications on spirituality and about social reform, requiring the political authorities to create provisions to defend girls from the insidious predations of those who managed prostitution.

This is where we now place our principal question for the theme of this article: After his return to Naples, did he work as a Redemptorist or simply as a Neapolitan member of the Congregation of the Apostolic Missions? This is all the more a question because he continued to participate in its Monday meetings as often as he could. Or, more simply, of which congregation was he a member: the Redemptorists or the Apostolic Missionaries? To answer this, there is one further point that it is necessary to consider: namely, a peremptory decision of the Archbishop of Naples, Francisco Cardinal Pignatelli, the ecclesiastical superior of both Alphonsus and Sarnelli.

ARCHBISHOP PIGNATELLI'S DECISION

On February 23, 1733, the authorities and members of the Congregation of the Apostolic Missions had decided to dismiss Alphonsus from membership in the Congregation and to deprive him of a chaplaincy that he enjoyed as a member. Why? The reason was that by founding the Congregation of the Most Holy Redeemer, he could no longer be a

---

[167] Alphonsus de Liguori, *"Scritto sulle virtù,"* in AGHR.

member at the disposition of the superiors of the Apostolic Missions. At this point, however, Cardinal Pignatelli intervened by an extraordinary action in virtue of his position as "Superior of all the Superiors" of that Congregation,[168] and blocked the dismissal and privation of the chaplaincy. This decision in Alphonsus' favor was brought about by the interventions of Alphonsus' great friend, Don Giulio Torno.

The act of peremptory authority by the archbishop, using his supreme authority in the Congregation of the Apostolic Missions, was of great importance from a juridical viewpoint. That is, Alphonsus, simply by being a member *de facto* of the Apostolic Missionaries and therefore maintaining a chaplaincy under its auspices, could still continue, if he chose, in his personal venture of founding the association of missionary priests, he had planned freely as a private person [*And this could happen*] without the intervention of the authorities of the Apostolic Missionaries and without the project becoming in some way "diocesan."

On the basis of this important decision, Alphonsus' position was ambivalent but clear: he remained a secular priest of Naples dependent as such on the archbishop and was a member of the Congregation of the Apostolic Missions, but in such a way that he could be autonomous in having responsibility over the foundation he was attempting. His membership in the Apostolic Missionaries was real but limited; it could not stand in the way when Alphonsus acted, as he believed, to establish his project. The double and simultaneous membership was possible because the two institutions were not formally religious, but associations of diocesan priests dedicated to missionary preaching, operative associations, even if the Congregation of the Apostolic Missions was not an association of private persons, but recognized and promoted by archdiocesan authority.

In the Congregation of the Most Holy Redeemer, technically the director of the association was the Bishop of Castellammare, Bishop Tommaso Falcoia, not as a bishop but as an expert in the organization of missionary and spiritual communities. He was also Alphonsus' spiritual director, freely chosen by him. But right from the start, Falcoia assumed all authority absolutely. He even presented himself as the founder, almost setting aside the real charismatic founder, the one chosen by God, namely

---

[168] Tannoia, *Della vita*, lib. 2, cap. 3, pp. 88–89.

Alphonsus, who was recognized as such by the highly regarded spiritual figure, Father Ludovico Fiorillo, OP, when asked by Alphonsus' spiritual director, Father Tommaso Pagano. The presumption on Falcoia's part stemmed from the dramatic situation of the Congregation until 1743, when he died. The blind obedience of Alphonsus was heroic virtue for him, but in fact the birth and growth of the Congregation of the Most Holy Redeemer was made very difficult because of Falcoia's absolutism.

Sarnelli could benefit as well from Alphonsus' status of being both a true Redemptorist while still belonging, in some form, to the Congregation of the Apostolic Missions, a status declared valid by the Archbishop of Naples, his true ecclesiastical superior. Sarnelli was also a Neapolitan priest, subject to the archbishop, who obviously knew him as a member of the Apostolic Missions. By associating himself with Alphonsus, he too enjoyed fully the status of being a Redemptorist, living and actualizing its charism while, at the same time, belonging to the archdiocesan congregation, since he also was permitted to be a Redemptorist autonomously. It was in this juridic condition of a Neapolitan priest that, from September 1733 to April 1736, he was a missionary with Alphonsus and lived in the Redemptorist house in Scala, while still going to Naples occasionally to attend the Monday meeting of the Apostolic Missions. When he returned to Naples in 1736 because of his health, his attendance at these meetings became more frequent, but his status as a member of the Redemptorist association remained unchanged.

It is possible to object that his evangelizing and social work in saving girls from prostitution was not an activity according to the Redemptorist missionary charism, while it could be that of a Neapolitan priest who was a member of the Congregation of the Apostolic Missions. However, in a certain way, it is consistent with the Redemptorist charism as found in a letter from Falcoia to all the Redemptorists written on April 8, 1738. He declares:

> Since His Divine Majesty remains pleased to assist one of our brothers [Sarnelli] and to bless him for his great efforts to rein in the insolence of the dissolute women of the world... we have considered it a good thing to exhort and beg you all, as the superiors of each residence *pro tempore* and all the subjects of our blessed Institute, that in the future you seek to prudently take up such a timely service for the Lord and

for people and to stand behind the zeal and sweat poured out by anyone who is called to the same task.[169]

Thus, Sarnelli labored in Naples as one "called to the same task," that is to the vocation and charism of the Redemptorists: to evangelize the poor, giving to the term "evangelize" its biblical broadness that embraces all the work of Christ willed by the Father as his "Mystery," in which the "missionary preaching to the spiritually poor" is made concrete in a special field. Indeed, the girls that Sarnelli evangelized in the many areas of eighteenth century Naples were in extreme spiritual poverty, for there were few people who effectively interceded for them.

Certainly the truth of Falcoia's thought about the Redemptorist charism is problematic; given that he will show that he was against the missionary efforts of the Redemptorists in the environs of Naples, he should have had much stronger reasons for considering the work of Sarnelli, in saving the girls in peril in the very city of Naples, to be non-Redemptoristic. But, as far as the solemn letter of 1738 in Sarnelli's favor is concerned, it is possible that it was another Redemptorist, Sportelli (whom Falcoia considered his unique spiritual son) who promoted this action, considering that this solemn text is composed in his handwriting, as it still appears in the keeping of the Redemptorist General Archives in Rome.[170]

SARNELLI'S THOUGHTS REMAIN ON CIORANI

So he kept working in Naples. Even while he was occupied there, he wrote to Alphonsus in 1738, saying:

> Naples is like a hell for me. But it is right that I stay here as long as it pleases God. I will come and go for the greater glory of God. As soon as the book on the devout life is completed, I can leave for good. As far as my love for the Institute, I have all the love and commitment possible. I would like to see it reaching to the skies, spread throughout the world, and I promote it even to the cost of my blood. But I do not know what I can do to bring you joy and blessing; I

---

[169] *Carteggio*, I, #221, p. 506.

[170] AGHR, 0503: EadSA, 475.

can do no more than the nothing I do. The Institute would do the same for me as I do for the Institute.[171]

So Sarnelli has a clear conscience that the work he is doing in Naples is work for the Redemptorist Congregation. If it is carefully considered, by doing this he is collaborating with the Institute for, precisely by his actions that are approved by Alphonsus, he is interpreting and defining the meaning of the true Redemptorist charism. His letter continues:

> For the missions, I will do what I can to help you if it pleases the Divine Majesty. Your Reverence sees that here I refuse a thousand offerings and invitations that are tempting, easy and at no cost. And although I got an invitation from one of the brothers of the Congregation for a Mission of the Holy Spirit, I excused myself from it and will continue to excuse myself if they put pressure on me as I am sure they will.[172]

Here Sarnelli's juridic status (if we wish to call it that) is clear. His superiors are not those of the Congregation of the Apostolic Missions and he does not respond to all their invitations. His superior is Alphonsus at Ciorani; even in Naples he is in strict collaboration with the Institute, for which he does whatever he can. Nevertheless, in the same letter he says that he wants to respond to Falcoia "not to include me as a member there [that is as a member of the community at Ciorani], either on account of my countless illnesses or the many very heavy duties here." He adds that Ciorani, since it is the baronial feud of his father "is not the proper place to exercise my ministry except in extreme necessity."

THE REDEMPTORISTS MOVE FROM SCALA TO CIORANI

On August 27, 1738, at Falcoia's order, against the wishes of the bishop and clergy of Scala, and even of the monastery of Redemptoristine Nuns, the Redemptorist missionaries, always at Falcoia's command, leave Scala permanently and move as a group to Ciorani into a spacious house built shortly before. The superior appointed for the community was Alphonsus, but in fact the internal ordering, even in details, depended on Falcoia, giving direction for the most part through

[171] *Carteggio*, I, #223, p. 512.
[172] *Ibid.*

Cesare Sportelli, who had been ordained for hardly a year. Falcoia wrote him, probably in September, determining the officers of the new community, formed by the members who had come from Scala. Sportelli was designated the zealator for the Congregation and overseer of the bishop's dispositions.

That September, Sarnelli was supposed to come to Ciorani temporarily because Falcoia told Sportelli: "Be sure to say to Don Gennaro and to everyone that you choose: 'Conquer yourself'."[173] Who knows what Sarnelli had to say about these orders given by Falcoia and passed on by Sportelli? Where was Alphonsus, the superior of the community? A letter of Falcoia probably from October 1738, the time of the individual retreats before going on the mission, gives us the answer.[174]

From this letter, we surmise that Alphonsus was gone in August and September for "holy visits to sanctuaries of the Blessed Virgin" and "for retreat." Falcoia rejoices in "all your spiritual delights." He says that he could not write earlier because of his ills and because "my letters would not have found you at Ciurani [sic] or they would have caught up with you while you were on your retreat." Why all these excuses for his silence with Alphonsus? Perhaps the answer is in what follows in the letter. He continues:

"I believe that you can imagine what is in my heart over the collapse of the monastery in Scala...I cannot put it all into the words I write." This laconic note makes us think that Alphonsus, while in the "holy visits to the shrines of the Blessed Virgin" and on retreat was not informed by Falcoia, either about his breakup with the nuns or about his order to close the house at Scala, an action almost unexpectedly imposed on the priests on August 25, 1738.[175] The previous month he had written to Sportelli whom he had sent to examine the very critical situation with the bishop and the nuns: "The nuns are obstinate in their feelings and I am determined in mine." He finishes: "It seems that I have no other alternative, but you can wait for some other further news and advise me of it so that I can resolve your comings and goings."[176]

Alphonsus knew nothing of all this; he was left to make his "holy visits to the sanctuaries of the Blessed Virgin." A silence that should

---

[173] Falcoia, *Lettere*, 387.

[174] *Carteggio*, I, #224, p. 514.

[175] Falcoia, *Lettere*, 386–387.

[176] *Ibid.*, 380–381.

cause amazement. But for someone who is well aware of the history of how Falcoia thinks about Alphonsus, such comportment does nothing more than confirm the words that the latter had taken from Falcoia's letter of September 5, 1732, that is, seven days after he had chosen the bishop as his spiritual director: "Conduct yourself as a child in the arms of his father or mother."[177] In truth, Falcoia was very solicitous for the physical health of Alphonsus and of the others; it was almost maternal. His letters at times are very moving in their concern. But in their spiritual life as religious, they need to be babies, even if they are priests and, even more so, if they are nuns at Scala. If these latter were not "childlike," Falcoia became, as we already said, "hard as a rock."

FALCOIA'S VS. ALPHONSUS' VIEWS ON THE APOSTOLIC MISSIONS

The Redemptorist Congregation in Ciorani, and radiating out of Ciorani, finally started taking on the more stable external form and interior community vitality of a missionary congregation. The Archbishop of Salerno, Fabrizio De Capua, issued a decree through his vicar general on September 12, 1735: "We, therefore…grant your congregation of missionaries a house with its own church, in which to praise God and where you can peacefully fulfill your service, along with the statutes we have revised and approved."[178] Notice: This was a revision and approval of a house and of the carrying out of the divine services and not of a rule of religious life; there was not yet a written rule, and so the congregation still remained at the level of a private association. Alphonsus was always aware of this legal status of his congregation. This is why he was then, and indeed always, conscious of the fact that he was bound to the Archbishop of Naples as his superior and in communion with the Congregation of the Apostolic Missions and with so many priests, especially Don Giulio Torno, his theology teacher. This created in him an attitude of respect, which was always natural for him, given his well-known affectionate nature. But around the years 1738–1739, Alphonsus' attitude was not to Falcoia's liking.

---

[177] *Carteggio*, I, #40, 174
[178] AGHR, XVIII, A. 1bis.

As early as 1733, he said that the relation between the Apostolic Missionaries and the Redemptorists ought to be a "distant alliance."[179] But in 1739 he wrote the following somewhat agitated letter:

From what you tell me about the priests of your present congregation [*i.e., the Apostolic Missionaries*], my dear son, I cannot tell you otherwise than that this blessed congregation can offer you—and I mean this in a good sense—the greatest temptation. It is certain that you must not *claudicare in duas partes: et deficit ambobus, qui vult servire duobus.*[180] The great dependence that they want to demand of you really does not please me, and under various pretexts they will surely marginalize you little by little. What I think is worse is that your regard and concern about the chaplaincy, etc. are the cause of this kind of dependence…My son, you have in your hands such a sublime work, a work totally from God, a work that will bring to the Church of God the most immense results: *Age quod agis*[181] and do not desire to divide yourself *in duas partes*[182]…if afterwards they want to take away the chaplaincy, divine providence will still not run out.

It is necessary to recall that this vision of the sublimity of the work that Alphonsus has in his hands is valuable and that the Congregation of the Most Holy Redeemer must be thankful to Falcoia. But it would have been better if Alphonsus could have really "had in his hands" a little more than what Falcoia would allow. The latter also wanted a clear separation from the Congregation of the Apostolic Missions because he conceived the Congregation of the Most Holy Redeemer in Ciorani as a form of community in the sense explained by the first historian of the Congregation of the Most Holy Redeemer, Giuseppe Landi, CSsR, in 1782: he wanted the Redemptorists

…mainly at home studying and engaged in a holy retreat, and carrying out a contemplative life rather than an active one. Meanwhile, in addition to that, he wanted them engaged in conducting retreats for the persons who would

---

[179] *Carteggio*, I, #90, p. 274.

[180] One who wants to serve both sides, will serve neither.

[181] Attend to what you are doing.

[182] *Carteggio*, I, #226, p. 520.

come to reside in the house any time during the year, besides occupying themselves in the few tasks in their own church. In addition, he then desired that the subjects of this Institute spend all their time in contemplation and mortification. For that purpose he planned that every year each confrere would make twenty, thirty or forty days of retreat before going out on the missions. Moreover, he wanted more time each day for mental prayer, choir recitation of the Office and four disciplines a week. Lastly, every week, Friday and Saturday were to be days of fast and there were to be other exercises during the day.[183]

Because of his concept of religious life, what the association would become when it was a true "Order," he got to the point of complaining even about Alphonsus, because he was out of the house doing too much preaching. Finally, in February 1739 he wrote Alphonsus: "Your return to your nest lasted only a few days and I desire that while in the nest, you fully rest your feathers so you will fly without danger of crashing due to the weakness of your wings."[184]

But in Alphonsus and Gennaro Maria, Christ lived through his Spirit in an intense way and, for them, missionary activity was also growth into mutuality with Christ. That is, their personal growth in apostolic holiness was not just a simple, individual perfection. There was no danger of weak wings.

For them, the imitation of Christ consisted, not in reducing Christ to a simple model of virtue for individual holiness as Falcoia conceived it, but in the continuation, precisely through a kind of symbiosis or mutuality, of the mission or project of "sum[ming] up all things in Christ, in heaven and on earth" (Ephesians 1:9–10) as willed by the Father. This was a continuation, always *specified and supported by Christ and his Holy Spirit*, that for Alphonsus and his Congregation the spiritually most abandoned people had to be their special field of action. This applied especially to the people who dwelt in the countryside, where

---

[183] AGHR [G. Landi], "Istoria della congregazione del SS. Redentore, parte prima o sia prima epoca della prima formazione della congregazione del SS. Redentore," (unpublished, composed in two volumes during four months of 1782, in the Redemptorist house at Gubbio).

[184] *Carteggio*, I, #226, p. 519.

other missionaries did not go with organized missions to bring about a firmly rooted conversion to Christ.

Surely this particularization of an apostolic field of action could not be realized if the Redemptorists did not live a true life of prayer in their house. Indeed, the apostles, when they created the first deacons, declared that their "apostolic life" had to be devoted entirely "to prayer and to the ministry of the word" (Acts 6:4). But this life of prayer, for Alphonsus, Sarnelli and the authentic Redemptorists was always strongly centered on Christ. This meant that Christ was not seen simply as a model of individual perfection but as a living person always acting among the people to save them, especially among the "poor sinners," as Alphonsus would say, or "the poor little souls" of the girls trapped in prostitution, as Sarnelli would put it.

Only by means of this contemplative mutuality with Christ, both transformative of the individual and community oriented, which is the Father's mission or project, is the apostolic character of Redemptorist life inseparably, and at times simultaneously, the prayer through which Christ is seen and lived as well as the missionary preaching that, in a different way, radiates Christ. This is the reason that at home the Redemptorists, with Alphonsus and Sarnelli, did not enclose themselves in a hermitage. Rather, always growing in mutuality with Christ by more intense "contemplative prayer," they evangelize by radiating Christ to the people even at home.

Their program, indeed their rule was: evangelize by letting themselves always do so through the living person of Christ who dwells amid the people. Often with the voice of their own true needs, the people suggest to the Redemptorist how to evangelize. In this way Sarnelli heard the voice of the girls in the so-called "Spanish Quarter" of Naples, trapped by organized prostitution; then he evangelized them as their poor social and spiritual condition demanded. Sarnelli explained this to Alphonsus in July 1733 before leaving to take refuge in Scala. Alphonsus, the Founder, was in agreement. For this reason, besides that of poor health, he could return to Naples in April 1736 with Alphonsus' consent.

SARNELLI'S PLAN: TWO CONGREGATIONS
TOGETHER IN MISSION TO NAPLES

This living communion of Sarnelli with Christ, the eternal Savior, always in action, led him, not to accentuate the separation from the Congregation of the Apostolic Missions as Falcoia wished, but rather toward a mutual project of extraordinary missionary collaboration for the poor people who were not well cared for spiritually in the environs of Naples. Sarnelli understood their spiritual condition very well and was convinced that a large mission for them was in accord with the proper charism of the Redemptorists *as it was lived by Alphonsus*. Considering his friendship with Alphonsus, he spoke to him before Falcoia was contacted. It was the Archbishop of Naples, Cardinal Giuseppe Spinelli, who would speak authoritatively to the latter. Spinelli was the actual superior of Alphonsus since January 17, 1735, after the death of Cardinal Pignatelli on December 15, 1734.

On February 18, 1741, then, Sarnelli wrote Alphonsus:

My Most Esteemed Father:
It is time to sanctify this diocese [Naples].

How? He had decided to propose to the archbishop a great round of missions in the environs of Naples, of which Alphonsus was to be in charge. "This morning, I had a long conversation with His Eminence, who was gently complaining that he had not seen you yet. I told him everything, the dependence on Bishop Falcoia. I explained to him the way to handle it, the letter he should write to Bishop Falcoia and to mention that he does this with my knowledge." The cardinal understood the obstacle of the "dependence on Bishop Falcoia" and even accepted Sarnelli's suggestion of the style of the letter to Falcoia as a way to get things going. He agreed and so Sarnelli exclaims: "Blessed be God. In an hour they got things done, in God's name, that once would have taken ten years. All to his glory...I say come in obedience to Falcoia. I told His Eminence that I will reside with you and thus not waste seven months this year, when the whole house is moved outside [to Sant'Aniello di Barra, designated as the center for the mission?]... Be of good heart: I see a great field open for spreading what you desire and the Institute."[185]

---

[185] *Carteggio,* I, #268, pp. 594–595.

On February 24, 1741, the cardinal sent the letter to Falcoia in which he says, among other things:

I ask Your Illustriousness, therefore, to direct the said association to follow my said intention, while assigning them [the Redemptorists] to quickly respond to my decision that is so much in conformity to the spirit of their vocation, which they said Sir Don Alphonsus and his companions have followed with such devotion.

He ends by requesting that [Falcoia] "command" the Redemptorists to come "through obedience." Thus, by doing this, he will promote the very great honor of God and greatly oblige me."[186]

We underline the statement of the cardinal that the mission to the environs of Naples was "in conformity to the spirit" of the vocation that Alphonsus and his companions were following. It seems that this letter, composed by Canon Fontana to carry out the agreement between the cardinal and Sarnelli, was composed "with the knowledge" of the latter, and therefore was according to the idea he had of the proper charism of the Congregation of the Most Holy Redeemer that had filled him with enthusiasm and that he promoted. In this, there is no way he could not have been in accord with Alphonsus, but at the same time knowing that he was in complete disagreement with Falcoia. From this, as was just noted, the tone of the letter was calculated to block Falcoia's resistance. The confidential letter Sarnelli wrote Alphonsus on February 18, which must certainly have remained a secret as far as Falcoia was concerned, makes all this clear.

Falcoia quickly responded to the cardinal with a very long letter, laying out in detail many reasons against the idea and ended: "Eminent Lord, I am prostrate with my face to the ground at your feet and humbly beg you to deign to leave these blessed persons in peace," referring to the Redemptorists at Ciorani. He says, among other things, "I am...a poor little twig broken and fallen; it is only out of great humility that these servants of God wish to lean on me for support, and if I fall or if they must remain far from me, everything could be lost, either through the clash of their different opinions or through other causes of the inconstancy of human hearts."[187]

---

[186] AGHR, XXVII, D. 11.

[187] Falcoia, *Lettere*, 127.

The fact is that a good seven years, three months, and two weeks had passed since November 15, 1732, and Falcoia had never once convoked a community meeting to discuss the community's organization or life. Besides, Sarnelli, Rossi, Mazzini, Villani and Sportelli could hardly be called men marked by "inconstancy of the human heart" and the "clash of their different opinions." They were not people like Mannarini and Tosquez and Di Donato in the battle of November 8–15, 1732. They could and should have been brought together to discuss their opinions, which differed from those of Falcoia. But he did not admit "diversity" from his opinions.

In truth, we must say that Falcoia often called upon Sportelli, but how? Not to discuss, but rather to receive *[Falcoia's]* "oracles"—the term is Sportelli's—either to pass on to the confreres and to the nuns to carry out in dealing with others or for the eventual new founding of religious houses. One example will suffice. On January 20, 1742, Sportelli went to Pagani to treat of the foundation of a new Redemptorist house, but Falcoia was not happy about it and so wanted to delay it. "Upon arrival at Pagani," Sportelli writes, "according to the oracles of Your Illustriousness, I began to drum my fingers on the table in order to break matters off discretely and in a plausible way." Thus, we have oracles of Falcoia and the play-acting of Sportelli so as, not to discuss, but to follow a planned way to postpone the project. But there was no need to tap his fingers, because, says Sportelli, "Bishop De Dominicis [the Bishop of Nocera e Pagani] had gone to Naples to hand in his resignation."[188] Therefore, this was the method: proceed according to the oracles. This must also be kept in mind to interpret the history of the origins, both of the Redemptorists as well as of the nuns.

One of the reasons for this way of acting was a disposition of Falcoia's character; he confesses it himself in September of 1733 on the occasion of a very important matter: "I have great difficulty in getting myself to listen to a variety of opinions."[189] He was not a man of dialogue. Even with the nuns, when they wanted to discuss something about their rule or about other problems in their regard, it reached the breaking point. This also explains why he always refused permission to Sister Maria Celeste Crostarosa, whom everyone now recognizes to have been a true mystic, to ask for counsel from other

[188] Falcoia, *Lettere*, 418–423.
[189] *Carteggio*, I, #103, p. 291.

priests about whether her doubts regarding her interior life were valid or not. This is something strongly censured by the mystical theologian, St. John of the Cross.[190] What was the reaction of Alphonsus when Falcoia had to officially notify him of the cardinal's proposal? Tannoia says that Alphonsus excused himself, adducing, among other reasons, that there were plenty of qualified missionaries in Naples. "When the cardinal received this response from Alphonsus, he was disgusted and getting serious said, "I am your superior; I want to be obeyed!...and getting very forceful,"—Tannoia continues—"he said that he had more right than any other bishop because [Alphonsus] was his subject and his diocesan [priest]."[191] Thus, up to the death of Falcoia on April 20, 1743, poor Alphonsus found himself caught between obedience to Falcoia and obedience to the Archbishop of Naples. After 1743, his wisdom found a way to manage and in 1748 it will be Cardinal Spinelli himself who will present to Pope Benedict XIV his priest, Alphonsus de Liguori, with the Institute of the Most Holy Savior and its Rule for pontifical approval. It was received and approved, something that Falcoia was never able to accomplish.

THE CRISIS WITH FALCOIA REACHES ITS PEAK

From May 1741 to June 1742, the faithful in the environs of Naples were being evangelized, first by Alphonsus and Andrea Villani, later by Paolo Cafaro and Sarnelli. The work was enormous but most successful. Alphonsus, however, could not be involved in the life of the community at Ciorani that was undergoing not a few troubles due to his absence and that of his companions for more than a year. On June 22, 1742, he wrote to Sportelli: "My Dear Don Cesare, pray that Jesus Christ frees me from Naples...When the cardinal gets back, I will speak with him, but I have it in my head that it will only be with the greatest difficulty that he will actually let us leave. At least, as we said, we may be able to succeed in going back and forth." [192]

---

[190] San Juan De La Cruz, "Llama de amor viva," Canción 3ª, n. 61, in *Obras completas* (Burgos 1987), p. 1027.

[191] Tannoia, *Della vita*, lib. 2, cap. 12, pp. 124–125.

[192] *Carteggio*, I, #275, p. 608
In a draft of the letter dated June 30, Falcoia states this differently: "...moving on according to his [Falcoia's] ideas."

Sportelli naturally passed the matter and its limited hope on to Falcoia. But the latter decided to go after Alphonsus with a heavy hand, using Sportelli as intermediary. So he makes him write on July 6: "It pains [the bishop] that he does not see the Congregation moving on towards its proposed goal,* since it is moving away from its mark of the imitation of Our Lord Jesus Christ in evangelizing the poor amid the most needy dioceses and for the good of the most abandoned souls. And therefore, he never felt an inclination toward foundations in the aforesaid suburbs." Here he adds that if there is thought of a foundation "in that case, the foundation there would have to be separated from the one here [in Ciorani] and the members left free either to go along with Your Reverence there or to stay here under his [Falcoia's] direction."[193]

It is clear that he is speaking of "a foundation there," that is, in Barra. Yet, in fact, Alphonsus was against such a foundation because, if we believe his biographer, Tannoia, such a foundation would be a distraction and something foreign to the Redemptorists.[194] But Falcoia's real reason was very different. He said that the founding of a missionary house at Barra was the same as founding a new Congregation, separate from the one in Ciorani, and in such a case Alphonsus would have to make up his mind: either at Ciorani under the direction of Falcoia or with a new congregation under obedience to the Archbishop of Naples.

What is the precise reason for such a separation according to Falcoia? Notice: to found such a house would be to depart from the "characteristic of the imitation of Christ." This imitation consisted in founding houses amid needy dioceses to house missionaries dedicated to evangelizing the poor in the midst of these dioceses. The immediate consequence of this decision of Falcoia was very grave: continuing to give missions in the suburbs of Naples means one is no longer a Redemptorist and in that case one is removed from the congregation at Ciorani. In this way, Falcoia actually cuts off the attempt of mediating with the Archbishop of Naples that Alphonsus was attempting to do in accord with Sarnelli and he rejects the possible "coming and going" thought up by both Alphonsus and Sportelli. Poor Alphonsus, subject of the

---

* In a draft of the letter dated June 30, Falcoia states this differently: "...moving on according to his [Falcoia's] ideas."

[193] *Carteggio,* I, #276, p. 609.

[194] Tannoia, *Della vita,* lib.2, cap.13, p. 128.

cardinal, carefully evaluating the situation, delicately working with a sharp *scalpel*; Falcoia, on the other hand, intervenes with a *hatchet*.

Faced with this threat by Falcoia on July 6, 1742, Alphonsus could not escape: he had to bend to Falcoia. He turned to Canon Giacomo Fontana, "someone in very good graces with the very eminent Spinelli," to convince the latter to free him and his companion to return permanently to Ciorani. Fontana knew how to convince the cardinal and on July 20, 1742, Alphonsus "went to the Most Eminent Spinelli to resign…"—as Tannoia paints the picture—"riding his little mule and crossing Naples with Father Villani, he entered the courtyard of the archbishop's mansion and dismounted." As the cardinal received him, he asked "what do you think, Don Alphonsus, is my diocese not as needy as all the rest?"[195] The question is a clear reference and response to the statement of Falcoia and so, once more, Alphonsus finds himself caught between two opposed obediences, just as in February of the previous year. At that time, however, Sarnelli was there to deal with the cardinal in a way to neutralize Falcoia. Now the conditions of the community at Ciorani gave Falcoia the trump card so that he even had objective reasons. But the latter wished to win hands down over Sarnelli and took the occasion to put him completely out of the game.

FALCOIA: WHAT ABOUT DON GENNARO MARIA?

In a letter of July 7 [or maybe 8], Alphonsus must have written to Falcoia about the continuation of the mission by Sarnelli. It was easy for Alphonsus to presume that the cardinal, if he decided to allow him to leave for Ciorani with his companions, would want his successor to be Sarnelli. Indeed, that is what actually happened. We do not possess this letter or the later one of July 10 that we shall discuss shortly. Sportelli, who often served as Falcoia's secretary, should have saved something, but he did not. Alphonsus, on the other hand, kept many of Falcoia's letters.

On July 9, three days after his notice to Alphonsus to return to Ciorani with Villani and the two lay brothers, Falcoia wrote a letter which turns out to be the last letter he ever wrote directly to the saint. It begins: "My Dear Father Don Alphonsus, be sure that I esteem you as the apple of my eye." Then he repeats that it is necessary that

---

[195] *Ibid.*, lib. 2, cap. 15, pp. 138–139.

he return and realizes that "earlier, in dealing with the direction you had undertaken, it was necessary to treat it in a skillful way in order not to create more damage and disorder," and then he adds: "I do not consider your remaining for eight or ten days more to be a drawback, mainly for the reasons behind it."[196] These final words give us to understand that Alphonsus had responded immediately to Sportelli's letter of July 6 with its strong threat if he did not return to Ciorani from the mission in the environs of Naples. He assured him that he was preparing to return and had to be prudent in arranging things so as not to compromise what had been accomplished thus far by the mission.

But in this letter written in Falcoia's own hand on July 9, Alphonsus read some thoughts about Sarnelli that troubled him very much, so immediately by return post he replied to Falcoia on July 10 to express his "perplexity." Falcoia received this last letter and, in his own words, it "made my head spin." He did not answer Alphonsus, and a week later he wrote the following to Sportelli in the greatest confidence: "My Dear Father Don Cesare, I received your much appreciated letter dated July 12, after receiving the enclosed letter of Father Don Alphonsus, dated the tenth; I must tell you that his perplexity and concerns made my head spin. I have not responded and do not know if I will respond, but I beg you that, after you have read it, you return it to me immediately."[197]

What were Alphonsus'"perplexity and concerns"in the letter of July 10 that made Falcoia's head spin? Unfortunately, we do not possess that letter but we will try to interpret what these things are, arguing from Falcoia's letter of July 9 that Alphonsus was answering.

In that letter, Falcoia, after saying that Alphonsus could remain in Naples for "eight or ten days" more, spoke of the future condition of Sarnelli in a way that could not help but raise grave "perplexity" in Alphonsus, to say the least. Actually Alphonsus knew that the cardinal had the highest regard for Sarnelli but, above all, he knew it was Sarnelli who had moved the cardinal to inaugurate the mission of the environs of Naples and confide them to Alphonsus' care. And Sarnelli was also the one who had suggested the way to overcome Falcoia's resistance. Moreover, he had designed the pastoral masterpiece that became the *Istruzione per li missionarj deputati a scorrere la diocesi*

---

[196] *Carteggio*, I, #277, p. 615.

[197] Falcoia, *Lettere*, 439–440.

di Napoli per introdurvi and *piantarvi gli esecizj e le opere della pietà e religione, e mantenerle in viva osservanza.*[198] Also it was Sarnelli who wrote the letter of presentation of this instruction to bishops and prelates.[199] This letter exhorted the missionaries to introduce to even the lowliest people a profound spirituality, with mental prayer mornings and evenings in the church.

We can deduce that Alphonsus' letter of July 7 or 8, 1742, must have explained this possibility of Sarnelli's continuation, for Falcoia's letter of July 9 states: "I hold the person of Signor Don Gennaro and his virtues in the highest regard; but you cannot agree with his plans under any circumstances." It is clear he knew Gennaro Maria's plans from Alphonsus' letter and by his handwritten letter responded with a clear-cut "No."

"Signor" Don Gennaro's Plans

What could these plans of "Signor" Don Gennaro Maria be? From what we can easily surmise, these were the plans: he would remain to direct the missions at Barra as a true Redemptorist. This being the case, a Redemptorist lay brother would be able to stay with him as a real confrere, taking care of the house and watching over his very fragile health, all the while praying together, all this being done in the apostolic charity of Christ, in accord with the Redemptorist charism.

But in Falcoia's letter, he immediately puts Sarnelli, and therefore his missionary work in Naples, as the central problem by asking: What kind of a *figura*[200] would he show being alone with a lay brother of the community? Wouldn't this give the impression that he belongs to the Congregation of the Most Holy Savior, as he lives there alone when your rule intends that a single priest never live alone? And

---

[198] [*Instruction for the Missionaries Deputed to Traverse the Diocese of Naples in Order to Introduce and Plant there the Exercises and Works of Piety and Religion, and to Maintain Them in Active Observance*]. This instruction of October 12, 1741 was reedited by C. Sarnataro as *Le catechesi a Napoli negli anni del Card. Giuseppe Spinelli (1234–1754)*, Materdomini 1989, pp. 166–176.

[199] APGR, FS.

[200] To an Italian, one's *figura* is a very delicate issue that the English word "figure" does not easily convey. Basically, it means how a person appears to others, as can be seen in such expressions as: far figura, to look extremely nice: *far bella figura*, to look good, to make the right impression; che figura!, how embarrassing! Almost nothing in natural life can be more important to an Italian than *far bella figura*.

then, what kind of activity of our Institute, either in the house or in the church could he perform? Who is going to pay the rent for the house? What will be the role of the lay brother? Is he to be a member of the Congregation or a servant? Look at how, in one way or the other, all kinds of great problems arise! Not even the least of our brothers should be put at risk in this way; you should keep an eye on them, take care of them, esteem them. A misstep of even the least brother can bring down dishonor on each and everyone. They should not demean themselves by being servants to anyone who wants them to do so, otherwise there will be objections raised by all the brothers who would claim to be offended in the treatment of just one of their number. No, do not even think of it. The success and the conduct of Signor Don Gennaro can be taken care of in a thousand ways.[201]

Falcoia's thought is clear: Sarnelli, continuing the mission by himself, is no longer a Redemptorist and therefore no other Redemptorist can be permanently assigned with him on the basis of religious life and for the sake of the dignity of the brother who should not be obliged to be a "servant."

It is hard to believe that this letter was conceived and written by Falcoia. But unfortunately, it is in his own hand. Still, in the solemn letter of April 19, 1738, to all the members of the Congregation, he had exalted Sarnelli's work in Naples in defense of the girls in danger as a true Redemptorist work, even though Sarnelli had then already been at it alone for two years, living in his father's house, and certainly could not be observing the "activities of the Institute prescribed by the rule." How is it then that now, by living with another member of the Congregation, he should stop "giving the impression that he belongs to the Congregation of the Most Holy Savior?"

What is even more astounding is what he says about the lay brother who would have stayed to help Sarnelli in the missionary work that Sarnelli, always in a poor state of health, was finding very heavy. Right at this time—July 8, 1742—Gennaro Maria writes to Sister Maria Angela, who had asked him for news about his "troubles":

Ah, Most Esteemed Sister Maria Angela...I do not know what to say except that God knows: I am caught up in every kind of problem. My life, especially for some time, is not

[201] *Carteggio,* I, #277, p. 614–615.

118

life, but agony and suffering. Enough. I need a lot of prayer, because no human means will relieve me; in every aspect of my suffering, the remedy has to come from on high.[202]

It was Alphonsus, nearby and personally aware of this situation at the time, who thought of getting him a Redemptorist brother to help, but Falcoia's response was, "No, do not even think of it." And why? Because, as he put it, the brother would be simply a "servant."

To support a missionary, with his physical and psychological strength in crisis, so he can preach, hear confessions, administer the sacraments: is doing all this "being a servant?" Is it not, rather, to assist with the missions that the missionary is preaching? Besides, there was the fact that brothers at the time of Alphonsus also did formal missionary work, especially among the poor. Think of St. Gerard Majella. Falcoia would defend the dignity of the Redemptorist lay brothers! But writing this way, did he not realize he was in fact discrediting all the work of Redemptorist brothers? For them, in fact, more than being something physical, their work was apostolic and therefore properly Redemptorist, over and above their constant "doing the pious exercises" prescribed for Redemptorists. At least that was the thought of Alphonsus, who lived the true charism of the Institute. It is fortunate that now theology gives us the key to a better reading of the events of the eighteenth century. We take notice that Falcoia did not grasp this Alphonsian charism, since he reduces the imitation of Christ above all to Christ being a model of the ascetic life for personal sanctification. From that, so many misunderstandings!

"You Cannot Agree With His Plans Under Any Circumstances"

How does Sarnelli, then, create problems, granted that Falcoia admired Gennaro Maria's virtues and merits? Falcoia's response is that Sarnelli's plans to conduct missions in the suburbs of Naples were not properly Redemptorist plans: Alphonsus wanted to consider these plans and work redemptoristic, but to do this was, as far as Falcoia was concerned, to risk the identity of the Institute. We have already discussed the reason for the disagreement: they did not have the same understanding of

---

[202] APGR, FS, Lettera 37.

the Redemptorist centering on Christ. So the conclusion of Falcoia: Alphonsus could not go along with "Signor" Don Gennaro if he wished to be a true Redemptorist. Liguori remained silent. But he continued to consider Sarnelli as a real Redemptorist and, if he kept himself in check, he suffered in silence. For him, Sarnelli continued to be a real Redemptorist priest as he always had been, alone or in community.

In reflecting on this sad episode for Sarnelli and Alphonsus, I believe we can see the importance of Sarnelli's role in determining the charism that God had given to the real founder he had chosen, namely Alphonsus de Liguori. Sarnelli had intuited this clearly right from July 1733. He had completely embraced this charism along with Alphonsus and had interpreted it and lived it, despite Falcoia's deviations. The two were aware of their mutual agreement regarding the plan of God on the mission of Christ to save a world fallen into so many forms of poverty and ultimately into death.

At this point, I am not going off on a tangent if I recall two similar episodes found in the later history of the Congregation of the Most Holy Redeemer: one, at the beginning of the nineteenth century with St. Clement Mary Hofbauer in Poland, and the other, in the United States of America, with St. John Neumann in the middle of the same century. They lived out the authentic charism of the Redemptorists to engage in an intense apostolic life, which emerged from a true mutuality with Christ, and built both elements into a true life of contemplative prayer and varied missionary action in its many forms, whether at home or beyond.

Still, in Falcoia the conviction and criterion of religious direction existed that one could not be truly Redemptorist if one did not actually observe the ascetic community exercises found in his prescriptions for individual religious perfection. It is precisely for this that it is necessary to be at home, *except* for the times of going out on missions. Right from the beginning he had determined in detail the exercises of prayer, mortification, meditation on the twelve virtues, of which Jesus was the *model to be copied* in life and preaching. Yet a real and suitable rule of such a life he never succeeded in developing.

The clear proof of this mentality of his about asceticism in detailed acts during the day at home solely for the perfection of the individual can be found in an admonition that he gave Alphonsus in September 1737. The latter was the novice master of Andrea Villani, and he took

Villani with him on a mission. Therefore the novice (who was already a priest) could not "practice observance and learn the spirit of recollection" by staying home.[203] At the time, the house in Ciorani consisted of four rooms, while on the floor below were four more rooms: two serving as a jail and two as a pub. So much for recollection![204]

In the end, as far as the mission in the environs of Naples is concerned, it continued with Sarnelli as director and inspiration of the most effective members of the Congregation of the Apostolic Missions. He continued alone, without any Redemptorist brother.

He did not cease, however, to assist the Redemptoristine Nuns at Scala, especially and in a unique manner, as the spiritual director of Sister Maria Angela. In what role did he write and at times intervene in matters of the Redemptoristines of Scala? As a Redemptorist? The question is not marginal for our topic because precisely on July 8, 1742, two days after Falcoia had declared that he was not a Redemptorist if he did not return to Ciorani, Sarnelli wrote to Sister Maria Angela: *"I esteem the priests of the Most Holy Savior, and I help them, but I am not living strictly according to their rule and under their Institute."*[205] It is easy to see why this expression, in the way it sounds, would stir up doubts as to whether Sarnelli had not stopped considering himself a Redemptorist, at least from 1742 on. It is a fact that not a few have thought so and perhaps still do. What is the truth?

What has been said up to now makes us realize, for solid reasons, that the expression is at least ambiguous. But because this expression was under discussion not only in circles of historians, but even in the canonical process of Sarnelli's beatification in 1906, it is necessary to pay attention to the time, reason and therefore the sense of this 1742 statement to the Redemptoristine Nuns of Scala. To do this it is necessary to recall briefly the relations of Falcoia and of Sarnelli, as a Redemptorist, with the nuns of Scala.

---

[203] *Carteggio,* I, #216, p. 498.

[204] Tannoia, *Della vita,* lib. 2, cap. 7, pp. 104–105.

[205] APGR, FS, *Lettera* 37.

FALCOIA, REDEMPTORISTINES, REDEMPTORISTS, SARNELLI AT SCALA

Falcoia was the director of the nuns right at the founding of their monastery in 1720 and later from 1730 when, after his election as bishop, he could again take up their direction. In 1738, he fell into conflict with the Bishop of Scala, Antonio Santoro, who in November 1732 had approved the Institute and the Rule of the Nuns and therefore was their actual juridical superior. Because of this conflict, the Redemptorists, under orders from Falcoia, left Scala on August 27, 1738, and all of them went to Ciorani, where they were known during the 1700s and 1800s as the "Padri Cioranisti." A substantial number of nuns, taking their bishop's side, also got into conflict with Falcoia. It is to be noted that Sarnelli, while indeed exhorting the nuns to respect and stay united with Falcoia, said to Sister Maria Angela that, in conscience, she could dissent from Falcoia whenever he took a position that Sarnelli judged was unjust, but only as long as she continued to respect him.

The outcome of the break in relations between Falcoia and the Bishop of Scala in 1738 was that the latter entrusted the spiritual direction of the community to the Pious Workers, a decision that became permanent in 1739. On June 16, 1739, Sportelli wrote Alphonsus: "His Illustrious Lord [Falcoia] has cut himself off from the mind of those servants of God, both individually and as a community, and thinks that you should do the same. When you get letters from them, if you do not wish to spare yourself the trouble of reading them, you can respond briefly that they should take it up with their prelate."[206] Their prelate, as we have noted, was their actual ecclesiastical superior. Likewise, Sarnelli and the other Redemptorist fathers also left the spiritual care and direction of the nuns to the Pious Workers.

In May 1741, Santoro died; he had been Bishop of Ravello and Scala since June 1732. The new bishop, Biagio Chiarelli, was not consecrated in Rome until December 9, 1742. During the interim, the Chapter Vicar directed the diocese. The Pious Workers continued to direct the monastery because it was the bishop who had called them, in place of Falcoia and the Redemptorist priests. So the latter sensed they should not interfere in their direction. It was actually a Pious Worker who, in 1749, saw to the editing and pontifical approval of the nun's Rule.

---

[206] *Carteggio*, I, #232, p. 533.

Therefore, since Sister Maria Angela was without a director, she again turned to Sarnelli. He responded in a letter of September 5, 1741, promising that he would write her, but adding: "That this correspondence is not called or seen as individual spiritual direction as if you are entirely dependent on me *[as your spiritual director]*. I will answer you the same way I answer others who write me."[207] This reserve is understandable from the fact that Sarnelli wanted to avoid suspicion that he was inserting himself into the spiritual direction belonging to the Pious Workers.

This letter of September 5, 1741, had not yet reached Sister Maria Angela after seven months. This can be deduced from a second letter from Sarnelli on March 31, 1742. In this letter, he repeated that he does not intend to act as if he were her spiritual director.[208] On July 8, 1742, he responds with the aforementioned very long letter that has two parts: first, encouraging her spiritually and giving her instructions on how to proceed to conquer confusion and scruples, before passing on to other matters.

One of these matters is of great interest here because it was on this, as we have said, that the *Promotor fidei* latched onto. To those who affirm with certainty that Sarnelli was always a Redemptorist, he opposed Sarnelli's own explicit statement contained in this letter that we have alluded to. He comments on the words, "I esteem the priests of the Most Holy Savior, and I help them, but I am not living strictly according to their rule and under their Institute." That is: Sarnelli esteems and helps them; he does nothing more; therefore consistent with this, Sarnelli himself adds that he does not live strictly according to their rule. Also, previously the *Promotor fidei* had established the principle that, even setting aside the issue of public or private vows, "no one can be considered a member of an ecclesiastical or civil society, except those who accept the laws by which the society is regulated."[209]

The text immediately surrounding this sentence in Sarnelli's letter reads:

As far as being silent about your direction, for a thousand reasons, it is wise to be quiet... As far as advising you to take on spiritual direction from Father [Barbieri], I will certainly

---

[207] APGR, FS, Lettera 33.

[208] APGR, FS, Lettera 34.

[209] *Novissima positio super virtutibus ven. S. Dei J. M. Sarnelli*, Rome 1906, n. 21, pp. 1–12; n. 23, p. 12.

do so, and I would do so for all [the nuns], if the occasion arises. This is because I do not have any inclination or other thoughts or interest in proposing other directors. *I esteem the priests of the Most Holy Savior, and I help them, but I am not living strictly according to their rule and under their Institute.*[210]

The conjunction "because" makes it clear that he wants to say that he does not intend to propose other directors among the Redemptorists even though he esteems and helps them. As Sarnelli writes this he is well aware that the Pious Workers were the spiritual directors of the monastery that the bishop wants in place of the Redemptorists. The same reason is behind his request for silence about his direction "for a thousand reasons."

But how can we explain what follows: *"but I am not living strictly according to their rule and under their Institute."*? The immediate motivation for Sarnelli is the importance that both the Pious Workers as well as the clergy of Scala be certain that the Redemptorist priests are not giving direction to the nuns and if he does help them, he is not seen as one of them.

Can he, however, say this in good conscience unless he had a real intention of no longer being a Redemptorist?

We must attentively consider the date of the letter: July 8, 1742; the missionary campaign for that year has stopped and would be taken up again only in October. He knew that, by the peremptory command of Falcoia, Alphonsus and his companions had returned to Ciorani. He was also well aware that the cardinal wanted him to be Alphonsus' successor as head of the mission, and he, always ill, did not have much energy. So he had to decide. Besides, he realized that by staying on as a missionary in the suburbs of Naples, according to Falcoia, he was no longer a true Redemptorist.

It was at exactly on the same day (either July 7 or 8) that he writes the letter to Sister Maria Angela, the second part of which reads:

> Recommend me to Jesus Christ, especially now that I have to make a great decision to accept the heavy weight of an enormous work for the sanctification of this diocese of Naples that I was carrying on with Don Alphonsus and other missionaries. But now Don Alphonsus and his companion

---

[210] APGR, FS, Lettera 37.

are gone and so there is the danger of losing this infinite good that is being done, but to accept it is beyond my strength." [Then he adds the text we have been studying:] "As far as being silent...I do not incline otherwise or have other thoughts nor would I choose to propose a different director. *I esteem the priests of the Most Holy Savior, and I help them, but I am not living strictly according to their rule and under their Institute.*

If we take account of Falcoia's decision, could Sarnelli, who was himself at one time a member of the Pious Workers, write to Maria Angela of being, in good conscience, what he was according to Falcoia? That is, by using the expression "I am not living," does he also mean, "I am not a Redemptorist?" Let's see.

SARNELLI: A REDEMPTORIST AFTER JULY 1742?

The *Promotor Fidei* underlined the following expression of one witness in the canonical process mentioned above: "When he was [a member] of the Congregation of the Most Holy Redeemer," and argued "Therefore, for some time he was a Redemptorist, but then he left."[211] This statement is not referring to Sarnelli's departure from Scala in 1736 because Alphonsus had made it clear that he was leaving *Scala* and not the Congregation of the Most Holy Redeemer. So does this pertain to July 8, 1742? Let us see.

The basic question that must be asked seems to be: by reason of what action, did he cease to be a Redemptorist? Was it by reason of his own choice expressed in this letter of 1742 as the *Promotor Fidei* and others thought? No, because on the same day he wrote those words, at the *very same time, he was in accord with Alphonsus on staying at Barra with a Redemptorist lay brother,* and this action, as Falcoia himself was to admit the next day, was the same as recognizing Sarnelli as a *"figura di Redentorista,"* something that he, Falcoia, did not want to admit. This attitude of Falcoia is what led to such great "perplexity" for Alphonsus that he immediately expressed it to Falcoia who was so opposed to it that "it made his head spin" and he never responded to Alphonsus. From then on, it was shuttered in silence.

Externally Alphonsus submitted to the decision of Falcoia, but his later conduct says he always remained convinced that Sarnelli was

---

[211] *Novissima positio,* n. 26, p. 14.

a real Redemptorist, as he implicitly, but clearly said two weeks after Sarnelli's death. This proves, I believe, that the expression of July 8, 1742 does not indicate a free choice of Sarnelli, but only his *external situation* imposed by Falcoia's authority.

We will reflect on this episode that reveals so much for the history of the origins of the Redemptorists.

Here we find ourselves facing different decisions: one in the executive power of Falcoia's command and the other in the dissent, although unspoken, of Alphonsus. Which reality, which authority has prevailed in the life and history of the Congregation of the Most Holy Redeemer: that of Falcoia, which was followed in the majority of these early cases, or that of Alphonsus that was mostly silent and endured?

From the facts, it seems that Sarnelli recognized Alphonsus as the real superior, willed by God, even if Falcoia made himself not only director but actually superior and therefore founder. What is revealed by the way Sarnelli acts in planning and bringing about the great mission in the environs of Naples? He had first discussed this with Alphonsus and they kept it secret from Falcoia. Above all, what is seen in his way of dealing with the inevitable opposition of Falcoia's authority and in his suggesting to the cardinal the way of composing a letter to Falcoia? I believe these show two things. He was aware of Falcoia's authority, both tight and peremptory. But at the same time he knew of the wider view that moved Alphonsus right from their first meeting at Scala at the beginning of June 1733. This is clear from the letters to him in that June and July when he pondered the charism that moved the latter to the foundation, despite the apparent collapse of the first attempt directed by Falcoia. Moreover, had not Sarnelli understood it in February 1741, as the field of the mission to Naples' suburbs opened up, with the expression "Be of good heart: I see a great field open for spreading your desires and the Institute"? Why be of good heart? Because Sarnelli knew the breadth of Alphonsus' desires were in dreaming of his Institute, and he realized that this wideness of the latter's vision was now before them. This explains, so to speak, Sarnelli's audacity in going against Falcoia's vision that, as far as the apostolic outreach of Alphonsus was concerned, was opposed to the latter's vision. Falcoia saw the Congregation as a means of personal perfection and Christ, on the ascetical plane, is reduced to a kind of supersaint, and therefore a supreme model to imitate precisely for personal sanctification. "I speak of Christ on the ascetical level": so says Falcoia.

It is a fact that no sooner had Falcoia died on April 20, 1743 the Congregation took off through the christo-apostolic dynamism that had been enflamed and determined the breadth and force of Alphonsus' aspirations when he became aware that God had called him to it.

Sarnelli's expression, however, raises a question in relation to the biography of Alphonsus to which, I think, there is no easy answer: how could this christo-apostolic dynamism, which today we recognize as the charism-gift of the Holy Spirit of Christ, remain hidden after August 1732, when Alphonsus put himself under Falcoia's direction, until April 1743, when the latter passed away? Silence out of the virtue of obedience? What is signified by the breaking of this silence brought about by Sarnelli and announced to his friend as founder: "Be of good heart: I see a great field open for spreading your desires and the Institute?"

Both Sarnelli and Alphonsus esteemed Falcoia as a saintly man. But this was not reason enough for them to consider his ideas holy, even if Alphonsus blindly obeyed in silence. Sarnelli instead decided at times to say no. Who was acting better, [we can ask] given that Sarnelli was also declared of heroic virtue, as the Church has recognized? It is about this "nonsanctity" of Falcoia's ideas and his related comportment at the origins of both the Redemptorists and Redemptoristines that historians need to take greater account in their research, even if it is in fact critical.

SARNELLI A REDEMPTORIST AFTER MAY 9, 1743

On May 9, 1743, after Falcoia's death, the Redemptorists took vows of poverty, chastity, and obedience. Sarnelli, who was absent, did not make them. Because of this, did he cease to be a Redemptorist? Here too, in order to respond, we must follow his living out of his own history.

In October 1742, he again took up the missions for seven more months. To become aware of how he lived out his daily actions, we read what he wrote to Sister Maria Angela on March 14, 1743:

> For the last sixty days I have been so sick and overwhelmed, always on my feet, in the midst of concerns and tired, with no way out whether I want it or not. During this time, I have had to go to more houses, more places, experienced more climates, and hurried from one mission to the next, or to say it better, from one battle to the next. Beginning next Saturday I have to go to another distant place and mission, by force of necessity, and I cannot do anything else. Your Ladyship, do

not tell me to take care of myself. Always say: God takes care of us. Because, even if I want to take care of myself, the Lord has put me in such a situation and circumstances that I can't. I have no way or means, spread all over the place, dying and in agony. My heart is no longer of flesh, but of stone, and my spirit is in me as if it didn't exist. Enough! God knows...I'm done. I am writing in the midst of a fever, I will retire for the night...I have become *pauper et dolens [poor and sorrowing]*. I do not even have a place to rest away from these missions, going from one countryside to another, well, or sick, or dying, or dead. You would be astounded if Your Ladyship knew the particular situations I encounter and in which I find myself.[212]

This is the real Sarnelli in 1742–1743.

On May 9, shortly after Falcoia's death, the Redemptorists at Ciorani took the usual vows which religious make, even though they remained simple diocesan priests or lay brothers. They took the vows freely, *without any approval, even by a bishop*. In 1735, Archbishop De Capua of Salerno in approving their residence and apostolic work at Ciorani, had read and approved only the statutes regarding "its own church, in which to praise God and where you can peacefully fulfill your service."[213] The Congregation continued living its independent life, based on the authoritative permission of the Archbishop of Naples given in February 1733, but based on remaining in communion with the Congregation of the Apostolic Missions.

Tannoia, speaking about the taking of the three vows (but with a grave error on the date: giving it as July 22, 1741, instead of May 9, 1743), notes that "the only one missing was Sarnelli, because he was again involved in Naples with the Most Eminent Spinelli."[214] In the canonical process, the *Promotor Fidei* includes the statement of a "most authoritative consulter" according to whom, if Sarnelli had had the intention of taking the vows, he could very well have gone to Ciorani, easily getting the permission of the cardinal.[215] But was that really so?

[212] APGR, FS, Lettera 48.

[213] AGHR, XVIII, A. 1bis.

[214] Tannoia, *Della vita*, lib. 2, cap. 14, p. 136.

[215] *Novissima positio*, n. 27, p. 15: *"si vovendi intentione minime caruisset."*

In fact, on May 9, 1743, Sarnelli was involved or performing duties for the cardinal at Naples, as Tannoia's expression would have us understand, but was moving from area to area, with great effort and without a moment of rest. His nonattendance was not a deliberate choice not to take vows as a Redemptorist, but an obligatory absence from a free personal action of the confreres. An obligatory absence because he was burdened with the work and sufferings entailed in the missions. And it is worth noting that the nontaking of these vows did not change the status he already had in the Congregation.

This was always a free association of priests who followed the Neapolitan priest, Alphonsus de Liguori, in apostolic ministry. The *Dichiarazione del Card. Pignatelli del 23 febbraio 1733* was of the greatest importance for the simultaneous membership of Alphonsus, and later of Sarnelli, in the Congregation of the Apostolic Missions while retaining an autonomous freedom to found the Congregation of the Most Holy Redeemer. Nothing more. The vows made before 1749 changed the spiritual personal relationship to God of each individual. Only the oath of perseverance, made in 1740, bound them to the association; but even this was personal and free. It was also of no import that in 1743 the decision was made at a general meeting and the members made the vows "in the hands" of the Rector Major, Alphonsus de Liguori; they were still private vows. If the vows were meant "to exclude," it would have been necessary to have an explicit statement by each member, including Sarnelli, or by the chapter or by the Rector Major Liguori; but this did not happen. Rather, as we shall see, the Rector Major, Alphonsus, continued to consider Sarnelli a member.

It will be quite otherwise when the "religious profession of the three vows" will become an act by which one will become a member of a Congregation, in some way recognized by an ecclesiastical authority. But this would only happen on October 1, 1749, after the Congregation and the Rule received the approval of the Holy See on February 25, 1749. It was on the first of October that the Redemptorists, convoked by Alphonsus, the acting Rector Major, in a constitutive assembly or chapter, formally accepted the decree of approbation of the Congregation and Rule given by the Holy See, and pronounced the three vows according to the evangelical counsels.

It is helpful to read one of the articles from the *Acta*:

All the professed subjects accepted the Rule already approved by the Holy See and according to its intentions renewed the vows of chastity, poverty and obedience, and the vow and oath of perseverance in the Congregation. Then they proceeded to the election of the president of the chapter (since it was thus considered that our Congregation was now being born, after the approval of the Rule and Institute received from the Holy See). He who was Rector Major, that is Father de Liguori, renounced his office in the hands of the Congregation, with the Chapter accepting, and so there could be a legitimate election by all the members of the same.[216]

Thus, the chapter was aware that the Congregation was then being born as a real Congregation of priests and lay brothers according to the Rule approved by the Holy See, in the Institute likewise approved by the Holy See. We are no longer dealing with a simple association of priests and lay brothers, begun in Scala by the initiative of Alphonsus, with the members freely joining him. Nor is it any longer a matter of the permission Alphonsus received in 1732–1733 from his superior, the Archbishop of Naples, by which he could remain a member of the Congregation of the Apostolic Missions while attempting to found a new Congregation that would remain his private one. All the vows and ties made before 1749 were private, in no way recognized by Church authorities. Falcoia was not an ecclesiastical authority for the Congregation who had to be recognized with an obligation of conscience; this he never was. The Bishop of Scala, likewise, had not recognized and approved them but only granted them the right to perform priestly functions at Scala. This was the same in 1735 with the Archbishop of Salerno and then ordinaries of other dioceses.

In the *Acta* of the Chapter of 1749, it is said that the members of the Congregation "renewed the vows of chastity, poverty and obedience." The term "renewed" only indicates that they were already bound to God theologically, but on the juridical level these were completely

---

[216] *Acta capituli generalis apud Juranos [Ciorani] anno 1749 celebrati*, in *Acta integra capitulorum generalium CSsR ab anno 1749 ad annum 1894*, Rome 1899, pp. 4–5.

new actions.[217] Beyond the juridical issues, of more importance are the theological and spiritual reasons behind the vows of May 1743. Just as the theological and spiritual reasons underlying these vows gave inspiration to the Redemptorists, who were living at Ciorani in that time, they also moved Sarnelli to go on these missions, not out of some commitment to the cardinal at Naples, but as a true Redemptorist, even while lacking physical strength and without rest, journeying from one suburb to the next in a missionary activity that was truly self-sanctifying, just as were the vows taken at Ciorani.

SARNELLI DIES AS A REDEMPTORIST JUNE 30, 1744

The life story of Sarnelli after May 9, 1743, confirms his status of a Redemptorist in communion with the confreres at Ciorani. This is clear from a letter of June 21 of that year to Sister Maria Angela. To appreciate it, we must situate it in the events of his life during that month.

We have a document written six weeks after the taking of the vows on May 9; that allows us to deduce that, without doubt, Sarnelli was always a Redemptorist.

During May and June of 1744, Naples was under the threat of a serious plague-epidemic. "Poor Messina suffering plague and Naples

---

[217] J. Pfab, "De indole juridica in congregatione sanctissimi Redemptoris, ante annum 1749 emissorum," in *Spicilegium* 19 (1971): 280–303; especially pp. 280, 302, 303. Father Joseph Pfab, Superior General emeritus, in a study he did in 1971, corrected the statement made in the historical introduction to the new Constitutions and Statutes of the Congregation of the Most Holy Redeemer approved by the Redemptorist General Chapter of 1967–1969. This stated that the vows of 1743 were "private religious vows," and those taken in 1749 were "public religious vows." After an analytical historical-juridic explanation, he concluded that the vows of the Redemptorists, as is the case for all religious congregations that pronounce simple (not solemn) vows, only assumed the character of "public religious vows" by force of the apostolic constitution *Conditaea Christo* of Leo XIII on December 8, 1900; this is when the Congregation could juridically call itself a clerical religious congregation by pontifical right and religion. Consequently, the simple vows made before 1749 were only private vows. The simple vows taken after 1749 and accepted in the name of the Church, are characterized differently by different jurists: private vows, public vows (at least, de facto), non-public vows, recognized vows, acknowledged vows. Pfab prefers the last term. His recommendation was accepted by the Redemptorist Chapter of 1982, and so the text of the *Constitutiones CSsR* reads today "A quo tempore [this refers to February 25, 1749, but should be understood as: *de jure*, because *de facto*, it should say: from October 1, 1749], *confratres vota simplicia ab auctoritate pontificia agnita emiserunt.*" Pfab also dealt with the reply of the *Promotor Fidei* in Sarnelli's cause insofar as he did not take the private vows in 1743 at Ciorani with the other Redemptorists.

on the verge of the same," Sarnelli writes to Sister Maria Angela on June 21, 1743. Sarnelli is thinking "of leaving for this diocese" to allow the priests to be "at the service of their people." But he does not have the strength himself: "I run the danger of falling over dead there." Not only that, but if the plague comes and if he goes out to help the infected, "I would be the first one to die. I do not know what to do before that, whether to go back with the priests at Ciorani, but I find it difficult even to do this."[218] The following day at Naples, there was a huge penitential procession with the cardinal dressed in poor clothes at its head. Sarnelli also took part in it, but he went home in very bad condition, which reached the point that, in October, he could no longer direct the mission of which he was the chief architect and inspiration.

He spoke of this condition and the penance taking place at Naples to Sister Maria Angela, but of interest to us is only the expression "*I do not know what to do before that, whether to go back with the priests at Ciorani....*" As it turns out he did not go back because, from October to June, his life was an even more pain-filled journey toward his death. However, the fact remains that on June 21, 1743, even after the taking of vows by the Redemptorists at Ciorani, he knew that he could also go back with the priests at Ciorani. He would not have believed this if he were not still a Redemptorist. In this case, though, he would have had to go back to Ciorani where his father, who after his wife's death at Naples where his son Gennaro Maria attended her, was now living in his own home.

In June 1744, Sarnelli, who was staying at his brother Domenico's house in Naples, entered into the last month of life from an irreversible sickness. Alphonsus, advised of his condition, immediately sent Redemptorist Brother Francisco Tartaglione and, later, Brother Francisco Romito to care for him.

Shortly after Sarnelli died on June 30, 1744, Alphonsus, at the request of the Neapolitan priest, Antonino Sersale, a friend of both Sarnelli's and Alphonsus', organized in a "written form" some memories and sent them to Naples to be printed. On July 17, just two weeks after Sarnelli's death, he wrote to Don Giuseppe Sparano: "The most important thing I ask of you is to urge the Lords of the Congregation [of the Apostolic Missions] to have them printed." He was referring

---

[218] APGR, FS, Letter 54.

to "the writings" on the life and virtues of Sarnelli. Sparano would have had to "request" the Apostolic Missions, for Alphonsus immediately added these words: "*It would truly be our responsibility*, but God knows how we are doing, and Don Gennaro left us in charge of his books with the accompanying obligations and commitments."[219]

What does Alphonsus mean to say by this final statement: "It would truly be our responsibility?" Why was it not the duty of the Congregation of the Apostolic Missions, but rather ours, the Redemptorists, to publish the biographical news of his life and virtues? There is only one answer: the Redemptorists had the responsibility because Sarnelli was their confrere, with greater right and obligation to make the announcement. And likewise, three years after the death of Sarnelli, August 11, 1747, Sportelli, in a letter to Alphonsus, asks the Redemptorist Brother Francisco Tartaglione "to obtain from the Lord Baron Sarnelli a portrait of our Father, of his son, Don Gennaro, for the monastery at Scala."[220] "*Nostro Padre*" says Sportelli: that is to say a Redemptorist priest confrere.

SARNELLI AND ALPHONSUS: MEMBERS OF TWO CONGREGATIONS

The expression of Alphonsus: "It would truly be our responsibility" [to print the obituary] expresses what is the correct ecclesial position of Sarnelli for 1733 to 1743. He belonged simultaneously to the Congregation of the Apostolic Missions and to the Congregation of the Most Holy Redeemer, but his *position* lies more with the latter where Alphonsus was the charismatic superior, to whom he was spiritually bound and obedient. From the juridical point of view, both Sarnelli until his death, and Alphonsus until 1749, were dependent on the Archbishop of Naples because they were always his Neapolitan diocesan priests during that time. The archbishop granted permission for the simultaneous membership in the two associations and therefore a certain collaboration, from the active missionary point of view, was very possible. The mission in the environs of Naples was the expression and confirmation of this situation of mutual collaboration. It mattered not that this was not pleasing to Falcoia; he was not the charismatic founder of the Congregation of the Most Holy Redeemer.

---

[219] Alfonso de Liguori, *Lettere*, I, 94–95.
[220] Sportelli, "Scripta quaedam minora," a cura di I. Low, in *Spicilegium* 5 (1957): 232.

But this pleased Sarnelli. Why? Because he, unlike Falcoia, had understood the true charism that had moved Alphonsus to found his Congregation. He had understood and lived it well for eleven of the twelve years of his priesthood (1733–1743). This is why the Holy See in its decree of 1906 on the heroicity of his virtues affirmed: "The illustrious Congregation of the Most Holy Redeemer, which glories in the Doctor of the Church, St. Alphonsus de Liguori as its founder, right from his birth (i.e., his birth into glory at death), has numbered, among its members, an apostolic man, such as the times demanded…this friend and imitator of Liguori…the venerable Servant of God, Gennaro Maria Sarnelli."

Indeed this authoritative eulogy is no more than an echo of another authoritative voice that, on June 30, 1744, was raised at the moment of his death. Canon Antonino Sersale, his great friend, subsequently Archbishop of Naples, was near him at that moment. In a voice filled with sobs, he exclaimed at his passing:

"Naples and Don Alphonsus Liguori have lost a saint, and the Neapolitan clergy has lost its gem."[221]

This was indeed the affirmation of the real identity of Sarnelli, Redemptorist with Alphonsus, priest of the Neapolitan clergy in active collaboration with the Congregation of the Apostolic Missions. This is the solution that this research offers to the reader. Therefore, it does not seem necessary that history choose between the two alternatives: either the Congregation of the Most Holy Redeemer or the Congregation of the Apostolic Missions.

---

[221] F. Alfano, *"Lettera del 1° agosto 1864 al P. La Notte, sulla testimonianza di Romito reguardo la morte e I funerali di Gennaro Sarnelli"* (manuscript), Naples 1864, in APGR, FS.

CHAPTER FIVE

LETTERS OF GENNARO MARIA SARNELLI

There are eighty-eight known autograph letters of Sarnelli, usually signed "Gennaro Maria." In this chapter are included translations of forty-eight of them. Ten of these are written to Alphonsus at the time of the beginning of the Redemptorist Congregation; thirty he wrote to Sister Maria Angela de Vito (a Redemptoristine nun in Scala); the eight others are written to various Church authorities. By means of these, we wish to cover the whole horizon of his spiritual world: his missionary vocation, his appreciation of religious life, his spiritual discernment and his interest in the major issues of the Kingdom of Naples. At the same time, we can notice the simple and concrete matters of daily life. The original manuscripts of these letters are found in the Archives of the General Postulator of the Redemptorists in Rome.[222]

TO ALPHONSUS DE LIGUORI (JULY 8, 1733?)[223]

The rumors in Naples are affecting the reputation of the new Institute. Sarnelli tries to put out the fire there although he worries over the situation of the missions and of the house in Scala.

---

[222] This translation is based on the following sources: the first five letters to St. Alphonsus are from *The History of the Congregation of the Most Holy Redeemer,* Vol. I/ɪɪ, ed. by Francisco Chiovaro and J. Robert Fenili, translated into English by J. Robert Fenili, Liguori: Liguori Publications, 2010, "Appendix 1: Selected Documents, A. The Protagonists of Scala," 174–191. Footnotes to Sarnelli's first ten letters are taken from *Carteggio.* The letters to Sister Maria Angela de Vito are translated from *Lettere spirituali di Ven. Gennaro M. Sarnelli,* Naples: 1851. 1851. The final eight letters are from the 1888 Edition of the *Opera omnia.*

[223] *Carteggio,* Lettera 79, pp. 250–251. Original [signed manuscript letter] 2 ff., 20.5 × 14 cm, in Archivium Generale Historicum Redemptoristarum, Roma [Hereafter, AGHR], EadSA, 021; copies in AGHR, CK [F. Kuntz], 8–10; Archivio Della Postulazione Generale dei Redentoristi, Roma [Hereafter, APGR], CD [B. D'Orazio], 11–13. Ed: De Meulemeester, *Origines,* I, 272–273.)

Most Esteemed Father,

I received your much-desired letter. I am filled with the greatest consolation and confusion, I tell you with all my heart, since I was with you like Judas among the apostles. Fine, your charity has made up for my own lack. As to money, I know that you can help me, but I do not think I should trouble you, since I found some more in the luggage. Later, with God's grace, I will manage to get some.

I have already written you two letters, one at Castello a Mare, the other in Naples, and because Mr. Giovanni [Olivieri] has come home, I am including this third one with the others I wrote.

I repeat to you that it was the will of the Lord that I had come there and now to Naples. Even the best people here say that the foundation has gone up in smoke, since it was based on the visions of a woman who told lies. I assure you that this Celeste, may God make her a saint, has dealt the Institute a severe blow. But I hope in God that these evil allegations disappear, and in the meanwhile with the permission of my spiritual director, I will go around proclaiming everywhere the true reasons for things and for my departure, and with the letter that I beg you to send as fast as it can be copied, I will make everyone read it to remove the error about the revelations and about the Institute with new pink habits that till now a lot of people have been told about.

Today I fired one shot (pray the Lord that it hits the mark) by talking with a pious young priest, a friend of mine, as a way to fire it. He heard me with tears in his eyes and thanked the Lord that what these rumors are saying was not true.

My Dear Father, keep recommending me to Jesus Christ and the Most Holy Mary, since I already see that your prayers can make me come to you and have now smoothed over many difficulties. This morning I was again at the Giesù to speak with Father Manuilo, but it was not possible. Tomorrow, God willing, I will go there [again].

Let me know why you do not have the Blessed Sacrament in your poor little chapel, as Don Giovanni [Mazzini] asked me. If it is because you lack a pyx, I would like to get you one.

I will stay here for a few months to put my things in order and those of the poor girls that I am dealing with. Pray the Lord to allow me to have another chance to find someone to take up the task of helping them. For the rest, look, I am totally carried in the adored arms of Divine Providence. Whether living or dead, wherever he wants me, I will go. Prayer, my father, prayer is what will get me endless graces, not only for me to come to you but to destroy the countless evil thoughts in everyone's minds in Naples. I have not been able to unburden myself with Father Superior, because I am again waiting for the answer of Father Manuilo that I am sure will indeed be favorable.

Give my most humble greetings to Father Superior, Don Cesare [Sportelli], and Brother Vito [Curzio] and to all, to the holy nuns, since I base all my hope on your prayers and theirs, for I deserve nothing other than to be the poisonous tree cut down and thrown into the fire, and I say that before God with all my heart and with tears in my eyes.

May the Most Blessed Sacrament and the Most Holy Mary be praised forever.

[Gennaro Maria Sarnelli]

To Alphonsus de Liguori (July 9, 1733) [224]

Sarnelli manifests his desire to enter the new missionary Institute and what is being said in Naples about Sister Celeste and the monastery at Scala.

Live Jesus and the Most Holy Mary

Naples, July 8, 1733

Most Esteemed Father,

From the conversation I had with Msgr. Falcoia, I clearly realize that he wishes to establish the foundation in Scala, where there will be time to acquire the spirit of the community and to conduct missions for that area, and then to move to other areas in Chiazza and elsewhere, meeting the hopes among the many prelates who seek foundations.

Today, Thursday, I spoke with Father Manuilo about my situation. He listened to me very attentively, and then he gave me the good news that it is the will of God that I join the Institute, but that the matter needs a great deal of prayer, and in fact, he promised me that he would

---

[224] *Carteggio*, Lettera 80, pp. 252–256. Original (signed autograph letter) 4 ff., 20 × 13.5 cm, in AGHR, EadSA, 038; copies in AGHR, CK [F. Kuntz], 1–8; APGR, CD [B. D'Orazio], 1–6. Ed: "Documenta coaeva circa originem et fundationem nostri Instituti," *Analecta*, 6 (1927): 105–107; De Meulemeester, *Origines*, I, 267–270).

warmly recommend me to the Lord during holy Mass and that six days from now we would talk over the matter again. I hope the Lord grants me the grace.

Meanwhile, may Your Lordship, along with all the other servants of God there, please, for the great love you have for Jesus Christ, for the sake of the good that you seek from the Virgin Mary, recommend me ardently to the Lord that he hear me, begging him to grant me the grace. And I especially ask you as you offer holy Mass that when you place the fragment of the consecrated host into the sacred chalice, you also place there my heart with it, praying Jesus Christ that he removes the poison of self-love as well as certain passions that torment me greatly and that he give me the necessary spirit and strength for that holy Institute.

I spoke with Don Giovanni [Mazzini] and gave him your letter. He burns with desire but is still at peace.[225] Hope in the Lord for good results. He was so very consoled when he learned from me what I have told you, and I have not finished, since he is spending a long time with me this evening. And he has thanked the Lord in a special way.

Here the rumor is that the Institute is in fact dead since it was built on the revelations of a deluded soul, and that the Mother [Superior] gave Celeste three options or she would go: a year in [the convent's] prison, submitting to the rule of Msgr. Falcoia, or leave on her own. I have spoken out about everything as it truly happened.[226]

They say that Your Lordship should give it up now, since it is clear everything went up in smoke, and that you will always be there alone. That the bishop has little use for you and lets you stay only because you are Don Alphonsus di Liguoro [sic] and he no longer considers you as part of the Congregation and Institute.

They say that the mission we gave was heard about, and that Carace[227] said that the superior had written me a strong letter for me to quit and come back there. I have not spoken with Borgia.[228]

---

[225] Giovanni Mazzini could not participate in the gathering at Scala that founded the Institute. In fact, neither he nor Sarnelli had obtained the authorization of their spiritual directors. F. Chiovaro, *Il beato Gennaro Maria Sarnelli*, Materdomini, 1996, 73.

[226] *I have spoken...happened*: on this matter, see Crostarosa, *Autobiografia*, 259–260, 262–264; Majorano, *L'imitazione*, 82–83. See Lettera 93 [of *Carteggio*].

[227] This refers to Tommaso Carace, a celebrated preacher, who guided Alphonsus in his first missions. See De Meulemeester, *Origines*, II, 100; *Lettere*, I, 94, 107–108; Tellería, *San Alfonso*, I, 108, 302, 381; II, 222.

[228] This refers to Canon Nicola Borgia (1700–1779), the future bishop of Cava (1751–

It is truly a grace from the Lord that I came there to remove these many errors not only from the ill-wishers but even from our dearest friends. God knows what effect this resolution of mine will make in all the storms and in the poor estimate in which the Institute now stands.

On my part I do not want anything that is not pleasing to God, let the world say what it will. Meanwhile, I beg you anew out of pity: recommend me to the Lord and to Most Holy Mary and have others do the same because I have great need, and from now on inscribe me among your own, although I do not deserve it, but because I have firm confidence in the infinite mercy of God who will give me the grace.

However, I do not say this out of humility but in truth, you will receive a lowly subject, full of vices and deficiencies, and very weak; think very carefully so you do not have to repent of it and do not have to take on too great a burden. I am not saying this because I have little desire to come to you, but only to unburden my conscience so that I can be excused before God and the world, that you are willing to accept me as I am. Your prayers, and those of your companions, of the nuns and of all those worthy souls there, can make me very happy. I have great confidence in you, take pains to do it, do it always, and I hope that this resolution of mine, made with the approval of such a man as Father Manuilo, will shut the mouths of many and stimulate others to come to you. Don Giovanni tells me that his spiritual director holds Father Manuilo in the greatest esteem and depends on him to see what divine providence disposes. May God always be blessed who promotes his honor in so many unexpected ways. I am only sorry that my demerits will impede the fruits that could be reaped if this would have happened to some other person less unworthy than I. May the mercy of the infinite God, out of love for the Most Holy Mary, be such that it will enlighten me and make me worthy of such beautiful grace. Prayer, my most esteemed Father, prayer; it is what can do all things and make me hope for all things.

Monsignor Falcoia read the letter, approved it and said that he needed to modify it a little about the matters of the Congregation. I said that I would have it read only by some friends, but he said it should be put in everybody's hands. Right now my Father Manuilo has it.

1765), and later of Aversa (1765–1779). A friend of Alphonsus, Sarnelli, and the Institute, he was at the time a very active member of the Congregation of the Apostolic Missions. See *Hier. cath.*, VI, 111, 158; Santamaria, *Historia collegii*, 528, 582, 583; Tannoia, II, 263–264; Tellería, *Prima S. Alfonsi palaestra*, 411; Villecourt, I, 293.

Then I will give it to Don Giovanni. After that, so everyone may read it and have their many prejudices and false suspicions removed, please have it gradually copied by Don Cesare [Sportelli]. You can be sure that this could make many people happy. On the top put a title: "Let Jesus Christ be our light," and then, "My Very Esteemed Friend," and then begin the letter.

Remove the part where it says: "In this new Congregation nothing happens with as much reserve as in yours." Also take out where it says "the fruit of our missions seem like rain in summer," along with what follows in the same sentence.

At the end, conclude: "All that I write you, I do only for the honor of God and out of the desire I have to see that so many of the poor abandoned souls of our neighbors, yours and mine, are helped as well as to see you advanced in perfection; I am moved by no other motive than what pleases God. He who is the examiner of hearts knows if what I say is true. To him alone be praise, honor and glory forever, and may he be known, feared and loved by the whole world. To conclude, I remain offering you the most humble reverence."

At the end, put the signature of my name in this manner, as Msgr. Falcoia ordered:

Y[our] Most Affec[tionat]e and Ob[edie]nt Ser[van]t,

Gennaro Maria Sarnelli

P.S. Most esteemed Sir Don Alphonsus, tell Don Cesare to be patient in his difficulties. As soon as [the letter] is finished, send it to me. Answer me and give me courage and console me with the hope that such is the will of the Lord and advise me if you wish me as I am, and all the worse for what I have written you and for what you have known of me, so that I should not have to regret any error I may have made. I conclude, most humbly kissing your holy hands. I pay my respects in a most special way to Father Superior, Don Cesare, Brother Vito [Curzio], and all the priests and gentlemen there. Let Father Superior pay my most humble respects to Mother Superior and all the nuns to whom I will have the honor to write a few words when I have time. May they meanwhile not stop praying for me for the infinite mercy of God and of the Most Holy Mary.

May the Most Blessed Sacrament and Most Holy Mary be held in eternal praise

Y[our] Most Hu[mbl]e and Ob[edie]nt Ser[van]t,

Gennaro Maria Sarnelli

P.S. Everybody here is saying that our Congregation was founded on the revelations of a deluded lady visionary (these are the exact words). Praise God that I got here so I can straighten everyone out. I have already begun, but little by little, because I have not yet declared myself. I am waiting for another answer from Father Manuilo. I have not yet spoken to Borgia about it, or with the Superior, and I am avoiding a meeting until I have a new response from my Father [Manuilo], who has my letter to read. I beg you to hurry, as fast as you can, the letter of Don Cesare, and let it be written on a single page of Genoa paper[229] and nicely penned, so that (since I cannot unprejudiced everybody verbally) I can do it by the written word. If it seems a good idea to you (although I have already told my spiritual director) that I come there permanently, as I hope [you will], advise me if I may go throughout all of Naples telling everybody that I am going with you and mail the letter to disabuse them and make them know that you do not remain entirely alone, as they are saying. Answer me explicitly, console my embattled heart and yourself command all heaven on my behalf, please. To Don Cesare: I have already given the letter to his sister, and have told her that he is on a mission, and that he is well and happy.

To Alphonsus de Liguori (after July 9, 1733)[230]

In addition to his work and the rumors floating around Naples, Gennaro Maria feels discouraged and tired. He nevertheless plans to go on the missions he is preparing for.

Live Jesus and Most Holy Mary
[Naples, after July, 9 1733]

---

[229] "Paper of Genoa" or "Genoese [paper]" was a type of paper suitable for writing or printing. See Assante, *Amalfi e la sua Costiera*, 193.

[230] *Carteggio*, Lettera 81, pp. 256–259. Original (handwritten letter) 2 ff., 20.5 × 14 cm, in AGHR, EadSA, 024; copies in AGHR, CK [F. Kuntz], 31–35; APGR, CD [B. D'Orazio], 19–22. Ed.: "Documenta coaeva circa originem et fundationem nostri Instituti," *Analecta*, 6 (1927): 110–111; De Meulemeester, *Origines*, I, 275–276.

My Most Esteemed Father,

Don Giovanni Mazzini most humbly sends his respects. He tells me that I am to say in his name that he cannot participate in the mission there. He is, however, in good spirits and [*asks that*] you pray and have prayers said for him because he hopes in the Lord that you will have him as a constant companion shortly. What is good must come from heaven and it does not come without prayer. Have prayers said to the Lord for this and thus things will go well by the Lord's grace.

Three things have made an impression in Naples that explain why our Institute has lost respect: 1. the revelations; what is heard often: revelations and nuns, nuns and revelations; 2. the pink habit; 3. that you want to found a religious institute. On the other hand, I always avoid all these matters, and I shut all their mouths by saying that we are a congregation of priest workers who are going to help the souls of the most abandoned poor places and we go to see that those who do not know God may know him, and nothing more. They have no answer for that.

This morning I had a long talk with the Bishop of Minuri, who wants missions in his diocese.[231] He has again offered S. Nicola[232] to serve as our retreat. He will give us all the faculties. He has placed the whole diocese in our hands; he offers us his mansion for the mission. But it is necessary to have the city ask for this so as not to make it seem that it is the prelate who wishes to arrange these things.

The city is truly in extreme need, I do not think that there are confessors or anyone. And there is a religious who serves as pastor by the bishop's leave. He well justifies his cause and he says that he is right now sending it to the Collateral [Council], and that whatever he did, he did it all with the public authority of the tribunals of Rome and of Naples.[233] The truth is that the city and clergy are in need of a great

---

[231] Minori, a city on the Amalfi coast of 2,200 inhabitants, was an episcopal see at the time. Alfano, *Istorica descrizione*, 43–44. The bishop from 1722 to 1761 was Monsignor Silvestro Stanà (1687–1761); *Hier. cath.*, V, 270.

[232] This refers to the ex-convent of the Augustinians that stood on a hill above Minori. Mansi, *Illustrazione*, 28; V. Criscuolo, *La chiesa e Il convento San Nicola in Minori. Storia e cronaca*, Minori 1997.

[233] This is an allusion to the argument between the bishop and some of his clergy who, on November 26, 1732, had induced the Holy See to name an apostolic visitor in the person of Giovanni Fabrizio de Capua, Archbishop of Salerno. See ASNa, *R. Camera di S. Chiara, Bozze di Consulta*, vol. 30, Incarto 42.

deal of help. Tell Don Tommaso Sasso that the city calls us to go there as soon as possible. I must go to the Bishop's house where the vicar will prepare a letter for me and give us all the faculties.

My Most Esteemed Father, the missions are many and right now there is the retreat at Scala. The missionaries are few right now (I hope in the Lord that there will soon be many), help is needed there. I have told this to Don Giuseppe Porpora, in case he would be needed. He said that it might be possible in October. Likewise, if your Lordship thinks so, I would like to tell de Alteriis.[234] And in turn, I can speak to Father Gregorio Rocco of S. Spirito di Palazzo about help;[235] he ardently wants to give missions and work tirelessly so he might be able to help us at present while we are so few.

The other missionary priests are better and therefore we can hope to get them and they would be as good as our own. But to move any of them one needs the hand of God. On the other hand, we can have this Dominican priest whenever we want him. As far as zeal is concerned, his desire to put out indefatigable effort is the same as ours. And he's also capable. Let me know. It would seem to me to be good because, if he comes to Naples and finds success, he could also do something for us here.

And then Your Lordship wants to go to Caiazza, but if these missions aren't finished first, you cannot go. On this matter, it seems expedient that you get some help to be able to sanctify these places with divine grace. Then the Congregation will have more credibility after those places have already been sanctified and you can more easily go where the Lord calls you, I mean, to Caiazza. Let me know when the mission at

---

[234] On Michele De Alteriis (1703-1775) from Panicocoli (Villaricca, since 1871), see Berthe, I, 173, 174, 232; De Meulemeester, *Origines*, I, 98; "D. Michele De Alteriis," in *S. Alphonso,*" 21 (1943): 22-24; Tannoia, I, 38, 44; II, 126; Tellería, *San Alfonso,* I, 122, 137, 250, 256, 274, 302; Id., *Sancti Alfonsi adscriptio militiae ecclesiasticae,* 328. De Alteriis, who was a companion of Alphonsus since the time of the Evening Chapels, had to leave the Institute "forcefully removed by his father in the midst of an armed invasion." Rey-Mermet, *Il santo,* 393. See De Meulemeester, *Origines,* II, 112-113; Tannoia, II, 100; Villecourt, I, 147-148.

[235] On the Dominican priest Gregorio Rocco, see E. Giardino, *Il predicatore delle strade di Napoli: P. Gregorio Rocco,* Napoli 1987; G. Cioffari-Miele, *Storia dei Domenicani nell'Italia meridionale,* II, Napoli-Bari 1993, 454, 465-468. Regarding the convent of S. Spirito di Palazzo, see M. Miele, *La Riforma domenicana a Napoli nel periodo post-tridentino (1583-1725),* Roma, 1963, *passim*; G. Provitera-G. Ranisio-E. Giliberti, *Lo spazio sacro. Per un'analisi della religione popolare napoletana,* Napoli 1978, 42-45.

Gerola (Agerola) will take place, because I must arrange several things here and see how many could be brought at best.

Most esteemed Father, yesterday was a very disturbed day, there were several temptations and battles and I was very worn out. The demon fought me. I hope in God, in Mama Mary, in your holy prayers, in those of the nuns, and of those good people to whom I profess my eternal obligation.

I spoke with Don Peppe[236] and Don Nicola Borgia about the bishops of Cilento[237] and the one of Capaccio, who all have large dioceses. It was at Odoardi's place,[238] the Benedictine monk in the community of S. Severino of the Cassino,[239] where it seems to me you have a brother.[240] Write a letter to anyone you want and I will take it to them. But if you can't, I will see to it in some other way.

As for the diocese of Satriano,[241] tomorrow, with the Lord's help, I will speak to the duke of the place, who is a good friend of mine and my family, an excellent Christian, namely, Don Antonio Laviano. He would give us all the help and arrangements for the mission in his territory.

Tell me (although I already know and said) if it is true that the nuns have thrown Celeste out. But I said that the Mother [Superior] got on her knees and begged her not to go. It is said that they put her out without any clothes and that the nuns of S. Cataldo gave her some things out of charity.[242] Tell me specifically about this so that I can

---

[236] "Don Peppe": This probably refers to Don Giuseppe Cerchia.

[237] Cilento is part of the central Apennine Mountains (Campania), covering the peninsula along the Gulf of Salerno (to the north) and of Policastro (to the southeast). Its inhabitants were especially in need of spiritual care, to the extent that Celestino Galiani called them almost savages. See De Meulemeester, *Origines*, I, 151; G. De Rosa, *Vescovi, popolo e magia nel Sud*, Napoli, 1983, 66, 94, 117–119, 129, 130–131; G. Galasso, *L'altra Europa*, Milano 1982, 28, 90, 184, 339; A. Lerra, *Chiesa e società nel Mezzogiorno. Dalla "ricettizia" del sec. XVI alla liquidazione dell'Asse ecclesiastico in Basilicata*, Venosa 1996, 34–35. See also Lettera 104 [of *Carteggio*].

[238] Agostino Odoardi, OSB (1674–1741), was Bishop of Capaccio from 1724 to 1741; *Hier. cath.*, V, 142.

[239] See J. Mazzoleni, *Il monastero benedettino dei SS. Severino e Sossio*, Napoli, 1964.

[240] Antonio (1698–1739), Alphonsus' brother, entered the Benedictine Order in 1716, and took the name of Benedetto Maria. He was later master of novices in the monastery of SS. Severino e Sossio in Naples. See Swanston, *St. Alphonsus*, 12–17, 20, 25, 33, 47, 58, 61, 318; Tellería, *San Alfonso*, I, 70–71.

[241] This probably refers to present-day Satriano di Lucania (Potenza), an ancient episcopal see later joined to the diocese of Campagna.

[242] Crostarosa, *Autobiografia*, 265–267.

give [your letter] first to Porpora[243] and then to Carace to read, for they are badly caught up with this and the whole town with them.

I am in the midst of troubles, but my troubles are mild because I foresee that I will easily knock down the obstacle [?] ....

[Gennaro Maria Sarnelli]

TO ALPHONSUS DE LIGUORI (JULY 17, 1733) [244]

The desire to enter the community at Scala meets an obstacle in the plans to teach in the rural schools that the missionaries are now taking on. Moreover, such tasks would impede his work of protecting the helpless youth of Naples. Nevertheless, Gennaro Maria dreams of the missions and wants to come as soon as possible.

Let Jesus Christ be our Light

Naples, July 17, 1733

My Most Esteemed Father,

Since I am already one foot into that holy Institute and have the desire that, after I get in, I may live with blind obedience to the indications of whoever is in charge, it seems right that I first briefly explain the difficulties involved in coming to the Institute that cross my mind along with other things.

First was the fear I have that if I am required to teach school, it would seem that I would not be able to pursue my ardent desires to lead many souls to God, while on the missions I would be able to teach countless children, hear their confessions and lead them along God's way, besides so many other things that are accomplished by the holy missions. Yet, on the other hand, if I teach school I would lose myself among 30 or 40 students. Just thinking about it, I feel I would die.

---

[243] This refers to Giuseppe Porpora, a companion of Alphonsus in the Apostolic Missions. See Berthe, I, 44, 346; Dilgskron, I, 312; Rispoli, *Vita del B. Alphonsus*, 115– 116; Tannoia, I, 31, 38, 44, 61–63; II, 128, 197, 201; Tellería, *Sacellum Scalense*, 358.

[244] *Carteggio*, Lettera 87, pp. 268–271. Signed handwritten letter, 5 ff., 20 × 13 cm, in AGHR, SAM/17, 1105; copies in AGHR, CK [F. Kuntz], 17–21; APGR, CD [B. D'Orazio], 6–11. Ed: De Meulemeester, Origines, I, 270–272.

The other difficulty was that, finding myself committed here to rescue the girls who are at risk and to write in their defense to reveal the endless damages done them because of which they sell their honor while still children, it appears that by entering this Institute, gaining this great good, at least by my [current] writing, could be impeded. Coming there, I would be hard-pressed to have the time and place to finish it so as to be able to give help to so many poor little souls, something that I could not in fact do if I was stuck in school.[245] And this is all the more so in that I am laboring on another work on Christian doctrine that Borgia asked from me in order to give it to the Secretary General of Doctrine here.[246] This work would also help those who come to the Institute to realize the great necessity and the powerful effectiveness of Christian doctrine and the means to insure its fruitfulness.

I mention this therefore before entering there in order to make you aware of the desires that the Lord gives me for his glory and from which I foresee great joy, if the Lord blesses it. For the rest, see that I have thrown myself on the bosom of divine providence and am totally at rest there and in the hands of the one who commands me in the Lord's place. Let them throw me into hell and I will be most content, if there I believe to be following the will of God.

If I come there, as I hope, does it seem good to Your Lordship that I do so at the beginning of August and then, when the novena to the Holy Cross is finished,[247] return here to finish arranging my affairs? Or am I to arrange everything and [provide for] these girls as best I can, and then once and for all come to you and not return to the city? If I must arrange everything first, my coming would be toward the end of August, please God. So will your Lordship, as clearly and possible, advise me of the dates for the mission at Gerola (Agerola) and if by coming at the end of August, I would be on time.[248] If this aforementioned mission would begin much earlier and I would not have finished my business here, by getting Don Giovanni Mazzini to come, I could pass up the mission at Gerola, and so be there all set for

---

[245] This work, titled *Ragioni cattoliche e politiche in difesa delle repubbliche rovinate dall'insolentito meretricio*, was published in Naples in 1736.

[246] Was referring to the unpublished work titled *Istruzione circa i costumi, e le verità della Fede*. See Chiovaro, *Il beato Gennaro Maria Sarnelli*, 147.

[247] The feast of the Holy Cross fell on September 14. That year Sarnelli preached the novena in the cathedral of Scala in preparation for this feast; *Ibid.*, 76. See Lettera 104 [in *Carteggio*].

[248] On the back of the page we read: "Agerola near Amalfi Au(gust) 11–18, 1733."

the novena of the Cross and, with the help of the Lord, continue right after with the other missions. Let me know everything in detail, so I can thus take care of my affairs and settle them according to what you write me.

My Most Esteemed Father, this very evening I got your letter and it brought me to tears for its tenderness and consolation. I do not fathom, nor can I express, the obligations that I feel in my heart toward you, Don Cesare [Sportelli], Don Pietro [Romano], the holy nuns and all the people there. I endlessly tell the Lord to repay all the great charity that you have for me, something that I truly do not deserve. Things are going very well, as you already know from my other letter that by now you have received. Due to all your love and so many prayers, it is impossible that the Lord would not want to answer them, and although my faults are great, they are not greater than the infinite divine mercy, and our Mama Mary Most Holy we must not forget.

Keep me in mind, but continue to pray to the Lord. My spiritual director[249] still holds onto the letter I wrote; you would hardly believe how many things he has to do! But I hope in the good Lord to remove the prejudices of the whole city with its thousands of false suppositions, not only on my own but especially by means of this spiritual director of mine who recognizes that it is all from God. Pray for him because he deserves it. He has great love for God and for you.

As to Don Giovanni: he responded briefly and said that he could not come to the mission. Still, trust in God and pray that you find God's mercies and the marvelous and loving signs of his divine providence. Don Giovanni will probably be [a member] of the Institute before me and will certainly be more useful than I.

Ah, my dear Signor Don Cesare: a thousand very humble greetings and pardons if I do not write him due to lack of time since I must immediately hurry the person off who has to deliver the letters. I am sending a letter from his honorable mother to whom I spoke when I dropped by her house; she is indeed a godly soul. The schools are moving ahead, and I will send a girl to them, my sister's daughter.[250]

---

[249] Father Domenico Manulio was in Naples during a break of the canonical visit he was making to the Neapolitan Province of the Company of Jesus, of which he was the provincial. See ARSI, Neap. 59 (Epp. Generalium, 1732–1733), ff. 181–186.

[250] There is no indication which of his sisters Sarnelli is alluding to: Lucrezia Maria or Maria Anna.

With the Lord's help, I will bring not only what you told me to, but everything. But pray to the Most Holy Mary that I also bring a new heart and a new life which I ardently desire to reform.

Happily then, my most esteemed Father, I say again and again: *Nolite timere pusillus grex, quia complacuit Patri vestro dare vobis Regnum.*[251] I always, night and day, pray to the Lord for everyone there and for the growth of this holy Institute. Answer me about all that I write, and reread my letters before you respond so that you can answer all my questions.

I will bring the large Calapino[252] if the Lord permits. If there is anything else that I am not aware of, let me know so I can bring it. Finally, excuse the length [of this letter]; it's something you can use for the recreation time.

I also long for the little grotto, a pleasure to the Lord.[253] I resolutely try to do what God wants of me. May his infinite mercy be blessed that he chooses to share with me so many graces not only without any merit of mine, but even with my real faults. Ah, that our Mama Mary may do a great deal for me before God and that she does it now through your prayers. May the Most Blessed Sacrament and the Immaculate Conception of the Most Holy Mary be eternally praised.

Tell my Signor Don Cesare that I hope his faith in the blessed God about my coming is realized. The letter that he just sent to his mother I have not yet received. If I get any more letters from her I will get them to him at the first opportunity.

I am now giving your letter to the mail. Give this letter to Msgr. Falcoia and the other one to mother [superior] who has written with such great charity and has made me very happy.

Finally, I remain, most humbly kissing your sacred hands,
Your H[umb]le and most ob[edie]nt s[erva]nt and br[oth]er

Gennaro Maria Sarnelli

---

[251] "Do not fear, little flock; it has pleased God to give you the Kingdom of Heaven" (Luke 12:32).

[252] *Calapino: Dizionario della lingua latina (e di altre lingue europee), II,* 541. Named after Ambrogio Calepino, OSA (1435–1511), the author of a celebrated Latin dictionary.

[253] See Capone-Majorano, *I Redentoristi,* 183–202.

P.S. In my name, [give] Father Superior my countless greetings. And also say hello to Brother Vito [Curzio], and ask him to pray for me as I do for him at holy Mass.

TO ALPHONSUS DE LIGUORI (AROUND JULY 20, 1733)[254]

Unfounded rumors that are circulating through Naples about the foundation. Problems he is facing before entering the Institute. He asks for prayers.

Live Jesus and the Most Holy Mary

[Naples, around July 20, 1733]

Don Ciccio Carrafa[255] was named superior of the Congregation [of the Apostolic Missions].

Everybody I speak to brings up "the Nun" or "Celeste." I staunch the conversation immediately and say: "Let's just let it lie! We churchmen will deal with it among ourselves." That way I can lessen the impact of having to answer a million questions. They are asking me if Tosquez is with us.

My Most Esteemed Father, please don't stop recommending me to God and having others recommend me to the Lord and Most Holy Mary. I need them so much, now more than ever, to overcome so many obstacles and to generously obtain the grace of the Lord to come among you although I do not deserve it. But I hope you will allow me to ask for your prayers. Just today I had so many temptations of hesitancy, but I have always trusted and wish always to trust in the infinite mercy of my God, the Infinite Goodness, and in the merits and intercession of our

---

[254] *Carteggio,* Lettera 88, pp. 271–273. Signed handwritten letter, 2 ff., 20.5 × 14 cm, in AGHR, EadSA, 022; copies in AGHR, CK [F. Kuntz], 23–26; APGR, CD [B. D'Orazio], 13–16. Unpublished.

[255] This refers to Francisco (diminutive: "Ciccio") Carafa (1685-1754), friend of Alphonsus and future bishop of Nardò (1736-1754). See *Hier. cath.,* VI, 307. At the time of his episcopal nomination he was chaplain of the Treasury of St. Gennaro. See Tellería, *Rev. D. Caietanus de Liguoro,* 333. On his election as superior of the Apostolic Missions, see Id., *Prima S. Alfonsi palaestra,* 440.

Mama the Most Holy Mary. But the devil does not stop tormenting me, and if he hides for a while, he immediately returns to trouble me. May the will of God always be accomplished. Please do not forget to beg the infinite mercy of God to complete his work since *Dei perfecta sunt opera.*[256] And if he wills to call me to this holy Congregation out of pity, he will tear down the obstacles that I may come. It is true that for my sins both past and present I will always be undeserving of his grace but pray that he will have patience with all I lack in his divine sight.

I am striking a great blow of joy for the Institute. Pray that the Lord assist me and brings success for his glory. When I think how it is possible that the Lord wishes to make use of me in some way for this magnificent work and by coming to be among the first [members] as well as to promote it here even amid so much hesitancy and so many doubts, I comfort myself by remembering what St. Paul wrote: *Quae infirma sunt mundi, quae stulta, quae contemptibilia sunt mundi elegit Deus ut confundat fortia,*[257] and that the Lord called to his apostolate even the tax collectors.

Your little book of hymns is on sale in a shop. I would like to know exactly how much a pack of one hundred copies comes to, and if it would be possible to allow them to reprint more at half the price you received before, because, if that is not possible, it would be necessary to pay what the book seller wants for them.

Be patient, send the copied letter quickly, because Father Provincial Manuilo has kept the other copy and due to his great amount of work, he has not finished reading it. As for justifying the Institute and also me, it is necessary to show it to a lot of people, especially to Don Giovanni Mazzini's spiritual director, to clear away the reasons that he adduces for not giving him permission. Be of good heart, however, that the Lord is arranging matters well in his adored and marvelous providence in ways that we can only trust.

I hope nevertheless to come, the Lord willing, and I come to you in good spirits because no other motive moves me to come but to do the

---

[256] Based on the Vulgate (Deut 32:4): "The Rock—how faultless are his deeds, how right all his ways!"

[257] The Vulgate (1 Corinthians 1:27–28) text actually reads: "But God has chosen the foolish of the world, so that he may confound the wise. And God has chosen the weak of the world, so that he may confound the strong. And God has chosen the ignoble and contemptible of the world, those who are nothing, so that he may reduce to nothing those who are something."

will of the Lord and become a saint in order to please God. Still, I have innumerable emotions, even good ones, to overcome. And now I have no external disturbance or battle, as I had months earlier which gave me so little urge to leave here; but in parting, I only leave to find God closer and to make him this ultimate sacrifice of denying my own will, even in holy and good things.

Always pray for me, while I suffer and act for the whole Congregation or Institute as you will understand later. Prayer, prayer, prayer, please, my only hope for removing those obstacles that burden me before God with my ongoing imperfections. Pray to the Lord to give me a new heart so that I can truly begin to love him and sacrifice myself completely for him. And like a child throws itself entirely into the arms of its loving mother, so may I too throw my whole self on the bosom of his divine providence. May the Most Holy Mary, my only hope, obtain for me by means of your prayers more than what I ask. Let me know about everything going on there, console and comfort me with your words.

A thousand greetings to Signor Don Cesare [Sportelli], and tell him that I was at his mother's house, and she was very grateful and sent her greetings.

Gennaro Maria Sarnelli

TO ALPHONSUS DE LIGUORI (JULY-AUGUST 1733) [258]

Unfounded rumors that are circulating through Naples about the foundation. Problems he is facing before entering the Institute. He asks for prayers.

Live Jesus and the Most Holy Mary
[Naples, July-August, 1733]

I ask you to respond as soon as possible by sending me copies in your own hand of the letter that Father Fiorillo wrote that give

---

[258] *Carteggio*, Lettera 93, pp. 279–281. Signed handwritten letter, 2 ff., 20 × 14 cm, in AGHR, EadSA, 023; copies in AGHR, CK [F. Kuntz], 36–38; APGR, CD [B. D'Orazio], 16–18. Ed: De Meulemeester, *Origines*, I, 274–275.

me permission to leave for the Holy Work. In a separate letter enclosed with them tell me: "My Don Gennaro, this is the message that Father Fiorillo sent me, so I did not act willfully but through prayer and obedience." Or use your own words so that it can be read by people who assert the opposite. This will help.

At the same time, let me know how the superior of the monastery spoke to Celeste so that she would not leave and whose fault it was. Put this in the same letter to me and in which you write out the permission of Fiorillo and what happened with Celeste. This would help a lot, with God's help, to disabuse this Naples of the false beliefs and to demonstrate that you are not a fool nor have acted willfully and that the nuns were not tyrants.

I want to repeat. On a half sheet of paper write me how Celeste's departure occurred and what the superior and the other nuns said. And, at the same time, tell me that you acted under obedience in leaving Naples and write out word for word Father Fiorillo's letter in the same message, so I can have many others read it and your justification through obedience, and that the nuns were not as cruel as they say. This will be good for the greater glory of God and for the Institute, showing that it is from God.

My Dear Father, I received your letters Thursday just as the bell was sounding for noon, and I assure you they were a great comfort to me. I am here awaiting the arrival of Signor Giovanni Olivieri, just as the currier is about to leave, but I do not wish to omit telling you the *Lord sends help in due time*: the last time you wrote me, I was in the dumps and you consoled me. Now I have greater troubles and yet I am still relatively happy. May the infinite mercy of God be ever blessed.

I write in haste. I will write you more at length when I have another chance, and I will answer your letters and everything. I ask you to write me often so that the courier come a little sooner. I find things are going very well for me and I hope in the Lord that the same is true for Manzini. Enough. Prayer, prayer that can do all things, and we have no fear.

In the coming week, who knows, I will have many very detailed things to report to you. I have great internal difficulties. Pray to the Lord to give me firm faith and great trust and to the Most Holy Mary to help me. I have not had time to read your letters. I am writing another letter in which I say that the Lord appeared to Solomon,

Tertullian, Origin, Saul, and then later they failed. Then I add the words of St. Teresa that you wrote me; then you will understand it all. Finally, I thank you endlessly for the great charity that you show me, something that, to tell the truth, I really do not deserve.

Greet Signor Don Cesare [Sportelli] for me, Father Superior,[259] Brother Vito [Curzio] and all. Tell the superior[260] that I have not even been able to read a little of the letter she wrote me. I will answer her some other time. Pay my respects to Father Superior and to the Mother Superior and all the nuns and thank them for all their kindness to me. I received the copied letter and I appreciate it greatly. On that point, this morning Father Manuilo sent me the other one and said that it is well. I only need to specify a few more things about the rule.

For the rest, I most humbly kiss your sacred hands.

May the Most Blessed Sacrament and the Immaculate Conception of Most Holy Mary be ever praised.

I bought your leaflets at 33 grains[261] per 100, and I managed to get *La Vera sapienza*[262] by Segneri printed, adding some short hymns if they fit.

From your Lordship's hum(ble) and m(ost faith)ful servant and son,

Gennaro Maria Sarnelli

P.S. I am very happy that the mission at Gerola for August 29 has been postponed, both because it is too cool and because I can get all my matters settled and also must have a meeting with the Bishop of Salerno.

---

[259] Pietro Romano, superior of the community and confessor to the monastery.

[260] Sister Maria Angela De Vito del Cielo.

[261] A grain (*grano*) is a copper coin minted in Naples.

[262] The book titled *La vera sapienza, ovvero Considerazioni utilissime all'acquisto del santo timor di Dio, disposte per tuitti I giorni della settimana* (s.l.s.d.), often attributed to Father Paolo Segneri, SJ (1624–1694) was actually the work of Father Giovanni Pietro Pinamonti, SJ (1632–1703), See C. Sommervogel, *Bibliothèque de la Compagnie de Jésus*, 9 vol., Bruxelles-Paris 1890–1900, VI, 763; VII, 1088.

TO ALPHONSUS DE LIGUORI (JULY 1, 1738)[263]

Sarnelli is sending him some books, paper, money, and figures. He asks him for suggestions on material to include in his books of prayers and he gives him some names of possible assistants in his missions.

Long live the Most Holy Trinity and the Most Holy Mary Immaculate

Naples, July 1, 1738

Most Esteemed Father,

I am sending you nine booklets on the Holy Trinity so that you can send three to each of the monasteries where you have given retreats. I think that the one in S. Georgio already has it. The one at Tramonti certainly does[264]. Send this to Penta,[265] Cava,[266] Pellizzano,[267] etc. If there are more than three, let me know so I may send you more.

My Lady Mother[268] wishes to have a small celebration in the chapel [of the Baron of Ciorani's mansion] both for the feast of the Most Holy Madonna of Carmine, as well as that of the glorious St. Anne. For that purpose she is sending two tarì[269] for Masses on the two feasts as well as a pound of candles for the Masses on these two feasts. Whatever is left over is for your own use. See that a lot of people come and that all goes well to the glory of the Most Holy Mary and for the good of souls.

---

[263] *Carteggio*, Lettera 222, pp. 507–510. Original (handwritten letter) 2 ff., 20 × 13.5 cm, in APGR, photocopy in AGHR, EadSA, 103; copies in AGHR, CK [F. Kuntz], 36–38; APGR, CD [B. D'Orazio], 16–18. Ed: De Meulemeester, *Origines*, I, 274–275.

[264] These refer to the Carmelite monasteries in the two towns.

[265] Penta is a town in the neighborhood of Fisciano (Salerno), in which from 1239 to 1807 there existed a monastery of Benedictine Sister of Montevergine under the title of S. Maria delle Grazie. In 1741, Alphonsus sought to place a young woman there as a boarding student. See. De Meulemeester, *Origines*, II, 1; P. Lugano, *L'Italia benedittina*, Roma 1929, 439.

[266] He is probably referring to the nuns' monasteries in Cava.

[267] Pellezzano was a suburb of San Severino with a population of 915. Alfano, *Istorica descrizione*, 46. Regarding a mission preached there by Alphonsus, see Tannoia, II, 117.

[268] Caterina Rosa Scoppa.

[269] *Tarì* are silver coins minted in Sicily.

Don Giovanni [Mazzini] wrote me that he sent there my box of three branches [of artificial flowers] for the little sisters of S. Gennaro de' Poveri, that the Vicar requested of me for the statue of the Most Holy Mary. If you have a safe way to do so, send them to me.

In the care of my brother, Andrea, I sent a figure of an *Ecce Homo* for the confessional. Now I am sending you another three for the front of all four confessionals; see that they get placed properly.

I received your letter [Giuseppe] Porpora told me that he wants to send [Michele] De Alteriis to Cava. That would be great, but I fear that his parents will not let him go for fear of you, etc. If he does not go, I will let [Giuseppe] Jorio know.

I would like Your Reverence to advise me about what I should write on the Most Holy Mary. It is a simple matter to find something in Grassetti, which I do not have on hand, or in *Alfabeto mariano*, which I don't have either, because they treat the usual things. I am looking for the story of the Most Holy Mary where she freed the Roman matron who had murdered the child who had been born incestuously. I think it was in Bovio.[270] Father Saverio [Rossi] related it to the people. This would be very helpful for me in a very important matter.

I sent a figure for the confessional. You have not told me if you have received it. Tell Don Andrea, my brother, that I sent him a black sash, the book of Jorio[271] for the parish priest's nephew, and an *Ecce Homo* for you. I also have not heard if they were received.

As far as completing the review of the booklet for the congregation,[272] I am in no hurry. Do the revising little by little and with no rush as you have the time, and put in whatever you wish. And do not send it to me until I tell you; send it with every care and assurance that it is not lost. Because once things leave this poor battered head, I don't know if they will come back or be thought of anew.

---

[270] Carlo Bovio, SJ (1614–1705) was the author of *Esempi e miacoli della SS. Vergine Maria Madre di Dio detti nella chiesa del Giesù dal P. Carlo Bovio*, Roma 1701. This is a reference to Example VIII (II, 72–84): "A Roman lady fallen into the sin of incest and of parricide was freed, by the Most Blessed Virgin, from the nefarious condemnations of a demon."

[271] Probably G. Iorio, *Isturzione per gli confessori di terre e villaggi*, Napoli 1736.

[272] G. M. Sarnelli, *Le sagre congregazioni ad onor di Maria SS., utilissime al cristianesimo, colle regole facili, e brievi da osservarsi da congregati. Colle maniere da introdurre le congregazioni di spirito, che chiamansi segrete, e sue regole*, Napoli 1739.

Here we are in the middle of carnivals and parties. It makes me cry that we cannot get away from the multiple offenses to God and the loss of souls. Even the things that are innocent in themselves still have thousands and thousands of evil consequences. I never read or hear that people observe two Lents a year like they hold two carnivals. We must pray to God to illumine these poor sinners and for help to these poor seculars, who run around lost in vanities [As for me, by the mercy of God, I will not give up my efforts...][273]

I have prepared ten packets of paper for printing and along with them another sheaf of some scrap paper. I don't know if they can come by mule wagon. Please do not set them aside, but use them for the intentions (?) or some other good use because I have found them useful, especially the sheets for printing. The other sheets of folio size and half size, I mean the ones for letters, I can send out as you want them and it will be no trouble for me. Let me know if you need them.

Let me know what I can insert in the books I am now printing, such as other devotions published elsewhere, to improve the books and make them easier to sell. I already put in the four little rosaries: the Most Holy Trinity, the Holy Wounds, the Holy Child with the Steps of the sacred Infancy, and the Seven Dolors, and other very lovely devotions printed somewhere else. Advise me about other things that would make the book more profitable and easy to sell. I do not care about the greater cost. Please answer me about this.

We spoke together today, I, Porpora and that priest from Cava.[274] It was said that Porpora wants De Alteriis. If he cannot come, Jorio has promised me to send a good member who right now has gone to Procida to preach the month on the Most Holy Mary.

[Gennaro Maria Sarnelli]

---

[273] Unfinished sentence crossed out.
[274] Probably Don Paolo Cafaro.

To Alphonsus de Liguori (After July 1, 1738)[275]

He writes of his troubled state. His publication efforts and his fight against prostitution and blasphemy are described. He expresses his love for the Institute.

Long Live the Most Holy Trinity and the Most Holy Mary Immaculate
[Naples, after July 1, 1738]

Most Esteemed Father,

I had already written my last letter when I received one from Your Reverence. I sent by mule wagon half a package of paper for printing and a bunch of scrap paper. I suspect you have received them. I am enclosing here a key to the box in which there are three bunches of artificial flowers. Put the key in an envelope and tell the driver where it is in case the guards at the bridge want to inspect it. I told him that if he has to pay a tax (I don't think so), he should pay it and bring me the bill so I can reimburse him the costs. Tell him for the love of God not to lose the key.

As to the brochures for the congregations,[276] look them over at your convenience and I will be grateful for anything you add. At the end of the two books there is some advice for prelates and superiors; please check those as well.

I rejoice over the new house and the comfort you get through the Blessed Sacrament. I am also happy that this is the cause of your being able to forget everything else, because there is nothing that gives greater glory and honor to this Blessed Sacrament that desires to be recognized and loved by the whole world.

Regarding the book on the disrespected Jesus, it will be a while before I can use it because I cannot deal with it until I get the time to compile the book on the passion of Jesus Christ. But if you have any further need for it, let me know and I will send it back right away because I have no other use for it until that time.

---

[275] *Carteggio*, Lettera 223, pp. 510–513. Signed handwritten letter, 2 ff., 20 × 13.5 cm, in APGR, photocopy in AGHR, EadSA, 103; copies in AGHR, CK [F. Kuntz], 36–38; APGR, CD [B. D'Orazio], 16–18. Ed: De Meulemeester, Origines, I, 274–275.

[276] See previous letter.

Thanks be to the Most Holy Trinity and Most Holy Mary that Don Cesare [Sportelli] is feeling better.

About the novena in August, I'll tell you the truth, when I spoke to the priest in charge of the church, I did not make a commitment and I acted uninterested and reluctant. Since then he has not spoken to me, or I to him.

I am very greatly troubled and confused. May God's Most Holy will be done. I say this so that you will pray for me and ask others to do so because I have tried not to tell anyone about my depression, sufferings and pain except when I simply must speak so my heart does not break. I fear I may overexaggerate. Although life is a continual death for me and the thought of death brings me great fear. May God do something. I need effective intercessors who will please Mary Most Holy and make me able to see my errors and failings because, if I do not know them clearly, I cannot remedy them.

As to my book, it is making me sweat blood, but I am about to complete it. I lack time, health, obliging printers and money. May God take care of it.

Regarding the work here, it is still effecting some very good progress against some of the professional prostitutes, and in the dealings with the king and the cardinal.[277] Next, I hope to God to be able to make proposals against blasphemy that will prove to be an easy way to bring about a great diminishment of it.[278] Recommend all this to His Divine Majesty and have others do the same that it will have success even throughout the whole Kingdom. When we make an effort to stop prostitution throughout the whole Kingdom, we will need a great deal of prayer. I ask this of you. Bring it to the attention of the monasteries of holy nuns.

Naples is like a hell for me. But it is right that I stay here as long as it pleases God. I will come and go for the greater glory of God. As

---

[277] See F. Chiovaro, *A Life of Blessed Gennaro Maria Sarnelli, Redemptorist: 1704–1744*, translated by J. Robert Fenili, Liguori MO: Liguori Publications, 2003, Chapter 6; A. De Risio, *Chroniche della Congregazione del. SS. Redentore*, Palermo 1858, 93–95.

[278] [G. M. Sarnelli], *Opera contro all'abuso della bestemmia. Tomo unico, divso in tre libri: Colle regole, aniere et pratiche, ordinate per frenare quel delitto*, Napoli 1740. See A. Sampers, "Controversia quam S. Alfonsus sustinuit ann. 1746–48 «De malediction e mortuorum»," in *Spic. hist.* 14 (1966) 6.

soon as the book on the devout life is completed,[279] I can leave for good.

As far as my love for the Institute, I have all the love and commitment possible. I would like to see it reaching to the stars, spread throughout the world, and I want to promote it even at the cost of my blood. But I do not know what I can do to bring you joy and good; I can do no more than the nothing I do. If my prayers can do anything in Jesus Christ, I am already offering them continuously. The Institute would do the same for me as I do for the Institute.

The Baron, my father, says that in August he is coming there. If he comes with the Baroness, my mother, I will have to come also, and this back and forth in the middle of all my business will cause me a great deal of trouble. God's will be done.

As to the missions, I will do what I can to help you if it pleases the Divine Majesty. Your Reverence already knows that here I refuse a thousand offerings and invitations that are tempting, easy and at no cost. And although I got another invitation from one of the brothers of the Congregation for a Mission of the Holy Spirit, I excused myself from it and will continue to excuse myself if they put pressure on me as I am sure they will. I was only in S. Gennariello twice and God knows how hard that was for me and how threatening. And when I can, I will go twice a month, once for each part.

I am sending the letter of Bishop Falcoia who mistakenly thought that I had written it when it was my brother Andrea whom I had asked not to let him read because it sounds a little haughty, I don't mean about me but about him. Only about the rents and the income, as if they would not be paid. But Andrea tells me that they will be paid right on time. I would like this to be cleared up with Bishop Falcoia for the sake of the well-being of this foundation [Ciorani].

Please send this letter of Falcoia back to me later since I must answer him, and especially in my regard, not to include me as a member there [that is, as a member of the community at Ciorani], either on account of my countless illnesses or the many very heavy duties here, just as there. Since the people there belong to my father's feud, it is not the proper place to exercise my ministry there except in extreme necessity, etc.

---

[279] G. M. Sarnelli, *Opera illuminativa, e istruttiva, per secolari, ecclesiastici, e religiosi, per facilitare a ciascuno stato d'anime l'esercizio della vita divota, e per introdurre nelle parrocchie, comunità, e famiglie l'uso in comune della considerazione, e delle preghiera. Colle meditazioni sopra le massime eterne*, Napoli 1738.

Thank the Lord that the professional prostitutes have been restrained during this occasion in which half of the Kingdom is in the city and these events bring great excesses and give countless scandals.[280]

From Y[our] R[everence]'s M[ost hum]ble s[ervant] and b[rother]

Gennaro Maria

P.S. Please read everything and answer me about what is necessary. And indicate that you have received what I sent. I will give all your thanks to the Lord, my father.

I will not stop praying for Your Reverence at holy Mass, and for the Institute. May Your Reverence please do so for me and for the work at hand, and ask others to do the same.

TO ALPHONSUS DE LIGUORI (JANUARY 1741?)[281]

This letter was written when Alphonsus was involved in the mission at Serino. He speaks of his illness and of Mass intentions, as well as of the death of Brother Gaudiello and the difficulties the foundation faces with the government of the Kingdom.

Long live the Most Holy Trinity and the Most Holy Mary Immaculate [Naples, January 1741?]

Most Esteemed Father Rector,

I just received Your Reverence's letter. I am troubled; in the last week I had three attacks of a new illness; and last night a pain from the top of my shoulder to my chest, but today and this evening it has let up a little, by God's grace.

---

[280] Sarnelli is alluding to the ten-day celebration for "the public welcome of the Queen" Maria Amalia of Saxony on July 2, 1738. See *Correspondenze diplomatiche veneziane da Napoli*, XVI, (1732–1739), a cura di M. Infelise, Roma 1992, 562–563; I. Ascione, "L'alba di un Regno (1735–1739)," in *Carlo di Borbone, Lettere ai sovrani di Spagna*, 2 vol, a cura di I Ascione, Roma 2001–2002, II, 22–24.

[281] *Carteggio*, Lettera 265, pp. 589–590. Signed handwritten letter, 18.5 x 13 cm, in APGR, "Autografi di G. M. Sarnelli," LP 29; photocopy in AGHR, EadSA, 122; handwritten copies in AGHR, CK, 247–249; APGR, CD, 102–104. Ed: [Sarnelli] *Opera contro all'abuso della bestemmia…*, t. XII, libr. II, pp. 100–102.

Let me know when you want the booklets with the sixteen *carlini* exemption and I will send them. I will consign the letter to Borgia and tell him the rest when I get a chance to see him.

As far as the books are concerned, I will tell you about them now and then not mention them again. It is less than a year since I took care of a thousand [*intentions for*] masses gratis, as you know; and I was then given five hundred more. I immediately sent them to Don Giovanni [*Mazzini*] and to Don Saverio [*Rossi*] to be said, since the thousand will soon be completed. He was very pleased and sent me his thanks very quickly as he has quite often. Now Your Reverence sees how to react to this matter. The priests of the Most Holy Savior were clearly my first choice, that is, Don Giulio [*Cesare Marocco*] and Don Carlo [*Maiorino*]: two Masses more per day. During this year they also needed Masses to be said by the pastors in Carte, and so it was urgent that they receive my thousand extra Masses to satisfy the obligations in less than a year. Then, why will they not have the same need at least now when we are talking about a period of two years? Two priests are missing. There will not be help from the pastors of Carte and the Congregation by prolonging and delaying the missions has gotten a better name and publicity. Enough, let's not repeat it. I was begged on bended knee to give this chance to others. But I, who really want to help you, dearly want to give this benefit to your missions and houses, as I have done with the fifteen hundred Masses and on other occasions. Therefore, if I can continue with my books and opportunities to offer Masses, and if I have the chance to obtain some Masses to have celebrated for my intention, have your three houses ask me and I will put myself at your service. Indeed, since I am bound in justice to many people, and I am not allowed to use my publications to satisfy these obligations in justice, don't let Don Saverio think that I cannot have more free Masses to celebrate after these thousand that are already completed.

I heard that Brother Giacchino may have died, but I have had no news whatever about it.[282] There is a rumor that you cannot continue building because of a royal order to stop. But I do not know if this is true.

---

[282] Born at Bracigliano in August 1719, Gioacchino Gaudiello died at Ciorani on April 18, 1741. See Minervino, *Catalogo*, 231; Tannoia, II, 124.

Recommend me to Jesus and to the Most Holy Mary that I dedicate myself to the greater glory of His Divine Majesty and to the good of my soul and the souls of my neighbors.

Let me know when you are back in the residence. And inform me if my books are being distributed in the places where missions are being given. I don't get any news. Remember me to everyone, and I kiss your sacred hands.

Y[our] R[everend's]

[Gennaro Maria Sarnelli]

P.S. My greetings to Don Giovanni [Mazzini], Don Andrea [Villani] and Don Filippo [De Vito] and all. I sent twelve booklets for Communion to Don Andrea.

To Alphonsus de Liguori (circa February 15, 1741?)[283]

He speaks of the missionary projects that are being carried out in the capital, in particular about the general mission in the Archdiocese of Naples.

Long live the Most Holy Trinity and the Most Holy Mary Immaculate [Naples, circa February 15, 1741]

Most E[steemed] F[ather] R[ector]

I received the *Menologio*.[284] [Canon] Gizio told me that you received the 150 ducats from Piazza. Gizio has been sick but he is better now.

Please tell Don Andrea Villani that I have not received the twelve grains[285] so he will mention it to the parish priest. Thanks be to God that the practice of mental prayer in common is ever on the increase.

---

[283] *Carteggio*, Lettera 268, pp. 593–596. Signed handwritten letter, 20 x 14 cm, in APGR, "Autografi di G. M. Sarnelli," LP 30; photocopy in AGHR, EadSA, 125. Ed: De Meulemeester, *Origines*, II, 227–229. Bibl: Berthe, I 228; Dilgskron, I, 207; Rey-Mermet, 434.

[284] A liturgical book that contained more extended lives of the saints than those found in the Missal.

[285] A grain (*grano*) is a copper coin minted in Naples.

Bishop Filomario[286] is in Naples and he tells me that he has introduced the practice in his vast diocese with great success. He wants some missionaries to establish it in the villages; his diocese has 134 locales. His Eminence (May God grant him increase of spirit) has already instructed all the Lenten preachers in the city and its suburbs that he wants them to introduce common mental prayer.[287]

Now talking about ourselves, Most Esteemed Father, it is time to sanctify this diocese and then many other provinces. By God's mercy, now we have more than we were looking for and desiring. I kept the matter secret from my brother Andrea, but I think it is already decided and that it will happen. I spoke with Signor Borgia. He agrees with everything and is now considering a place to set it up and the way to support it. He is inclined toward the suburbs in order to be close to the whole diocese. He says that the parish at Arzano is vacant,[288] and has it in his head that Don Giovanni Mazzini be the administrator.

This morning, Saturday, I had a long conversation with His Eminence, who was gently complaining that he had not seen you yet. I told him everything, your dependence on Bishop Falcoia. I explained to him the way to handle it, the letter he should write to Bishop Falcoia and to mention that he does this with my knowledge. He freely agreed with it all and is now persuaded and determined. Tomorrow Fontana will come and he will have the task of writing the letter. Blessed be God. In an hour they got things done, in God's name, that once would have taken ten years. All to his glory.

If you agree, get to Bishop Falcoia ahead of time so his response does not displease the Cardinal of Naples who can be of help in your holy plans. His Eminence is pleased to have you and another, and now Borgia knows Mazzini, etc. Do not lay down any conditions, come and

---

[286] Marcello Filomarino (1692–1765), Bishop of Mileto (1734–1756). See *Hierarchia catholica medii et recentioris aevi*, cura R. Ritzler-P. Sefrin: VI (1730–1799), Patavii 1958, 288.

[287] See R. Giovine, *Vita del gran servo di Dio D. Gennaro Maria Sarnellli, Padre della Congregazione del SS. Redentore e di quella della Apostoliche Missioni eretta nel duomo di Napoli sotto it titolo di Regina degli Apostoli*, Napoli 1858, 259. Likewise, in his *Istruzione per li missionari deputati a scorrere la Diocese di Napoli...*, Napoli 1741, Cardinal Spinelli had dedicated a section to "Mental Prayer in Common." In it he suggested to the clergy to use these writings of Sarnelli: *Il mondo santificato, L'anima illuminata* and *Il Cristiano santificato*. See Sarnataro, *La catechesi a Napoli*, 54, 170–171.

[288] Arzano was a suburb of Naples with a population of 4,173. Alfano, *Istorica descrizione*, 6.

you will have much more than what you desire. I say come in obedience to Falcoia.

I told His Eminence that I will reside with you and thus he will not lose me for seven months a year, when the whole house is on the move. All that remains is a lot of prayer so His Divine Majesty blesses everything. Be of good heart: I see a great field open for spreading your desires and Institute.

I also inform you that Olivieri[289] is free, thanks be to God. I was afraid because the directors had defrauded the lottery of 100,000 or more ducats.[290]

And also: by the divine mercy, the Bishop of Nola has asked Torni for two missionaries of our Congregation [of Apostolic Missions] whose only task is to go around his large diocese and introduce mental prayer in common; Torni has agreed. Maybe I would like to escape there, but I am not sure.

All the missions by the missionaries of the Archdiocese result in mental prayer in common with them leading the meditation, and they do not go out in the morning until after they have made this prayer with the people of the place. Help me to thank Jesus Christ and the most Holy Mary for such great mercies. My health is better, thank God. Blessed be God!

Greeting to all. I kiss your sacred hands, Y[our] R[everence's]
Most H[umble] ser[vant]

Gennaro Maria Sarnelli

---

[289] Giovanni Olivieri was converted by Alphonsus from a sinful life as a youth and became a close friend and benefactor of the Saint. He housed Redemptorists when they were in Naples and underwrote the costs of some of Alphonsus' publications.

[290] On February 21, 1741, the Venetian ambassador to Naples, Aurelio Bartolini, wrote to the Senate: "Recently a considerable theft was discovered that the directors of this royal lottery had perpetrated, with tickets printed after the fact and counterfeit keys, to the extent that it appears the money stolen was a sum of 300,000 ducats, of which so far the royal treasury has been reimbursed about 75,000. The director and almost all the accomplices in the act are in prison and many of them have been convicted and are in danger of losing their lives by a well-deserved decree of justice. *Corrispondenze diplomatiche veneziane da Napoli, Dispacci*, XVII (1739–1751, a cura di E. Tonetti, Roma 1994, 223.

TO SISTER MARIA ANGELA DEL CIELO, SUPERIOR OF THE SCALA MONASTERY (FEBRUARY 25, 1737)[291]

He thanks her for her prayers on his behalf and for the consolation they brought in his suffering. He exhorts her to perfection: the love of God, glad acceptance of sufferings and contradictions.

Long live the Most Holy Trinity and the Most Holy Mary Immaculate. Most Esteemed Mother,[292]

I received your letter, and I thank you very much, and likewise, all the sisters, for the great kindness that you show me by recommending me continually to God along with my ministries and the people His Divine Majesty places in my care. I thank my guardian angel, and all your guardian angels as well, for remembering my tremendous needs to God, along with my deep misery. At the same time, I thank your charity and I never stop begging His Divine Majesty to repay you and all of them a hundredfold for what you have done, are doing and will do for me. Please continue wholeheartedly. Pray to His Divine Majesty that through the Most Holy Hearts of Jesus and Mary I am given a heart fully conformed to his divine will so that I forget myself entirely and so find my place in the situation, life and work where he will be most glorified.

As to the little I sent you, accept it as a sign of my good intentions because I really want to help you in every way but I am not strong enough to do so. Let's leave it in the good Lord's hands for he is our most loving father and knows better than we do what is good for us.

The Lady My Mother thanks you for your kindness and asks you to recommend her to His Divine Majesty together with our large family that has much need of his help.

I thank you for the encouragement that you have given me with your last letters. Would that it may please the Lord (and so then,

---

[291] *Lettere spirituali di Ven. Gennaro M. Sarnelli*, Naples: 1851 [Hereafter, *Lettere di Sarnelli*], Libro I, Lettera I, 13–16.

[292] This nun was superior of the convent at the time of this and the next three letters, so he addresses her as "Mother." In the remaining letters to her, he addresses her as "Sister" because her term of office had been completed.

certainly myself) that there be greater glory in my sufferings. Then it would not seem a martyrdom but a joy. Still, the one who is infinite Wisdom, Holiness, Justice and Truth seems to arrange the sufferings in a way that makes them seem to be, not for his glory, but rather out of his disdain. Nevertheless, may his infinite goodness be ever blessed and his admirable providence as well, which I adore whether I understand them or not.

Let your painful anxiousness to always belong entirely to God and the ardent longings of your wish to see him glorified increase ever more in your heart; these are a gift of God. May the pain you feel over your lack of response always grow but without disturbance in your heart. Be confident that the grace of God will always triumph in your soul. The lofty edifice of perfection is not built in one swoop, but little by little by suffering, by self-mortification, by doing violence to oneself in joyfully embracing our crosses and by loving the Highest Good. The more that holy love increases, so much the more does the loving heart seem overwhelmed by the mercy of God and desirous of responding so to please him. These desires have to be the continuous activity of our life. Happily, we have a God who is so good and generous with us! We have an infinite obligation to him, but through his mercy and blessing, he will always be the victor and we the conquered. In truth, we have the great consolation that, through Jesus Christ, we are able to satisfy the honor, praise and thanks due the Most Holy Heart of God. May Jesus Christ, his blood, his merits and his divine actions be a continuous offering to the most august Trinity; may they be a continual sacrifice to the divine honor. If it were possible, in every breath renew this gracious oblation. How great should be the honor, glory and praise you want to offer the Lord; all this you can give in every moment by means of Jesus Christ. Thus the Eternal Father will be pleased and eternally glorified.

You mentioned Sister Mary X[293] who wishes to become a saint. I also desire it and I recommend her to you. I would like to know how she is doing.

---

[293] As often happens in these personal letters of Sarnelli or Liguori, when individuals are mentioned their names are omitted from copies and translations as a way of preserving their privacy. This respectful action is a bane to historians and researchers seeking to accurately write biographies.

I will send the fruit[294] as soon as it arrives. But I am troubled by the fact that I have not received the shipment. It seems I am being cheated. It doesn't feel right to me. But may God's will be done. In these cases one always ends up losing, never winning.

Now to finish. I wish you and all your sisters a thousand blessings at every moment in the name of the Most Holy Trinity. I will not forget to pray for all of them, and for you, Sister, during my Mass. And I will also ask the same of all the people on the mission that I am presently conducting. Greet everyone for me and get them to remember me always. Accompany my works with your prayers; I put myself at your service in all that I can do. Long live the Most Holy Trinity, Jesus Christ and the Most Holy Mary.

Naples, February 25, 1737

TO SISTER MARIA ANGELA DEL CIELO, SUPERIOR OF THE SCALA MONASTERY (MARCH 7, 1737)[295]

Advice about physical mortifications, the spirit of penitence, denial of one's own will. Exhortations to pray for some of his works. The way to respond to divine grace.

Long live the Most Holy Trinity and the Most Holy Mary Immaculate

Most Esteemed Mother,

I received one of your letters in Ciorani. But the other one that you indicated you had sent me I have not gotten; how often I have asked Mr. X about it!

As to the penances that you want to continue, considering the serious health issues you are facing and your pale complexion, I do not advise this. It is enough for you to follow the community penances when you can. Since the Lord is troubling you from above with sickness and lethargy, it is enough to bow your head, adore and kiss the hand that strikes you and accept them with courage and joy. You should not add any more

---

[294] *Uncertain translation:* "fruits for the branches" *(pomi per le frasche)*
[295] *Lettere di Sarnelli,* Libro I, Lettera II, 16–18.

167

to them, except once in a while when you must overcome some serious temptation; otherwise your poor body may break under them. This is all the more true since the rule already prescribes some mortifications.

It is fine to foster your holy desire for the spirit of mortification and penance to grow, but not by carrying it out. The Lord, who will still encourage these good desires, will accept them as if actually practiced, just as he accepted those of St. Teresa as long as she desired to do them but was sometimes forbidden to do so because of her poor health.

Meanwhile, try to compensate for not practicing physical mortification by producing it interiorly by denying your own will in all things insofar as you can. In such mortifications you need never restrain yourself because they do not harm the body while they sanctify the spirit. Be alert to do many of these and let no occasion for exercising many such mortifications pass you by. But still, do so gently without a spirit of violence and in a tranquil way. Likewise, you can do some corporal mortification if it has no bad effect of the body.

Most Esteemed Mother, I ask your charity and that of your sisters in urgently praying and having prayers said to His Divine Majesty and to Mary Most Holy for the ongoing work that I am now dealing with in Naples and which is producing a bit of good, but slowly. Now I am distributing another book for that purpose.[296] Please pray several times a day to the Holy Spirit, calling out fervently so that whoever reads it be enlightened to understand clearly and eagerly how to practice the truth. And likewise pray and have prayers said to Jesus Christ for the other works that I am undertaking for the great glory of God. I already know that you and the sisters are doing so. I write about it to make you keep it in mind and to prompt your fervor and thus to have you do it with greater commitment.

You have good reason to want to correspond to the divine grace of seeing oneself as being ungrateful to the Highest Good. That is our reality. But console yourself that you can offer to the Holy Trinity [*the gift of*] Jesus Christ and so satisfy [*the debt*] of gratitude, praise, honor and satisfaction you owe. Continuously offer the merits of the divine Son: and so you will give infinite satisfaction. The Divine Goodness, Majesty and Grandeur [*the Son*] offers thanks to the same Infinite Goodness [*the Father*].

---

[296] *Ragioni cattoliche e politiche in difesa della città rovinate dall'insolentito meretricio,* Naples 1736.

Finally, do not forget to recommend me to the Lord while I find myself in the midst of battling against a corrupt world and I am forced to deal with half the world amid my great suffering. I do not stop praying especially for you and all the sisters, to whom I send my respects. I hope that you and all of them receive the fullness of the most tender heavenly blessings; that is what I beg His Divine Majesty for you.

I remain offering you my most humble respects.

Naples, March 7, 1737

TO SISTER MARIA ANGELA DEL CIELO, SUPERIOR OF THE SCALA MONASTERY (FEBRUARY I, I738)[297]

Scruples about celebrating Masses.

Most Esteemed Mother,

After I wrote my other letter, I now add that, sympathizing with your great needs, I am taking fifty Mass intentions that I have received and sending you the responsibility of having them celebrated according to my intentions. Therefore, you can tell the Most Illustrious Monsignor to see that these Masses are celebrated according to my intention and, once they are celebrated, that he send me notice. Moreover, tell Monsignor X or Father Confessor Y that these Masses must be celebrated *ex iustitia* [*out of justice*] because they have received a stipend for them. Thus they cannot be the kind of Mass intentions that some priest are accustomed to fulfill by deducting one day off each week although their obligation is for Mass to be said *quotidie* [*daily*] as the benefactor has ordered. All of these [*Masses*] must be celebrated to satisfy in justice the one who gave the stipend. I write this to unburden my conscience and to follow the Lord's will who does not wish that in performing a charitable act one does not have to pay any attention to justice. This worries me every time I forward some intentions. Please see that these fifty Masses are said as soon as possible according to my intentions. If I can send more soon,

---

[297] *Lettere di Sarnelli*, Libro I, Lettera III, 19–20.

I will try to do so even at my great inconvenience. Keep this letter so that when I send more intentions like this they will be celebrated according to the above directions.

The money for these Masses (I am talking about five ducats), I cannot send you right now because I don't actually have it. But when the person who has requested the celebration of the Masses gives it to me, I will immediately send it to you. I know I will have to wait a few months but the money is very certain.

Finally, I close, offering my most humble reverence not only to you but also to all the sisters. I wish you the fullness of blessings of God's kindness *de rore Coeli et de pinguedine terrae.*[298] I heartily commend myself to your prayers, both private and in community, for I have the greatest need of them for myself and for my work for the spiritual good of our neighbors. Long live the Most Holy Trinity and the Most Holy Mary Immaculate.

Naples, February 1, 1738

P.S. I am sending four ducats right now.[299]

TO SISTER MARIA ANGELA DEL CIELO, SUPERIOR OF THE SCALA MONASTERY (UNDATED)[300]

Consolation in God when one's words serve to comfort others. Response to the question of how it is possible for hardness of heart to be joined to the desire to please God. Invitation to humble oneself but not to be weak and how to incite the sister to zeal for salvation.

Long live the Most Holy Trinity and the Most Holy Mary Immaculate

Most Esteemed Mother,

I received your letter. I thank you very, very much, and all the sisters as well, for the great love you have shown me. They may be sure

---

[298] From the dew of heaven and the fullness of the earth.

[299] This postscript seems to contradict the statement in the letter that Sarnelli could not send the stipend. Probably, after finishing the letter but before posting it, he somehow acquired money to cover a part of the stipend.

[300] *Lettere di Sarnelli*, Libro I, Lettera IV, 20–23.

that the more they pray for me to the Lord, ever greater good will descend upon them. I will write a letter to all of you together that you can read to them and remind them often what I suggest in it. I say this not less to all the sisters than to yourself to whom I recommend myself.

I am sending you the disciplines you requested, one for Sister Maria W and the other for Sister Maria X. I also send the holy cards for those who are dying to Sister Maria Y and the dyes for Sister Maria Z.

My Lady Mother offers her most humble reverences to you and all the sisters, and she warmly recommends herself and the whole family to your prayers. It was all right not to write directly to her; I will act as your secretary.

I never stop feeling consoled in the presence of Almighty God and of thanking him when my words are of some comfort to others. Everything comes as a gift of the infinite love of God that he shows through your trust and merits, even though I deserve nothing but hell.

As to your desires, they are all holy and meritorious. If it seems to you that you are not reaching the level of virtue that you want, do not be upset nor upbraid yourself because the Lord wants you to realize who you are and who he is. Therefore seek to desire great things, to pray, to suffer, and to embrace the Cross of Jesus Christ, and have no fears. His Divine Majesty will console you greatly, very greatly and amid your pain and coldness of heart he will evermore see that you acquire self-awareness. The foundations of the building are being laid, the building he wants to construct in your soul.

You asked me how coldness of heart and the desire to please God can exist at the same time. I answer that this is the effect of the desolation and interior pain, and these are the trails that spiritual persons must undergo, trials that do not show any external effects but only internal ones. If you were having tender feelings of heart, brilliant lights and a sense of grace, there would be no cross, no suffering. But the Lord wants to keep you on a cross, not on cushions, and in this way to strengthen your desires. You want to suffer for God and glorify him. The great desires you have to please your God, these are your reward, these are your glorification of God. The pain that you find in coldness of heart, in aridity and in desolation, is precisely what it means for you to suffer to be pleasing of God. Therefore always cry out: *Blessed be God; thanks be to God; praise be to God however he treats me. It is enough that he fulfills his will in me and that he remains glorified and pleased in me.*

Be full of joy: embrace the cross of your Spouse and hug it to your heart. Pray to him that he give you great love for his holy cross. Don't you see that by the way of the cross, His Divine Majesty wishes to lead you to himself, to conform you to his beloved only begotten Son whom he sent into the world to live amid crosses and to die on the Cross?

You are truly doing the right thing when you sink yourself into the abyss of your nothingness and give yourself over to the recognition of yourself. But I do not want such a thought to be so intense that it makes you become cowardly. After you have realized your nothingness and your lack of dignity, forget your own being and throw yourself entirely on the immense bosom of your dear heavenly Father. Open your heart and be very confident. Say with St. Paul, *I am all-powerful in the God who comforts me: I can do all things through him who strengthens me.*[301] Remember always that God is God and cry out continuously: *You are my God. O God, your mercies are infinitely greater than my misery.*

Finally, I recommend that you always enkindle a holy zeal for salvation in your sisters, and always keep them in mind of it. I do not cease to pray to His Divine Majesty for you and I hope to do so as long as I live and never to forget to do so. Thus I am sure that you do the same for me and for all my work for God and for my holy plans and desires that require a great deal of prayer in order to succeed.

I close by offering my most humble regards and begging His Divine Majesty to fill you with his dearest and most abundant blessings every hour, everywhere and at every moment. Oh, let us have the greatest desire that the Supreme Good be known and loved by all the world; then I will be happy to die!

Blessed and glorified be Jesus Christ and the Most Holy Mary.

---

[301] Philippians 4:13.

TO SISTER MARIA ANGELA DEL CIELO, MEMBER OF THE SCALA MONASTERY (UNDATED)[302]

Sister Maria Angela has completed her term of superior. Sarnelli gives her advice on the difficulties she has in observing the Rule and in the controversies that have arisen among the nuns.

Long live the Most Holy Trinity and the Most Holy Mary Immaculate

Most Esteemed Sister,

I am answering your past letter. I sympathize deeply with the community's difficulties. I have written two long letters to the superior giving some ideas about how to remedy such evils. I felt great satisfaction in hearing that you have withdrawn for a retreat; therefore, take courage to combat, resist and conquer, and do not be overcome by these tempests. I wish that all the sisters would do the same, one at a time, to find comfort and grow much closer to God as the devil seeks to divide them. Suggest this as best you can to avert the great storm that seeks to threaten you all and so you can lessen the strong reactions that then follow to disturb you. This way you will all get closer to God and deal more effectively with the matters of community peace and quiet before God who alone can lead you to a happy ending. I hope that he does so in his own time out of his goodness. Moreover, I desire that the sisters not commit sins and omissions since the Lord only permits these problems in order to test your virtue and so see if you truly love him with all your heart.

I thank the Lord for your spiritual peace. May His Divine Majesty increase it ever more. It is a gift of God; so thank him. I want this same peace to come to all the sisters during this turmoil. Let this peace which you feel not cause you to forget the common good; do your part to bring this about as much as you can by your prayer, advice, good example and other human means so that it returns to your house of God.

Do not stop helping everybody with every kind word, even those who are the most contrary and needy, no matter how much these seem to you to be the cause of the entire disturbance. David, while he fled

---

[302] *Lettere di Sarnelli,* Libro I, Lettera V, 23–25.

as his own son was hunting him to put him to death, met a man called Shimei who beat him down with insults and who even threw stones. David's captains wanted to get even. No, said David, "I do not want that. Leave him alone so that he may speak evil of me and mistreat me. God wishes that I be mistreated by him."[303] Therefore always try to hint at the way of truth and of peace in their awareness. Have pity on the most contrary ones and try to lead them back to a good conclusion.

I do not feel very well and this evening I suffered a terrible loss of blood from my head that is still bothering me. May Jesus Christ be ever blessed. Perhaps I will not give the mission of the Holy Spirit because of this malady. If they make me give it, I will expose myself to death. Help me with your prayers that I may determine the Most Holy Will of God.

I pray for you and for the whole community and I also asked others to do the same. May the Lord grant my desires and yours.

I wish you a flood of blessings from the Most Holy Trinity.

TO SISTER MARIA ANGELA DEL CIELO, MEMBER OF THE SCALA MONASTERY (UNDATED)[304]

He continues to give her advice on the same topic. He urges her to penance and asks that she pray for him.

Long live the Most Holy Trinity and the Most Holy Mary Immaculate

Most Esteemed Sister,

This morning I received your letter from which I understand that His Divine Majesty has willed for my last letter to you to add more suffering to those you already have, instead of relieving them. You should also offer this as a sacrifice to the Lord. But I tell you and assure you that that letter was not in fact intended for you but for some of the other

---

[303] 2 Samuel 16:11: "Let him alone, and let him curse; for the Lord has bidden him."
[304] *Lettere di Sarnelli*, Libro I, Lettera VI, 25–29.

sisters so that, when you had the chance, you would tell them aloud what I had written you. I have heard from other sources that there is a sister who is a bit resentful and is opposed to the orders of Bishop X [*Falcoia*], and who speaks willfully with little propriety about her own feelings. I also figured this out from many clues. You may speak to them at the opportune moment about my observations; that is why I wrote you. If they do not listen to what I say, and they are not getting the advice of others, they will surely fall into the error of following their own will and impulse without objectivity and therefore dangerously. I do not say this to you, not even implicitly, because I know that you do not act in even small matters without taking precaution or without the regard for the guidance which the Church and spiritual writers have based on the Holy Scriptures. I must write that way for the sake of the common good and to rein in any resentful and discontent person. Yes, the present situation may be a little bitter; it is necessary to offer this bitterness to God and suffer for the common good in order not to fall into something worse, more bitter and more widespread. You should go speak very nicely to any of the sisters who usually seems to be most guilty so that when another occasion arises she will be more moderate.

I appreciate your virtue of excusing the sisters, but in this matter, when a correction is necessary, it is not proper [*to excuse her*] since the sister's fault can bring damage to the whole community. In these cases, what is needed is correction, a kind and charitable one, yes, but not an excuse. Indeed, I already know that you have not said something that is not the case, since some of the sisters have created their own resentment, and have sided with those whose opinion or attitude does not agree with yours even though they are aware that you are against it. But no matter what they feel, correct them because that is what God wants. That's enough of that.

You do well to write once in a while to Bishop X, but not often, either about matters of conscience or other matters; appreciate your good fortune whether he replies or not, even if you feel seriously offended. Just raise your eyes to heaven and offer it all to Jesus. While you offer a sacrifice of praise to God, if Bishop X thinks you are guilty or wants to test you, he is making a different kind of offering to God because he believes he should act in this way for the common good. Keep on going and thank His Divine Majesty no matter what happens. Also write to Father Don Alphonsus once in a while and tell him what you tell me, namely that you do not understand what you are missing in dealing with Bishop X, that you write him and try to take good care of the sisters and that they exhibit true humility. For your part, do what you can and then live quietly and secure, whatever happens.

As to yourself, I am saddened over your sufferings, but I rejoice at your progress because I assure you that in your sufferings you are truly glorifying the Lord and that Jesus Christ remains pleased with your stricken soul. Take heart and do not fear. This is the way you become a saint: suffer greatly, suffer always and suffer in every way. I remember that in the last letter you wrote me during the novena for the feast of the Annunciation before going on retreat, you told me that what you especially want from Mary Most Holy is the grace of true humility and of belonging completely, completely to Jesus. Look at how our dear divine Mother has heard your prayer. This is exactly the means to completely fulfill your desires by suffering what you have to suffer, to suffer it with faith, hope, love, joy and thanks, even if it means bearing the pains of hell. Be of good heart because the Lord wishes to give you great graces and prepare you by this fire to strengthen you more and to perfect you in order to make you capable of receiving even more of the treasures of his grace.

I feel I must tell you that now you are nothing before God or before the sisters. Thank the Lord who is giving you this awareness and who keeps you in this state because this road leads to total emptying of yourself, true detachment from every created thing and perfect abandonment into the divine blessing and the profound knowledge of the very being and greatness and mercy of God. Repeat often: *Pater, non mea voluntas, sed tua fiat.*[305] Then with merely a glance but with deep thought, place everything in you into the bosom of God's good will. The devil will tell you that in this suffering you are neither pleasing God nor are you glorifying him. In response to this temptation, open your eyes to the immense embrace of the divine goodness and rest in that.

Moreover, do not forget to pray steadily for me and for this work of God that I am promoting. When you can, read a little of my new book that I sent you,[306] especially the section on prayer. And entreat the Most Holy Trinity that it draw all people to holy prayer and make this world a world of prayer. Beg the Lord to enlighten prelates to promote this work

---

[305] "Father, not what I want but what you want" (Mark 14:36).

[306] *Il mondo santificato.*

of common mental prayer in their dioceses so it may sanctify them, and pray for the people that they respond and give themselves to prayer and profit from it.

Finally, rest with Jesus Christ. I want endless blessings on you from the Most Holy Trinity. I never stop recommending you to the Lord.

Greet Sister X for me and tell her that she should desire to be holy and that she not follow the example of any of the resentful sisters but follow your example. Tell her I pray for her and that she should do so for me and that she may profit from her retreat.

If there is anything that I can do for you in any way, let me know. Long live Jesus and Mary.

TO SISTER MARIA ANGELA DEL CIELO, MEMBER OF THE SCALA MONASTERY (UNDATED) [307]

He mentions problems with the mail, the way of self denial and how to face community problems.

Long live the Most Holy Trinity and the Most Holy Mary Immaculate

Most Esteemed Sister,

I have been worried because I have written you four times and received no response and I had no idea why. This was bothering me since, knowing your problems, I wanted to offer some help but I could not do so if you did not give me a chance. I just received your long letter dated August 11, but the one you sent me on the fourth I have not received. I have not gotten any other letters after the one in which you asked about a matter of conscience.

I wrote the superior in response to her letter; I think she has received it.

---

[307] *Lettere di Sarnelli*, Libro I, Lettera VII, 29–32.

I have written an additional letter that you can have the Canon [*Romano*] read.

Read it in my name to the superior and to the others as your prudence dictates, and keep it so that anyone can realize that I do not defend the Canon, but rather seek truth and the common good. Read it also to the sisters who favor the Bishop [*Falcoia*] and are opposed to the Canon. I say "opposed" because they believe that is what they must do; they all know their own consciences. If this succeeds, I hope that the entire disturbance will end.

I wrote you to inform the Bishop of what happened because he did not take your side, and I wrote that even Sister Maria X would also write him because the Bishop considers her objective, so she would be listened to with greater attention. There is more reason that the superior write him because she favors the Bishop's position (something I want for all the sisters, except in this case that offends against justice because the Bishop is poorly informed about it) and so will be favorably heard.

Tell me, who is now the Vicar?

Meanwhile, I advise you to make sure the superior, and all the sisters who do not already understand, that what you are doing is not attempting to disobey but only to keep this point of justice inviolable which the Bishop does not understand because he has been poorly informed. And [*let them understand that*], except on this point, you trample down all consideration of gratitude, worldly honor, pity, your own inclinations, whatever anyone may say, everything even to the point of shedding your blood or losing your life. Just do not betray God and your own soul by agreeing with a manifest injustice demanded by the Bishop because he does not understand the case. In factual matters, even the pope can make a mistake. Make them understand that, since you have clearly established this truth in your heart, namely, that the Bishop is not well informed of the facts and that the law of God does not allow you to demand it of others [*Let them know*] that this is your only intention for having undertaken this opposition.

Let everyone, the sisters and others, know what I am writing and bring it to their attention at the right moment: the superior, the sisters, the Bishop, Father Don Alphonsus, and Don Giovanni [*Mazzini*]. You have to wipe out of their minds the evil thoughts they have about you, not to justify your own glory, but for the sake of the good example that you must give for the common good and because the glory of God demands it. Justify yourself, but with peace, humility, resignation and truth.

I am happy to hear about the attempts made with the Canon to make things turn out well, and I also feel good that the sisters have not said anything to you except to follow the Bishop's orders even though he is ill-informed. The superior, the superior is obliged to inform him of the truth if the Bishop does not believe you.

I suspect, I am speaking in general, I do not know particulars of the case. I fear that in your community there is someone with an imagination full of wild ideas who, while meaning well, writes down your remarks for the Bishop and creates more than one misconception that the saintly old man takes to heart. Or perhaps there may be someone who has his confidence from whom he is misinformed and basing himself on the information received from this zealous and sincere soul to whom he is attached and partial, he believes everything said absolutely and questions your innocence. If such a person exists, she is the ruin of the community and the destroyer of the holy love of God and of neighbor. Indeed, zeal is holy if it notifies a superior of disorders. But one must do so with countless reservations, cautions and prudence. And such a person who does this must be, so to speak, ten times more holy, ten times more prudent, ten times more zealous and completely full of proper charity that is not disordered; she must be a woman ten times wiser than any other woman and a lot wiser than a wise man. Otherwise her reports are like weeds.

I end now by paying my respects to all, the superior, the sisters, the boarders. I recommend myself to the prayers of all. I do not cease to pray for all and to ask others to do the same. I pray and I wish thousands and thousands of blessings at every moment from the Most Holy Trinity.

I am greatly consoled that Sister Mary Y is getting along well. Offer her my respects and tell her that I do not stop praying to the Lord for her. May she do the same for me and may she not draw back from the promises she made to Jesus Christ and to the Most Holy Mary. May the Lord bless her always.

To Sister Maria Angela del Cielo,
Member of the Scala Monastery (Undated)[308]

He congratulates her over the peace reached in her community and gives further advice on that topic. He urges her to respond to her holy desires and divine inspirations. He mentions his own problems.

Long live the Most Holy Trinity and the Most Holy Mary Immaculate
Most Esteemed Sister,

I heartily thank the Most Holy Trinity for the peace and grace granted to your community. I hope in the Lord that he may choose to prove to you the truth of that great saying of the Apostle that, for the chosen ones, all things will work together well; even sins are the motive to humble themselves all the more, for lowering pride in themselves, for being more cautious, for more tears, for more confidence in God and for more love of the Infinite goodness.

Now the sisters must realize that they should not become upset over events, but rather trust in God and wait for his help with faith, patience and peace.

Meanwhile, I ask, at least for my sake, that those sisters, who might not yet be entirely satisfied, be well disposed. I tell them that, otherwise, they would be showing stubbornness because it has become clear that all the events of the past were disposed by God for the greater advancement and cautioning of the community. Say to them as well that, not only should they not find a problem in asking the Bishop for Father E as a substitute, but they should be willing to do so and thank the Lord. The difficulties they are having with Father D are frivolous. If they are not totally pleased with him, for this very reason they should obey him if they are spiritual souls as I believe. Such persons know very well that their pleasure should be directed toward the Creator and not the creature, toward heaven and not earth. One of the first rules of the spirit is to mortify and deny oneself, renouncing all the laws and rules of self-love and self-will, and to see to it that these products

---

[308] *Lettere di Sarnelli*, Libro I, Lettera VIII, 32–35.

of our heart die to all that regards our own inclinations, even if they are spiritual and innocent. There is no other means. But if then they wish to have Father E… in place of Father D, they will be quickly heard. But they must decide between one of the two. If they think the other will be more conducive to the common good, then they have reason to ask for him. But if they do not get the one they want, they must always thank God for the decision. In a happy eternity all their desires will be met, but in this valley of tears, in this exile, it is enough that they can be guided in the way to heaven in the best way possible. And in my opinion, they will find that in the advice of Father E… Tell them all this in my name and, at the same time, tell them to ask the prelates for Father E… I do not think at all that even one [*of the nuns*] will find him unsuitable.

I am sending more chocolate. When you need some and have no other means, I will not fail to send you some when I can.

Finding an hour glass is driving me crazy. I have tried many and none of them is what you want. The half-hour timers were large, made of walnut and worked well. But you asked for a one hour timer.

As to your desires, actions and divine inspirations, thank the Lord and respond faithfully. I believe it is well that you would like to be freed of the prison of the body and to give your soul over to the desired rest. But in this world what you want is not possible. Up to our last breath, we must bear the burden of the body that the Lord allows us to feel in order to see how we strive to run to him, to bring it about that we do violence to ourselves and so conquer by combat. We go on drawing nearer to that Highest Good as if we were rowing a boat by the strength of our arms. That way, by keeping before our eyes this unwieldy mortality, we always recognize our own nothingness and, by setting aside self-trust, we then trust in that Infinite Goodness that is the whole reason for our hope. The time will come when you will see this weight lifted.

Now we come to my own troubles what will surpass your belief. Only God knows them and can understand them. Up to now I have felt your troubles, I mean the ones of the community, and I have shared in them. Reason and sisterly charity wish that you also share in my difficulties. I will not explain them for countless just and reasonable motives, but I assure you that all of them, old and new, new and old, are incredibly intense *usque ad mortem*,[309] long-lasting, without a break, and innumerable. But, with all that my heart can express and for every possible reason that I could bring up to spur you on to greater commitment and fervor, I place them all in your hands and beg your prayers for all of them. Commit yourself to begging the Lord and the Mother of God for me, for the sake of his greater glory, for my greater good, for the Church and for my neighbor that he enlighten me to deal properly with many things that I desire and that I need, but lack the understanding of why or how to do so. Enough: the strong, loving light of my God can do all, knows all, and reaches all. Tell the other sisters the same thing so that they act with all their strength. I also wrote to the superior to offer community prayer for me. I urgently ask the same thing of you and tell you that in all this I long to see the effect of your prayers. Remember me and speak of me to the Most Holy Trinity, Mary Most Holy and all heaven. Pray to the Most Holy Trinity through Jesus Christ. Nevertheless, I say this in every way I can: since general grace is for the greater glory of God, these things could not happen unless God wants them or if they were not worthwhile. It is only my faults that can lay down obstacles and it is because of these I beg heaven and your merits.

TO SISTER MARIA ANGELA DEL CIELO, MEMBER OF THE SCALA MONASTERY (SEPTEMBER 5, 1741)[310]

He urges her to read the book on The Holy Rosary of Mary and The Desolate Soul. Advice on that topic. He advises her to perform her tasks with a sense of confidence and he agrees to guide her in spiritual direction but he wants to explain the conditions of this direction, especially at this time that he is involved in the great mission in the suburbs of Naples. He asks for her prayers and those of the community for various reasons.

---

[309] *Even unto death.*

[310] *Lettere di Sarnelli*, Libro I, Lettera IX, 35–38.

Long live the Most Holy Trinity and the Most Holy Mary Immaculate.
Most Esteemed Sister,

I received your letter and, since a new book of mine on the holy
rosary of Mary has just been published, I am now sending you a copy. I
ask you to have it read in common.

I sympathize greatly with your sufferings and troubles. Take comfort
in the Lord and have no doubt that it is entirely God's love for you that
is leading you in this most secure and meritorious path of suffering.
Revive your faith that His Most Divine Majesty arranges everything
for his greater glory and for your greater good. Do not give up precisely
on this point of confidence in the infinite good and live with the greatest
assurance that the Lord will, even in this life, enable you to understand
how uniquely and kindly you are regarded and that these storms
are sent because of the great love God has for you. May the loving
Mary, Mother of Mercy, reach into your heart and be your comfort in
suffering.

I am happy to hear that you are reading my books and that by
God's goodness they are of some comfort to you. I urge you not to
omit reading the entire important one, *l'Anima desolata [The Desolate
Soul]*. Let me know if the other sisters have read it and what impression
it made on them. I recognize and thank the goodness of the Lord that
has allowed me to produce this little work to bring comfort to many
persons. I do not think that any other work has proven more effective
for people of every state in life.

I appreciate that you live without direction and contacts and that
you have desired some of my help, even though I am so poor at it that I
appreciate the good fortune of having someone direct and help my poor
soul. In fact, I have obtained the permission of the one who stands in
God's place for me for you to be allowed to write me every so often
and that I can reply only about what you ask me. I therefore offer to
be of as much help as I can and whenever I can. Just so you know: I will
be leaving in November to scour all the towns and suburbs of Naples
giving missions at the command of our cardinal, who has assigned me
a stable residence in one of the places that is very close to Barra so we
can then visit and journey throughout the diocese. Thus, I will not be in
Naples all the time but come and go for short periods. You can address a

few letters to Mr. X who is responsible for my belongings and he will let me know about them or give them to me when I go to Naples.

So these are the conditions under which you may write me and I may reply:

1) That you mention this plan only to the superior to whom you must report. No other sister is to know you are writing me and I am responding, except when I send you a book for the community because then it doesn't matter that they know.

2) That this correspondence is not called or seen as individual spiritual direction as if you are entirely dependent on me [*as your spiritual director*]. Then I will answer you the same way I answer others who write me. And I will do it more generously with you because I am sure of three things: a) that you will always pray to God for me; b) that you will profit from them by the Lord's help, and c) that you are writing for your spiritual wellbeing, and not just to pass time or to let off steam, and it will be done soberly and at the proper time.

Meanwhile I ask you to recommend me most warmly to the Lord, since I find myself in mortal anguish both interiorly and exteriorly. Just a short time ago I got news that was so bitter and of such disturbance that I don't even know where I'm at. I can only say: "Your will be done, O my Lord!" Moreover, I want to let you know that His Eminence has made me responsible for all the people of these towns and environs, which means about 100,000 souls. So, since I have to start up this great enterprise, pray to His Divine Majesty for me so I have divine assistance, and if I am unable to carry this enterprise out but rather should be spending my time publishing other spiritual books, that His Divine Majesty arranges things so I can undertake whatever will work out for his greater glory. Meanwhile, yesterday something pertaining to another matter came up that sidetracked me from this work in the villages, and it brought up some more problems. I ask you, and others whom you can persuade, to recommend to the Lord that I can complete it all for his great glory, for my soul and for the good of my neighbors.

I am saddened over the death of Bishop Santoro. Still, the will of the Lord is the great cure for all ills to which we must always resign ourselves.

Give the superior my compliments. For my part, I always pray for the spirit of the community and I ask her to pray for me as well as have her community do the same, begging the Lord and the Most

Holy Mary for me while I do the same for her and for all the good sisters there. Also pay my respects to all the sisters and especially to those whom you mentioned in your letter; recommend me again to the very warm and efficacious prayers of all. To all the students I send my blessings and above all I profess my desire that you and all these servants of God become truly holy.

Naples, September 5, 1741

TO SISTER MARIA ANGELA DEL CIELO, MEMBER OF THE SCALA MONASTERY (DECEMBER 31, 1741) [311]

He tells of the bout of sickness he is experiencing and mentions items he is sending her. He congratulates the community on its peace and unity.

Long live the Most Holy Trinity and the Most Holy Mary Immaculate

Most Esteemed Sister,

I should have written these lines on a separate page along with the other one I sent but I did not feel able to do so. After I wrote to the superior, I was overcome by a worse illness that forced me to go to bed and to stop offering the Holy Sacrifice. I am in the Lord's hands. I do not know where things will end up. May God's will always be done. I refer to what I wrote in my other letter to the superior about my health. I am sure of your kindness.

Ten cruets were sent but two of them were broken and another one I made them change. I do not know if they are what you like, but I do not know what else to do since I went to the glassmaker and had them made to order and was insistent. Naples has become impossible, especially for someone who uses few words and doesn't haggle.

I sent two pounds of chocolate. I hope to soon send you more. When there is something in which I have the ability to help and for which you are depending on me, please feel free to ask me because I am happy to assist you.

---

[311] *Lettere di Sarnelli,* Libro I, Lettera X, 38–40.

I am happy over the unity, peace and charity that I hoped for and was announced from the heavens: *Gloria in excelsis Deo et in terra pax hominibus bonae voluntatis.*[312] I surely hope that all the defects and nastiness work together for the good of all. I appreciate the penances, humiliations and confessions of each one's shortcomings. May they glorify God. I suspect that by your example and your suggestions you had a helpful hand in such holy actions.

Let me know why Sister Y, Sister X and Sister Z wrote me, that is, what prompted them to write without your saying anything to them.

Also tell me if all the sisters are fully docile to the suggestions of Bishop [*Falcoia*]. If anyone has not given in, out of charity convince her and induce her not to disturb the common good, because I have never discovered, nor do I see, any other way than this for you to arrive at unity and peace. Moreover, to help her see this, ask her what she thinks, what would she do to bring peace. If she can find a better way, great; but if not, she will have to give in. I believe that by your power of persuasion and her docility to the grace of God, she will agree.

Give my respects to all. A thousand blessings on all. May they pray for me. Etc.

The last day of the year.

TO SISTER MARIA ANGELA DEL CIELO, MEMBER OF THE SCALA MONASTERY (UNDATED)[313]

He begs her to have her community make a novena for his ministry and his health. He asks their assistance in preparing some holy cards.

Long live the Most Holy Trinity and the Most Holy Mary Immaculate

Most Esteemed Sister,

---

[312] "Glory to God in the highest heaven, and on earth peace among those whom he favors!" (Luke 2:14).

[313] *Lettere di Sarnelli*, Libro I, Lettera XI, 40–41.

I received your two letters and answered them at length some time ago by means of Signor X. I later sent you another folder for the holy novena.

I just got another one from you with the letter from Sister X enclosed to which I am responding and including with this one.

I am in Naples. I am sending you twenty-eight candles for the holy novena; I will get them off to you as soon as I can.

I send a little box of very fine chocolates for the pleasure of your community. They weigh about six or seven *libbre*.[314]

It is now clear how important it is for you to pray to Jesus Christ and the Most Holy Mary for me. Otherwise, you would soon lose me. My troubles and difficulties increase day by day. I am totally at a loss how to get out of them successfully. I have never found myself in the state I am these days, without relief and knowing no way out except to pray and trust and have prayers for me said to his Divine Majesty and the Most Holy Mary.

So I recommend this very grave trial of mine to your prayers and those of your whole community. I well recognize that they are bringing bad effects on my neighbor. Nevertheless, I adore the very lofty divine decisions and resign myself to his will. God knows what to do. Meanwhile, I have prayers said for me because I know that is what God wants. For the rest, I suffer and remain quiet. May God be ever blessed; he sees to it that a small heart may suffer so much and still remain standing. May his holy will be done and glorified.

May you keep well. I extend to you countless heavenly blessings and I realize that your life is always accompanied by the blessings of holy obedience.

P.S. I wanted to send the enclosed letter unsealed so that Mother Superior might read it. But then I thought it over a lot and I cannot in conscience do so. Indeed, it is your rule that the superior can open letters of conscience that come to her religious sisters and read them; she can open them, read them, then she can put them back in the envelope, seal them and hand them on to the addressee so that she does not know or suspect. I think that the superior can do this according to your rule.

I am sending a stack of small printed holy cards of the Immaculate Conception of Mary. Please do me the favor of cutting them apart, then placing them in the Blessed Sacrament tabernacle as is the custom,

---

[314] Approximately 4 lbs or 4.2 kg.

accompanied with your prayers, and then forwarding them to me just as you did for me before. However, if nowadays it would seem shocking to put them in the tabernacle, don't bother so as not to upset anyone. Instead, put them rather in the hands or at the feet of the [*statue of the*] Madonna in the monastery.

TO SISTER MARIA ANGELA DEL CIELO, MEMBER OF THE SCALA MONASTERY (MARCH 31, 1742)[315]

He sends some booklets and other devotional items. He speaks of assisting her in her spiritual direction and begs her prayers and those of her community in his difficulties. He expresses his concern over the superior's sickness and offers advice on remaining trustful in the Lord.

Long live the Most Holy Trinity and the Most Holy Mary Immaculate Most Esteemed Sister,

I received your letter with the note saying you received the booklets and the candles. I thank you and your dear sister religious for having done me the great favor of offering the novena you just began. This has given me great comfort amid all my grave difficulties. I am sending along an envelope containing three different kinds of rosaries so you can take the one you like and share the rest with the others. I am also including five of the booklets you asked for and a good many sheets of the holy cards of the Immaculate Conception of Mary. This way you can pass them out to your community as a favor to me. Since I have arranged for my book to be printed, I find myself in such poverty and shambles that at times I do not even have enough for my own upkeep. Blessed be God that at the cost of some pain of every kind for me, he has given me reason to do good for so many people.

It has been several months since I sent you another packet of booklets like these along with a letter in response to your earlier one. But I don't think you received either the booklets or the letter.

---

[315] *Lettere di Sarnelli*, Libro I, Lettera XII, 42–45.

In your letter to me you say that you had at times wanted to write me since you found yourself without any permanent direction for a spiritual advisor. I told you, and I tell you again now, that the Lord placed me here on earth, not for my sake, but for the good of others and I have committed myself to others. Thus, I do not hesitate in the slightest to give myself and whatever poor strength I have in service to you as well whenever you wish to write me and need a response. I am well acquainted with your discretion and prudence in avoiding taking up my time with useless matters although I am not properly your spiritual director, but only an advisor and comforter in matters of conscience. This is what I am for many others when I can do so without detriment to my ministry and if I am capable of helping. I lay this before your judgment and I will not refuse you insofar as I can offer some small part of my effort. I do this for many others to whom I am not under the same obligation as I am to you because of your constant prayer for this poor person standing before His Divine Majesty.

Rather, I have to thank you very much because you do not leave off frequent and even daily prayers for me to the Lord. You cannot imagine the great need I have; only God knows.

That Infinite Good, as you know, who sees that my prayers for help do not match my needs, inspires and moves others to pray for me. Still, I beg your charity in not overlooking your fervent prayers for me to the Most Holy Trinity, our Lord Jesus Christ and the Mother of God. There is no other hope in this world except in God alone, no other comfort except in the sacred prayers you make for me. For my part, I promise you again my weak prayers to the Lord for your spiritual growth. This I have done in a special way, I do it now and, with God's help, I will continue to do so.

I am sorry to hear that Mother Superior is so ill. Be sure to have no doubt: suffering while not dying is a grace from the Lord. Tell her of my concern and ask her to recommend me to the Lord as I do her.

I rejoice greatly over the peace and unity in your community. I thank the divine goodness for it and I pray that it may remain permanently and always increase. This is the ordinary working of divine Providence: to send calm after the storm. Blessed be God!

I am pleased that you read my books, mainly *l'Anima desolata* and *l'Anima illuminata*. See to it, as well, that they are read in common and especially by other women religious, as is done in almost all monasteries of religious in this city and in other places, with great comfort and profit through the mercy and goodness of God.

Meanwhile, make efforts to trust evermore in the divine goodness and grow in holy confidence and rest secure in the bosom of that great love. He who began the work will bring it to completion. Firmly believe that the Lord helps from very near and has special care for your soul. May you recognize this so you know how to thank him and to respond ever more jealously to his infinite love.

I urge you to pay my respects to all of the other servants of God there. Tell them to pray for me, while I also beg the Lord for their good during the Holy Sacrifice. I also thank you for the holy novena you offered with fervent prayers for this poor soul and his life. I wish you and to all the fullness of heavenly blessing now in this life, in the hour of your death and for all eternity in blessed glory where I hope to see you all.

Finally I remain, offering you my most humble reverence.

Live Jesus and Mary.

Naples, March 31, 1742

TO SISTER MARIA ANGELA DEL CIELO, MEMBER OF THE SCALA MONASTERY (MAY 18, 1742) [316]

He writes requesting prayers for the health of Father Domenico Manulio, a respected Jesuit spiritual director, who was also Sarnelli's director [Manulio was likewise one of the people Alphonsus consulted about beginning a group of missionaries to the countryside in 1732]. Sarnelli speaks about his own health and also asks her to write.

Long live the Most Holy Trinity and the Most Holy Mary Immaculate

Most Esteemed Sister,

I am sending you this letter along with the five booklets you requested in your letter. What is moving me to write you is that Father

---

[316] *Lettere di Sarnelli*, Libro I, Lettera XIV, 48–49.

Don Domenico Manuilo is in poor health and I owe no greater debt even to my own father than I owe this holy man.[317] Thus I beg you and all your dear servants of God to offer special prayers to God for his health and for his soul, since you have great merit in the eyes of God. I am sure that the City of Naples will lose a great help if it loses Father Manuilo, this holy man, full of charity and zeal that have benefited all. He now needs prayers. So besides my own weak intercessions, I ask again for your individual and community prayers. I hope you can do so and that blessed priest will return the charity, especially when he is crowned in heaven. I owe him much; now is the time to repay him love for love.

As to myself, I can say it in a couple of words: I am full of ills and more dead than alive. I am forced to take some medications. Pray for me that I enjoy a reenergizing of my forces for the glory of God, for the profit of my poor self and for the good of my neighbor. That way, by God's favor, I can accomplish many works of great consequence for the eternal salvation of all peoples, if it please Jesus Christ.

Whenever you want to write, feel perfectly free to do so, especially this month when I cannot study much because of the medications. That means I have more time to read your letters and to answer them without having to turn aside to other work.

Stay well. I am writing in a hurry. I send to you and to all countless blessings in the name of the Holy Trinity and of Jesus Christ, our Lord that his holy spirit ever increase in you. Let us take care to bring happiness to our God. *Tempus breve est*,[318] so may the deserving and infinite goodness be loved and served wholeheartedly.

I end humbly reverencing you and desiring to see you holy.

Naples, May 18, 1742.

---

[317] Father Manuilo was a Jesuit who was Sarnelli's spiritual director.
[318] Time is short.

TO SISTER MARIA ANGELA DEL CIELO, MEMBER OF THE SCALA MONASTERY (UNDATED)[319]

Sarnelli tells of Father Manuilo's death. He also speaks of his own health and fatigue as well as the difficulty he finds in satisfying all the requests made of him by the nuns

Long live the Most Holy Trinity and the Most Holy Mary Immaculate
Most Esteemed Sister,

I received the letter that you sent me and I replied about your [*question of*] conscience in another letter I wrote you. However, I did not actually get those letters to the mail carrier and so I am enclosing them in this letter.[320]

As to the blessed Father Don Domenico Manuilo, that pious soul, who now rests in his blessed eternity (that is my sure hope), yesterday the Lord called him to himself and he passed from this life. I felt terrible sorrow over it, but this is what we are all born for, he today, we tomorrow. May the most wise will of the Lord be ever adored. We can say that in the past few months His Divine Majesty has chastised the City and Kingdom by taking to himself many of the most zealous missionaries and prelates. Regarding Father Manuilo, I thank you and Mother Superior for your charity; you all will have your reward from him as he now repays you from paradise for all the prayers you said for him; they have in no way been lost. I am sure he that he received some special help and comfort from them in his last days, all of which aided him even more to deserve a more blessed life. Indeed, you may be sure that his holy man lives with God in paradise. Do not hesitate, I beg you as well as your whole community, to offer prayers for his soul, confident that you are offering them for a saint. He will not forget to pray for all of you from heaven. Since his charity toward all was so admirable while he was on earth, how much more will it be in paradise?

I thank you that you are recommending me to the Lord. Truth to tell, I am very, very worn out and sick. I have passed a year full of fatigue

---

[319] *Lettere di Sarnelli*, Libro I, Lettera XV, 50–52.

[320] *Translator's note: The letter he refers to follows below as Letter 26.*

and trials together, such that it is only by a miracle of God and by the intercession of the Most Holy Mary that I am alive. The medicines have given me some relief to the fierce obstruction in my bowels, but my chest is still in pain. May God do what he pleases. I have sustained myself for many years in this way, not so much by medicine but more with fatigue and pain. And in this way the Lord has sometimes eased and sometimes increased the difficulties apart from any human help that proved entirely useless when it was the moment for me to suffer. I beg you and all the community to pray for me that the will of God may be fulfilled in me, and that he have pity on me even though I do not deserve it. I am very sure that both you and all those dear servants of God are doing so for me just as I do for you. Let me know at your convenience when you can make another novena before the Blessed Sacrament exposed so I may send you the candles. I always desire for you to make these novenas but not in the periods in which they conflict with novenas that are customary for you to make in your community, so that there may be a particular honor paid to the Blessed Sacrament and a special appeal for my poor self.

I am sending along ten more of the usual books so that you can distribute them to the nuns that do not already have a copy. I take this occasion to give you this private confidence that I am not displeased if you ask for something that I can take care of; I do it happily. Would that I could do more. On the other hand, I usually find it more than a little inconvenient if I must go to Naples to do [*a lot of*] errands or shopping, since I don't live in Naples any more but out in the countryside and am often running around the diocese without anyone in Naples to take charge of these inconvenient tasks. Do not say anything about this right now, but when there is an opportunity mention in general that I no longer live in town and so it is very inconvenient for me to procure things unless I have them where I live, since it is my nature to not deny anyone anything, even in small matters. Indeed, this is not a matter of cost, but it is due to the planning and effort and to the amount of time it takes since I very seldom go to Naples, just every now and then.

I am enclosing a note for Sister X along with the two books she asked me for.

Stay well. I send you countless blessings as well as upon all your works, actions, thoughts and rest; may they all be directed to God, the greatest good, who deserves to be loved and glorified in his infinite bounty.

TO SISTER MARIA ANGELA DEL CIELO, MEMBER OF THE SCALA MONASTERY (JUNE 21, [1742]) [321]

Sister Maria Angela had asked for some practical rules of life. Sarnelli answers in this and the following three letters, giving her instruction on the way to deal with herself and others. He comforts her in her troubles, counsels sincerity without scruples, and points out the difference between confidence and fear in life's battles.

Long live the Most Holy Trinity and the Most Holy Mary Immaculate
Most Esteemed Sister,

Yesterday, June 20, I received your letter. Today, the 21st, I am responding. This first page deals with your own conscience, while the second regards the questions of your community.

I feel your grace-filled discomfort. I am sorry for your suffering, but I am pleased that the Lord has so much care and concern for you to make you aware of your small faults. Always pay attention to the profit from them that the Lord, in his very personal care, wants you to find by not willingly deviating a bit from your aim and your focus. And thank the Lord for them as a blessing given you.

Keep yourself well centered in the duty given you because the Lord has placed you there through obedience.[322] Have no worry about the person assigned to your care as long as you do what you are required to do in acting for her wellbeing and instruction. When you accepted this charge under obedience, it was up to the Lord to give your spirit strength and virtue to act properly as long as you cooperate well and proceed with the proper diligence. While you may be desolate for your soul's sake, your words will not have a debilitating effect on your novice's spirit. But if God wants them to have that effect, that is best for you and for her. Do not doubt, however, it is one thing for a person to suffer in themselves and it is a different matter for that same person, through God, to succeed in instructing others.

---

[321] *Lettere di Sarnelli*, Libro I, Lettera XVI, 53–56.

[322] Sr. Maria Angela had asked Sarnelli to give her some practical guidelines for her life and her role as a novice director. In this letter and the next three, he responds to her request.

As to your sincerity, it is necessary to be very sincere without getting scrupulous, to express oneself as best one knows and can interpret what is happening, and not to go quibbling interiorly about whether to tell everything or not, to act this way or that. Whoever does not wish to voluntarily hide and pretend, the God who is faithful will not allow to be fooled; he will supply in some other way whatever you do not know how best to put into words. Sometimes it happens that you have not thought that I have understood because you did not know how best to explain it, but the Lord has seen to it that I understood you perfectly. Do not want anything else; about this matter you are scrupulous for no good reason. Explain yourself without worry as best you think you can and before writing, commend yourself to God, write in his name and forget everything else.

As to prayer, since there is nothing new here, it is not necessary to add something special on the point. Just walk faithfully along that tried and true way that the Lord is leading you. Constantly ask the Divine goodness to assist you in the great journey and guide you along the best road. Focus your mind, as far as you can, on the consideration of the life and example of Jesus Christ in order to imitate him, but not in a way that you shut out or deviate from other spiritual traits belonging to the divine Spouse amid the immense greatness of his adorable attributes.

These urges that you are suffering or, to say it more correctly, these spurts of growth for your spirit by which you want to belong entirely to God are good. But after desire there must follow action and effect by seeking out the aspects and ways that make them totally God's and not your own. And indeed in so doing, I do not want you to worry so that you become disquieted, with "how am I sure I am not doing it…how do I know if I am responding…" Just respond and pray to God that he bring it success; then you are properly responding.

The fact that you feel one minute contradicted and then next consoled, one minute moved by temptation and the next drawn to God, this is not unusual nor is it extraordinary in the spiritual life. Although this mortal journey is a battle, that does not mean it should be a battle for you, if you do not cause the rebellion, the uprising, the fight, the contradiction. Since we are made of spirit and mud, the mud has to act like mud, and the spirit has to act like spirit overcoming the shocks of its own particular mud by its virtue through the grace of God. Since our own humanity is still acting on us on one side, and on the other the Spirit of God, we sense the movements of our nature and of God's spirit. When our lower side is reluctant, when the heart wants to go the other way, when the human side seeks relief, that is "you" speaking. When the spirit seeks eternal things, looks for mortification, tramples down created things and flees creatures, that is God [*calling*]. So that the confidence is truly in God and from God, it must be accompanied by a suitable fear of one's own evil side. Therefore, we must not discard a well-regulated fear that does not disquiet but that springs from God and brings the soul to cling to God more faithfully and confidently.

It is not necessary when you give an account of your life to go around examining the fine points of each hour of your life and all your motives. It is enough if you mention what you recall when you write, because if there is something important in the past, it will surely stick in your memory. When there is nothing major and needing advice, there is no need to pick at yourself to find something.

When you feel those movements and passions, lose your spirit in the bosom of God, turn to God, think of God, and your heart will say that it wants nothing but God alone. You are right that to fully possess God and be possessed by God, you must rid yourself of your own person by denial and mortification of your own will so that it should not deviate the least bit from the will of God. It is with the action of prayer and obedience that you arrive at this with God's grace. Deepen yourself in these activities to arrive at your desire.

As to God, surely he will not cease to move you toward greater good. As to me, I will not prove lax in giving you proper advice. As to you, it is your responsibility to follow both the inspirations of God and the orders of obedience.

There is nothing left to say in response to your letter about your conscience, except to advise you to always push yourself to move forward to arrive at the understanding of the Supreme Good by the kind of perfection and denial of your own will that the Lord plans for you. The road is long, the time short. Match your diligence and your fervor to the shortness of time and brevity of life, so that you can also say: *Consumata in brevi explevit tempora multa.*[323] May the Lord accompany and bless your life, your suffering and your every relief, but on the condition that you recommend my spirit to the Lord. May the Most Holy Trinity

---

[323] "Being perfected in a short time, they accomplished many years" (Wisdom 4:13).

increase the virtues that are necessary for you to accomplish the work of your election. Stay well.

I bid you my most humble respect.

June 21, [1742]

TO SISTER MARIA ANGELA DEL CIELO, MEMBER OF THE SCALA MONASTERY (JULY 8 1742) [324]

Sarnelli expresses his commitment to the good of the community and speaks of the need he has for their prayers in his suffering and works of ministry. He continues the topic of spiritual direction. (He uses the term "Fathers of the Most Holy Savior," as the Congregation of the Most Holy Redeemer was known from 1732 to 1749.)

Long live the Most Holy Trinity and the Most Holy Mary Immaculate

Most Esteemed Sister,

After responding in a separate letter about what pertains to your conscience, I here add everything else.

I have not in fact received a letter from Mr. X; but indeed when I happen to go to Naples, I will make every effort to take care of your business. You can be sure that I desire to provide every care and help I can. May it please God and may I be able to do so. The publication of my books has brought me to such a [*financial*] state that at times I find myself without food or clothing. Blessed be God who wishes to bring success to his work amid poverty and pain!

I think you want to know my difficulties. Oh, Sister, I am nothing before God and human beings; I am not worth life or death! I do not know what to say except that God knows: I am caught up in every kind of anguish. My life, especially now for some time, has not been life, but agony and suffering. Enough. I need a lot of prayer, because no human means relieves me; in any kind of suffering, the remedy has to

---

[324] *Lettere di Sarnelli*, Libro I, Lettera XVII, 57–60.

come from on high. The only thing I have not lost is confidence in the goodness of the heavenly Father through the merits of Jesus Christ and in the intercession of the Most Holy Mary. So I beg you to pray, and ask others to pray, always and fervently for me because I have extreme need for prayer. I thank you deeply for the charity that you show in praying for me and for the novena you began. You said that the novenas are about finished unless I write you. But in that case I would have to write you every month from now on so that you keep them up. I only received your second letter (your last one) the day before yesterday and I wrote you immediately. Therefore you can forego the inconvenience of continuing this devotion of the novena on my behalf; it is enough if you frequently remember me to Jesus Christ and the Most Holy Mary, especially after Holy Communion. The Lord will reward you generously. Especially now that I have to make a great decision to accept the heavy weight of an enormous work for the sanctification of this diocese of Naples that I was carrying on with Don Alphonsus and other missionaries. But now Don Alphonsus and his companion are gone and so there is the danger of losing this infinite good that is being done but to accept it is beyond my strength.

I think that Sister Mary X wants to write me. I tell you the truth but in confidence. I am not used to ever denying a response to anyone. But I do not appreciate their writing to me, especially a woman who does not write with the desire to gain something from it and to have advice in a necessary matter. They only do it to blow off steam without gaining any profit from my response; this gives me great pain because it seems to be a waste of precious time. However, if they do it only once, it is not important; and I beg the superior not to give them permission too easily.

As to the matter of not talking about my direction, there are countless reasons why it is good not to mention it. From the beginning I asked you for secrecy with regard to all the other nuns, except for Mother Superior. Therefore, I insist on it all the more. When I send some booklets or something else, you can say that I sent the booklets or I asked for some novenas, and on that occasion you can give them all my respects and recommend me to their prayers.

As far as being silent about your direction, for a thousand reasons, it is wise to be quiet....As far as advising you to take on spiritual direction from Father [*Barbieri*], I will certainly do so, and I would do so for all [*the nuns*], if the occasion arises. However, I do not have any inclination or other thoughts or interest in proposing other directors. I esteem the priests of the Most Holy Savior, and I help them, but I am not living strictly according to their rule and under their Institute.[325]

I am sending the booklets that you requested for the convent students and novices; there are six of them, just as you asked, and I send them gladly. Whatever I have, I am happy to share. I can send what you want for the rest of the community. Indeed, if there is need or usefulness in sending a second copy of *Mondo santificato* that was just published (there are a lot of copies available) or a another one of *Anima desolata*, feel free to ask, because I am very happy to do so, just so that they are put to good use and profit and are not left to die on a shelf.

The next time you write me, remind me of some suggestions I should give you regarding your office. Do not be troubled that you make me take time away from others when you write discretely about something necessary. Then, in return for the time I spend in counseling you, your prayers must take on the task of obtaining for me from the Lord the strength and virtue to be able to gain a great deal more benefit for the other people I serve.

Considering the situation I am in, it is like swimming in the ocean, battered by waves on every side. Nevertheless, I do not stop praying often for you so that the Lord will direct and accompany my thoughts and advice that I give in his name and for his honor.

Give my regards to Mother Superior. I have not ceased recommending her to the Lord in her grave illness that saddens me. Greet all the sisters if you have a chance, and recommend me to their prayers, telling them that I pray to the Lord for all of them.

Keep well. Love with all your heart the Infinite Goodness and the Mother of God. I bless you in all your thoughts, words, works and joys; may they all be for the glory of God and for great profit to your spirit and the greater good of your neighbors.

From S. Giorgio a Cremano July 8, [1742]

---

[325] See the discussion of this remark by Domenico Capone above in Chapter Four.

TO SISTER MARIA ANGELA DEL CIELO, MEMBER OF THE SCALA MONASTERY (UNDATED) [326]

He warmly recommends himself to her prayers in his current sufferings and duties for the Diocese of Naples and also that he may avoid the scourge of plague. He asks her and community that they not forget to beg the Lord's mercy in the face of this impending punishment.

Long live the Most Holy Trinity and the Most Holy Mary Immaculate

My Most Esteemed Sister,

Now that I have written to you about your own conscience and about your community, it is time to write about your neighbor.

Because among these neighbors, I have to be first because of my role in attending to your spirit; thus, I will speak to you first about me. You must realize that I do not know whether I am on earth, in purgatory, or in hell. There are so many evils and troubles of all kinds that fall upon me that I suffer rather than live. My difficulties are known only to God and they never let up, with no comfort or respite for a single day: bitter days, frightful nights, moments of torment are what make up my life. God knows what else he sends me. All I can do, then, is suffer. I die every hour, and if I am alive, I don't know whether this state is life or death. I regret every breath I take and I fear I will die from the fear itself. If God does not do something special to help, I'm finished. The only hope I have lies in God through Jesus Christ and the Virgin Mary. But even with all the hope, I still don't find even a little relief, neither from heaven nor earth nor from creatures. I must confess, however, that God's grace keeps me going.

At the same time, besides these problems, new pains, fears, and worries continue to grow, and I do not know how to pull myself together. The plague comes ever closer bringing a clear danger in traveling to Naples and this leaves me in extreme worry. First, I have agreed to go around this province to preach, especially to the priests and clergy to dispose them to assist their people. But in this extreme heat

---

[326] *Lettere di Sarnelli*, Libro I, Lettera XVIII, 61–64. This letter is obviously part of the same packet of letters as the preceding ones dated July 4, 1742.

after eight months of constant travel and movement, and with so many problems on my shoulders, I run the risk of falling over dead. But it is better to die wearing oneself out for God because this preaching can be of extraordinary success and I must do it since there is no one else to do so. Still I am anguished and very fearful that I am exceeding my strength because I am worn out.

Another great torment is that since the pestilence is almost to Naples, which is nearby, I do not trust myself to go around ministering to those infected, because I would be the first one to fall down dead. At this point, I don't know what to do, whether to retreat to the priests in Ciorani, which in itself presents problems that trouble me even more. I seek light from heaven but a thick darkness surrounds me and I do not know how to decide. I am asking wise men here on earth but when I do not know how to explain myself, they do not know what to say to me; so I fonder battered by the most bitter waves.

For all this and for all my other greatest needs, I beg you, Mother Superior and all the community to make another ten-day novena before the Blessed Sacrament exposed beginning on Saturday July 6 and ending on the 15th. During this, all of you double your prayers for me, and you especially, first over this dangerous departure to preach, as well as for the second question, about the threat of pestilence. Please pray for me in my fear that this may be the end of my life, both that if I were to die, it would be for God and in his peace, and that it will be when and how it is pleasing to God. When I leave, you can write me if you wish because I can answer you since I am going to the areas and lands in the diocese close to Naples.

Since I have this chance, I am giving Mr. Y fourteen carlins to purchase four pounds of candles and send them to you for this novena. I am also giving him a little box with forty very beautiful little drawings that I just had printed; the craftsman made them to order; there is one for each sister. I am also sending you some sheets of holy cards; cut them apart when you get them and send me a handful. I am also sending another six pounds of chocolate.

I have recommended my soul and my life to your prayers and those of the whole community that I may sacrifice myself perfectly to the divine will.

I now recommend to you and to your community the whole world that is about to be lost. The poor city of Messina is filled with plague and Naples is on the verge. Now is the time for continuous prayers, penances, meditations, expositions, mortifications and for putting each one's conscience in order before God because the danger is everywhere and universal. Tomorrow in Naples there will be a great procession, one of penance such as has never been seen before. The cardinal will be there in penitential dress together with all the missionaries in the city of Naples. All the nobles will also be there in penitential attire; then will follow fifteen days of mission. Throughout the countryside there will be many other penitential processions, sermons, novenas, and expositions. It is your responsibility to commit yourselves to the task of placating God. You do not preach, nor hear confessions nor care for the sick. Do you want to be useless within the Church of God in assisting those of your neighbors at this time of terrible punishment? I am thinking of writing to all the bishops of the Kingdom as well as to your own bishop to have them seek this goal of placating the angry God. Call on the divine promises; pray at every moment to the Eternal Father through Jesus Christ, and to Jesus Christ through the intercession of the Most Holy Mary. Whoever loves God, now is the time to approach them. What I am writing to you, I say to all your nuns; and I send them my respects.

TO SISTER MARIA ANGELA DEL CIELO, MEMBER OF THE SCALA MONASTERY (UNDATED)[327]

He gives various points of information, state of his health and recommendations for prayer. His plans for two works he wants to publish.

Long live the Most Holy Trinity and the Most Holy Mary Immaculate

My Most Esteemed Sister,

I am writing separately about what does not pertain to your spiritual direction and its guidelines so you can keep the other letter separate and read it at the opportune time.

---

[327] *Lettere di Sarnelli*, Libro I, Lettera XIX, 64–67.

I first mention that so you can more easily correspond by writing a letter early. Indeed, if your letter is not ready when the courier comes, let him leave and then send the letter the next time. Or, if there is some urgent news or need for advice, then you can write only what is pressing, and keep the rest for another time.

As to the matter of Mr. D, I do not clearly understand what you said. I guessed that you wanted me to make a recommendation to Mr. D, on behalf of the help you had asked for the your monastery building. As you know, I do not live in the city, but outside it. So when I do go into town, I will try to oblige you, and when I get the chance I will write you about it.

With my last letter, I sent twenty-eight wax candles to use for the holy novena. I believe you received them and that you are now making the novena as I asked you, Mother Superior, and the entire community.

In the matter of your own person, you can let me know at your convenience how your health is doing, how you are getting along in your difficulties, what is giving you the most worry and suffering, and whatever is worth knowing so I can better assess how to counsel you in God's name.

I am sorry to hear of the superior's troubles. I pray to the Lord for her, begging for her good health so she can better be able to oversee and fulfill her office since the wellbeing of the sisters in the community depends so much on her care and attention. It is necessary to pray to God and to place oneself in the hands and will of his divine providence.

I say the same for myself. Believe me: I am forty years old and I don't think I have ever seen myself in such a state of continual trouble and poor health that has reached the point that everything bothers me and nothing gives me relief. What is human has not been any help for me, I mean human help and remedies. Only and always, what is divine and heavenly helps, and now more than ever. God has sent me these evils and God lifted them when he pleased. I was struggling when [*the human efforts*] came, and still struggling when they left. I have never been cured by a change of air, or medications or a health regime. God sends them himself. If it is for his pleasure and glory, I hope for and await his infinite goodness in the meantime. So I beg you and, so you may receive a greater reward, I place you under obedience but without scruple to say some special prayers for me, directing them to the Most

Holy Trinity through Jesus Christ and to Jesus Christ through Mary Most Holy. Especially make a novena for me privately and in particular, praying and praying again to the goodness of the Lord for me. Make it a point especially in this present novena to Our Lady of Grace. I promise you moreover that, besides the prayers I have said and will say to His Divine Majesty for you, to take very special care and help in your guidance as far as the goodness of the Lord allows me.

I am on the point of beginning another project, that is, publishing a book of great usefulness and importance for this diocese, this Kingdom, all Italy and (I hope) all the holy Church of God. But I do not have much strength and I feel distressed because of my weakness and dangers. Still, this was the case for all the books I have, but now the effort is much more demanding and heavier. After this volume, I must publish another that many people are asking for and awaiting; I have already begun it. It is a book in three volumes on the glories, greatness, life and mysteries of the Mother of God, titled *Maria glorificata* (*Mary Glorified*).[328] Pray to the Most Holy Mary that she may be pleased for me to glorify her by this work and by all the people who will read it. I hope and think it will result in great glory for the Most Holy Mary.

Enough! I give myself to God; it is into the hands of the Blessed Virgin that I place my cause and that of my neighbor, or to speak more correctly, the cause of God himself. I know that the Lord demands prayers to make gold issue from this mud and water from this rock. In the meantime, I request your prayers and those of all the servants of God in your community. I again promise all of them my own poor prayers and assure them that the greater will be the success of my labors and of the help for my neighbor to the extent they pray for me.

Finally, I give my holy blessing to all you are doing and will do every moment of your life. I wish you all the blessings of the Most Holy Trinity, of Jesus Christ and of Mary Most Holy.

Give my regards to all the nuns for me and stay well.

---

[328] This work promised by Sarnelli was never completed.

TO SISTER MARIA ANGELA DEL CIELO, MEMBER
OF THE SCALA MONASTERY (SEPTEMBER 27, 1742)[329]

He asks for a novena on his behalf in the church because of his present difficulties. He also speaks of the installation of the new Bishop of Scala.

Long live the Most Holy Trinity and the Most Holy Mary Immaculate

My Most Esteemed Sister,

I wrote you a long letter about the way to quiet your conscience, once and for all. I have gotten away now from the mission in which I am engaged. Meanwhile, my needs are always pressing me and my troubles growing, and I have no other relief except to have prayers said for me to move God to his mercy for me even if I do not deserve it. I am sending you the usual twenty-eight candles for a novena that I ask you to hold in your church beginning the first Friday after you have received this request of mine and finishing it on Sunday, the eighth, which is ten days. My custom has been to sponsor this novena in honor of the Most Holy Trinity and Mary Most Holy and Immaculate. However, since the octave of the novena in honor of the Holy Rosary is already near, I desire and intend for this novena to honor the Most Holy Mother of the Rosary. I urge you, Mother Superior, and all the nuns that during this holy novena you fervently recommend me to the Lord and to the Most Holy Mary. I promise you my poor prayers, which are nevertheless rich through Jesus Christ in the Holy Sacrifice of the Mass.

You cannot believe the extent of my troubles and the crush of all kinds of difficulties without any relief; sometimes a little more, sometimes a little less but truly without relief. I hope in God. May the divine will, to which I entrust myself, be accomplished through me. It is because I know that divine providence wishes prayers and more prayers for the accomplishment of his graces. Thus I do not stop trying to gain them in every possible way. Help me now that the tribulation is weighing me down and killing me.

---

[329] *Lettere di Sarnelli*, Libro I, Lettera XX, 67–68.

This morning I heard from a canon in Naples, a friend of mine, that the bishop for your city is just named and that he is a friend of his. I told him to recommend your community to him heartily. I then wrote the canon that I would like to have a talk with the new prelate. If I have the chance, I will do my part for the good of your ministry.

Give my regards to the reverend mother. When you want to write me, you can do so now that I am away from the mission.

Keep well. Attend to the perfection of your spirit and to serving Jesus Christ with zealous purity and fidelity. May the Most Holy Trinity bless you. I wish to bless all the actions, moments, and consolations of your life in the name of the Lord.

Massa di Somma
September 27, 1742

TO SISTER MARIA ANGELA DEL CIELO, MEMBER OF THE SCALA MONASTERY (OCTOBER 26, 1742)[330]

He thanks her for the novena said in his behalf. He gives her norms for spiritual exercises and frequent confessions. He urges her to keep silent about his giving her spiritual direction.

Long live the Most Holy Trinity and the Most Holy Mary Immaculate
My Most Esteemed Sister,

I received your two letters and I am now answering the first.

I am very grateful that you have made the novena for me while those severe difficulties of all kinds were pressing on me. Blessed by God! When you make such novenas for me, I beg you to also recommend me to your whole community, as best you can, so they fervently pray the Lord for me. You already understand this, and I hope your charity has no need of my further protestations. You cannot imagine my situation. May the Lord's will be done. Enough; I will not go on. Pray for me always and at every moment and do not doubt that the Lord

---

[330] *Lettere di Sarnelli*, Libro I, Lettera XXI, 69–72.

will reward you. I do not cease praying for you at Mass, just as you have written.

It is best to make the retreat during that holy novena if it does not upset the devotion of the other sisters. You can do so during the novena for the Immaculate Conception of Mary and, all the more so, if it does not disturb the community or its duties. Indeed it is always proper to think of God and of one's own soul. I do not mean during the novena before Christmas, because that novena follows a special spiritual routine, less rigorous but more devout.

You do well in wanting to satisfy the Lord when he is offended; you also do well to make a point of following the exercises as if they were the last of your life with all the attention and fervor possible. As far as exterior mortifications are concerned, taking note of your delicate health and without running the danger of aggravating your constitution, you can double your ordinary daily mortifications during the retreat. Beyond that, your greatest efforts are to be directed to interior recollection and internal mortification of your own will against which you must always battle with great vigor.

If you did not go to confession more frequently during the time of the special exercises, it was not a case of disobedience, but of discretion. If it had been disobedience, it would not have been true charity because charity is something regulated, and so it is ordered when it is regulated by obedience. But I repeat, I required you to go to confession frequently, but I did not mean it in this situation, nor in similar cases; rather, that you must not omit frequent confession out of scrupulosity or fear of not developing proper sorrow and purpose of amendment. And I tell you this as a general rule in all cases of obedience; when you have a doubt due to any circumstance that changes the previous state of things and you ask the superior about it and do what she tells you, you are being obedient to me and to the will of the Lord. On the other hand, it is disobedience if the situation has not changed from when you were given the obedience and you act against obedience. But if this is not the situation if the circumstances have changed and there is no time to ask the superior again, you act prudently in a different way by doing what you think your director would tell you to do. I am telling you this not just for this one case but as a general rule in all matters so that you will be at peace and not act in a state of confusion but with that holy freedom of spirit that accords with the divine plan and the conscience of saints.

I recommend that you continue to keep my spiritual direction of you secret from the other nuns, not only for your community's good, but also for mine for I have very serious requests from other monasteries and I have legitimate reasons for saying no. You have done well in responding as you have; keep doing the same when the question comes up because it is the truth. I realize that these dear servants of God would not take it ill if they understood, but it would not be convenient either for me or for you if they find out. Beyond that, whoever finds out, finds out; it is enough we are just careful not to publish it all over the place. It is only necessary for the superior to know, as I have said from the beginning, and I say it once and for all.

As to the second letter you wrote me about your conscience, rejoice that you can present to the Lord these new blessings of obedience and of confusion. However, I want, and I command you, that after you have written, you do not keep thinking about what you wrote, at least not beyond asking God's pardon in general and always thanking him for the generous blessings and the great care and attention that he has for you. I read your letter attentively and I assure you that you should have no doubts of conscience nor repeated confessions because I have understood it all, and your conscience does not need any further confessions. Rest secure in this and turn your mind to ardent love of Jesus, the Highest Good.

In regard to your new prelate, I will not stop doing my part in favor of your community whenever I get the chance and I can meet with him insofar as I can while I am in charge [*of the mission*] outside Naples. If there is need, I will surely let him know at another time.

Keep well. Give yourself truly to God, for God wishes all things for himself. Recommend me continuously and fervently to Jesus and Mary. I give my respects to the superior and the nuns, to whose prayers I recommend myself. I bless you in all your life and works with the blessing of the most lovable Trinity, and of Jesus and Mary.

October 26, 1742

TO SISTER MARIA ANGELA DEL CIELO, MEMBER
OF THE SCALA MONASTERY (NOVEMBER 7, 1742) [331]

He informs her of his place of residence outside Naples. He gives her some news about spiritual relationships he has made. He tells her of the state and burdens of life he finds as well as his confidence in God and in the prayers of others.

Long live the Most Holy Trinity and the Most Holy Mary Immaculate

My Most Esteemed Sister,

Today, November 7, I received your little note. I also mention that I received both of the letters and answered them about fifteen days ago.

You ask when I will return to Naples. But I wrote you that I have not lived in the city for a long time but in the suburbs of Naples, three miles from the city and that I often go into town in the morning and return during the day, but that my home is outside it. And I am always leaving here to go around these areas of the diocese of Naples for the missions with my companions as our Cardinal commands. But whether on mission or at home, I am always close to Naples, and since our neighbors go back and forth from Naples almost every day, they are therefore able to carry letters or pick them up.

Now tell me what effects the report you gave me has had on your spirit, and how it has worked out for you. Has it caused scruples, something I would not want to happen. Has it produced humbling and gentle disturbance, or something else. Let me know about this and try to draw out of it the profit that the Lord seeks by rejecting the scruples, quieting the unrest and overcoming the temptations by faith and obedience.

Since you want to know some news of my health and situation, I must mention that I am grateful to the Most Holy Trinity who treats me thus, because this is the divine will that I adore and to which I resign myself and want to resign myself all the more. But for the rest, being a mere human, I must say my heart has never felt such a painful situation and life than the present, due not only to its length but also for

[331] *Lettere di Sarnelli*, Libro I, Lettera XXII, 72–74.

its intensity and for the variety of troubles. I see no way to get any light or hope of relief outside of the great overall mercy of God in general, in the goodness of the heavenly Father through the merits of Jesus Christ, in the intercession of the Mother of God. Every solution turns out to be useless for me and brings no comfort. Blessed be God forever and his adorable judgments!

In the meantime, since you wish to know how I am doing, please help by bringing your charity to bear on the means to help my being and my tragic state. Make a novena precisely for me and beg His Divine Majesty to give me light, to let me know what his will is for me now amid this darkness I do not understand, and give me the grace to deal with it perfectly. Through the merits of Jesus Christ and of the Most Holy Mary may he give me the grace and open for me the gates of his wide mercy, not to make me happy (something I am not looking for nor want, for I am not looking for joys, either material or spiritual), but to breathe in his loving goodness and to find his holy will and his greater pleasure. I do not deserve this. But Jesus merits it before the heavenly Father, and the Most Holy Mary before her Son. Join them in your fervent and constant prayers, just as I in turn promise to do for you in return by praying especially for you in the holy Mass and by carefully attending to your guidance.

The present and past happenings that have for so many years been going on here are so tense and confused that nothing can be done to resolve them if the Lord does not take them in hand and open the way. This is because no one, not even the wisest, knows the sure answer when things are in such a mixed-up state. If one thing is settled, something else falls apart; and if some important matter is ruined no one knows what will happen. So everyone, I included, decide that what is needed is prayer, resignation, patience and new light from the Lord. This I beg and for this reason I ask you to offer the most special prayers, above all, during the upcoming novena of the Patronage of the Holy Mary, and during the retreat that you will make during the novena of the Immaculate Conception. My health likewise is worn out and keeps me disturbed and my life in no way gets any better. Enough! Only trust in God is left for me, and in Jesus and Mary, from whom I trust in faith for every mercy.

May the Lord bless you abundantly. And I want to bless you in all your life and works and actions, whatever they may be. Grow in the holy fear and love of God; now is the proper time to hurry along the way of the divine will.

Keep well. Give my regards to the superior and the sisters as best you can when you have the chance and recommend me to their prayers.

S. Georgio a Cremano, November 7

TO SISTER MARIA ANGELA DEL CIELO, MEMBER OF THE SCALA MONASTERY (NOVEMBER 24, 1742)[332]

He encourages her to have little confidence in her self but to have it in God, in gratitude to God amid suffering. He gives her advice about confession and communion, about giving advice to the sisters, about vows, etc., and cautions her about the future.

Long live the Most Holy Trinity and the Most Holy Mary Immaculate My Most Esteemed Sister,

Here I am, on the mission; however, I received your letter in Naples delivered personally by Sir N. I am answering, not at length, but I think sufficiently.

First of all, I hope in the Lord that the report you sent me brought joy to your soul. In what you detailed there, I behold the great mercies of God, the highest blessings of the divine spouse, your deep obligations and the gratefulness that you owe to your supreme benefactor for such singular goodness with which he has graced you. I discern the sorrows, the weaknesses and the shortcomings of the mortal creature. All this moves me to urge you all the more to a great diffidence in yourself, a great confidence in God along with a great detachment from every earthly creature, no matter how spiritual and holy it may seem, and an intense vigilance in your conversations and interactions, as well as in your writing and speaking with anyone at all. Always have on your lips and in your heart: *For God alone and nothing else*, and regard and

---

[332] *Lettere di Sarnelli*, Libro I, Lettera XXIII, 75–81.

appreciate creatures according to the rules and measure of a Faith purely ordered toward God.

I am not going to give you advice about what else you have told me in your letter because, by divine grace, your heart already knows the disorder and danger involved and now the situation and case are no longer the same. Thus, I have nothing more to say to you about all this other than to thank His Divine Majesty ardently for having kept his hand over you, for never turning away his gaze full of special love, and for not allowing any greater damage as human nature tends to cause and quickly overwhelm us. Keep asking pardon of the Lord with a childlike heart, with confidence and love, with humility and thanks.

As far as confessions and communions are concerned, I order you out of obedience and in the name of Jesus Christ, to think no longer about the past, nor worry about a general confession, nor repeat faults already confessed except to repeat the worst faults in a few words so that you can be assured of sacramental absolution. Beyond that, your soul is already justified before God and you are already forgiven through the confessions you have made, whatever may have been your faults, for they were conducted properly according to the rules of the sacrament and the will of God. Again, I forbid you to go back willingly to thinking about past sins in order to see whether they have been confessed or not. It is enough to just cast a general glance back, and by gaining a horror in general over the past disorders and new thankless actions, weep in a spirit of contrition at the feet of our dear heavenly Father, and near to the wounds of our lovable Redeemer that burn away and cleanse all your stains with his precious blood in which you must deeply trust over and over.

As far as the vows, I think that, for the present, they are already dispensed or changed. As to the scruples over the past, forget about them. If there are any that still give you trouble or scruple and you do not know if you have been dispensed, let me know. For the future, do not make any promises without express obedience and permission. Make the intention that from now on, whatever you say or promise the Lord, you do not intend to oblige yourself by vow without the express permission and obedience of your director. Nevertheless, I now change them, as far as I have the power, into being promises that are not obligatory except for an act of gratitude to the Lord.

As far as advice you gave the sisters when you were superior in matters you did not understand, you have already dealt with the substance of them by indicating this to your confessor. In accordance with the general and well-founded principle, such actions could not have involved voluntary assent and so they were free from any fault, at least any grave one, and so you have legitimately addressed them sufficiently. I am not getting into the details because you are no longer superior and you are not obligated by matters already completed. No longer think about the past.

As to temptations by which the demon wants you to do so and urges you to examine yourself scrupulously about whether you committed a fault, I tell you this: I knowingly confirm that it is the devil who is suggesting all this, and you are not to examine it at all, not to question it, not to think of it or question it. This is because the fault, if there really was a fault, would be so clear to you that you would not need to investigate it. So do not think about it anymore and laugh at the temptations of hell.

Regarding the oath you made, because it was made with a conscious decision that was very clear, there can be no scruple. I believe that if you have already confessed it, one time was enough to clear up any defect or lack of attention.

I tell you the same in regard to the rest of your scruples: If you would have needed to do anything about matters of the past, I would be giving you more exact and pertinent advice. But what is done is done, and since it was done with a good intention, and even more since whatever was improper in the action was confessed once, quiet your mind and your absolved conscience, and stop thinking about it.

There is only one thing I want to know: I mean, there were some alms about which you spoke to me, if I recall, when I returned from the mission at Consa, and I answered you orally and then wrote you about them. It seems that I said that it was all right and that there was nothing further to do; I now repeat the same. However, I do not recall what you told me about whether or not the superior, according to the monastery's rule, could make such a large donation without the approval of the twelve [*consultants*]. I tell you with certainty that if the persons in question paid the monastery back for the help they had received, there is nothing for you to worry about any more. I am also sure that Mr. X did repay; I do not know about the other person. Also, you do not have to worry whether the alms came from the monastery funds or were obtained from some outside source, or whether only that portion of the money came from the monastery that the superior had the authority on her own to give as alms. I say this not to give you scruples, but to decide how to protect the role of the community. Nevertheless, you have no obligations in the matter because nothing can be done now. It might be handled this way (if it is a case of the limit for giving things from the community being exceeded) that the present superior would write Mr. X that when he sends them some assistance, he indicates he is sending it to the community to repay that which the community gave not only to him but also to the other person. But I believe that, in any case, you have no need to worry as long as there is no clear news and what has been done was done in good faith.

You are not to worry that I may not understand you because you did not know how exactly to explain the case. The Lord makes me understand whatever you may think that you did not know how to explain. It is enough that you did not voluntarily keep silence and hide things, or exaggerated them. I already know that is not the case because you have intended to explain yourself sincerely and correctly; we must trust that the Lord's goodness will make me understand. I am saying this once and for all.

I clearly realize that your merits are God's gifts and that whatever good you have done or whatever evil you have avoided, all was the work of divine mercy and that, on our own, we cannot gain wisdom or produce anything that is not evil. So you have no reason to glorify yourself but only to glorify God's mercy and grace that accompany you, fill you and follow you.

As regards that remark made by those confessors that you have not lost your baptismal grace, it really is not our place to make absolute judgments about this. I think they said this to allay your scruples and to encourage your trust. So don't think about it; it is much better to place yourself in the abyss of one's nothingness and always recognize the great abundance of one's miseries and of one's past faults and so detest them as they appear before God. Indeed, in human estimation many faults are light or venial, but before God they are very grave and weighty, especially in souls enlightened, blessed and helped by grace with such abundant aid.

Suffering is the surest part of your life and most meritorious. And for this blessing you ought to continually thank the divine goodness.

All that is left for me to say is that past disorders serve as a caution and reminder not to trespass in the least for the future. Indeed, you have known, and still know, how the evil spirit and human misery hide self-love under the appearance of good and of spirituality and how these simply nourish your own desires. Be careful, very careful with everyone. Be jealous, very jealous of your heart, whose affections and leanings must tend toward and rest in God alone. The neighbor must be loved, but with the charity of a sincere heart, with reverence, with detachment, with ordering toward God and with every caution; it is easy for self-love to become mixed into it. Always purify your intentions and proclaim at the Lord's feet that you have no desire for any other affection or inclination except for his divine love, his will, his desire. In your actions, always have recourse to God and recommend yourself to the divine goodness.

I see that your soul owes a great deal to the Mother of God, the Most Holy Mary. Therefore, nourish your filial devotion toward so lovable a mother and protector.

As for myself, I have great need of prayer. I still have immense troubles and fatigue, although somewhat abated but only by a thread. May my Lord be blessed! Do not forget to invigorate your prayers for me to the Most Holy Trinity, to the adored wounds of Jesus, and to the Mother of God, your Mother and mine, because I pray for you during Mass as you once wrote to me to do. Pray all the more during the next two holy and important novenas for the Immaculate Conception and Christmas, and also during the time of your next retreat.

May the Most Holy Trinity bless you at every moment. May Jesus and Mary always remain in your heart. I offer you my respects.

Portici, November 24, 1742

TO SISTER MARIA ANGELA DEL CIELO, MEMBER OF THE SCALA MONASTERY (JANUARY 21, 1743) [333]

On his sickness and on the difficulties met in the missions. His requests for prayers.

Long live the Most Holy Trinity and the Most Holy Mary Immaculate

My Most Esteemed Sister,

I answered your earlier letter, and right away I received your last letter with the note about the prayers and vocal prayers to offer for you. I do not think I can answer your letter now, but I have read it. I have now been greatly afflicted by sickness with a fever for seven days. Half-dead, with my heart in my mouth, I have celebrated [*Mass*] every morning and I am in such toil in the mission, and it is a large one, that it is a continual fight: terrible housing and no shelter. I am completely exhausted. Meanwhile, I hope and wait for the needed help from heaven while the earth and the world crumble beneath. I beg you, Mother Superior and the whole community to offer for me a devout novena of ten days to the Most Holy Trinity and Most Holy Mary Immaculate. I am sending you the usual twenty-eight candles. I ask all the sisters to pray very fervently for me and for this work that I have entrusted to me that I do not think I can leave because it is for the great glory of God and the infinite benefit of this diocese of Naples. But I do not think I can move forward because of such troubles, sickness and weakness that I cannot keep on. So in this state of contradiction please implore the abundant mercy of the great Father of lights through the merits of Jesus Christ that he effectively relieve me; I am resolved for his greater glory, the greater good of my neighbor and that of my poor spirit together with my body *usque ad mortem*. [334] Please also pray Our Savior Jesus through the merits of his Blessed Mother Immaculate.

Therefore, I ask you, first of all, for a fervent novena of prayers for me to the Most Holy Trinity, to Jesus Christ Our Lord and to the Most Holy Mary Immaculate. If you feel you owe me for the services

---

[333] *Lettere di Sarnelli*, Libro I, Lettera XXIV, 81–83.

[334] "Even unto death" (Philippians 2:8).

I have rendered and am rendering you by my spiritual direction, now is the time to repay me for them; this is the only pay that I request or will ever request and nothing more. Do so then under the virtue of holy obedience and reinforce your prayers and offer them up amid your most difficult troubles. Tell the Lord that since I do not know how to pray and cannot do so, I send your spirit to pray for me at the feet of His Divine Majesty. I said fervently: I did not mean emotional fervor which is not the Christian virtue and the heart of petition and mental prayer. By a fervent novena, I mean one with intensity of heart and will, begging the lovable goodness of the Lord on the basis of reasons embraced by his infinite mercy from the blood and merits of J[esus] C[hrist], by the intercession of the Mother of God, of the heavenly saints and angels of the dear Church Triumphant and of the just ones of the earth, as well as from the motive of holy zeal, firm charity and your obedience.

I am telling you the truth. It has been three years (although my whole life seems martyrdom) that I have found myself in the most unceasing storm, the most horrible of my whole life, with no pause for even an hour of the day or night. There is no kind of suffering that I have not endured and continue to endure. During such a long course of the most intense sorrow while I await, not deep consolation (which I do not seek), just a little bit of comfort or pause, but instead a hurricane most unexpected arrives. It is little in comparison with my sins, indeed I know I must say to myself, *Non contradicam sermonibus Sancti*;[335] only one ray of light is left to me: I hope in God; let God take care of it. Do not be surprised at my words that slip out of a heart pierced *usque ad mortem*. I fear that my great weakness makes me exaggerate. I recognize clearly that I am weak, very weak. But I cannot deny that I am breaking down under the burden, since my spirit, my life and my whole being is less than that of an ant.

Take care. May the Lord bless you. As a sign of my gratitude, give my respects to Mother Superior and to the sisters for me, especially during this opportunity of the holy novena.

If you are in the midst of conducting another novena in the community, you can postpone mine, since I want a novena entirely for myself, my resolutions and doubts that are not very urgent.

I hope to answer your letter and note as soon as possible.

---

[335] "I have not denied the words of the Holy One" (Job 6:10).

I request that you direct this novena for the intention that the Lord will establish over me and over all these works what most pleases him since I find myself in constant confusion over the news that arrives. And I cannot leave my responsibilities in the hands of the directors if I do not get some heavenly enlightenment since I do not know what to say, nor do they know what to answer, except be patient and wait for God.

Secondigliano, January 21, 1743

TO SISTER MARIA ANGELA DEL CIELO, MEMBER OF THE SCALA MONASTERY (FEBRUARY 16, 1743) [336]

On his sickness and on the difficulties met in the missions. His confidence in God.

Long live the Most Holy Trinity and the Most Holy Mary Immaculate My Most Esteemed Sister,

I wrote you two letters and in the second I enclosed a packet of holy cards. I answered everything both about your conscience as well as about my situation. Now I beg you to pray for me and have others do so, for nothing is lessened of my troubles; in fact they have gotten worse. I am in God's hands, indeed I have gotten out of bed but weakly. I have been gravely ill for twenty-four days, and this morning I saw a doctor for the first time. He found me with a fever, with my innards in a mess and with a chest twisted and injured. I am in the countryside and tomorrow I am required to vacate this house and move on to another place and house. See what a very bitter and deadly vocation and duty I have! Whether alive or dying or suffering, I must pass from one journey to the next. Neither a hint of an idea appears nor advice from experts to give me any relief. If heaven does not speak, I will follow my agonizing course and my consummation. Whenever you feel that my body and my life has no need of more prayer, that is the time to offer a prayer

---

[336] *Lettere di Sarnelli*, Libro I, Lettera XXV, 84–85.

for my soul. Only heaven can help me if it is pleased to do so. In the meantime, the earth is all death and thorns. There is no person or place that can give me a moment's peace. Blessed be God! I am resigned in the adored hands of the Lord. Double the prayers for my intense and nonstop gasps. I do not know if these gasps are the pains of hell or of purgatory, of martyrdom or merely natural and earthly. I do know clearly that I can do no more and that I am dying and in agony. All that is left me is hope in God the Father through Jesus Christ, and in Jesus Christ through the holiness of the Most Holy Mary along with the prayers of holy people. For the rest, let God do with me [*what he wants*]; it is for him I am consumed, as well as for my neighbors who are the cause of my extreme pain, I mean, over their eternal well-being.

Recommend me to your community. Let me know if you received the candles and if you have made the novena, when it began and when it ended.

Keep well. May the Lord bless you always.

Casavatore, February 16, 1743

TO SISTER MARIA ANGELA DEL CIELO, MEMBER OF THE SCALA MONASTERY (MARCH 17, 1743) [337]

On his health, which is better. He wants to publish a book. Problems in the handling of his correspondence and fear of thieves. On the frequency of communion.

Long live the Most Holy Trinity and the Most Holy Mary Immaculate
My Most Esteemed Sister,

I received your latest letter. I cannot deny that this morning I feel a little better, to the point of being able to preach to the people attending this mission where I arrived yesterday. But I also cannot deny that it is a divine miracle that I am not dead from being constrained to move from one battle to the next with such discomfort and disadvantage, dangers

---

[337] *Lettere di Sarnelli*, Libro I, Lettera XXVI 85–87.

and fatigue, poor lodgings and worries. I have covered four regions during my long, serious illness and in twenty days I move on from this one to the fifth. Pray the Lord for me that he gives me peace and security and that he puts me into the situation of his greatest glory, the wellbeing of my soul and that of my neighbor. While this manner of living is destroying me, I cannot change it on my own unless the Lord opens a way for me. Fervently beg him that he restore the inspiration for writing and publishing books that I think of much greater profit than missions. Pray and thank the Lord however he treats me.

I am very troubled to hear that our letters are being opened. Yours arrive sealed, but I am not sure they are sealed the way you do. I am sending back the last letter you sent me so you can see whether that little layer of red attached to the white one is yours. If it was not put there by you, then it is clear the letter was opened and then the red layer was added, something I know that you do not usually do. I think, therefore, that I will send this letter of mine by a different route so that you can be sure of its security. But I am in doubt as to who to ask; I wonder if it involved Mr. X. If you have any idea who opened it, choose another way of sending them to me and of getting my responses. This is a great crime for whoever did it; no one has the right to open my letters. I have written this with a suspicion about Mr. X. I seal my letters solidly when I send them. Although mine and yours could be opened without our noticing and then reseal them.

I have sent you another letter, the length of a folio, in which I responded to your previous one. Let me know when and how it arrives.

I share your fear about thieves. But I trust in God that they will do no harm. Listen, for five months a year I live with this fear every night when I am at home where I live during the period when there are no missions and is located in a place three miles from Naples. I passed those nights without sleep. Pray to the Lord also for me since there is nowhere that I rest secure. Blessed be God.

Regarding receiving communion, do not have any more scruples or difficulties, for the love of God; and don't write me anymore with doubts. You should go to communion once a day. If it were permissible for you to go to communion a hundred times a day, I would order you to go to communion a hundred times a day! The more you feel tempted and distracted, the more you should receive the One who knows and wants to give you victory and comfort, and sees you at all times. Whether it involves an emotional experience or not does not matter.

Keep well. I give you a thousand blessings. It is very late and I am tired. Excuse my handwriting because I am writing fast. Many thanks for the prayers. Thank Mother Superior and all the community for me. God will repay them.

P.S. I add here, that it would be a good idea for you to speak with Mother Superior and watch to see if by chance it might be that someone in the monastery opened your letters or mine. I do not know what to say, but it is necessary to find out where this came from and security is necessary for the future. May the Lord always assist you and accompany you. Again I give you my respects.

Melito, March 17, 1743

To Sister Maria Angela del Cielo, Member of the Scala Monastery (April 8, 1743) [338]

Advice about fear of thieves. Desire to enjoy a little peace amid his problems. Advice about keeping her spiritual direction secret and about the approval of the Rule.

Long live the Most Holy Trinity and the Most Holy Mary Immaculate
Most Esteemed Sister,

I received your letter. I have set aside my suspicion that our letters are being opened. I could not doubt Mr. X because I am sure he is an honest man. My doubt was whether the courier had allowed them to pass into other hands. Now I will post them through the usual channel of Mr. X, by whom I usually send them to you and whom I likewise recommend that you use as well for our exchange of letters back and forth.

I sympathize with your worry about thieves. I have suffered a great deal from them as well. But do not have doubts. The Lord mortifies us

---

[338] *Lettere di Sarnelli*, Libro I, Lettera XXVII 88–91.

but will not let us perish. Pretend not to notice these evildoers and do not change your usual routines, but rather remain more prayerful and more trusting in his goodness and protection, since I think that is what good religious do in these trials. I put a holy card at every door and window and by the grace of God I have suffered no hurt in my house. But I am indeed afraid of them, although I trust in God and in the protection of the Blessed Virgin. So put some bars in the shape of a cross behind all the entrances. I offer this as a human means because the thieves find it difficult to get in if they find the door blockaded from within; without bars it is very easy to get the door open without a key.

As for myself, by God's grace, I am no longer hindered from celebrating holy Mass. Still, I remain in so many and so deep troubles that, if the Lord does not grant me a remedy, they will drag me down and completely finish me. There is nothing in which I do not suffer. Blessed be God! One trouble no sooner ends than another one arises. Enough: pray to the Lord for me, and have your community pray as well. What extreme need I have, and at times I feel just about to fall over and come close to expiring. May God's will be done! But I tell you the truth: I desire and hope for a little peace in these final years of my life, but it is God's peace, so I can take care of the work for God that I planned and finish the books I have begun so I can publish them for the good of all. Pray urgently to the Lord that in my remaining days, after the seven months of the missionary campaign, I can find a little free time and make up for what I have neglected because of so many difficulties and troubles, if it so please God.

So then I recommend that you keep entirely to yourself all of the advice that I have given you about how to deal with Mr. X[339] so neither he nor others know what my advice was. This bothers me a great deal; they cannot find out if you keep it hidden from all of them so that none of them can learn of it from me or from you.

Now we come to you matters of conscience. Again, I urge you to the exact following of the obedience I gave you about the holy Sacraments of Confession and Communion.

Do not agonize over the various feelings and movements that test your spirit, because we all have to pass along this road to arrive at what we desire, some in one way, others in a different one. These emotions and

---

[339] *This remark seems to refer to the earlier letter of January 21, 1743*

movements of feeling are a test to make us aware of ourselves and of God, and they are the foundations of perfection when we reach the depths of this holy recognition.

Regarding the advice you want about the rule, it is true that this is an important point and must be trod with full reflection and much prayer so that ruptures or disturbance does not develop. As far as I am concerned, I know clearly that the best side to take in this matter is to follow the proper procedures before the Holy Congregation in Rome for the approbation of the Rule that you are presently living and observing and in the observance of which your community is already finding great spiritual profit. If God wills, Rome will approve and finalize it; if, on the other hand, it does not wish to accept it, it is a sign the God does not will it, either. Make the whole community understand that, if it turns out that the Holy See does not agree, they must leave the matter in your bishop's hands and in what the sacred Congregation decides. In that way, you will be following the means given by the Lord and you will be receiving the results and the end of the matter from the hands of the Lord. This way no nun can com plain because you did not decide it; the Holy See did, or better, the Holy Spirit decided it through them.

Due diligence is necessary, but it must be discreet and ordered. It is enough that everything be awaited with indifference. Show yourself before the others as indifferent, in that you desire the approval as you should desire it but, at the same time, be resigned over the results that you will accept as the will of God. Above all, pray about this, and leave it up to God who takes your establishment more seriously even than you, but who wishes that his works follow their regular course.

I have the news about Bishop Falcoia in my heart. If you find out anything more, let me know. I am always away from Naples and know very little about such things, although I have heard about it briefly. Don Alphonsus rarely writes me, since I am in places far away from him.

I also have always had this grand view of the Institute of the priests of the Most Holy Savior being a work of God, not founded on private revelations, but on the basic reality of things and an Institute according to the Gospel and way of the Church of God, and seeing in it the great fruit and real profit for its members and for our neighbors.

May the Lord bless you at every moment, and may the holy feast of Easter bring you the fullness of his graces.[340] But, whether they be troublesome graces or peaceful graces does not matter; it is enough that they are graces from God and plentiful graces. Ask for the same for me. My weakness is great, nevertheless I will whatever pleases God.

Give my regards to Mother Superior and to all the nuns. If they want any good wishes, tell them I wish them also all the same graces from God that I wished you.

Keep well. Grow in holy fear and in self-denial.

Capo di Chino, April 8, 1743

TO SISTER MARIA ANGELA DEL CIELO, MEMBER OF THE SCALA MONASTERY (APRIL 28, 1743)[341]

He speaks of Bishop Falcoia's death (April 20, 1743). The bishop had indicated in his Will that his body was to be buried at the nun's monastery in Scala while his heart was to be buried in his diocese. But the people of Castellamare refused to give up his body and even buried it under a huge pile of stones to prevent its theft. Sarnelli makes an ironic play on words in this letter because Falcoia had suffered from kidney stones while he lived [Later on, his successor as bishop had him buried in the cathedral].

Sarnelli then offers advice on detachment from creatures. He continues to seek to give her comfort in spiritual aridity.

Long live the Most Holy Trinity and the Most Holy Mary Immaculate Most Esteemed Sister,

Out here in the country last night I read your letter and the two enclosures.

---

[340] Easter was celebrated on April 14 in 1743.

[341] *Lettere di Sarnelli*, Libro I, Lettera XIII, 45–48 [*In the 1888 edition of Sarnelli's works, this letter is place among the letters written in 1742; the manuscript itself indicates only the month and day, not the year. However, this letter could not have been written in 1742 since Falcoia's death mentioned in the letter did not occur until April 1743.]*

I had already heard of the death of the holy Bishop Falcoia but I had not yet received the details you mentioned, which succeeded in consoling me about the mercy that the Lord bestows on his servant after his death to make him appreciated. The stones, if they had been miraculously placed in his heart, would have indicated the steadfast heart of this devout dead man; but since they were piled on his poor body, they show he was a martyr of suffering and patience.

God willing, tomorrow I will go to Naples and seek to engage the lawyer Borgia for the business I have been put in charge of. But I'll tell you the truth. Although justice is on Scala's side since this is the burial site indicated in the will of the deceased, nevertheless I think it will be difficult to contest and win over an entire city that bears the motives of piety and devotion for its pastor. I hope in God that justice will be done and I will do what I can in the city tomorrow. But the conditions of my health and my work demand that I come back tomorrow evening and then leave for some new places. Tell Mother Superior and the religious that I know I am obligated to them for the prayers they have said and are still saying in my behalf. If it depended on me, I would do, not only this, but even greater things for your community.

Regarding Signor Y, I have not seen him for almost two years. I saw him only for a few days the first time. He made me great promises and told me that his business was going well and that his state of mind was getting along by God's usual mercy. I thanked him, I was pleased and praised the Lord for all this. I hope that he would choose to release the mortgage right away, although neither one of us stated that to the other. I urge you act in this matter with the prudence and discretion you suggest. Although I do not foresee getting any news and little attention from him, still act in a way that he does not get aggravated and you do not waste time over the matter. The man is of good heart and has good will, but he is too quick in attaching himself to pious people, although for good purpose. But as far as I see there will be no recollection, but only loss of spirit and personal satisfaction involved. As for the rest, do not write him unless the superior tells you to. When he writes you, answer but in a few words and not without the usual charity and politeness; pay attention to your detachment and mortification.

Do not trouble yourself over the stirrings you feel, even when they are undesirable or the upsets you experience in your emotions, since these are the ordinary course of events the one who loves God must face. I have written you many times that it is through these different situations that one learns by experience who is the creature and who is the Creator, which is, as they say, the foundation of a holy life. These are a great gift from the Lord even though onerous and bitter in the body and the emotions which suffer and find no relief. Let me just say that I can assure you that your spirit gains more in these setbacks and storms of passion that in your moments of fervent devotion. These fervent moments are granted by God as a reward for the desolation and pains that the soul has suffered with virtue and his merciful grace. They are received with greater detachment and clearer understanding that are the simple gifts of God and movements of his merciful grace and are not the offspring and result of our weak humanity that seeks only what is wrong and, without the grace and the mercy of the Lord, would not do anything that is not evil. So comfort yourself and be sure that what the Lord demands is better for you; receive it humbly, patiently, by the power of grace, indeed without failing in the confidence that we should have in the goodness of the Lord. While this goodness always stays the same, it has infinitely differing results.

As to me, I am not as near death as I was, but I am under great pressures and have all kinds of troubles. Ask God to give me his peace, especially at this time when I am dealing with some very important matters, about which all I can say and do, humanly speaking, is risk my life.

I do not forget to pray for you. But I fear that the flood of business and worry do not help my poor prayers: May Jesus Christ in the Eucharist that, by God's mercy, I celebrate every morning, make up for what I lack and may the heavenly Father, through the infinite merits of Jesus Christ, grant me his mercy together with all those for whom I pray, and for you as well.

Stay well and keep fighting. I am in the field and you in your solitude. Raise your hands and with your prayers help me succeed for the glory of God and the good of my neighbor.

May the Most Holy Trinity bless you at every moment, every step and every moment of rest. Etc.

From S. Giorgio a Cremano

April 28, [1743]

TO SISTER MARIA ANGELA DEL CIELO, MEMBER OF THE SCALA MONASTERY (JUNE 29, 1743)[342]

Description of his sickness and sufferings. He explains why he tells her of these sorrows.

Long live the Most Holy Trinity and the Most Holy Mary Immaculate

Most Esteemed Sister,

I wrote you a long letter and sent it eight days ago. But I did not have time to send you what I mentioned in it. I went into Naples for the Procession of Penitence that was being held, and I spent three hours going without a hat in the heat and cold with a wind and it ruined me. I got back here late at night with a cold and fever. I was so sick that I seemed on the verge of death. I have remained so worn out that all I feel is agony and death. Pray the goodness of God that I either live or die according to his Most Holy will. Please busy yourself in prayer to Jesus Christ and to the Most Holy Mary that they end this life of great suffering I am enduring; Let me live or die, as always according to the Most Holy divine will. O God! I have comforted the agonies of so many poor souls who were suffering in body or soul and yet here I am now in agony abandoned out here in the countryside without finding anyone to comfort my sufferings of body and soul. Blessed be God who out of his hidden judgment has reduced me to this deplorable state that I am sure nobody could envy. I celebrated Mass this morning beyond my strength, almost killing myself and I was on the point of passing out at the altar. Why do I bother telling you my ills, or even a little bit of them? It is because I want to urge you to pray to God for me, as well as to the Most Blessed Virgin, that she finally take pity on me, because she is my mother and I am her son, the Mother of God who is the Mother of Consolation for others, the Mother of Health, and the loving mother. She is my mother, but only as the Sorrowful Mother; and my queen, but as the Queen of Martyrs. The Most Holy Mary pours out these titles on me with such force that I think my soul will depart and my life will end in its last breath.

---

[342] *Lettere di Sarnelli*, Libro I, Lettera XXVIII, 92–94.

What I am leading up to by this account is you should not put your hopes on the spiritual direction of a man in such hard misery and buried in such darkness as I am. Rather, depend on God who acts with the most marvelous wisdom, making light shine out of darkness, water from the rock and fire out of ice. Therefore, it is not I, but God; not my virtue, but entirely God's, that assures your direction.

Moreover, realize that when you deal with suffering, with painful desolation and contradictions, you can do so with the greatest freedom.

Although I fear that my suffering is different from that endured by spiritual people, this does not mean I lack all experience of suffering. Therefore, be content to pay attention to my lessons as those of someone who in this suffering has all the experience necessary.

For the rest then, the Lord gives me the grace to be one person suffering within himself and another in guiding and advising others.

Indeed, who knows, I hope and have confidence that one day a kind ray of that divine light will explode over me that will speed me along the way to God's holy mountain! I do not desire consolations, rather I feel pain in thinking about them. I do not seek sensed delights or extraordinary things that I abhor. God knows: *Dic animae meae, salus tuus Ego sum.*[343] Enough! May the deep abysses of God's judgments be blessed, which I endorse now and forever. *Non contradicam sermonibus Sancti.*[344]

I recommend myself to you, and I recommend myself to the whole community. During the holy novena reinforce your prayers, please, so that the Lord grant them. I have great need of prayer and this is what I ask of you.

May the Lord bless you. Give them my most humble respects.

From S. Giorgio a Cremano, June 29, 1743

---

[343] "Say to my soul, 'I am your salvation'" (Psalm 35:3).

[344] "I have not denied the words of the Holy One" (Job 6:10).

TO SISTER MARIA ANGELA DEL CIELO, MEMBER
OF THE SCALA MONASTERY (SEPTEMBER 21, 1743)[345]

He requests prayers during a novena for the feast of Our Lady of the Rosary.

Long live the Most Holy Trinity and the Most Holy Mary Immaculate

Most Esteemed Sister,

A little while ago, I sent you a letter with an enclosure for Sister Mary Y and then the other day I saw her here in Naples, when Mr. X was here. Send the messenger for the letters to Z at the bell tower of S. Liguori.

I am sending to Mr. X's house a package of candles together with this letter. I beg Mother Superior, you and the whole community to please make the usual novena in honor of the Most Holy Trinity and the Most Holy Lady of the Rosary with exposition of the Blessed Sacrament and prayers for me, along with the usual litany. I ask you to begin the novena on Saturday so that it lasts for the whole octave until Sunday. Please speak in my behalf to Mother Superior and the other nuns so that they make this holy novena for me fervently.

You will not believe how troubled I am with difficulties. I have great need of prayer for my soul and for my life because I feel completely ruined and I cannot find a remedy for my ills beyond waiting for help and remedy from heaven. I do not know how to pray, and so I ask you to pray for me with prayers made valuable by your charity and obtain for me from the Lord what I ask for but do not deserve. Enough! I place myself in your hands and I, for your greater merit, impose on you especially to pray fervently for me to the greater glory of God and to my comfort, since I can bear no more. Still, may the Lord be forever blessed and his holy will be done.

My respects to the superior and the nuns.

May the Lord bless you at every moment. Keep well. Love Jesus and Mary.

Naples, September 21, 1743

---

[345] *Lettere di Sarnelli*, Libro I, Lettera XXIX, 94–95.

TO SISTER MARIA ANGELA DEL CIELO, MEMBER OF THE SCALA MONASTERY (MAY 3, 1744)[346]

He gives instructions about handling mail. On the election of officers of the monastery. His health.

Long live the Most Holy Trinity and the Most Holy Mary Immaculate

Most Esteemed Sister,

Speak to the courier and do not spare your words. He promised the bookseller to return the same day to get the answer that I prepared as quickly as possible and I also got the candles ready, and then he did not come that day. The next day I sent the letter and candles to Mr. X's house, and he told me that the courier had already left that morning. Talk to him because at times the letters get delayed and it's his fault.

I want to know how things stand regarding your illness and I want you to obey the superior and the doctor so you will be cured.

I am already moved to make fervent prayers to the Holy Spirit and to the Mother of God for the new elections to the offices of your community, since this is a matter of great consequence. You are to go along with whatever the will of God and the common good demands without attending to your own inclinations but the good of the community. Let me know the outcome.

As for myself, there is nothing else to do than to sigh from the depths of my pain. I have not been able to celebrate Mass for the last several days. Yesterday, the feast of Sts. Philip and James, I went by sedan-chair to the nearby church to say Mass, and it turned out that after the *Gloria*, I fainted half-dead at the altar, and I passed out without being able either to say or hear Mass. This morning, Saturday, I have not suffered, but I fear the danger of doing so tomorrow on Sunday and I don't know what to do. I have never seen myself in such a terrible situation,

Do not say anything more about my condition, or that I should pay attention to my health and take care of myself, because these are useless words and this [*kind of talk*] bothers me. All my woes come

[346] *Lettere di Sarnelli*, Libro I, Lettera XXX, 96–99.

from heaven, even the physical ones, and make everything win out that is contrary to all my attempts and hopes for health, rest, shelter and sleep. Pay attention. I strive to do the things that are good for my health and rest; nevertheless, the very opposite comes about. This gets to the point that if I would try my best to bring these ills about, I could not have things come out worse than they are now when I am trying to do the right things. Everything goes wrong and turns out worse so as to lay me low and steal my life away. I said they come from heaven because I have this belief: if all hell is marching against me and creatures themselves are moved and arranged this way, this is by God's permission, for without it, all of this would not be able to touch even one hair of my head. If I have to name one cause, the cause would be my sins and ingratitude that have brought these ills on me.

The death of my mother, the care that I gave her, the contradictions I had to bear. The dispossession of houses over my head. The retirement of my parents to Ciorani. My remaining alone and abandoned. The need to plan for a crumb of bread that turned out to be stale. The turning of everyone against me for no reason. Deep sadness. All food makes me sick; every medication turns my stomach. I call the doctor, he does not show up. See if it is my fault! I repeat: it is entirely my fault because of my sinfulness. But in all this, I want to hope in the infinite mercy of God, in the blood and infinite merits of Jesus Christ, in the intercession of the Most Holy Mary, in the pity and love of heaven, that all will turn out well. I adore the divine judgments: I recognize that God is holy and just. Just and holy is God, most wise, most provident. He knows what he is doing. *Non contradicam sermonibus Sancti.*[347]

I write all this so that you will pray most fervently and have others pray for me in these very bitter times in which I lack strength for faith, hope, love, patience, and fortitude. I hope you will do this, and the nuns will do this, most of all during this holy novena. I write this to you in confidence and secrecy because I do not want my evils to be made public. May the Lord be blessed!

Then, let me finish [*by saying*] that these deep tragedies come from heaven and only heaven can comfort me, can enlighten me, can free me from them. This is the grace that I seek by means of fervent and persevering prayer such that others can obtain for me what I am incapable

---

[347] "I have not denied the words of the Holy One" (Job 6:10).

of deserving. I write in mortal fear and each bad day is followed by a worse one. May God's will be done forever!

I am about to leave for my usual residence where the climate is better and I do need a change of air. Still my hope is no longer in earthly things but in those of heaven.

This morning the courier heading for your area arrived at my house. I told him that my letter and the candles were at X's house and that he should come here to my house today where I will await him. I will send this letter with him along with an eight-pound box of chocolate that is of very good quality and was made especially for me. But I am no longer able to partake of such a delicacy, hot water and herb tea is enough to upset my stomach fit to die. Let the chocolate serve your community that can enjoy it.

I send my respects to the superior and the sisters.

Keep well. May the Lord bless you. Now is the time to put your effort into prayers for me if you want me to stay alive on this earth.

I pay you my most humble respects.

Naples, May 3, 1744[348]

TO FATHER GIOVANNI MAZZINI, CSSR (N. D.)[349]

He speaks of the celebration of Masses. He seeks some notes and books in order to compose some medications on Christmas.

Long live the Most Holy Trinity and the Most Holy Mary Immaculate

Most Esteemed Father Don Giovanni,

I have not yet received the letter you spoke to me about. If I had received it, I would have answered it.

---

[348] Sarnelli died June 30, 1744, less than two months after writing this letter to Sister Maria Angela del Cielo.

[349] *Lettere di Sarnelli*, Libro II, Lettera II, 287–288.

Regarding the Masses, I am truly sorry: because I had already received several intentions before them, and when I returned to Ciorani, I forgot about them. Thus, besides just a few more, the number of intentions has not gone beyond the five hundred, plus the twenty that you already celebrated for me. Beyond these, I have accepted about thirty, but I expect notices and inquiries. During the summer not many intentions are given because day-to-day work is strong. But in the winter and during Lent they come in greater numbers. The same is true of the sale of books.

I will send the booklets to the other confreres if they want them. Let me know if Brother Vito [*Curzio*] is there.

Ask Father Rector [*Alphonsus*] for the [*book by*] Nie[re]mbergh on scruples. I do not need it right now. Tell him that. Rather, what I would like right away is some good book of novenas for Christmas, because I must prepare a novena, that is, print one at the end of the treatise on the gifts of God. I have to take care of it quickly because the book has to see the light of day at the beginning of December, God willing. I am doing this novena out of necessity and I am shortening the book where it has to deal with the Passion because I do not want to spend more time on it. So I am putting together a short novena like those meditations on the Most Holy Mary, with the practices and pious examples. I know a bit about [*the book of Giuseppe Antonio*] Patrignani [*SJ*]. What I am hoping for is [*to produce*] a worthwhile, well-done book with few words but which says a lot that would elicit affections.

Tell me what you think about this kind of novena: points [*to treat*] and material that you think might be good to use.

Please also tell Father Rector to give me some notes for this little novena, not only about the baby Jesus, but also Jesus' Incarnation, that is, his Sonship to the Father. And along with them, let him write some devout, affectionate and tender sentiments toward the child Jesus. But I am in a hurry, because, as I said, I have to rush this for the beginning of December.

Stay well. Recommend me to His Divine Majesty.

Let me know how things are with Father Don Servio [*Rossi*].

Give my regards to all the fathers and brothers. Recommend me to their prayers.

I kiss your hands.

TO FATHER GIOVANNI MAZZINI, CSsR (UNDATED)[350]

He expresses his thanks for gifts. He asks for prayers in his present needs.

Long live the Most Holy Trinity and the Most Holy Mary Immaculate

Most Esteemed Father Don Giovanni,

I received thirty-six carlins from Mr. X of Cava. I thank you for your help and for the task you undertook for Mr. Y. God knows the extreme need in which I find myself. Ask His Divine Majesty to grant some little peace to my extremely turbulent and afflicted heart, that I can quiet it according to his greater glory and pleasure.

I wrote a letter to Father Rector [*Alphonsus*] on behalf of Mr. Z, who will come tonight. If you want to read it, do so, and if you want to give me a response, I would appreciate your doing so because I really want some good news.

My Dear Father Don Giovanni, I want to make up my mind once and for all, and I ask His Divine Majesty to enlighten me. Please also pray for me yourself and ask others to pray as well. This life is eating me up. I think that the devil is tormenting me in order to drive me away from here and from this work that is so destructive of his evil plans. I do not want to give him the victory just to find peace in my own life and I do not want to leave such a good thing, so I am being eaten up. But if it is the will of God, I want to be where God wants me. Please pray and ask others to do the same since I am a monster of miseries, miseries and pains neither grasped nor understood.

Fiat voluntas Dei in omnibus et super omnia.[351] Amen. Greet everyone for me. I am sending the letter for Brother Gennaro that he asked me for with Father Rector's permission, and I recommend myself to his prayers. As usual, I send my respects to all the priests and brothers; recommend me to their prayers as well.

---

[350] *Lettere di Sarnelli*, Libro II, Lettera III, 288–289.

[351] May God's will be done in all things and forever.

TO FATHER GIOVANNI MAZZINI, CSsR (UNDATED) [352]

He tells about the progress of his book. He speaks of his severe troubles.

Long live the Most Holy Trinity and the Most Holy Mary Immaculate
Most Esteemed Father Don Giovanni,

I am enclosing a note from the administrator about the books. Do not
lose it. I do not know what book he has distributed to the community
mentioned. I will find out, so there is no need for you to deal with it.
Twenty-five carlins are what I have kept with me.

I did not get from Mr. Z the money that he owes me for the last
ones. I cannot believe the complications. I hope to God this all ends
because I have reached my limits; they are at an end. God be blessed
for whose sake I am not only poor, but it is mortal anguish, and I do not
know what to do! May God illumine me for his greater glory.

I am happy about the building; I thank His Divine Majesty and
want to cooperate with all my heart. Would that I could see it finished
tomorrow, but I am happy with the progress.

By the mercy of God, I am very sick, but less gravely than has been
the case up to now. I go about often half-dead; but then I manage. I do
not know how things may go.

My regards to Father Rector [*Alphonsus*] and to all the priests and
brothers.

Don't forget to promote the books in the mission we spoke of. If
there is need for a good number of them, send someone here and I will
take care of it but send along a letter that indicates the number of each
title as well.

I am sending three booklets for the other three brothers there, since
Brother Vito [*Curzio*] forgot them. But on the condition that these
good brothers pray for the benefactor and for the author.

Keep well. Recommend me to the Infinite Goodness. I kiss your
sacred hands.

---

[352] *Lettere di Sarnelli*, Libro II, Lettera IV, 289–290.

TO FATHER GIUSEPPE CHIERCHIA (JUNE, 1733?) [353]

He urges him to go to Ravello and Scala to exercise his ministry.

Long live the Most Holy Trinity and the Most Holy Mary Immaculate

I received your most welcomed letter. But I am sorry that Fr. X is not coming. Nevertheless, I console myself with the hope that you can come here for fifteen days and meanwhile Fr. X can fill in on Fridays. That is very worthwhile here and will be a great help because I cannot do it and no preaching has been done here for a long time. You would give the great sermon in the church and then other exercises. That would bring a great deal of joy here and would produce a lot of good. If you do not come, these exercises would not be held since right after Easter I must go to Naples with God's help. I will wait for you here. I will not offer you a stipend but I will send you home with a good part of the collection; and if in coming you have to incur any expenses, I will surely pay you back. *Nemo propheta acceptus est in patria sua.*[354] Thus, they little appreciate someone who is always there and comes again, but they need someone who is a stranger. I hope your presence here will be the answer to this request. I wrote the same thing to the bishop [*Falcoia*]. That's it.

P.S. I would like to know, if you cannot come now, would you be able to come for Holy Saturday this Easter. I can attest that this bishop wants you to give the retreat to the priests in Ravello. And, at the same time, you would give the great sermon in Ravello and then something more in Scala. This is not certain, however, but what I am asking you now is certain, because if there is to be peace, it is necessary that I go quickly to Naples. Therefore, it is safer for you to come now. If you cannot come right away, come Sunday or Monday because there is still time.

---

[353] *Lettere di Sarnelli*, Libro II, Lettera V, 290–291. Father Chierchia was a priest of the Diocese of Naples who assisted the members of the new Congregation of the Most Holy Savior on some of their earlier missions. There were hopes he would also become a member but he did not choose to do so.

[354] "No prophet is accepted in the prophet's hometown" (Luke 4:24).

[TO THE MOST ILLUSTRIOUS BISHOPS AND PRELATES OF THE CHURCH] (1736) [355]

He urges them to stamp out the vice of prostitution.

May Jesus Christ be our light.

Since a book has been published in this city about reining in carnal licentiousness, the author has seen it as an opportunity to make a gift to Your Most Illustrious Personage. The main purpose of the author was to provide a remedy to the public scandal and that the individual perpetrators be found out and stopped as diligently as possible. A secondary purpose was that young people be moved by curiosity to read of the process to be carried out against these scandalous women and so have before their eyes the horrid image of this lascivious vice, its great dangers and evil consequences. This would cause them to restrain themselves from it if they are already contaminated, while those who are still innocent may be kept from this vice and be moved to the holy uprightness that the writings ably suggest. There is hope for great success in those who attentively read it, by means of that divine light that usually vividly illuminates and speaks to the heart through the promises of Holy Scripture and from the thoughts of the Holy Fathers, both of which fill the book.

Your Most Illustriousness knows well that this is necessary in every locale and village, even though there is the myth that in these places the populace is less infected. But this impure vice, one that loves hiddenness, darkness and secrecy, makes great inroads even there where everyone thinks virtue rules. Although in those places there may not be prostitution, these damnable practices are not absent and cause some half-public scandals, the bad odor of which appears and is smelled all over the place where such scandals are quickly known and, even if they are not so obviously public, are at least whispered about. Even worse, since in a small town, locale or village, a half-known scandal is all the more harmful than a thousand cases in a large city because among a small group as opposed to a large one, evil is a pestilence

---

[355] *Lettere di Sarnelli*, Libro II, Lettera IX, 128–131.

that needs nothing more than closeness and contact in order to grow and infect those nearby. Thus, young people who usually lack caution are eager for lasciviousness and mischief and do not wait for anything more than an opportunity for doing evil. O God, what ruin is not caused to proper custom and reason? What a mess is not made for souls? And what damage does not befall the Church in one scandalous harlot who lives in the neighborhood? This is the vice that by itself has robbed and still robs the Church of more of her children that all the rest put together. The very penetrating thought of St. Remigio is verified by the all-too-universal damage, confirmed by Scripture, by the Holy Fathers, and by experience (that great teacher of all things): *Demtis parvulis, ex adultis, propter carnis vitium, pauci salvantur.*[356] Thus, the more this fire from hell spreads, the greater is the increase of God's outrage, the prejudice to religion and the damnation of the people.

Thus, the author is persuaded that Your Most Illustriousness will receive with open arms and with the great pleasure of your zealous spirit this little book and the respect that comes with it. Since you love the honor of the Almighty, the decency of Christianity, the uprightness of social customs, the eternal well-being of the people committed to your care, you will not cease to promote what the work intends with as much zeal as you can muster, not only by seeking a remedy for carnal corruption, which along with the most terrible vice of blasphemy has become almost universally spread, but also, after having read it all, you will want to pass it on and give it to others to see, and especially to use your authority to charge pastors with reading it. It will awaken them to stand guard with all care that such corruption not take root in their parishes, or if it has already gained a foothold, attend with greater effort to eradicate it and to immediately inform their prelates of it. And also it will benefit them so that from the altar and in the confessional they work with due prudence and caution to help the people to understand that this vice is not just a small evil, nor just a weakness, as is now being bandied about among the seduced young people to their great damage, but that it is an excess of the highest order and by reason of its evil effects, is a grave outrage to the Almighty and proves to be very pernicious to souls, many of whom may hold evil and hell in their hearts.

---

[356] With the exception of children, among adults few are saved because of the vice of the flesh. *(San Remigio, Ex Loh. V. Luxuria, 3, n. 41.)*

The second volume of the work, where I propose practical measures to put reins to prostitution and how to keep the power of carnal filth out of the Kingdom, will be sent to your Most Illustriousness in due time.

Because all the author's hopes right from the beginning have been in his God who inspired the enterprise, he has confidence that by his omnipotent grace he will bring success to such a great purpose which at the same time is most just, necessary and useful to all the Catholic and civil cities. Encouraged by being under the auspices of that infinite goodness, he lives more than certain of overcoming the many burdens that such libidinousness usually brings with it. Thus I beg Your Most Illustriousness with the greatest respect and with all the depth of my heart to commend this work to the Lord and to recommend the task of prayer to the men and women religious and to the lay people of your diocese, so that by means of this unified prayer of the faithful, heaven will be ever more favorable to this cause that is now being brought before His Majesty (may God protect him) so it will be brought to a very effective success. Our most pious prince along with his most zealous main ministers has already given the most obvious evidence of wishing to remedy the situation most effectively. Therefore, the truly wisest of every class of society of our glorious city ardently desire it and are committed to it. That is what we wish here and in the entire Catholic world. Then, as this city shows its desire for it, it will become easier for holy prelates and the whole municipality (this comes about automatically) to obtain the best order for the whole Kingdom.

Finally, the author prostrates himself at the feet of Your Most Illustriousness, and devoutly begs you to accompany this enterprise with your blessing. He remains continually asking His Divine Majesty during the great Sacrifice that he fill Your Most Illustriousness' soul with his dear lights and favors, so you may always grow in zeal and fervor and may be able to lead to heaven all the sheep of his flock. Amen. May the Most Holy Trinity and the Mother of God, the Most Holy Mary Immaculate, be known and loved by everyone for all ages.

Your Most Illustriousness' Servant, Naples, 1736

[TO SIR BISHOPS OF THE KINGDOM OF NAPLES] (MARCH, 1740) [357]

He is sending them some books and pamphlets and recommends books he has already sent.

The author of the book titled *Il mondo santificato*, which he has twice sent to Your Illustriousnesses in the last year along with some circulars, now sends you several pages which contain a summary of the Supreme Pontiffs' pastoral letters in which he commends and approves the practice of daily mental prayer in common and earnestly urges bishops to introduce this pious institution and the faithful to attend it [They also contain] the practices that St. Charles Borromeo followed in the orders he gave to introduce and establish mental prayer in common in his diocese. I therefore ask your Most Illustrious Reverences, after seriously considering the thoughts and blessed expressions of the Supreme Pontiffs and seeing the practices held by St. Charles Borromeo, to be pleased to order that they be observed by all their churchmen and then to publish them in all their churches.

I am also sending a booklet that contains the practices conducted in this metropolitan area and in various other provinces, as well as the programs put into practice by Cardinal Paleoto, Archbishop of Bologna, upon introducing into his diocese the practice of mental prayer in common with the approval of the Supreme Pontiff at the time who enriched them with indulgences for anyone who attended these holy services. And, even more, to urge the leaders to resolutely establish common prayer, he therein responds to all the problems that could arise against doing so. May you holy prelates consider it worth your while to examine these few pages that contain truths of great value and very useful practices for your dioceses. Please do not deny this kindness to the author who strongly desires them for the good of all persons and for no other reason and who most humbly begs you through the depths of the mercy of Jesus Christ.

I am sending several copies so that bishops may spread them throughout their dioceses and may pass them from hand to hand among all the churchmen

---

[357] *Lettere di Sarnelli*, Libro II, Lettera VI, 291–294.

in rotation so that each may read the notices carefully; only good can come from this reading, whether mental prayer is introduced or not.

As far as the books already sent, again I beg the kindness of you Illustrious Prelates to take note of them and I ask that you spread them in your zeal, especially the little work [*Il mondo riformato*] on the care and education of young people along with the practices to raise them well, which are recognized by the wise as most useful for the world and worthy of passage before the eyes of all churchmen; such practices can easily result little by little in a universal reformation within families and in their steady sanctification.

Also, what is explained in the extremely important Tract II of the second volume of Il *Mondo riformato* is worth noting and being read by their churchmen. It deals with irreverences committed within the Church, with the manner of effectively eradicating them and contains very abundant material for preaching to the people about the reverence proper in sanctuaries and for making them fear possible sacrileges. Please have the Ecclesiastical Hierarchy seriously read and consider this task that is so very necessary and glorious for the Catholic religion which is being deeply harmed and aggravated by that detestable abuse. On this matter, I know that many Christian provinces nowadays need instruction, attention and reform. Who is unaware of this? Who among the wise does not weep over it? In fact, all your holy prelates, zealous for the honor of the Almighty and for the uprightness of the Holy Faith have felt the deepest regret over such a disorder. Burning with holy zeal, they have not spared the means and the effort to exterminate (or at least, to lessen) this great evil in their dioceses. Among them the great Cardinal Borromeo stands out. He proposed laws, guidelines and prohibitions based on papal authority and on the holy councils, especially the Council of Trent, to the pastors of souls so that they imitate this most glorious examples and follow the practices.

All of this would show better results [*if done*] during the visits that they pay their dioceses, both regarding the introduction of the exercise of mental prayer in common as well as by proposing to their churchmen to take note of the books I am sending and by providing them for their use.

If, unfortunately, some prelate would not wish to be pleased to attend to these works of God (although it has pleased thousands of other most venerable and most learned personages) either because of the cost of the work, or because he does not consider the tenor of the works to be worthwhile, or for some other reason, may he not leave the books to die on a shelf, but give them to his most zealous assistants so that they may peruse them entirely, form an idea of them and then make a full and detailed report on them. May these same assistants be given the task and the concern, in the name of their prelate and with his authority, to let the other churchmen of the diocese know of them and thus promote their use everywhere.

It is therefore hoped that pastors of souls do not feel bothered that, from time to time, I send you these various works so that they will be patiently read. They are being sent to you for no other reason other than to promote the glory of the Lord of All, the advancement of the holy Church and the salvation of persons. If the author, for the sake of the common good, has not spared himself from trouble, worry and cost for the sake of love of God, may holy prelates not withhold their committed cooperation in this holy project for the real advantage of their dioceses, even if it costs some inconvenience. Be sure that this is not time lost, but rather the best of commitments since all of this brings advantage to Christian people. Indeed, it is already a fact now clearly seen in those provinces whose wise bishops have gratefully received these works with considerable attention and with active zeal.

May Your Most Illustrious Lordships excuse this manner of writing as well as any lack of proper politeness and respect for your most worthy persons, not only in this instance but also in all other similar occasions. You know very well that those who are holy, enlightened, and loving of the eternal and true do not attend to worldly ceremony. Therefore, the number of personages of different kingdoms for whom these works and notes are intended, along with the value of communicating with them, the great amount of ministry for the good of others, and the overwhelming occupations which continually bear down on this weakest of writers do not permit him the use of finer manners and distinctions. Let him end, prostrate at your feet and humbly kissing them, and recommend himself and his poor efforts most heartily to your holy prayers and those of your people. Likewise, even he, poor in virtue and spirit such as he is, offers continuous prayers to the His Divine Majesty for all you Lords and for all your dioceses. He has also requested prayers of the people and of exemplary and fervent religious communities, for the very profound purpose that you may be seen to be totally aflame and effectively moved to renew everywhere this ancient salutary institution and to educate the people with the proper means to keep them inflamed in holy prayer such that when they have become souls full of prayer, we will see "The World Sanctified."[358]

Naples, March, 1740

[TO SIR BISHOPS OF THE KINGDOM OF NAPLES] (OCTOBER 1740)[359]

He introduces them to some of his works. He exhorts them to read and distribute them, to introduce mental prayer in common into all churches, and to combat the vices of blasphemy and corruption.

The author of the works sent to the Most Reverend and Illustrious Bishops and Prelates of the Church both in the past and in this present mailing was moved and encouraged by the zeal of many of those who received them with singular gratitude. They provided copies for their dioceses and introduced the devout activities proposed in them. He has returned again, with reverence, to present these new efforts prepared for the greater glory of God and for the good of souls with the hope that they will be embraced with no less good will and with equal results for the common good that they promise.

I am sending you the second little volume of the work against the contemptible vice of prostitution with a synopsis of the same work and with a new appendix of the laws, edicts and provisions recently published in this metropolis; the first volume of these was sent to you Illustrious Gentlemen in past years. Again I send some notices meant not only for the Ecclesiastical Hierarchy but also for the civil authorities and magistrates. These can be of no little use if they are read not only by the Ecclesiastics but also by authorities and magistrates who, when they see a synthesis of their duties and the abuses ruling in the world to the grave loss of the Christian and public

---

[358] *Il mondo santificato* is the title of one of Sarnelli's writings.

[359] *Lettere di Sarnelli*, Libro II, Lettera VII, 295–299.

government, will be moved (at least some of them) to rein them in, and to be vigilant in exterminating from their provinces such evils. Therefore, I am sending several copies to each of you.

I have included an additional little work on the abuse of blasphemy and of perjury, no less important to the Christian world, especially for some provinces horribly dominated by these excesses. In it there are found reasons, rules, customs and practices that can be applied to disperse these other abuses. This is a very useful book, also for providing instruction and illumination for the Christian people in their obligations. In that way, it will be pleasing to the Almighty that the parish priests and preachers, considering seriously these clear arguments full of substance and eternal truths, would be able to formulate their sermons, preaching and catechism on these models and in their tenor so that, instructing and illumining the people at the same time, they might become wise in knowledge and understanding of the holy law and holy in their observance of it. God would be pleased to see all confessors use the suitable guidelines provided in the work in dealing with sinners who are habituated to these vices..

All of this will work out happily if it would please the Holy Prelates to read these works. Truth speaks for itself, but it must be carefully reflected on and considered, especially in order to note how easily it may be brought to success if the proper means are put into practice, ones both easy and efficacious. This reading would also serve to disperse those clouds and those doubts which at first sight appear about it. Therefore, then, when the proposals I mention are read, it is clear that these feared difficulties really have no force. Nor should the burden of many grave matters impede the reading. Among other matters that cause caution, one of the most dangerous is this: no one ever wants to believe that these disorders reign in their provinces. But the experience of experts demonstrates that no matter whether there are few or many, vices win when they are committed unobserved. Too much evil reigns nowadays and the huge torrent of abuses truly needs to be blocked and resisted. From the beginning the demon has managed to inject into some people, who are otherwise very intelligent, a diffidence and a lack of concern in promoting holy undertakings. But later, when they have seriously noted these actions under the light of that divine truth and in the sincere exposition of the state of things, they have learned what before they did not realize. This made them change their attitudes and advice when they have assured themselves and been persuaded that the world lives in grave self-deception and is in the greatest danger. Thus they become resolved and moved to put an end to all the evils.

The author comes with the most profound respect to render endless thanks from a sincere heart to those very zealous and holy prelates and honorable personages, not only of this Kingdom but of others, who deserve a reward before God to the extent that they went to the trouble of providing these books even to their furthest provinces, and, all the more, for introducing into these areas the holy practices of mental prayer in common that has brought great profit for their people. So all the more do I commend them for their zeal, so that their number may grow and this holy initiative be spread further.

Other holy pastors of souls are also humbly asked not to refuse the trouble of providing in their provinces these works and to establish the exercise of mental prayer in common. Through the depths of the mercy of Jesus Christ, may they not permit their dioceses to be left deprived of means so necessary and effective for eternal salvation, namely, to think of and pray to God daily in this manner. This is what the Christian world needs these days, and in the absence of which we can cry *desolatione desolata est omnis terra*.[360] Wherever the people are instructed as well in these proposed means, they become devoted to holy prayer and the opportune and easy ways to maintain the exercise of thinking of and praying well to God are conveyed to them. In fact, those holy and enlightened persons who have promoted these activities for eternal life have thanked the Almighty for the chance to introduce them and have ended up very satisfied and grateful to those who had proposed the idea to them. The people themselves have thanked the Divine Goodness a thousand times a day that he has provided them with such easy and effective means for sanctifying their own souls, and thus attached to God and to heavenly things hurried along the way of the divine commandments and assured their eternal salvation.

Therefore may all Prelates and Churchmen, for the love and honor of God, agree to hurry to cooperate on these holy plans and receive these suggestions as being in the interests of God and his divine will that they promote these works of his in their provinces. And at the same time, may they give themselves to eradicating those other two most pernicious and

---

[360] "With desolation is all the land made desolate" (Jeremiah 12:11, from Latin Vulgate).

ruinous abuses, dishonesty and blasphemy. The first changes humans into brute animals and tumbles them into every excess. The other sin, more diabolical than human, aims directly at wounding the honor of the Almighty and the destruction of religion. It is only through the lack of those who instruct the people properly and make them see their obligations that they drink from this torrent of iniquity as if it were water. Oh, if all Ecclesiastics would arm themselves with zeal and virtue to combat the abuses and vices, as it is their duty to do, how virtuous and sober would be countless Christian provinces that are not that way now! Rather, iniquity and libertinism now triumph because ignorance of the Holy Law reigns along with the absence of consideration of the eternal maxims. The infinite goodness of God, that is so committed to the sanctification and salvation of his elect, wills these eternal truths to be actively held by the world so that everywhere the monsters of vice may be combated and that holy prayer, that faithful and fruitful mother of all true virtue and Christian perfection, be spread throughout the universe.

May you Illustrious and Reverend Lords excuse my bothering you. Please receive with a good heart these offerings as that which has as its purpose praiseworthy objectives without human interest or earthly reasons. May you be pleased as well to pass these works and notices into the hands of your Churchmen, so that all of them may profit by them. Be sure that their author appreciates your kindness as he prostrates himself at your feet, and humbly kissing them, begs you to accompany with your holy prayers and blessings his plans and holy efforts for the common good. Likewise, miserable and unworthy though he is, he does not cease to petition the Divine Goodness for your eternal wellbeing and for the salvation of the souls committed to you.

Naples, October 1740

[TO THE ECCLESIASTICAL HIERARCHY, PRINCES AND MAGISTRATES] (NO DATE)[361]

He urges them to impede the vices of blasphemy and corruption.

Since the current disorders have spread too far and the abuses and corruptions of the Christian world have become so well known, it has become necessary to decide once and for all to make an effect response, especially to the terrible crime of blasphemy and to the abominable vice of public disorder *[prostitution]*. Both are the gravest and most ruinous of evils and are exceedingly hateful. The first contains a horrible sin that seeks to directly wound the honor of the Almighty. The second, because of its very evil consequences that turns humans into beasts and throws them into an abyss of every kind of evil, especially when these excesses become widespread and scandalous as is sadly the case nowadays.

Therefore it is time to unite force with strength and for the ecclesiastical and secular leaders to join in blessed harmony by a confederation of holy commitment and will, each in its proper authority and jurisdictional administration, so that each acts with true zeal in its proper tasks to put into the field an army of salutary and efficacious means to combat and dissipate, to beat down and destroy the army of vice and crime that threatens to devour the earth and ruin the universe. By doing this, what might not be attainable for the good of the Church and of the political government? In this way, the ministers of justice, the lieutenants of God, laying aside human fastidiousness, pressures, complaints and respect, with generous Christian courage will take up the sword of rigorous and exemplary justice, disperse the clandestine plottings of the impious and punish the evildoers; this way they will free the innocent from the damage and danger of being perverted. This is the reason that the Almighty has given authority to princes and the latter have appointed magistrates so that they may act to maintain the provinces that have been committed to their care in peace and tranquility and to defend the divine honor, especially when it is publicly reviled by the brazenness of mortals. *Non enim sine causa gladium portat. Dei enim Minister est, vindex in iram ei, qui malum agit.*[362] Recalling their eternal and indispensable

---

[361] *Lettere di Sarnelli*, Libro II, Lettera VIII, 299–308.

[362] "Authority does not bear the sword in vain! It is the servant of God to execute wrath on the wrongdoer" (Romans 13:4).

obligations for which they are to render a strict account to God in that supreme, true tribunal from which there is no appeal where the works of justice are examined and discussed with the highest rigor and where even the least omission is punished severely *Audite Reges, intelligite et discite Judices... Data est a Domino potestas vobis, et virtus ab Altissimo. Qui interrogabit opera vestra, et cogitationes scrutabitur.*[363]

Thus the purpose and intent of this work is to produce a remedy for many of the carnal liberties, both public and private, not only in the City but also in the surrounding area and villages. And in order to do so completely, it requires that the ecclesiastical hierarchy and the magistrates are fully aware of the disorders that are ruining the behavior of the provinces and have at hand the means to remedy them. This should not cause anyone to panic into thinking that there is a wish to invent something new and thereby feel that some novelty would decrease the value of holy plans and bring distrust of the leadership. Both the reverend prelates and the most worthy administrators of justice know that nothing is being requested from them except that they put into effective action with force and zeal what is already stated in the divine scriptures, what the sacred Councils have ordered, what the Holy Fathers have taught, what has already been established by canon law, civil law, municipal law, politics and what wise magistrates have already accomplished; [*in a word,*] by all who are jealous of the Almighty's honor and of the advancement of the people for whom they must care, something well-regulated societies have held closest to their hearts.

Here it is proper to quote from the most holy and provident documents founded on the eternal truths that the venerable Father Master Avila [*St. John of Avila*], an apostolic man, who was no less a learned and serious theologian, a zealous and holy man, sent to a gentleman who was an assistant minister of Seville. Father Avila wrote to urge him to exercise his duty, as well as he could, of applying a remedy to the dissolution and abuses. Here is what he says in short: *Judicium durissimum his, qui praesunt fiet.*[369] Philosophers affirm that the obligation of the one who governs is to provide the following benefits: Magistrates are to see to it that the citizens live virtuously in a way that gives honor to the Almighty. Otherwise anyone who would assume

---

[363] "Listen therefore, O kings, and understand; learn, O judges of the ends of the earth... For your dominion was given you from the Lord, and your sovereignty from the Most High; he will search out your works and inquire into your plans" (Wisdom 4:2, 4).

such a position would be acting in grave wickedness: *Noli quaerere fieri judex, nisi valeas virtue irrumpere iniquitates.*[364] The acts of the Council of Cabilonium [*Chalon-sur-Saône*] [365] affirm that those who govern the people should take counsel with the bishops in important matters that concern the public wellbeing. The same thing is insinuated by the Emperor Justinian in a truly Christian spirit. The King of Castile was accustomed to do so very often and one of those regents saw to it that a number of holy prelates were gathered in a provincial council in Toledo, asking them to please enlighten and counsel him on the ordinances and laws by which he should govern his realm in the most virtuous way.

After this the Venerable Father adds what follows, speaking to the same ministers and getting right to the point:

Public places for prostitutes are tolerable due to human weakness. But it is proper to demand that no one may establish or maintain brothels there. The reason is that such occasions excite desire and thus the evil that is tolerated to avoid a greater evil has the opposite effect and destroys the purpose for which it was permitted. In this way, prostitutes do not become the occasion and stumbling block to human desire. Thus brothels should not be allowed to be established in such areas, nor should prostitutes be permitted to lounge at entrance to their houses, *and all the more, not be allowed [to stand around] in public places soliciting innocent passersby to scandalous lives* so that they stop them from provoking sexual desires. It sometime happens that they not only incite men to evil by words but excite them by gestures as well. *O dear! It is not only by word and gesture that these perverted women today scandalize the whole world!* It is bad enough that unfortunate young people know that there are such places around without having these lascivious women wandering outside them to be seen and noticed. Your Excellency has already ordered and enacted a law that dishonorable women may not be employed in cafes and taverns. It is not right that prostitutes be allowed to live among upright families but they must be kept completely separate in assigned places. Nor should they be allowed to

---

[364] "The mighty will be mightily tested" (Wisdom 6:6).
[365] Deliberation 813.

go out as a mistress or escort, nor elegantly dressed, because the apparent prosperity of such women is a greater danger and temptation to weaken honorable women.[366]

In fact, this great soul (I am referring to Father Avila), saw to it that what others just suggested was put into practice; thus we find stated in regard to his zeal: "He brought it about that in the whole estate of the Marquise of Priego, wherever there were very populous places, there were no houses of public women, which were brothels of sin and locations of scandal. This remained the case for years and years."[367]

Therefore, it would be pleasing to the Almighty for every prince, every gentleman, every magistrate to read seriously these divine truths and scrupulously enforce them in each point: *Qui legit, intelligat.*[368] They should do so and reverently receive as holy prophecies these salutary and very justifiable requests of the sacred ministers of the Almighty; [*they should see them*] as the will of God and the duty of the Holy Catholic Church, their Mother, for the veneration of the Church is nothing less than the veneration of God! Therefore, the ecclesiastical hierarchy, specially assisted and illuminated by the Holy Spirit and fully instructed in the wisdom of the eternal truths, places these matters on the most carefully balanced scales of the sanctuary and knows and searches the truth, the crimes and the dangers so much better than others.

1. The holy prelates will thus make sure with apostolic courage and the most vigilant zeal to separate dishonest women from honorable association, to place all of them in sequestered confines. The magistrates will carry out the needed requirements. Consider the grave terms of disgust the holy Councils use to speak of this very dangerous mixing-in [with the general populace]. At the Council of Buda, after lamenting over other very grave disorders brought on the world by prostitution, concluded: *Cum ex vicinitate turpium*

---

[366] In vita, p. 1, Let. 11.

[367] *Ibid.*

[368] "Let the reader understand" (Matthew 24:15).

mulierum, et maxime meretricum, multis plerumque peccati occasio ministretur etc: et Religio Christiana, ac multorum bonorum honestas enormiter infametur.[369] The Enamense Council bitterly complained against prostitutes, exclaiming that these dishonest women are to be removed from Catholic realms as unworthy of living on earth: *Meretrices mortem inducentes et peierantes, tamquam terra indignas, et terra proiicite.*[370] Likewise, in small towns, neighborhoods and villages where such tolerance is not permitted, let them in fact banish prostitutes. The reason is that the purpose for which they can be tolerated is not present, because even one of these scandalous women is enough to contaminate an entire area. There is all the more at risk the smaller a location is since children, youths and young girls are tempted, as well as widowed and married people and so the amount of evil, serious and minor, increases.

2. Furthermore, note that those lascivious women are not to be employed in cafes, inns, and hotels. This is the kind of scandal by which many are lost, and many travelers will not be able to avoid giving in to the temptation, contaminating themselves by falling into the arms of these she-wolves. What is worse, this ruins the character of many young men who come from other places for studies and then return home for the holidays. It is to be greatly feared that many of them, finding themselves in those proximate and strong occasions with no fear of those who know them learning of their sins, will end up ruined and lose their health, the holy fear of God and their reputation. They will not only abandon all commitment to their virtue and education, but will return to their homes filled of vice and evil and there continue to scandalize their companions and honorable women. Innkeepers, who pimp wanton woman for profit and who

---

[369] "Because of the proximity of evil women, especially prostitutes, is the cause of very many sins...the Christian religion and the probity of many good people is enormously discredited" *(Canon XLVII, sub. Nic 111. An. 1279).*

[370] "Eject, as unworthy of the earth, prostitutes who are the cause of death and lies" *(Canon IV, An. 1009).*

draw regular customers [*for such a purpose*], should be rigorously penalized and made an example of. These innkeepers, who for a crust of bread destroy a mountain of people by a considerable destruction of human relationships, are truly enemies of God and of the Church, enemies of souls, enemies of propriety and of the public. If anyone deserves to feel the sword of human justice with all its strength aimed at wicked disturbers of the common good, who would it be if not these evildoers? Oh, for God's sake, use every power you have in all zeal to bring about an effective resolution.

3. All that I have said applies all the more in the case against those wanton traveling women, who thirsting for prey and conquest and seeking evermore pasture for their evil desires, like wolves from hell with unquenchable voraciousness, move from place to place, from one end of the land to the other, infecting the world, spreading everywhere the froth of their contagious poison. These temptresses leave with people rooted in more vice that last beyond their stay and what they themselves have done. This is what happens in those unfortunate places where the leaders are not vigilant with a hundred eyes and do not administer justice with a hundred hands. When such women are driven out by the zeal of those who are in charge of the surrounding provinces, they go to sow weeds in the other provinces where they find the leaders careless, leading a good life and resting so that they leave the field open and free for them to enter and stay and to do the damage for which they are talented. Thus, the populace becomes infected and is stimulated by their bad habits to mount the fiercest assaults upon honest women. Therefore, this universal pestilence must be snuffed out at all costs and such traveling women must never be permitted, especially if they are foreigners, to have housing or passage in the area; all the more, they must not be allowed to

stay permanently. How all too frequently does this ruinous sin exist! The leaders must remember that the Almighty commands that they do not allow a group of prostitutes to live among them, since even one of these guilty women is capable of infesting an area with abomination and inflame the world with sin: *Ne prostitutas filiam tuam, ne contaminetur terra, et impleatur piaculo.*[371]

4. Attend also to remedy the scandal of some loose women who live in small towns, neighborhoods and villages and have a bad reputation even if they are not public prostitutes. These infernal reefs, hidden beneath the surface, bring shipwreck to thousands and thousands of souls; they are like underground mines quietly tunneling away for the destruction of the place. Therefore, either they are to be converted or banished, since everyone in the area knows of them and gossips about them on every corner, almost endlessly, keeping the whole place in whispers and disturbance. It is certain that it would be a lesser evil for such a woman to be declared infamous rather than to let her pass as an honorable woman when she is dissolute. Oh, how many women pass themselves off as upright while they are worse than prostitutes! This abominable sin loves darkness, hiding places, secrecy, whether to preserve its reputation or for the danger that it bears with it. And so every small indication of evil turns out to be, in fact, an abyss of iniquity. Moreover, who does not know that a little yeast is enough to corrupt the whole batch? *Modicum fermentum totam massam corrumpit.*[372] So if some woman is in truth secretly sinful, she is to be corrected by the leader in secret and should be threatened with a serious punishment if the matter becomes public, while in the meantime there should

---

[371] "Do not profane your daughter by making her a prostitute, that the land not become prostituted and full of depravity" (Leviticus 19:29).

[372] 1 Corinthians 5:6 *(DR)*.

be some faithful informers assigned around her to be continuously attentive to gather information; if she is found to be guilty, the scandal should be removed by proper rigorous means.

5. Let the authorities also pay attention to admonish, correct, punish, and even excommunicate concubines, especially if they are married. Such damnable people can never be allowed or tolerated. *Si quis adulterium perpetraverit, morte moriatur et maechus et adultera.*[373]

6. Above all of the pious actions to be taken by holy prelates and the faithful, they should take to heart principally the task of protecting from the danger of prostitution poor young girls, orphans, runaways, indigents, vagabonds, those in peril of losing their virginity or who have already lost it. Above all, if these are the daughters, relatives or sisters of women of ill repute, [*they must be protected*]. If these latter girls and so many "prostitutes in seed" are not removed from danger and not helped in time, they will prostitute themselves and will ruin the province as well as themselves. Thus, every young girl in danger who is rescued, either by placement in a conservatory or in an upright household or by marriage, is one prostitute removed from the world and so dioceses will be freed from millions of scandal. What work of mercy could be more worthwhile? In place of building sumptuous and richly adorned churches! Instead by doing this, one protects holy virginity, one cares for the purity of the social fabric and one preserves faithful youngsters from contamination.

7. To protect purity that is endangered, one must watch that pimps (male or female) do not turn up in places to go about, under various false pretenses, seducing and kidnapping poor young girls. They take them into the cities and sell their purity to whoever

---

[373] "Both the adulterer and the adulteress shall be put to death" (Leviticus 20:10).

makes an offer, and then, after getting their money, leave them in abandonment burdened with vices and corruption; then these young girls, finding themselves left with lost virtue and modesty, turn into prostitutes and die in their sins. Oh, how much evil in one sin! Authorities should realize that this is not a rare happening, especially in the neighborhoods and villages near to large cities. What horrendous sins, excesses impossible to believe, appear if this growingly extreme wickedness is not preached against in the loudest voice: *Et puellam vendiderunt pro vino, ut biberent.*[374]

After hearing all this, if people do not pay attention to the eternal divine truths, and for the sake of worldly and political purposes, human respect, pressure or shock do not resolve to put an effective end to these public abuses, we will see who speaks the truth in the Valley of Jehoshaphat; will it be the world? Or God? Be aware therefore that the saintly Cardinal Borromeo, who after he had recommended to the prelates and parish priests to have recourse to the magistrates and beg their authority, principally to destroy the execrable sin of blasphemy and to punish that sacrilege with the rigor it deserves, added that if the magistrates avoid this, they will be guilty before God of all the sins that they left unpunished or did not punish to the extent they deserved. As well, the sacred Lateran Council, under Leo X, defined: *Quod si saeculores Judices (quod minime futurum speramus) blasphemiae convictos iustis poenis non afficiunt, sciant iisdem poenis, quas de sontibus sumere neglexerunt, vi Concilii Lateranensis se teneri.*[375]

Authorities should be worried and be moved to rein in such damnable license and such pride of morals by what the Supreme Pontiff Innocent III says: that Ecclesiastical Authorities as well as secular ones who observe the rising of abuses and the triumphing of error and do not oppose them, do not resist them, do not exert all possible force to dissipated them are guilty before the Tribunal

---

[374] "They sold girls for wine, and drunk it down" (Joel 3:3).

[375] "Civil judges who do not punish with just penalties those guilty of blasphemy (and we hope that there will be none in the future), should realize that by virtue of the Lateran Council they are liable to the same punishments that they neglected to apply to the guilty" (Act. Med. to. 1, pag.6, col. 2.)

of God the same as if they consented to, cooperated in such evil and fomented these sins: *Error, cui non ristiture, approbatur; et veritas, cui minime defendatur, opprimitur, negligere quippe, cum possis deturbare adversarios, nihil est aliud, quam fovere.*[376] The Holy Fathers considered that no matter how honest and circumspect in his ministry he may be, an authority who acts leniently and remissly in punishing the dissolute is condemned. The world does not think about this and fears it even less.

If there were no other reason, all authorities and every one of the faithful should, as much as they can, commit themselves to the destruction of these abuses, to dissipate the sinfulness, and to severely punish the evildoers. In this way, they may offer some compensation to the divine justice so wounded by the guilty world and so avoid the tremendous scourges that an offended Being who is Almighty would usual afflict on his sinful people, including as well, remarks St. Augustine, their leaders who did not oppose evildoers, who did not admonish the corrupt, who did not make efforts out of real zeal to keep the people among whom he lives in the holy fear of God.

---

[376] Error that is not resisted is approved. And truth that is little defended is denied. Not to oppose enemies when it is possible is nothing other than taking their side.

CHAPTER SIX

AFFECTIONS AND PRAYERS TO THE MOST HOLY TRINITY

The Redemptorists of Ciorani[377]

[Translator's Note: This chapter is a translation of the first part of a booklet published by the Redemptorists of the community of Ciorani as part of the celebration of the 300th birthday of St. Alphonsus Liguori. The booklet is an edited reprint of a work published by Sarnelli shortly before his death, Devozioni alla SS. Trinitá e a Maria SS. per apparecchio a una buona morte, da farsi una volta al mese.[378]

The booklet had its origin in early 1743, during the great mission outside Naples that Sarnelli was directing. His labors and the advance of tuberculosis forced him to take to his bed. He believed that he would never outlive this painful moment, so he began to journal prayers of praise and petition in preparation for death. After a time, his health improved and he was able to take up some of his work until his death the following year. During his recuperation, he wished to continue his commitment to make the whole world know of God's plentiful redemption, so he organized his notes into this booklet, setting them into prayers for each day of the week. This work, probably more than any other of his writings, shows us the fundamental elements of his spirituality, not in theory but as he actually lived it.]

---

[377] *Elevazioni e preghiere alla SS. Trinitá del B. Gennaro M. Sarnelli,* [Published Privately], Ciorani, SA, Italy, 1997.

[378] *Devotions to the Most Holy Trinity and the Most Blessed Mary as a Preparation for a Good Death, to be Practiced Once a Month*

FOR MONDAY: ACTS OF FAITH

"I believe; help my unbelief!"[379]

How deeply I thank you, O my God, a Trinity of persons and one in essence, for the gift of our holy faith that you have freely given me simply out of your goodness, the merits of my Redeemer Jesus Christ and the intercession of Mary! You have given me this grace, even though you foresaw that I would be unappreciative and not live according to the teaching of so holy a faith, even though you did not do so for many people outside the true Church, the Roman Catholic Apostolic Church, in which alone reigns the true Faith. This faith is a gift so divine and glorious that if we were to make a comparison, a thousand lifetimes would not be enough to gain such a treasure! I therefore thank you for so great a gift and I profess to believe with my whole mind and heart all that has been revealed to the holy Church.

I believe in you, three really distinct persons so that one is not the other but, as I believe, you are all equal in total majesty, power, wisdom, goodness and all perfections because the three of you form one sole and same God [*This is so*] because you, O Father, possess being of yourself, without receiving it from the other persons because you are unbegotten and ungenerated; and you, O Son, receive the same divine nature from the Father because you are begotten by him; and you, O Holy Spirit, receive it through the eternal and natural breath of the Father and the Son. I also believe that this difference in the way you act brings no inequality of perfections, power or goodness among you because I believe that the whole divine nature, which is a boundless sea of all that is good, lies entirely in you, O Father, entirely in you, O Son, and entirely in you, O Holy Spirit. I believe that all the same fullness that may be found in each person is not duplicated or multiplied and so you are all totally perfect whether as one person or two, or, as you are, all three.

I believe that although you, O Father, exist of yourself, and you, O Son, receive the being of the Father, and you, O Holy Spirit, receive

---

[379] Mark 9:24 [*DR* 9:23].

it from both of the others, you are all totally equal among yourselves because your Divine Nature essentially demands that the essence of the Father is such as not to be received from another, that of the Son is that it must be received from the Father by generation, and that of the Holy Spirit is that it must be received by the breath of the other two. And all of this is without any precedence in time or seniority of perfection because I believe you are co-eternal, of the same being, most highly exalted together, co-omnipotent, and matching in every glory.

The Catholic Faith consists in the veneration of a single God in Trinity, the Trinity in Unity, without confusion of persons, nor separation of substance; indeed, the Father is a different Person, the Son is a different Person, and the Holy Spirit is a different Person; but the divinity of the Father and of the Son and of the Holy Spirit is one, equal in glory, co-eternal in majesty.[380]

That is what I believe and since I have lived by your grace in this Holy Faith, which is uniquely true, infallible and divine, so I now profess that I am willing to die without paying attention to any deceit of hell; and I declare to wish to change into acts of the most living faith all the suggestions of the devil. I do not comprehend the mystery of how you are one God in substance and three in Persons; but the more I lack comprehension, all the more do I believe; and I rejoice in subjecting my intellect in the deference to your Faith, and indeed I am happy to believe while not comprehending so that I can give you greater honor and greater glory, as I confess you to be a God above anything that all created minds can understand.

Therefore, I confess you to be the true God because you surpass in your superiority all thoughts of any creature, inexpressible in any tongue and uncapturable by any mind. I confess it is through your mercy that I believe; but because I know that my faith is weak, I beg you, O Lord, to stimulate my faith in you to the extent that it is worthy of you, the first and unspeakable Truth, to whom all trust is due. Still, because it is impossible for me to possess an infinite faith that a God of infinite wisdom and truth deserves, I unite my faith with that of your Church, of all the patriarchs and prophets, of all the apostles and martyrs, of all the teachers and virgins, of all the saints and angels *[when they were]* in

---

[380] See the Athanasian Creed.

the state of pilgrims [*I unite it*] with the faith of my Mother, the Most Holy Mary who, beyond all others, had a faith worthy of a God. I offer you this faith; by reason of the love and merits of this faith that brought your Son down to earth, I ask you to take my unworthy self out of this earth and into heaven to see face to face without a veil and by means of the light of glory, what I now only believe.

I believe that you, the only begotten Son of God, Jesus Christ, the Son equal to the Father, became the true son of Mary; born from all eternity by a Father without beginning, born in time of the Virgin Mary. And so I believe you are true God and true human, perfect God and perfect human for you became human in such a way that you did not cease and could not cease to be God; and the very God that you always were, you will continue to remain with your Father and with your Holy Spirit. Although you are the same God, it is only you who was incarnated and made human for me, not the Father or the Holy Spirit, although they by the divine will produced the mystery of the Incarnation.

I believe that you are the Redeemer of the world and of the entire human race because I believe you died for the salvation of all human beings without excluding even one from the power of enjoying the fruit of your Passion and death. And I believe that you died, indeed not as God, but as a human being because as God you cannot suffer and are immortal by your nature; but as you are a God become human, in this way I believe in a God scourged, burdened, murdered and dead for me. And I believe that your death is the life of the world. If a God had not died for humans, no one would have hope of salvation; so your death is my life; your sufferings are my eternal salvation.

I believe that you, Son of God and of Mary, are the founder and master of your Church, which is your Kingdom on earth, that you have furnished with the seven endless fonts of grace that are the seven sacraments in which the fruits of your passion and death are applied. Among these, I believe that the Eucharist is the greatest of all [*the sacraments*] because it contains you, author of grace, as divine and human; and I believe it contains your body and blood with your soul and divinity, and together with you it brings your Eternal Father and the co-eternal Holy Spirit since they are inseparable from you.

I believe that you sacrifice yourself on many altars by the hands of your ministers, your priests, to the glory of the Father for the benefit of the whole world, renewing the same sacrifice that you made on the cross. The one on the cross was in blood, that of the altar is bloodless; but it is the same sacrifice because in both you are the victim, you are the priest. All the sacrifices offered and to be offered until the end of the world, I offer to you for me through the hands of your Mother Mary from whom you received the material for the sacrifice: your body and blood. And I beg that you offer [*this sacrifice*] to your Eternal Father in satisfaction for all my sins and for those of the entire world [*Offer it*] in thanksgiving for all the graces that have been granted to my unworthy self and to all that is created [*Present it*] to beg for me and for all your creatures whatever temporal graces that will work favorably for the good of the soul [*Offer it to beg for*] all spiritual graces but especially that of a holy death, on which depends our truest good since our eternal well-being depends on it. Please offer it to the sovereign majesty of the Father in the name of all creatures as recognition of him as the Lord, Protector and Sovereign of all creation [*O Son of God*] at your feet the whole universe should empty itself as should all creatures before their Creator; and you, as the High Priest of the Father and Supreme Pontiff of the universe who made satisfaction for all.

At every moment, I must wish, and do indeed wish, to be dissolved in your love, O my Beloved Lord, totally consumed in honoring you.

I believe that your Church, which is the Roman Catholic Apostolic Church whose visible head is the Roman Pontiff, is the only true Church in which alone the Truth lives and reigns, and that this Church which boasts of you, the eternal and true God, as its author, protector and defender, is the foundation and pillar of truth in which there can never be room for any shadow of error, despite the machinations of hell by means of many heresies; nor can it ever waver no matter how much many tyrants have struck against it. And I believe that this Church is always kept undefeated amid countless enemies and is always a glorious victor over all sects; you keep it steadfast in the midst of so many storms and invincible in a world of enemies; your word alone will support it until the end of the ages to your glory and to the shame of all our enemies: *the gates of Hades will not prevail against it.*[381]

---

[381] Matthew 16:18.

I believe, O my beloved Redeemer, the only begotten Son, that you are twice begotten and twice born: born of the Father as true God and of your mother as true human. Nevertheless, you are only one Son who was always born as Son because you were born God from God, virginal Son of the Father without the aid of a mother, and born as God by your Mother *[Mary]* without the aid of a father by the working of the Holy Spirit. Only a God could be born of an eternally virgin mother, virginal before the birth, virginal in giving birth, and virginal after the birth. Such a magnificent Mother is proper for a God and so it is indeed fitting for you to have formed her in such a way as the only virgin with out corruption, alone free by grace for all sin, including original sin. For a Son holy by nature and sinless in being, it was proper that she be holy by grace and sinless by singular privilege.

Therefore, I believe in the Son of God in the bosom of the Father, the human-divine Son in the womb of the Mother, omnipotent and immense in the bosom of the Father, the Lord clothed as a slave in the womb of the mother; unable to suffer and immortal in the bosom of the Father, unable to suffer and yet subject to suffering, immortal and yet condemned to death in the womb of the mother. I believe you are God the Creator in the bosom of the Father; I believe you are the human-divine Redeemer in the womb of the Mother, come down to earth for the universal salvation of all humans beings, in a way that no one is condemned by your fault, because you will all to be children of your Church and to all you have applied the infinite efficacy of your blood shed to wash away all sin for the salvation of all. Whoever is lost is lost by their own fault. By your grace, I believe in such a truth so glorious in you and I detest with all my heart the horrible blasphemy of those who accuse you of being a Redeemer only partially, who saves only those you capriciously pick [*I believe*] you should not permit me to be lost so that I become the object of the curse that sinners would throw in my face: *Look, here among us is someone who believed in a God who died for the salvation of all: how did he get condemned?* Do not permit it, O Beloved Lord.

I believe all this because my mother, the holy Church, commands me to believe it for you have revealed to the Church all that it commands me to believe. What I believe it's as certain as are you, God of infinite wisdom who cannot lie because you know whatever exists and, as a

God of infinite truth, who cannot lie since you present things as you know them. So it is through faith that you give me a share in your wisdom and truth by learning, without fear of deceit, truths that are beyond my limited capacities.

And I believe that you have given this revelation to your Church while equipping and sustaining it by means of clear and evident credibility by which it is enabled to recognize how divine and certain are its dogmas, infallible its doctrine, heavenly in the laws it imposes and the teachings which it gives, adorable in the beliefs which it proclaims so that no one, not even an atheist or a total fool, could call them into doubt. It is so clear and so evident that you, God of eternal truth, are the author of our Faith that there is no way that you can condemn us for what we believe because whom should we believe if not God?

Thus, all that Faith teaches me is as certain as it is certain that God is God, and it is as impossible that any shadow of error could darken our Faith as it is impossible that Truth can lie and God be an impostor or trickster. I live so sure under the shade of your Faith that with all confidence I can say: my God, if what I believe is an error, it is You, O God, who have deceived me. As sure as it is that you cannot deceive since you are holy by your very nature, so certain is my faith.

Increase our Faith [382]

Faith, my beloved Lord, faith! Spiritual goods grow in measure to this faith and every evil comes from lack of faith. I believe, O my God, I believe with all my intellect that I am happy to submit to what Faith teaches me. More than that, I firmly state that I believe all the more, the less I understand and the more you command me to believe, the mysteries beyond my very limited mind and that of every created intelligence. And so I offer you a respect that is worthy of a God as I conceive a higher esteem of you and your being because you reveal yourself as a God superior to all minds. I believe as much as all the patriarchs and prophets of the Old Law believed, but with this difference, that I believe it as something already completed while they believed it as future and so predicted it as what needed to happen. God alone can, with infallible certainty, predict future free and contingent events and reveal them to

[382] Luke 17:5.

the world. I believe that the many oracles and prophecies are historical because I believe the Son of God was made man and died for humans as was predicted. I believe the same Faith believed and spread through the world by so many apostles, authenticated by so many millions of martyrs, embraced by so many kings and queens, by so many princes and ladies, who were made happier by giving humble service to a crucified God than by the majesty of their thrones, defended by so many teachers of sublime genius and wisdom: Augustine, Thomas, Athanasius, Basil, Nazianzen, Chrysostom, Hillary, Jerome, Ambrose and countless others. It is impossible for a faith not to be true when it is defended with such commitment by the greatest minds in the world.

I believe a Faith proven by countless miracles, by the holiness of so many who have professed it and by the constancy of its dogmas, which were examined and discussed in so many councils; challenged by so many heretics, yet always triumphant over its enemies and able to clarify the truth which it teaches. Three prerogatives demonstrate the solidity of our true and divine Faith: it alone has power from God to work miracles; it alone makes its followers holy; it alone is changeless in its dogma.

I believe a Faith entirely conformed to right reason and to natural understanding, although the Faith is superior to it, but is not contradictory of it, because the same author of our Faith is the author of nature. I must exclaim in joy: *Thy testimonies are become exceedingly credible*.[383] So strong, clear and convincing are the reasons of our Faith that whoever does not believe is totally inexcusable; and although the mysteries may be obscure, by reason of their credibility, they seem to have lost the character of obscurity.

Let the peoples praise you, O God; let all the peoples praise you. The earth has yielded its increase.[384]

The virginal soil of the Most Holy Mary has produced the Lily of the Valley, its fruit the double substance, divine and human. Your Son has already brought about the redemption of the human race in much suffering and in a painful death and has poured out all the blood in his veins. May such suffering not be lost, O Father; may so much blood not be shed in vain; may these be the remedy for all evils; may they be the

---

[383] Psalm 92:5 [DR].
[384] Psalm 67: 5–6 [DR 66:6–7].

washing away of all the world's sins. Let all the nations recognize you, confess you, love you as the only true God with your Son and your shared Holy Spirit; may all people enjoy the results of the passion and death of our universal Savior.

May God be gracious to us and bless us and make his face to shine upon us…that your way may be known upon earth, your saving power among all nations.[385]

My sins, I know them well, Beloved Father, are an obstacle to your glory. Pardon me and all the children of the Catholic Church for all our sins. We offer you whatever suffering or death we may endure so that your Most Holy name may be gloried everywhere. Show all the beauty of your face, O Son, for you are the beauty of the Father and so it is impossible to know you and still not love you. Open the depths of your mercy to all, O Holy Spirit, so that all may know the true way of eternal salvation which is the Catholic Church alone. Let all follow Jesus Christ—their Leader, Lawgiver, Redeemer, and Judge—the only way to salvation.

All the ends of the earth have seen the victory of our God.[386]

Oh, how my heart rejoices, O my God and Lord, that you are glorified throughout the whole world! Oh, how happy am I, my Savior, that you reign throughout the whole universe by having established your throne over so many heresies conquered and so many idols crushed!

All the errors that arise against your Faith only allow you to triumph over new enemies; persecutions against your Church do nothing but make your glory shine more resplendently.

O apostles, martyrs, teachers, all the saints, I thank you for having toiled and suffered to spread the name of my Jesus and his Faith through the whole world. All your fatigue and suffering are graces given to you by my Jesus; you are the greater in debt to the extent that you have stretched yourself for his glory and have suffered the more for his honor. But all these are benefits done for me because I confess and recognize that all the glory of my Savior, Lord and Master, Jesus Christ, is for my own good. My God, enlighten everyone with your Faith or grant me all that I request for all unbelievers.

---

[385] *Ibid.* 67:22 [*DR* 66:22].
[386] *Ibid.* 98:3 [*DR* 97:3].

Would I had died instead of you.[387]

O Most Holy and Lovely Faith of my Jesus Christ! I wish I were worthy to lose my life for you and to shed all my blood by means of a generous martyrdom in your honor! Oh, that I could convert all false sects by some suffering of mine, dissipate all errors, draw all the nations of the world to adore you, fight all heretics and schismatics and unbelievers under your glorious command!

Oh, that I could speed through the whole world and preach your truth everywhere so that all minds would adore, all tongues confess, all hearts love God the Father, God the Son, God the Holy Spirit, the God in three Persons while One in Essence! I am not worthy of the great grace of losing my life for you; that would make me exceedingly happy. Although I am not worthy of offering you so much, O my God, I offer you my life. Arrange it as you please, take it away in any way you wish. I proclaim and declare that I return this life of mine to you as an authentic testimonial to all revealed truth. I give it to you, O my God, in testimony to the essential divinity, consubstantiality, co-eternity and equality of all three Divine Persons; in testimony to the Holy Spirit proceeding equally from the Father and the Son. I offer it to you in testimony to the true divinity and true humanity of my Redeemer Jesus Christ, equal to the Father in as far as he is God because he is of the same substance as the Father, yet less than the Father in so far as he is human and Son of the same substance as his Mother. Therefore, I confess one sole divine Person, Jesus Christ, subsisting in two natures, divine by the Father and human by the Mother, not in a merely apparent humanity but truly so, true flesh, true blood just as is the case for the humanity of every human being descended from Adam, yet without Adam's guilt because he was conceived by the work of the Holy Spirit in the virginal womb of Mary, the true Mother of God and Virgin Mother.

I give you my life in testimony of the grace gained for the whole world by the divine Redeemer, the grace essentially necessary for eternal life; the grace that heals the nature corrupted by sin; the grace that gives vigor to the human will to be able to do good while not removing the will's freedom. I give you my life in testimony of the redemption achieved by my Jesus, dead for the salvation of all human

---

[387] 2 Samuel 18:33 [DR 19:2].

beings, both predestined and reprobate, in a way that each one is saved owing entirely to Jesus, but each one is condemned through his or her own fault, because my God does not save capriciously but wishes on his part for all to be saved.

I offer my life in testimony to the seven sacraments instituted by my Redeemer for the good and glory of his Church which is the Catholic [*Church*] alone, and of which he is the invisible head and the Roman Pontiff the visible head. And in this Church I profess the perpetual Sacrifice of the holy Mass in which is offered the body and blood of my Redeemer because, by means of the words spoken by the priest, the legitimate minister of the eternal High priest Jesus Christ, the substance of bread is changed into the substance of the body and the substance of the wine into the blood of my Jesus Christ, who remains in the Eucharist together with his Father and with the Holy Spirit with his entire divinity and soul, body and blood, so that the entire Jesus is in every host and in every little part of it, just as the soul is in our entire body, and entirely in every part of the body.

I proclaim, in summary, that I will give my life in testimony to each tenet, which the sacred Father commands be believed, and especially the principal truths: the Trinity of Persons and Unity of Essence in my God; my Redeemer Jesus Christ's Incarnation, death, resurrection and ascension to the right hand of the Father with the power of judge, who gives an eternity of glory to those who serve and who die in his grace, but an eternity of suffering in hell to those who offend him and die in mortal sin.

Beloved Lord, this is the life I offer you completely and entirely. I would lose it for your glory to repair in some way all the injuries you have received from sinners; in thanksgiving for all the graces given to the world; for the glory of the whole heavenly court; for the relief of all the souls in purgatory; for the increase of grace in all the just, for the zeal of all your ministers and the reform of all sinners; for the comfort of all those who are troubled; for help for all the poor and sick and for the conversion of the whole world to the true Faith. I would want to suffer many times a death filled with as much suffering as there are human beings and their sins and as much as there are graces to be given them. I desire as many deaths for your honor as there are perfections in your divinity, virtues of your most sacred humanity, thoughts of your mind, words of your tongue, affections in your heart, steps you have taken, drops of blood you have shed, tears you have cried, sufferings you have undergone, wounds you have received, injuries and insults you have borne, moments of your mortal life, agonies and troubles of your death. I would undergo as many deaths as there are splendors in your glory and in that of your divine Mother. But why? Such deaths and sufferings do nothing for you.

Yet, for all that I owe, and the whole world with me, I unite my death with yours and I offer them to the Eternal Father by Mary's hands. Your death was a perfect holocaust that paid the debts to God of the entire world and gave him glory infinitely surpassing all the sins of the world. Even if no one was saved, you would lose nothing, O my great Redeemer, of the fruit of your death and sacrifice because you have satisfied all the debts of the world and given the Father infinite glory.

FOR TUESDAY: ACTS OF SORROW

Let our dishonor cover us; for we have sinned against the Lord our God.[388]

I lie prostrate in this bed, annihilated before your majesty, O my God and my Lord, as I remember how often I have offended you with such contempt. I am covered with confusion seeing the offenses done to you, O my God. Remember, my Redeemer, that it was for me and for my sins that you died on the cross, covered with shame and wounds; offer them for me to your eternal Father so that for your sake he will be willing to forgive me, even though I am so unworthy of it. The mercy of the Father and the infinite power of your merits will shine out more resplendently to the extent that I am burdened by my faults and he forgives me.

---

[388] Jeremiah 3:25.

O Lord, pardon my guilt, for it is great.[389]

I do not wish to diminish the gravity of my sins. I do not want, I cannot, excuse the extent and number of my faults. I am a great, very great, sinner, the worst of the worst. I have unfortunately worn out your omnipotence by my weakness, O Father. I have too severely shown disrespect for your wisdom by my ignorance, O Son. I have too often reviled your goodness with my evil, O Holy Spirit. I cannot excuse my immense malice in so many sins when you mortify me, O Father, or when you enlighten me, O Son, or when you help me, O Holy Spirit to keep me from falling. But with all of this I do not want, nor should I, lose confidence of forgiveness. Rather, from all this, I have more hope the more I realize I am unworthy of pardon. So with all my heart, I beg your pardon, my beloved God! I would die of sorrow from all the evil I have done and disgust I have given you! I wish that my heart would break from pain; but that would be useless because every least sin is against you, who are infinitely lovable and loving, and should be wept over with a sorrow that is infinite. Pardon me, then, O Father, for the glory of your omnipotence, for only an omnipotent God can break the indissoluble chain of sins. Pardon me by reason of your Son's merit, whom you willed to be crucified for my sins.

And you, O Son, pardon me out of love for your Father and your Mother and for the glory of your wisdom that has known how to find the way of satisfying the divine justice for all the sins of the world by having the Son of God become a human son, weighed down with all our sins and weeping over them as if they were his own. Pardon me, too, O Holy Spirit, out of love for the Father, the merits of the Son and the intercession of Mary whom you have given to me as a mother of mercy. Pardon me for the glory of your infinite goodness and mercy, which will be all the more glorified in proportion to the enormity of my sins.

Most merciful and glorious Trinity, pardon me for the sake of your infinite glory. All the angels and the blessed in heaven will bring you the tribute of eternal praise and admire your incomprehensible mercy for having saved me who am so unworthy and deserving of damnation.

I again implore your immense pity, O powerful, O wise, O merciful Mother Mary because in offending God, I have also offended you who love me so much. I confess that I have abused your powerful

---

[389] Psalm 25:11 [*DR* 24:11].

protection, my Advocate, Seat of Wisdom and my Mother of Mercy. I detest my audacity and ingratitude with all my heart. I would like to cry tears of blood for them. Beg for me, O Mother, an immense grief over my sins.

Ask for me a sorrow proportionate to such evil that would wash me of all the filthiness since I cannot be saved without sorrow. O Mother of All Pity and Mercy, have pity on me! Show in me the greatness of your mercy. Your mercy is necessary for such a great sinner. Mother of Sinners, by your patronage, give a new birth in grace to the greatest of sinners, and then carry me to glory so that I can sing forever your mercy and that of God.

You have done all the evil that you could.[390]

What I see with my eyes seems incredible; what I have done seems impossible. Who could ever have thought that I would have room in my heart for more malice than can even be found in the demons, to do such evil to my God who has done and continues to do me so much good? To hate a God so good who loves me so much? To seek to strip away the being, life, and divinity from a God who has given me my being, preserved my life and made me a participant in his divinity by means of his grace? To burden with injury a God who loads me down with blessings? To trample down the majesty of a God who supports me by his cross?

No one hates a person who loves them; no one does evil to the one who does them good; no one kills the one who preserves their life. Only the demons and their followers hate God.

My beloved God, there is no adequate punishment for me. I would not fear hell if I could love and praise you there. But because hell, being the center of all sin, is behind all that is evil, I beg you, O Lord, to free me from it for your glory and the honor of your holy name. As a promise of such grace, pardon me all my sins because it is with all my heart that I ask your pardon for them and I unite my small sorrow to that of all those who are contrite, to the pain of my father Jesus and my mother Mary who although they had no personal sin to bemoan, weep over my sins and those of the whole world. Jesus as my Redeemer and Guarantor, Mary as my Co-Redeemer and Mother, weep over them as if it were their own. Then, O Beloved

---

[390] Jeremiah 3:5.

Father, by the value of such a magnificent Son and the intercession of such a daughter, pardon me what evil I have done, indeed, (excuse my boldness) pardon all my sins, I beg you, O Father, for Jesus' sake. I am the guilty one, but he has chosen to purge them in his Divine Person. He has borne them, and you have placed their burden on his back so he could satisfy all your justice. You cannot deny such a great gift to your Son and so you cannot deny it to me, the disciple of such a Leader, son of such a Father, the servant of such a Master, the slave of such a Redeemer, the one ransomed by his blood, the fruit of his passion, the reward of his death. Do not again hold against me his wounds that I have reopened by such excesses; instead, you must look at your Son *dead in my behalf*, not at Jesus *dead at my hands*.[391] Even if you choose to look at him as killed by me, remember, O Father, that it was for my sins that you had your Son die; it was to satisfy for my sins that a God died. So, for love of such a Son, pardon me and let it be known that you can and know how to forgive and that your Son can placate you more than I can offend you. I have done something impossible to believe: I have done evil to a God. Perform another impossible act, yet one that is not beyond your power, O God of Infinite Mercy: save this sinner, who is in every way unworthy of your pardon.

To convince you even more to save me, I offer you, along with your Son, the tears and merits of his Mother. If I have renewed for your Son his sufferings and death, his Mother supplies in her way for my evil. By the merits and love of such a Mother, please apply to me what will cleanse me of all my faults: the blood of your only begotten Son, Jesus the Redeemer, and save me!

I will recount to thee all my years in the bitterness of my soul.[392]

I glance at my entire life and I see that I have not passed a day, not even an hour, without offending you. My God, at every moment you have done something good for me, and at every moment I have responded by doing something wrong. Where did I get such a hard heart against my God, who is so good to me? We are playing a game: you always love me and I always offend you; you fill me with blessings and I burden you with injuries. I wish I could drown them by tears of blood that would create as

---

[391] Italics in original.
[392] Isaiah 38:15 [*DR*].

many oceans as there are days, hours and moments of my unworthy life; but even this would be nothing because every single evil done to you, O God, no matter how small, is too much for any creature to adequately weep over. Gaze at your Spirit, O my God, the Spirit of complete charity, totally inclined to bestow mercy; then for the rest of my life I can weep over the evil I have done to you and then, in eternity, love you always.

I reflect on my life. I do not have the heart to raise my eyes to heaven because of the number and gravity of my sins; I have offended you too much. But this is not enough for me to give up imploring your infinite mercy. Thus, even if my sins are countless and of such gravity, they are as nothing in the infinite sea of your mercy, in the blood of my Redeemer. Through the hands of Mary, my Mother of Mercy, I throw them all into the sea of your mercy, O Father, into the floods of your blood, O Son, and into the cauldron of your infinite love, O Holy Spirit. In these oceans all my sins and those of an infinite number of worlds are dissolved, pardoned, and reduced to ashes.

Who will give…a fountain of tears to my eyes? And I will weep day and night for the slain of the daughter of my people.[393]

O God, you condemned your only begotten Son to an utterly hateful death because he appeared before you burdened by all my sins and those of the whole world. O beloved God, it is I, I, not your only begotten Son: I am the one guilty of so many sins! His wounds, his suffering, his agonies are due to me. If, because of your mercy (that I do not deserve), you do not wish to regard them as mine, lay them on me out of justice because the one who has done the evil must bear the penance for them. Therefore, I present myself at the feet of your majesty bearing my Redeemer's thorns, scourging, cross and nails and I beg your mercy out of love for, and in view of, my Redeemer's worth. Show how much you love your Son by pardoning and saving me for his sake.

You, beloved Son, pardon me as well. I am the cause of your passion and death. Worse than Judas, I have sold you for a mere whim! I have obstinately bound and beaten you worse than your executioners! And all for a pittance! I condemned you to death in the tribunal of my heart for my own vicious interests. O head, throne of the Divinity, I crowned you with thorns by my pride! O face, more

---

[393] See Jeremiah 9:1 [DR]. Sarnelli gives the quotation as "Who will give my eyes a fountain of tears, so I may cry night and day over the Son of my God slain by me."

beautiful than the highest heaven, I have spat on you and slapped you by my vanity! O eyes, brighter than the sun, I have blindfolded you by my immodesty! O lips, full of sweetness, I have poisoned you by my gluttony! O hands that made creation, I have pierced you by my dissolute life! O heart, center of all love, I have wounded you with my hatreds and disordered loves! O Jesus, I crucified you, I killed you, not just once as did your enemies in Jerusalem, but as many times as I have sinned! If only I knew how to weep for such evil! O my Redeemer, let me share in your sufferings by which you wept over my sins and those of the whole world so that I can be a partner in the reward of your passion and death, that is, eternal life.

Whoever does not become like you in suffering cannot be like you in your glory. With good reason, you weep over me who increased your wounds and, with furious insanity, renewed your passion and death. I long to make amends for this great evil and bind up the wounds with my tears and affection. Grant me such a gift! I will do anything to imprint your passion on my heart so that I will always recall it and ever unite in compassion with it.

O my beloved Mother, I have caused you more suffering by renewing your son's pains. Please pierce my heart with your sword so that, by weeping with you over the agony of your son and the anguish you felt, I may die for the sufferings from my sins that are the cause of so much grief to your child, Son of God, and to you, his mother.

Be gracious to me, O Lord, for I am languishing; O Lord, heal me, for my bones are shaking with terror.[394]

O Lord, have mercy on me who am in worse condition in my soul than in my body; Lord, heal the interior wounds in my heart. You alone can do so; and for this I offer you all my bodily suffering.

Be gracious to me, O Lord. See what I suffer from those who hate me.[395]

All my enemies, the demons, mock me and throw back in my face all my past faults in order to incite me to desperation. Lord, have mercy on me for the sake of your glory and to the dismay of my enemies.

---

[394] Psalm 6:2 [DR 6:3].
[395] Ibid. 9:13 [DR 9:14].

Turn to me and be gracious to me.[396]

Glance at me with your eyes of love, O my God, and this will destroy all the fears of my heart.

Be merciful to me, O God, be merciful to me, for in you my soul takes refuge; in the shadow of your wings I will take refuge, until the destroying storms pass by.[397]

O my God, I have done every conceivable wrong but I have not committed the worst sin of losing confidence in you. I therefore hope for pardon from you. I will not stop hoping for forgiveness and asking for it until you have pity for me in your mercy.

Will the Lord spurn forever and never again be favorable? Has his steadfast love ceased forever? Are his promises at an end for all time? Has God forgotten to be gracious? Has he in anger shut up his compassion?[398]

Will it ever be possible that you would choose, in my case, to forget to be a God so good and merciful, when you are pleased to be and to show yourself in this way to sinners who come to you with their hearts? I may be full of sin and I may have offended you more than anyone else (something I confess to be true). Still, all my sins and all the sins of the whole world are as nothing before your mercy. Therefore, my Beloved God, do you have the heart to abandon me forever? Do you have the will to allow my sins to block the font of your great mercy to the point that you would forget your spirit of love, of mercy, of goodness in order to choose to punish me eternally? How can this be, O Lord, how can this be? I may have done you every kind of wrong; my iniquity may be bottomless and my iniquities countless. Yet, you have not ceased to be the God whose nature is goodness and whose spirit is love and mercy. Even if I have stopped being your child, you have not stopped being my Father. I beg your immense pity in which I hide myself. Please show yourself to me as the kind of God that I profess and that I call on.

---

[396] *Ibid.* 25:13 [*DR* 24:16].

[397] *Ibid.* 57:1 [*DR* 56:2].

[398] *Ibid.* 77:7–9 [*DR* 76:8–10].

Be gracious to me, O Lord, for to you do I cry all daylong. Gladden the soul of your servant, for to you, O Lord, I lift up my soul. For you, O Lord, are good and forgiving, abounding in steadfast love to all who call on you. Give ear, O Lord, to my prayer; listen to my cry of supplication.[399]

I have no other hope, my God, except in you and in your infinite mercy; I possess no other good than you and your boundless gentleness. So have pity on me who is nothing but hope! Bring happiness to this afflicted heart by assuring it of pardon because you are a God of all sweetness and gentleness who enjoys revealing the greatness of your mercy to anyone who asks for it humbly and confidently.

My days are like an evening shadow; I wither away like grass. But you, O Lord, are enthroned forever; your name endures to all generations. You will rise up and have compassion on Zion, for it is time to favor it; the appointed time has come.[400]

My days have passed like a shadow and the plant that is my life is as dry as straw. I realize, my God, that I am nothing and my life is like smoke. Still, I rejoice that you are eternal, without beginning or end, and that your being is not subject to change because you are changeless, immutable by nature and not bound by death, and because now, more than ever, I need your mercy. If you do not take pity on me now, I will never be more worthy to receive your mercy. Pardon me, save me, so that I may be made changeless and eternal with you in glory and may praise you for all eternity.

Bless the Lord, O my soul, and all that is within me, bless his holy name. Bless the Lord, O my soul, and do not forget all his benefits—who forgives all your iniquity, who heals all your diseases, who redeems your life from the pit, who crowns you with steadfast love and mercy.[401]

O my heart and all that is in within me, offer all your blessings to your God because he is a God so good and merciful that he forgives all my sins, snatches good for me out of all my evil, and to the extent that I

---

[399] *Ibid.* 86:3–5.
[400] *Ibid.* 102: 11–13.
[401] *Ibid.* 103:1–4.

have offended him, he has crowned me all the more with his mercy. He wants me to be a prize of his kindness because it is only through this that he wishes to save me and there is no other way for me to hope for eternal salvation.

The Lord is merciful and gracious, slow to anger and abounding in steadfast love. He will not always accuse, nor will he keep his anger forever. He does not deal with us according to our sins, nor repay us according to our iniquities. For as the heavens are high above the earth, so great is his steadfast love toward those who fear him...For he knows how we were made; he remembers that we are dust.[402]

Who could sufficiently understand the greatness of your mercy, O my God? By simply willing to do so, you could work every evil upon me; you have every reason for doing so because I have offended you by abusing your mercy. Instead of punishing me as I deserve, you have overwhelmed me with mercy. You have deepened your mercy by granting me more graces even to the point of sharing, my most beloved Father, in my weakness and misery when I did not merit compassion, O God of all mercy and of all patience, in waiting for me, in calling me to repentance, in bearing me up with such pity, in pardoning me with so much love. All the angels, all creatures join in with me in exalting your infinite goodness and proclaim endless blessings on your mercy toward such an unworthy son

I implore your favor with all my heart; be gracious to me according to your promise.[403]

I beg with all my heart for a kind glance, one that is fatherly and loving; this is enough for me because this cleanses me from all my sins as you have promised me so often in the Scriptures.

The Lord, the Lord, a God merciful and gracious, slow to anger, and abounding in steadfast love and faithfulness, keeping steadfast love for the thousandth generation, forgiving iniquity and transgression and sin.[404]

---

[402] *Ibid.* 103:8–11, 14 [*DR* 102:5–11, 14].

[403] *Ibid.* 119:58 [*DR* 118:58].

[404] Exodus 34:6–7.

O my Lord and my God, Lord God of all things, God of mercy and clemency, God of infinite patience and mercy, most truthful God who has kept his promise of being a God of all mercy, and of showing yourself to be such with sinners who humbly and contritely call upon your mercy; it is to you that I turn with this trust. If you see that my sorrow and contrition are not sufficient, make them stronger and able to cleanse me of all evil and ill will, for you alone can do so.

According to your steadfast love remember me, for your goodness' sake, O Lord![405]

Remember me, my God, All my good, All my hope; pardon me to the extent of your mercy that is without bounds; such is the great mercy I need.

Look down from heaven and see, from your holy and glorious habitation. Where are your zeal and your might? The yearning of your heart and your compassion? They are withheld from me. For you are our father, though Abraham does not know us and Israel does not acknowledge us; you, O Lord, are our father; our Redeemer from of old is your name.[406]

Would it be possible for my malice to be able to overthrow your goodness, and for my sins to be greater than your mercy? Oh no, this is not possible, not at all! Still it seems that you act toward me, O my beloved Lord, as though my sins have reached the point that they have slowed the course of your mercy to me.

Where is the zeal you have for my eternal salvation? Where is your omnipotence that can do whatever you want? Where are the depths of your mercy and multitude of your pardons? O Lord, please show me that you are the merciful Father, the kind Redeemer that you, in fact, are and I will cry out to you.

Yet you have dealt with us, O Lord our God, in all your kindness and in all your great compassion.[407]

Work your glory in me, my God and my Savior, in accord with all your goodness and the greatness of your mercy so that when I am purified

---

[405] Psalm 25:7 [DR 24:7].
[406] Isaiah 63:15–16.
[407] Baruch 2:27.

of all my sins by your kindness and am filled with the riches of your goodness I can love you as much as I have offended you.

Now therefore, O God, listen to the prayer of your servant and to his supplication, and for your own sake, Lord, let your face shine upon your desolated sanctuary. Incline your ear, O my God, and hear. Open your eyes and look at our desolation and the city that bears your name. We do not present our supplication before you on the ground of our righteousness, but on the ground of your great mercies. O Lord, hear; O Lord, forgive; O Lord, listen and act and do not delay! For your own sake, O my God.[408]

Hear my prayers, O my God, these prayers of your unworthy servant. Do not look on my enormous sins, but on your goodness and on the magnificence, the expanse and the glory of your mercy; this is where I rest my hopes of being heard for my salvation as one marked by your blood. For your glory, save me!

Jesus, Son of David, have mercy on me![409]

O Son of God, in order to fulfill all the promises and to see that all prophecies were realized, it was with the excessive love befitting a God that you chose to become a son of David by becoming the son of the Virgin Mary of the royal family of David; now have pity and mercy on me. I ask for a lot, but it is as nothing in the face of what you have done for me by pardoning me and satisfying for my sins. Though Son of God, you became the son of a human being. Make me, a slave subject to the penalty of hell, a son of God by grace and later in glory.

Have mercy on me, O God, according to your steadfast love.[410]

My God, now you are mine, even if in the past you were not so because I turned my back on you so often. You have never abandoned me, but rather, gazed on me with eyes of pity; otherwise, how could I run to you? I therefore rush to the throne of your mercy and hide beneath the wings of your kindness. I beg your pardon for all my sins and I ask you this in view of the greatness of your mercy. What I beg, what I absolutely need to beg for, is your infinite mercy to erase all my sins. You are generous in

---

[408] Daniel 9:17–19.

[409] Luke 18:38.

[410] Psalm 51:1 [*DR* 50:1].

pardoning, and you rejoice in showing yourself as such. Amid my misery, I rejoice because you are able to show how great your kindness is for all sinners, but especially in my case it is so much more worthy of you.

My God, how great you are; you know how to draw so much good out of so much evil! You know how to draw the glory of your mercy out of my chaos and your honor from the offenses that I have perpetrated! I do not deserve such grace, but you must still grant it because of the kind of God you are, whose nature is to pardon and whose glory lies in relieving the miseries of others. Pardon me, O Father, out of the love of your mercy, that is, out of love for your Son whom you have given me; for the sake of the love of such a great Son, you must not deny me pardon. Forgive me, O Son, through the merits of your mercy that flows over me from your many wounds and the suffering of your death. Pardon me, O Spirit, the love of the Father and the Son, because mercy overcomes you.

According to your abundant mercy, blot out my transgressions.[411]

It would do me no good, O Lord, if you restricted the effect of your infinite mercy in my case. So I beg for unlimited pity because my sins are countless. Do not let your pity grow weary of me. Blot out every trace of my guilt so that it no longer urges me to fall. Wipe out, O Father, all my bad thoughts; block, O Son, all my evil inclinations; pull out of my heart, O Holy Spirit, all my evil affections. No matter how much I weep, my tears do nothing of themselves, so I unite them with the blood of my Redeemer. In this bottomless sea, I sink my whole being. In this ocean of love and suffering, regenerate me, O Father, O Son, O Holy Spirit.

I know my transgressions, and my sin is ever before me.[412]

If I would dare to disguise and excuse my sins, I would not deserve pardon, but prostrate at your feet, I confess them, accuse myself of them, detest, abominate, and abhor them with all my heart. I desire my life to be a perpetual memorial to my sins; I do not want to live for anything except to cry over my sins and in this way to take upon myself the revenge and compensate for the honor that I have stolen from you. My God, forget the evil I have done and make me always recognize it better so I can always weep over it.

---

[411] *Ibid.*

[412] *Ibid.* 51:3 [DR 50:5].

Against you, you alone, have I sinned, and done what is evil in your sight, so that you are justified in your sentence and blameless when you pass judgment.[413]

I confess, my God, that the evil I have done is so great that there is no punishment I do not deserve. But instead, show yourself as God by giving me very great suffering for no other reason than that I may rue the offenses I have given you. Not to love you is already too monstrous. But to offend you, disrespect you, plot against you: what could you call a person who engaged in such actions? Who could explain and plan such hatred? I am the only one that reckless.

How enormous is the injury I have inflicted on you! I know that I am the least worthy of grace; so I demand you take revenge on me, but a revenge that befits an omnipotent God, faithful to his promises that he will take revenge by pardoning. This is what a God should do: to make a vendetta out of pardon and to do good to the worst sinners. There is no glory in an omnipotent being stepping on a worm, trampling on a twig; but your greatest glory is to change a worm, a nobody from hell, into a seraph of love, a prince in the heavenly court. If you would not forgive me, someone who turns to you humbled and truly contrite, you would give your enemies the chance to criticize you and ask what kind of God is it that goes back on his word, and to slander you as an unfaithful God who lies since you have given your divine promise to pardon whoever comes to you contritely and then you have not kept it, not fulfilled what you promised. Or they can denounce you as a powerless God who lacks the ability to pardon.

Confound all your enemies; convict them as slanderers and liars. Show by your pardoning of me that you can and will do so that all your divine attributes may be glorified while you take a revenge befitting a God: the revenge of pardoning the worst sinner of all.

Indeed, I was born guilty, a sinner when my mother conceived me.[414]

What could this earth, condemned by original sin, produce other than the thorns of sin? I have within me the incentives of fleshly desire, the origin and seedbed of all evils. It is therefore no surprise that I fall; what is a marvel is that I did not slip into the abyss of everything that is evil.

---

[413] *Ibid.* 51:4 [DR 50:6].
[414] *Ibid.* 51:5 [DR 50:7].

Yet I would have fallen if your grace had not sustained me, a grace always ready to help whoever desires to use it; this is something I confess to have failed to do as often as I sinned. Still, however massive my weakness may be or whatever war my passions may wage, even the smallest amount of your grace could triumph over any movement of fleshly desire, could turn away any enemy assault because supernatural grace can overcome both nature and hell. I bring my miserable state and weakness before you, not to excuse my wickedness but to move your spirit that is pleased to pity the miserable and to protect the weak.

You desire truth in the inward being; therefore teach me wisdom in my secret heart.[415]

My God, you are the eternal truth, the great lover of virtue both in yourself and in your servants in whom you look for the image of your own uprightness and sanctity. Therefore, pardon me in order to reshape your image in me that I have misshapen. If you love truth that much, I confess that I have done what is wrong, that I did not respond to your grace that was prompting me toward what is good. Do what you have promised to do by absolving the one who confesses guilt; let that person realize the truth of your promises to whoever confesses the truth of their faults. It is true that I have offended Truth by sinning even in the midst of the light that was bright enough for me to know my malice. Yet, it is this truth that ought to move you to pity because it will prove the infallibility of your word. I plead the Truth that I outraged as my defense so that it can triumph over my malice. A person will despair of you only if they do not know your spirit, but not I who know from holy Faith the secret and hidden judgments of your providence which you declare to be more offended by despair than by any other sin because for every other sin there lies pardon in the request for your pardon, while despair brings with itself eternal damnation.

Purge me with hyssop, and I shall be clean; wash me, and I shall be whiter than snow.[416]

O Eternal and High priest, wash with the hyssop of your own blood this poor soul covered by a leprosy that makes it abominable in the eyes of

---

[415] *Ibid.* 51:6 [DR 50:8].
[416] *Ibid.* 51:7 [DR 50:9].

heaven and earth. One drop of it is more than enough to make it whiter than snow as if it had never contracted any stain.

Let me hear joy and gladness; let the bones that you have crushed rejoice.[417]

For with such hope, moreover, I still grow fearful at the consideration of your inscrutable judgments. Strengthen my hope, O my God; let my heart hear words of jubilation that say: "Your sins are forgiven you." Tell this person that he will be with you and rejoice in you forever. Do I ask for too much? No, for before your great kindness this request is tiny. Out of fear that I have not recovered your friendship and will not enjoy it forever, I live a painful death; my spirit, oppressed by fear, cannot rouse itself to praise you. Revive it with a firm hope so that with all the powers of my spirit and all the senses of my body I can sing songs of praise, thanksgiving and love of your name.

Hide your face from my sins, and blot out all my iniquities.[418]

Pardon my boldness if I dare to ask for the impossible: namely, that you wipe the memory of all my sins from your mind.

Turn the severe stare of your justice from me, and turn toward me the look of your kindness, the glance that cancels all my faults, both hidden and open, grave and light, committed by me or by others through my fault. Purify me entirely because I am sorry for all these offenses and I resolve to suffer any grave punishment rather than commit a single evil, even the slightest.

Create in me a clean heart, O God, and put a new and right spirit within me.[419]

What is this, O my God, what is this? Before sinning I felt within me a heart so inclined to love you and a spirit so quick to serve you that loving you was delightful and serving you was my joy. But now my heart loves everything except you and my inclination yearns for everything except you. Change my heart, renew my spirit. Give me a heart that loves you as much as it has offended you and a spirit as close to you as it once was distant.

---

[417] *Ibid.* 51:8 [*DR* 50:10].
[418] *Ibid.* 51:9 [*DR* 50:11].
[419] *Ibid.* 51:10 [*DR* 50:12]. *Ibid.* 51:12 [*DR* 50:14].

Do not cast me away from your presence, and do not take your holy spirit from me.[420]

How do you respond, O my God, will you grant me a grace so immense? If yes, I am sure not to lose you ever again. If no, oh, I will fear I am abandoned by you! Any punishment, O my God, but not that one! Before you wish to allow me to fall into new faults as a punishment for my past, as I deserve, look! See me willing to suffer the pains of the damned but do not permit me to sin; this would be worse than hell itself. If there is no other way to avoid sin, I will throw myself into that fire so that I do not offend you again. Do not allow me, O Lord, to be separated from you; therefore, bind me to yourself by means of your Holy Spirit who, as the loving bond of the Trinity, may also, through grace, be an invincible knot between you and me.

Restore to me the joy of your salvation, and sustain in me a willing spirit.[421]

To have lost you once is a punishment that saddens me but it is lessened by the hope of having regained you. Still, the fear of being able to lose you forever with no hope of recovering you the worst punishment of all. O my sweetest God, remove this worry from me; give my afflicted heart the joy of your salvation that I had before sin; comfort me with your rejuvenating Spirit. Since the Spirit is willing to live in me, as I hope, by means of sanctifying grace, may this grace be stable, ongoing and final so that by it I will give up my last breath into your hands. Oh, that the Holy Spirit be my consolation in my agony, my comforter in my trials, my guide in this great journey toward eternity. May the Spirit be the absolute judge of my heart and my soul so that I will live by grace on earth and in glory in heaven.

Then I will teach transgressors your ways, and sinners will return to you.[422]

If it is in your will to prolong my life, with the strength from your Spirit, I will preach to all sinners of your mercy; if you wish me to die with some sign of my eternal salvation, may my death be a strong voice to

---

[420] *Ibid.* 51:11 [*DR* 50:13].
[421] *Ibid.* 51:12 [*DR* 50:14].
[422] *Ibid.* 51:13 [*DR* 50:15].

attract sinners to you so that all will hope in you by knowing the mercy you have shown me, the worst sinner in the world. Who else could ever despair if you save me?

Deliver me from bloodshed, O God, O God of my salvation, and my tongue will sing aloud of your deliverance.[423]

The urges of my flesh and blood are so fierce and I feel such inclination to evil that there is no taming of this monster. If you do not bind me to your feet with a strong and firm grace, I will create a catastrophe. Listen to me, my God, my Savior! Out of celebration for such a favor, I will bless and exalt your justice: that justice by which you keep your promises, that justice which satisfies you with the minimal repayment that allows you to sanctify me.

O Lord, open my lips, and my mouth will declare your praise.[424]

I have always been unworthy of praising you since the praise from an unclean heart is not fitting for God. Purify my heart; open my lips so that I can raise up songs of praise and hymns of thanks for such mercy and am able to repay all the injuries I have done to you in my life. If I cannot do so with my lips, I intend to praise you in my heart.

For you have no delight in sacrifice; if I were to give a burnt offering, you would not be pleased.[425]

Behold me ready, O God of Infinite Majesty, to offer you whatever sacrifice: life, blood and all that is in me in satisfaction for my sins. Even if I extracted a sea of blood from my veins, even if I possessed infinite lives and consecrated them all to you, if I forfeited myself for you through a terrible martyrdom, and even if all creation that is or could ever be destroyed itself for my sake, all this would have no value in view of the injury I have done you by one sin.

The sacrifice acceptable to God is a broken spirit; a broken and contrite heart, O God, you will not despise.[426]

---

[423] *Ibid.* 51:14 [*DR* 50:16].
[424] *Ibid.* 51:15 [*DR* 50:17].
[425] *Ibid.* 51:16 [*DR* 50:18].
[426] *Ibid.* 51:17 [*DR* 50:19].

The sacrifice that pleases you and that you ask of me is a grieving spirit, a contrite heart crushed by sorrow. You ask for this because it is something I can offer. I sorrow, therefore, with the sorrow of all penitents. I make a sacrifice to you of all I am, of my spirit and my body, of the whole history of my life. And to make it worthwhile for you to accept, I offer them with the sacrifice of your only Son, sacrificed once on Calvary and many times on the altar. You cannot refuse this; by reason of this divine sacrifice you cannot deny me your pardon because every offering of your only begotten is more pleasing to you than [*the offense of*] all the sins of the world that have occurred or that can occur.

Do good to Zion in your good pleasure; rebuild the walls of Jerusalem.[427]

I ask that you let me die happy: such is the way I would die if your mercy were spread over all people so that they form one Church Militant on earth and later triumphant in heaven. O happy me, if I were worthy of such a gift! I would not care about suffering anything, even hell, if I were to see you loved throughout the world and then glorified in heaven.

Then you will delight in right sacrifices, in burnt offerings and whole burnt offerings; then bulls will be offered on your altar.[428]

When my work on earth is finished, O my most Holy Trinity, may you be glorified in heaven with eternal praise and thanks there at your altar as we offer the eternal sacrifice of glory and blessing for all the ages. Amen.

---

[427] *Ibid.* 51:18 [DR 50:20]
[428] *Ibid.* 63:4 [DR 62:5].

FOR WEDNESDAY: ACTS OF PRAISE AND THANKSGIVING

Because your steadfast love is better than life, my lips will praise you.[429] I realize that my life has been a constant injury to your name and goodness. I want to compensate completely for this by my praise. But how could such a great sinner laud you, O Most Glorious Trinity? Nevertheless, because I trust in your mercy being infinitely greater than my faults and I hold it so dear to me, I want to praise and glorify you. I wish I had countless lives, all of which I could spend in exalting and glorifying you!

So I will bless you as long as I live; I will lift up my hands and call on your name.[430]

Not only with my lips, but with all my heart and soul, with everything I am in every moment up to the last breath I take in my life, with all my strength, I laud you! Because my whole body and all my faculties want to (and should) be engaged in your exaltation, in order to supply for all the faults in which they have shared, I raise my hands to heaven to make up for what is lacking in my heart, which, despite how much it praises you, still can never give you the honor that is your due.

My soul is satisfied as with a rich feast, and my mouth praises you with joyful lips.[431]

Fill me, Lord, with the abundance of your grace and spirit so that my whole being is so full and sated that it sings your praises. So infuse my body that, no matter how much it feels pain, it may render you continual songs of praise with the greatest rejoicing so that you may find them pleasing to your heart and worthy of your name and thus I may sing you my praises amid all this pain and I rejoice over you in my sufferings.

You are my God, and I will give thanks to you; you are my God, I will extol you.[432]

---

[429] *Ibid.* 51:19 [*DR* 50:21].

[430] Psalm 63:3 [*DR* 62:4].

[431] *Ibid.* 63:5 [*DR* 62:6].

[432] *Ibid.* 118:28 [*DR* 117:28].

O Most Holy Trinity, you are my God in whom I believe and whom I adore. See that I profess you and will always profess you as my God because of the great God you are. Oh, I wish I could exalt you and praise you as much as I owe you and as you deserve! I rejoice that you are greater than all created praise and that you raise all our praise to the level of being worthy of you.

Bless the Lord, O my soul, and all that is within me, bless his holy name.[433]

O my whole being, you were formed by the most Holy Trinity in its image, furnished with the three powers of memory, intellect and will: a memory like that of the Father, an intellect like that of the Son, and a will like that of the Holy Spirit. Thus you are able to know, bless, glorify and love it [the Trinity], so you may enjoy it forever. Commit yourself to laud and bless your God and Lord. You powers of my person, my limbs, my bones, my senses, each and every smallest part of my body prostrate yourselves before my Lord in praise and blessing and in exalting his holy name. Yes, my most glorious Trinity, I praise you and will do so as long as I live. I will sing your glories in every moment of my life. I proclaim that I do not wish to live for anything else than to laud and praise you. As many thoughts as I have in my mind, affections and emotions in my heart, words on my lips, steps, breaths and glances, as many actions as I and all creatures may perform: all of them I intend that they become hymns of praise and tributes of blessing to your majesty, O Father, to your greatness, O Son, and to your magnificence, O Holy Spirit. But because all of this adds up to nothing, I exclaim:

Bless the Lord, all his works, in all places of his dominion.[434]

All you creatures of the heavens, the air, the earth, the seas and depths, whatever has been made by his hands, glorify and bless our universal Creator, Caretaker, Lord and Master, since there is no creature that is so vile that in it does not reflect the infinite power, wisdom, goodness, dominion and providence of the Supreme Lord. Bless him in the name of all rational creatures who, more than you, are obliged to the universal Creature, but yet are so ungrateful.

---

[433] *Ibid.* 103:1 [DR 102:1].
[434] *Ibid.* 103:22 [DR 102:22].

Bless the Lord, O you his angels.[435]

Blessed Spirits, the most beautiful work of the divine hands, you assistants at his throne, faithful executers of his commands, I beg you out of your great love for the Creator we share, in so far as you live as his debtors, as far as you enjoy his glory, I beg you to praise, bless, and glorify him in my name and in the name of all human beings. I envy your lot, not just because you are happy but rather because you praise and love him without interruption, as well as because your life consists in loving, while I *[who live]* in this valley of tears…am so stingy in my praise of him! Nevertheless, I direct everything to your glory, O my God, and I proclaim that I desire paradise solely so I can praise you without end; from this moment on, I pledge to unite my praise to that of the Blessed forever.

I will bless the Lord at all times; his praise shall continually be in my mouth.[436]

Oh, how happy would I be if I could bless and praise you all the time, in every hour, in every moment, O my most Holy and Uncreated Trinity! I would like to be present everywhere, in every creature, on the tongue and in the heart of all, in order to laud you with everything, in everything and through all things.

O give thanks to the God of gods, for his steadfast love endures forever.[437]

Who will not exalt you, O my God, whose nature is all goodness and whose actions are all full of mercy? To whom other than you will I consecrate all the worship of my mind, all the praises of my tongue, all the affections of my heart which I owe you by your infinite right and for whom you are God with all being, majesty and glory in yourself? *[To whom else]* after you have chosen to make yourself known to me as pure goodness and mercy, pure love and patience, pure friendliness and blessing? How could I not laud your kindness which continually blesses me? Or your power that constantly upholds me? Your patience that is my constant support? Your wisdom that continuously enlightens me? Your charity that always shows me love? Your mercy that like a loving mother never stops protecting

---

[435] *Ibid.* 103:20 [*DR* 102:20].

[436] *Ibid.* 34:1 [*DR* 33:1].

[437] *Ibid.* 136:2 [*DR* 135:1].

me if I am persecuted, consoling me when I am afflicted, nourishing me when I am starving, strengthening me when I am weak, raising me up when I have fallen, pardoning me when I have sinned, readmitting me to your grace when I act as an enemy?

O give thanks to the Lord of lords, for his steadfast love endures forever.[438]

You are the only God, Lord of All Lords! Therefore, to you alone belong all praise, all blessing, all love and glory. There is no other God. You alone are the one, true, highest and eternal God because you are God by nature; you alone are the absolute Lord. You are the only almighty one, the supreme ruler over all rulers and claimant of dominion and majesty over all. In your eyes, everything is less than a grain of sand in the face of the universe, a drop of water before the whole ocean; they are as nothing, and whatever small nothingness they possess is a gift of your limitless freedom; all of them could be annihilated in a second. To you, then, who alone can perform marvels and wonders at your whim, to you who act simply by willing without the aid of anything else, to you on whom all else depends, to you belong all praise and blessing, all honor and glory.

Sing, O heavens, for the Lord has done it; shout, O depths of the earth; break forth into singing, O mountains, O forest, and every tree in it! For the Lord has redeemed Jacob.[439]

Heavens, earth, sea and all that is in them, laud my God and my Lord with me. Let us praise him in time and in eternity. Let us glorify him from east to west, through every part of the universe since he fills with this majesty, glory and greatness all that is created or can be created. Let us exalt him for his mercies that he chooses to spread through the whole world, among his people, with us his poor servants, and to me, the most wretched of all. Let all creatures bless you, O Lord, in my name: flowers of the field, grass of the plains, leaves of the trees, trees of the forest, sands of the sea shore, waters of the oceans, atoms of the air, stars in the sky; and above all this praise, let there be the praise of all the angels' hearts.

---

[438] *Ibid.* 136:3 [*DR* 135:2–3].
[439] Isaiah 44:23 [*DR* 44:23–24].

Praise him for his mighty deeds; praise him according to his surpassing greatness![440]

Let us praise our God and Lord in all his works. Let us glorify him for all he has imagined, for what he has done, does now and will do. Let us laud him in and for all the actions of his power and wisdom, his kindness and providence, his generosity and love, his mercy and judgment! Let us exalt him as much as we can for his immeasurable grandeur, for his endless majesty, for his endless perfections. How could we who are so weak and ignorant, so in misery and so petty, praise a God so great, so exalted? That is why we exclaim:

Let them thank the Lord for his steadfast love, for his wonderful works to humankind.[441]

All you, yes you, all you attributes of our grandest, best and Most Holy God, you can give God the glory that he deserves. My one and triune God, in my name and in that of all the creatures, allow yourself to be glorified by your majesty and grandness, your sovereignty and highness, your goodness and beneficence, your glory and divinity, your power and wisdom, your mercy and justice, your pity and gentleness, your sanctity and innocence, your endurance and patience, your light and truth, your liberality and magnificence, your thoughtfulness and providence, your independence and simplicity, your eternity and changelessness, your infinity, your blessedness. In short, may all your attributes and perfections praise you, since they alone can glorify you as much as you deserve.

The Lord is my strength and my praise.[442]

I will always weep, my God, over my emptiness and misery for I can never reach the point of praising you as much as I want or as you deserve. But no! O my God, will to strengthen my weakness and equip my ignorance so that I am able to exalt you and to know how to do it. Make yourself present to my mind, tongue and heart and bless yourself in me and through me. May you praise, glorify and thank yourself in me and for me. You, O my God, are my praise because you are the only object of my praise and because you praise in my name to satisfy my debts since no one else beside you is worthy enough to glorify you.

---

[440] Psalm 150:2.

[441] *Ibid.* 107:8 [*DR* 106.8].

[442] *Ibid.* 117:14 [*DR*].

Father, I thank you for having heard me.[443]

I owe you all laud and glory for being the great God that you yourself are, and I owe you all thanks for being a God who has chosen to be so good, generous, liberal, and merciful to me and every other creature. Therefore, I thank you for all the graces and blessings that have come from your omnipotent hands and much more from your boundlessly loving heart through the realms of nature, grace, glory, and the hypostatic union. I also thank you for all the benefits granted to the Most Holy humanity of your Son and my Redeemer Jesus Christ on whom, by your sheer goodness and mercy, you bestowed a personal union with your Word; on the basis of this, you must then, out of justice, give him all that is due your natural Son; for a son by nature is by justice heir to all the paternal goods.

I thank you for all the gifts and privileges conceded to the Mother of God, Mary Most Holy, and especially for the source of all her prerogatives, namely, the dignity to be the true and worthy Mother of God [*I thank you*] for giving her as Mother to all the children of the Church, and to me, the most unworthy and poorest of all. With my Queen and Mother, I thank you for all the blessings bestowed on all your servants and children, all the angels and saints in heaven, all the just ones in purgatory and on earth, all Catholics, all heretics, schismatics and unbelievers, all of whom were filled with graces, even though they do not recognize you and thank you.

I want to thank you for everyone and I want to fill in with my gratitude for whatever is lacking in any of them so that you reach the goal of these works, namely, your glory and our well-being. The former is due to the necessary perfection of your being; the latter is the effect of the unspeakable mercy and untiring goodness.

I thank you for all the graces wasted by this very ungrateful person that I am, and I confess them at your feet. I thank you for having created me although you foresaw that I would be such an ungrateful son. I thank you for keeping me alive in your great love until this moment even when I attempted to steal away your very being through my sin. I am grateful to you for seeing that I would be born a son of your Church, the one Catholic Church, and for letting me die in it, a blessing lost to so many others. I thank you for the infinite patience

---

[443] John 11:41.

that you have borne toward me, with the very long endurance you have shown by so often waiting for my repentance, and so freeing me from the hell that I so often deserved; for the unspeakable goodness by which you have loaded me down with so many blessings of your incomprehensible mercy that you have granted me even after such enormous thanklessness on my part.

I thank you for all your benefits from the first moment of my life right up to the present even though I did not deserve them. I thank you for the eternity without beginning or end in which you have loved me. I mean to unite my thanks and affections to those of all the saints in paradise and so thank you with them.

Additionally, I now intend to always change into praises, thanks, affections and eternal blessings all the injuries and curses, all the hate of hell. From now on, I intend to always thank, praise, bless and love you for all of them. Oh, how happy and delighted I am, O my God, that you know how to change into laud and blessing, thanks and love of your justice, all the insults, blasphemies and hate of evildoers against you! I rejoice that you are a God so great and powerful that you can turn into glory, not only the praise of your servants, but even the insults of your enemies.

I thank you, O my God, for pouring out on me and on the whole world, blessings known and unknown. How many graces you have given me in my unworthiness and to all human beings that we have not even noticed! For all this I thank you. I thank you for happiness and for adversity, for riches and poverty, for health and illness, for blessings in accord with my natural inclinations and for those that work against them, for heaven and hell, for all the benefits that flow from your loving and generous hands.

I thank you for all the blessings you have bestowed on me and on all the world that are found in the order of nature because you have made all things for us humans. I thank you for all these even more since most of the world abuses these gifts in spite of you and are more ungrateful to you when you bless them all the more.

I thank you for all the benefits in the order of grace, for such lights, inspirations and impulses you have given me and to all, most of which our ingratitude rendered useless and ineffective.

Above all, I thank you for the greatest of all your blessings, the font of all good, that is, for having given me the God-Man Jesus

Christ as my Redeemer and Master, my lawgiver and example, my every blessing, hope and glory [*Thank you also*] for having given them to me in the most loving and obliging way possible because you have given them to me through Mary, a creature of my bloodline and ancestry in whom and through whom you became human and died for me. I thank you for all the sacraments he instituted, for the Church he founded, for the perpetual sacrifice of the Mass he left with it. I do so as if you had given it to me alone because you have given it in that way to the entire world by giving it to every person, and because such blessings have brought me my Redeemer as if he died for me alone.

[He] loved me and gave himself for me.[444]

I thank you for the many times you chose to apply to this unworthy person the virtues and merits of my Redeemer in so many sacraments and sacrifices [*of the Eucharist*]. Because every bit of gratitude I feel is a new blessing that you give me, I beg my Redeemer to thank your infinite goodness and inexpressible generosity in my name.

I thank you finally for the judgment you will make over me at the end of this life of mine. But I ask you, emptying myself before your feet, to grant me a judgment that will allow me to thank you with all the saints for all eternity, and by which I can always thank you with the Church Triumphant just as I now thank you with the Church Militant.

You are God: we praise you; you are Lord, we acclaim you.[445]

We creatures, whose nature subjects us to you, praise and confess you as our Creator, our Lord and our absolute Master of the whole created universe and of any that could be created.

You are the eternal Father: All creation worships you.

As your children through your grace, we adore and confess you throughout the entire universe, Father of the divine Son by your nature and our Father by adoption. You alone are the natural Father of your Only Begotten; in

---

[444] Galatians 2:20.

[445] All of the headings from this point to the end of the section are from the hymn, *Te Deum Laudamus*. Translation is by the International Commission on English in the Liturgy as found in *The Liturgy of the Hours*, New York: Catholic Book Publishing Co, 1975, Volume I, 651–2.

union with him and the Holy Spirit you both share, we confess you to be our Father by creation and by grace. If our essence as your creatures inspires reverence in us, if being slaves makes us afraid, the fact that we are indeed your children consoles us because of your tenderness, revives us by your trust and enflames us through love.

All you angels, all the powers of heaven, Cherubim and Seraphim, sing in endless praise: Holy, holy, holy God of power and might.

How could we avoid presenting to such a Creator God our praises and thanks, to such a Lord God our adoration and reverence, to such a Fatherly God our love and tenderness, we who are vile creatures, yet ones chosen; unworthy slaves, yet so exalted; ungrateful children, yet so favored? *[How can we do otherwise,]* while all the angels, all the powers of heaven, all the cherubim and seraphim acclaim you unceasingly, confess you and adore you, Holy God the Father, Holy God the Son, Holy God the Spirit, yet all three *[are]* but one Creator, one Lord, one God of All?

Heaven and earth are full of your glory.

How could we not do this, we whom you have enriched by such graces, when the heavens and the earth with all they contain resound with the entire majesty of your glory? When they recognize you for the great God that you are? When they speak of you to us, when they preach your perfections in order to urge us to laud, glorify and love you? When they are created for us and for our service, since your omnipotence has involved itself in all creatures for our good and our service? Are you going to be glorified, O Lord God and Our Father, by all the creatures you have made, and not by us, the creatures uniquely made to serve and praise you and to enjoy you? No, may it never be so.

The glorious company of apostles praises you; the noble fellowship of prophets praises you, white-robed army of martyrs praises you.

How much we rejoice, O Lord, when we think of you being exalted with songs of praise by the glorious chorus of apostles, by the exultant crowd of prophets and by the army of so many millions of martyrs! We will offer to your inexhaustible generosity their songs of praise and unite ours to theirs.

The holy Church acclaims you: Father of majesty unbounded, your true and only Son…and the Holy Spirit, advocate and guide.

The holy Church Militant that is your Kingdom on earth, spread throughout the whole world and overcoming all persecutors spat out from the darkest abyss, echoes festively the Church Triumphant, joining it in cries of praise, songs of joy and grateful tributes.

Now we, with both these Churches confess you the One God in essence, yet three in Persons. We believe you are the Father of immense majesty and incomprehensible grandeur. We confess you to be the true and only begotten Son of such a Father. We acknowledge you, Spirit Consoler, substantial holiness of the Father and Son, Sanctifier of souls with the Father and the Son.

You, Christ, are the king of glory.

You, you, O Divine Son, you, the Word made flesh and so, even as a human being, King of Glory. You are the deserving font of all the good things which you have poured out on us in such wide and profuse abundance from the inexhaustible source of the benediction of the Three Divine Persons. All Three fill us with graces but we owe all of them to you, O Christ, who has earned them. From the Trinity they are given us, by us received, by you they were won.

Eternal Son of the Father; you were born of the Virgin's womb to set us free.

You, who for an eternity sat as upon a throne, one worthy of your majesty in the bosom of the Father, did not hold back from lowering yourself into the womb of a young woman, did not shrink from clothing yourself in human flesh from the blood of a virgin mother, and without leaving the bosom of the Father, did not spurn imprisonment within the limits of a mother's womb. You did all of this to free human beings who had betrayed and rebelled against you from the eternal slavery incurred by their sins. As we consider you as God made man in the womb of a young woman, even though you are immensely purer and holier than all the cherubim and seraphim, we confess this miracle, believe it wholeheartedly and adore you in her womb as our God!

You overcame the sting of death and opened the kingdom of heaven to all believers.

Your love was not content to ransom us from the slavery and death of hell and of sin, but chose to turn us slaves into princely heirs and to buy us scepters, crowns and a Kingdom that would be given to us in justice by your Father, to us who are worthy only of your disdain and your avenging justice. And what is more, you disclosed yourself as a God of infinite love, one who wished to free us from sin and slavery by making yourself a servant to be treated like a slave, an infamous criminal. You wanted to open paradise to your believers with the key of the cross. May you be thanked and loved forever!

You are seated at God's right hand in glory.

When in faith we contemplate you, even as human, at the right hand of the Father amid the immense splendor of glory, of grandeur and power, you snatch us up in joy and with you we exult, we rejoice in seeing our flesh and blood being deified in you.

We believe that you will come and be our judge.

Your name is terrifying, O Christ, Universal Judge of the world! You, God of majesty, grandeur, and infinite holiness, of goodness and generosity unspeakable, of tremendous and incomprehensible justice. You, our Judge! O Lord, our blood freezes in our veins for fear of your judgment! The Most Holy God must judge us, so stained and abominable because of our evil inclinations, vices and many faults! You, God so grand and yet not feared! God so rigorous and still not respected! God so powerful and yet not revered! God so good, so lovable and still not loved but rather hated, disliked, abominated, belittled and harried!...Ah, the sentence of death awaits us! But we implore you and cry out:

Come then, Lord, and help your people, bought with the price of your own blood!

We breathe again at these words. If you terrify us as God, you hearten us as God made human. As one offended by us you cause fear, as dead for us you bring us hope. As Redeemer Judge you are the object of our hope. Yes, yes, you are our judge. We want you, you who are of our family; you who carry in your veins our blood from a mother of our ancestry; you who pleaded our cause with so many wounds in the tribunal of your Father!

You who, to liberate us from the sentence of eternal death, wished to be condemned to the cruelest and most hateful death, namely death on a cross. It is you and no one else that we want for a judge of our sins. Do you have nerve enough to condemn to hell members of your own race? To see your own brothers and sisters eternally trampled down by your greatest enemy, Lucifer? Those who are the price of your blood, the fruit of your suffering, the reward for your death? Can you bear to see eternally separated from you those whom you have redeemed at the cost of your suffering? Do you want to waste such suffering, to destroy the value of all the blood you shed, the blood of a God, every drop of which is more valuable than countless worlds?...Ah, no! Douse the lightnings of your justice in the blood of our redemption so that you do not discover in us anything worth punishing in the final day of your vengeance.

Bring us with your saints to glory everlasting.

Out of love for the blood you poured out as a cleansing for our sins, use it to quench the eternal flames that we deserve and write our names in the Book of Life so we can enjoy eternal happiness forever with your saints.

Save your people, Lord, and bless your inheritance.

Enroll us in your happy crowd of the elect and write into the book of predestination, not only us but all those redeemed by your blood so that there may be no child of eternal damnation. And as a sure pledge of this great favor and as a down payment of the eternal blessing on the last day of nature, grant your blessing to all of us who are declared heirs of your Kingdom.

Govern and uphold them now and always.

Direct our steps so that we do not leave the right path until we enter into eternal glory.

Day by day we bless you. We praise your name forever.

We desire to prepare ourselves for the eternal joys by blessing and loving you everywhere on earth and every day of our mortal lives, at every hour and moment of the day. We want to begin to praise your name for eternity without end. From now on, through every moment, we pledge to laud you with every song that will be sung to you throughout the ages.

Keep us today, Lord, from all sin.

So that our blessings please you and our praise be heard, Lord, keep us immune from all offense for the length of our earthly life, which no matter how long it lasts is less than a day in view of eternity.

Have mercy on us, Lord, have mercy.

Keep us from all sin in the future, since we have offended you too much in the past. See us at your feet, humbled, emptied and confused. We detest our ungrateful past deeds, and we beg pardon of the sins we have committed, we implore from your kindness the remission of all the insults inflicted on you.

Lord, show us your love and mercy, for we put our trust in you.

The greater is your mercy over our sins, the more our hope in you grows, since it becomes greater the more we are guilty and unworthy of pardon. Show us, O Lord, the vastness of your mercy by pardoning me. By such forgiveness, how great will your mercy be glorified before the court of heaven! We are deeply sorry for all our sins. But at least we can find joy in giving you the chance to display the immensity of your pity.

In you, Lord, is our hope, and we shall never hope in vain.

It is with this hope that I draw my thanksgiving and my prayers to a close. I hope in you, O Father, because I am a creature of your omnipotence. I hope in you, O Son, because I am a servant purchased from slavery by your blood. I hope in you, O Holy Spirit, because I am adopted by your grace. With it founded on you, my one and triune God, my hope cannot turn out to be in vain. Grant that this be so!

Finally, I thank you, O my most merciful, sweetest and most generous Mother Mary, because I confess that it is through your very powerful intercession that I have received all these graces and mercies of every type that God, the Font of All Blessings, has shown me. The whole world must join me in confessing that it was through you that we received the Greatest Good, the incomprehensible Good, the Source of all good received or hoped for, namely, your Son, the God-Man, Jesus Christ. Without you, who are the only one among all creatures worthy of conceiving the Son of God in your womb, he would not have become flesh. Without your consent to the Incarnation, God would not have become human. I thank you, then,

O Mother, for this unspeakable blessing not only in the name of the entire world that is so often ungrateful to its Redeemer, but also in the name of each person because this gift was given in common to all and, at the same time, individually to each one. This is true because your Son would not have gained more for each one if he were to die for each than he gained in dying for all. He died for all in the same way as he would have died for each if that were what was needed for their salvation. It is to you that, after the most Holy Trinity, we owe such an inestimable benefit.

And I thank you *[Mary]* for all the blessings of creation and of its ongoing conservation, because it was for love of you that God created the world; it was by your intercession, while he left so many completely uncreated and in pure nothingness, that he granted me, though unworthy, my existence even though he could foresee I would be so ungrateful. He also chose to keep me alive, though he should have destroyed me, when I was guilty of my first sin, and to make me a child of the Church while so many others are left outside.

I thank you *[Mary]* for all the general and special graces that God has granted me because it is to you, after God, that I owe all my blessings. God provided them for me, Jesus gained them for me and you were the one who asked him to do so. I owe you for the patience in which God has supported me all my life and still does so; for the goodness by which he has frequently called me to himself; for the mercy with which, I hope, he has so many times and in such excess pardoned me; for the love by which he allowed me to be born into and live within his Church, and in which, I hope, he will allow me to die; for his omnipotence by which he has preserved my life for so many years, freeing me from so many dangers of a sudden and evil death that has befallen others; for the wisdom by which he has many times enlightened me; for the generosity with which he has loaded me down with gifts which I then used to offend him; for the providence by which he has aided me during many dangers of body and soul on so many occasions. To you, after God, I owe everything: with all my heart, I thank you for them because I am not worthy of any grace; all this I profess to have received through your intercession.

To you *[Mary]* I owe the joy-filled glory which, as I hope, I will obtain even though I am unworthy. Because my thanks are worth nothing, I unite it with all your children on earth and in heaven with whom I offer my thanks to you in gratitude for all the graces given me and the world, and for the eternal and infinite love of the Most Holy Trinity.

For Thursday: Acts of Humility and Acceptance

I have become like a broken vessel.[446]
I cannot explain my lowliness, O Lord. I have become a bowl filled with all kinds of iniquity and ungratefulness. No matter how much you generously pour out your blessings on me my whole life long, I have turned them all into evil by the abuse of your graces. You, who are infinite goodness, change all my evils into blessings, my vices into virtues, my sins into rewards. This is how you act as God, although I have acted like the miserable creature that I am.

Truly I do not know how to speak, for I am only a boy.[447]
You have commanded me, Lord, to serve you, fear you and love you. Yet, I recognize that during my whole life I have not done any good, but rather much evil. Without you I cannot do anything but what is wrong! The fault is entirely mine, since I have abused so many of your graces. If you would have lavished those graces on other sinners, all of them would have recognized it and been grateful to you. I should have realized how to humble myself in my great misfortunes! But instead I realize that I took a bit of pride amid such humiliations! I cannot imagine a person wrapped up in so many of your favors who would still have such great ingratitude as I. Yet, how could I arrive at such wonderful humility if you did not stoop to give it to me as a gift, at least before I die?

But I am a worm, and not human; scorned by others, and despised by the people.[448]
Amid such price and ingratitude, I ask you, O Lord, to expose my faults to everyone. Impress on all hearts and minds the low estimate, the hate and

[446] Psalm 31:13 [*DR*: 30:13].
[447] Jeremiah 1:6.
[448] Psalm 22:7 [*DR* 21:7].

detestation that I deserve. Let no one think of me except in horror, and no one be contaminated with love for me, as I am worthy of contempt and hate. Indeed, there is no humiliation, no affront, no punishment that I do not deserve as the most disgusting of vermin, contemptible before the world, the most abject being in the universe.

What is your servant, that you should look upon a dead dog such as I?[449]

Who am I, Lord, that you lower yourself to give me even a glance of pity? I do not know how the world can put up with me; how the heavens do not strike me down; how all creatures can refrain from uniting against me as the reason for all the punishments that fall on the world! All this is the result of your immense pity. I rejoice that at my death, this world will be freed of one pestilence.

The steadfast love of the Lord never ceases, his mercies never come to an end.[450]

What heart and tongue could I find by which I could thank and laud your mercy, O Most Merciful Trinity, for having freed me from hell every time I have sinned? I would certainly have fallen if you had not shielded me out of your sheer pity. May all the glory be yours, while all the blame be put on me for all the sins I could commit but which solely out of your mercy I did not do so, even though you could not expect anything else from me than every evil I could commit. I wish the entire world would know my iniquity, so that everyone would exalt and marvel at your mercy and resent me. I would reveal them to all if this was for your glory and I was not afraid to scandalize the whole world. I am glad that they will all know on the last day and that everyone will glorify the pity you have shown to the most ungrateful person in the world.

We have all become like one who is unclean, and all our righteous deeds are like a filthy cloth.[451]

I realize and confess, my God, to be disgusting, completely covered with malice. In my life, I have done nothing but evil; but if I have done

---

[449] 2 Samuel 9:8.

[450] Lamentations 3:22.

[451] Isaiah 64:6 [DR 64:5].

some small good by your grace, I have contaminated it so much that it became useless and only served to nauseate your very pure heart.

My lifetime is as nothing in your sight.[452]

O my Lord and my God, prostrate at the feet of your incomprehensible majesty, I profess that I am nothing. I am nothing, I can do nothing, I have nothing. My being is not being. My power is powerlessness. My actions are useless. And moreover, I realize that I am in this state of lifelessness. What is worse is that I have added to my nothingness an ever greater evil: the existence of such a great sinner that I can and must call myself in all truth "Sin Itself." With so many graces and mercies from you, I cannot find anything in my life except sin. I confess to be a monster of malice and ungratefulness. But you, O my beloved God, who rejoices in looking upon the humble, even if they are sinners, cast a glance of mercy on this very vile little creature who lies totally empty at your feet and begs your infinite pity.

The tomb is my house.[453]

If I were to consider that actions of my life, I would surely find myself the most unworthy of all, deserving only your punishments. But since no one who is humble is ever condemned to hell, make me, O Lord, humble of heart so that in this way I can attain salvation. I confess myself at your feet as not being worthy of any blessing of nature, grace or glory: unworthy of the air I breathe, of being treated like other human beings, of praying. The only thing I deserve is hell. But because I fear, that in the midst of such humiliation, there is hidden a bit of pride, I offer you, O Father, the humility of your Son mocked by the worst insults on my account. I offer to you, O Son, the humility of your Most Holy Mother, whom you exalted to become your mother and who confessed herself to be your humble handmaid. And I present to you, O Mother, the humility of all the saints. Thus I, who am trampled underfoot by all creatures, empty myself before your majesty, O God, before whom the seraphim prostrate themselves in reverence.

---

[452] Psalm 39:5 [*DR*: 38:5].

[453] Job 17:13. *The Clementine Vulgate* text reads: *infernus domus mea est (Hell [=Hades] is my house.)*

I was like a brute beast toward you. Nevertheless I am continually with you.[454]

I profess at your feet, O Most Glorious Queen and Mother of Mercy, exactly what I am: the vilest of creatures. Therefore, I beg your intercession. You, who transformed a God into human form, while leaving him unchanged in himself, revealed a God of justice to be the God of mercy and sweetness as he was from all eternity; change this hellish monster into an heir of paradise, this rebel into a child of mercy so he can glorify you forever.

Let us also go, that we may die with him.[455]

Go, all my being, take heart! When our God desires it, let us go sacrifice ourselves on Calvary! Let us accept death with all delight: as Jesus died for us; let us die with Jesus and for Jesus!

Let us then go to him outside the camp and bear the abuse he endured.[456]

Would it be possible for me to draw back from death when a God died for me? Would I refuse pain and sorrow in the face of a God dying in such a painful way for me? I accept with all my heart the death you choose to give me, full of pain, of torments, of disorientation, of dryness and of desolation. But, out of your sheer goodness, let it only be in your favor. Assist me, O my Beloved Crucified One, so that with your death in mind, every suffering and all turmoil becomes my glory.

My heart is steadfast, O God, my heart is steadfast![457]

I am ready and prepared, O my God, to suffer whatever punishment and death you choose to send me: accomplish your Most Holy will in me and in everything of mine now and forever. If I am not good at bringing you joy, I am content that you can find some joy in any suffering I undergo out of love for you, in giving my life for your glory, and thus showing you are the absolute Lord over every creature and Master of life and death.

---

[454] Psalm 73:22–23 [*DR* 72:22–23].

[455] John 11:16.

[456] Hebrews 13:13.

[457] Psalm 108:1 [*DR* 107:1].

Your will be done, on earth as it is in heaven.[458]

My God, how much I want and pray that your will be fulfilled both by me and by all humans everywhere on earth, and that it is done with the same perfection that it is followed in heaven. In this I find all my happiness and contentment! I do not want to be anything other than you will; it is with this level of love and exactness that I wish to follow it. All I am and have, I desire solely because you will it. I am happy to lack all goods because that is your pleasure. And if you wish me to be poorer, if you wish me to be blind, crippled, hated by everyone, trod upon, sick with every kind of illness, dying amid any kind of torment, covered by leprosy: behold, I am ready to do whatever you want. I wish to be entirely yours in time and in eternity, however, whenever and wherever you please. I ask for as much grace as it pleases you to give me. If I could surpass the sanctity of the seraphim in a breath, but realize that it is not your will, I would not choose it. I long to be saved because I know it is your desire, but if it were your will to send me to hell, because that is your choice, I would more than willingly leap into that devouring flame and there enjoy it as my paradise simply because I would be doing your most righteous will.

You are my God. My times are in your hand.[459]

My God, You are my every good, my every hope, my every joy. In you, I already place and leave every thought of myself, my body, my life and my soul. I turn all of myself over to your pleasure. I want to rest securely in the loving arms of your providence and in them draw my last breath, certain that I cannot fear any evil because I am sure that God, my Father, my Creator and my Redeemer, cannot work evil on a child who, with complete trust in him, places all he is and all he has in his hands. I so wish to place my fate in your care that even if you returned it to me, I would replace it in your hands because I wish to entrust myself to you, not to me, since I can be untrue to myself while you cannot be untrue to whoever confides in you.

---

[458] Matthew 5:10.
[459] Psalm 31:14–15 [*DR* 30:15].

In the scroll of the book it is written of me. I delight to do your will, O my God; your law is within my heart.[460]

My triune and one God, in you I entrust my entire will; I do not wish anything if it is not yours. This is the rule I have established in all my actions and have impressed it as a law in the depths of my heart: Do always your holy will. Grant me the abundance of grace to follow this rule in all perfection so that I do not give you any displeasure but, rather, give you every possible joy in the time that remains for me in this life.

Teach me to do your will, for you are my God.[461]

My God, I should find nothing easier and more enjoyable for me than following your will, the first, eternal and infallible law of all holy action; but this is not the case. I have a will that is so depraved that it has no other inclination than to turn away from you and follow its own direction. Teach me, O Father, the beautiful virtue of doing your will; impress on my heart that you are my God and you rejoice only in those who desire what you want. How is it possible that all the irrational creatures always do your will and I alone rebel against you? Teach me this, you, O Divine Son, by your example since you did your Father's will to the very death on the cross. You, O Holy Spirit, the loving bond of the Father and the Son, tie my will to yours, the same will present in all three of the Divine Persons. You proceed from the unified will of the Father and the Son as from a single inspiring principle, give me the grace of having the same will as yours.

I will not restrain my lips: O Lord, thou knowest it.[462]

My most loving God, I confess at your feet all my evil inclinations. In every contrary situation, my corrupt nature is resentful as it wants all things its way, and all the more so now that my weaker part [*i.e., my body*] senses death is near. But if I consider that everything comes from your hands, from your will, without which not even a twig could be moved, I cannot voice a lament. I embrace every adversity and kind of death, despite the repugnance of my nature.

---

[460] *Ibid.* 40:7–8 [*DR* 39:8–9].
[461] *Ibid.* 143:10 [*DR* 142:10].
[462] *Ibid.* 39:10 [*DR*]

My Father, if it is possible, let this cup pass from me; yet not what I want but what you want.[463]

These are the words of your beloved Son in his agony in Gethsemane. You could not but be pleased in hearing them. It is with them that I pray to you, my beloved Father. I do not blush to show a Father my misery and weakness, even though you already know all of them well. Such a deep fear overcomes me in every adversity and such a tormenting a pain as I face death that my nature resists with too much strength. If it is possible, O Father, if it is your pleasure, take away this anxiety from this son of yours who is suffering so much from it, remove this great fear of death, if you can do so without contradicting your own will, without prejudice to my salvation. Nevertheless, let your will now be done, not mine. Rather, if you know that it is to your greater glory or my greater good that I suffer more, bear down on me with the heavy hand of your will, but, at the same time, let your other hand support me so that I may suffer it all, not just with patience, but even with gusto and joy. Indeed, if you were to place in my hands the choice between life and death and let me know that they were both of equal glory, I would choose death in order to conquer my nature and to make myself like my Redeemer who died for me.

Am I not to drink the cup that the Father has given me?[464]

Oh, you perverse nature of mine, how can you refuse death as you look upon a God who died for you? How refuse to drink from a chalice of minor pains when your Redeemer and Lord drank a chalice that seemed to contain an infinite sea of suffering on your behalf? If death is bitter, it is enough to know that it comes from the hands of a Father who loves me to sweeten all bitterness. It is enough to understand that a God is dead for me and that by his agonies he has sweetened the agonies, he has divinized the pains, and has disarmed death to make me die contented so that I may be made to resemble my Jesus Christ. I do not choose to see any adversity, including death, as coming from any other source than from you because all of it is arranged though the greatest love. Armed by this truth, I will to receive pain and persecution and_death because it all comes to me from you and all of it arrives out of the greatest love, and the greater the suffering, the greater is the love behind it.

---

[463] Matthew 26:39.

[464] John 18:11.

FOR FRIDAY: ACTS OF APPEAL TO GOD

God, my God, why have you forsaken me? Why are you so far from helping me?[465]

Allow me, O my beloved God and Father, to call on you at this moment of my death in the same words and prayers that your only-begotten Son spoke on the cross. You had condemned him to this most painful and despised death precisely in order to lighten the agonies of my death, to free me from eternal death and reward me with blessed glory. I seek, O Beloved Father, to call you, pray to you and honor you with the same affections as those of your Son and my Redeemer, Jesus Christ. My God, my God, turn your eyes of your paternal kindness and compassionate mercy toward this lowly little creature. How can you have the heart to leave me abandoned? Even if my sins, without number or measure, have deserved it.

O my God, I cry by day, but you do not answer; and by night, but find no rest.[466]

My God, my sins cry out louder for revenge than my voice cries for help; while I turn to you day and night, it seems that you are deaf to my prayers. But I do not lose heart because of this. Since you do not free me from the agonies of earthly death, I hope you will free me from the pains of eternal death.

Yet you are holy, enthroned on the praises of Israel.[467]

It is true that I find myself in such great sufferings of death, but it is just as true that you feel an infinite happiness in your trinitarian life, the shrine of all the saint's praise and I hope to praise you with them for all eternity.

---

[465] Psalm 22: 1 [*DR* 21:1].

[466] *Ibid.* 22: 2 [*DR* 21:1].

[467] *Ibid.* 22: 3 [*DR* 21:2].

All who see me mock at me; they make mouths at me, they shake their heads; "Commit your cause to the Lord; let him deliver—let him rescue the one in whom he delights![468]

All our enemies, yours and mine, insult me and criticize my hope that I have always had in you. Let them remain totally deluded liars by saving me for the sake of your glory and by remaining faithful to your promises to save whomever trusts in you and for the sake of the value and requests of my Redeemer with and through whom I pray.

Yet it was you who took me from the womb; you kept me safe on my mother's breast. On you I was cast from my birth, and since my mother bore me you have been my God.[469]

You, O Loving Father, formed me in my mother's womb, from which you gave me birth to the light of this world. Still, you were not content with this, but you destined me to be still more noble by a supernatural birth in the womb of another mother, the holy Church, from which you had me born to grace and made me your son so that you might assist me as a Father and the Church nourish me as a mother on the milk of the true faith and piety. Right from that point, you were all my hope, and even increased it when, in another excess of love you appointed as my mother the true Mother of God.

For the sake of the joy of your fatherly sanctity and love as well as through the merits of my double mother, Mary Most Holy, Mother of Mercy, and the Church, please be my Father and do not abandon me in this moment of my death.

Do not be far from me, for trouble is near and there is no one to help. Many bulls encircle me…, they open wide their mouths at me, like a ravening and roaring lion.[470]

If you abandon me, who will help me in this moment of my greatest need? Even now my death with its pains, worries and agonies is near. The demons of hell like bulls and lions rage against me, and plot over my poor soul to snatch it away. I do not have the strength to resist them because of the weakness of my body amid its agonies and the internal grief of

---

[468] *Ibid.* 22:8–9 [*DR* 21:8–9].

[469] *Ibid.* 22:10–11 [*DR* 21:10–11].

[470] *Ibid.* 22:11–13 [*DR* 21:12–13].

my heart that melts like wax in the heat of your justice over my faults and ingratitude. No energy to pray to you remains, no tongue to call out to you: I am reduced to a dead corpse.

Help me, my God, assist me, my Father. Do not listen to the hellish baying against me nor to the plotting of the evil demons, O my beloved God; see me nailed to this bed of pain and wounds. They have already signed the sentence of eternal death against me, taunting me that the fate of my body is the grave and of my soul is hell.

But you, O Lord, do not be far away! O my help, come quickly to my aid! [471]

I do not request consolations; that would be unsupportable for me to have such temerity. I request only virtue and strength against all my tempters so that they cannot glory in having conquered a son of yours and of trampling down one of your images through all eternity.

Deliver my soul from the sword, my life from the power of the dog! Save me from the mouth of the lion! From the horns of the wild oxen you have rescued me. [472]

I do not care about any bodily suffering; I welcome every agony and complete death of my body. But do not permit, my God, that my very self become the prey of Lucifer, whom I see as a ferocious lion, bringing with him all the other demons as vicious rhinoceroses, in a frenzy to capture me and drag me to hell.

Contain their fury, O my God; humble their pride, confuse their haughtiness by leaving them discouraged due to one miserable little creature.

I will tell of your name to my brothers and sisters; in the midst of the congregation I will praise you. [473]

If you choose to save me, I will proclaim and preach your mercy and your victories in my case to all my brothers and sisters in heaven and, together with the Church Triumphant, I will sing your praise forever.

---

[471] *Ibid.* 22: 19 [DR 21:20].

[472] *Ibid.* 22:20–21 [DR 21:21–22].

[473] *Ibid.* 22:23–4 [DR 21:23].

You who fear the Lord, praise him! All you offspring of Jacob, glorify him; stand in awe of him, all you offspring of Israel! For he did not despise or abhor the affliction of the afflicted; he did not hide his face from me, but heard when I cried to him.[474]

So that the saints in heaven will exalt with full praise and glorify your infinite power and mercy with every accolade, I will propose this new reason: the revelation of the strength given me to conquer our enemies, yours and mine, by your granting the supplication of a poor derelict by gazing with clear eyes of pity at a sinner deserving of a thousand hells and saving him.

From you comes my praise in the great congregation; my vows I will pay before those who fear him.[475]

I have been ungrateful for so many of the graces with which you have enriched me during all the years of my life. If you stoop to save me, I will no longer be ungrateful for all of eternity. Within your great and glorious Church Triumphant, I will praise you and glorify you as my God, I will thank you as my most beloved Father and most generous benefactor. In the presence of all the saints who adore you with the highest reverence and respectful fear, I will render tributes of laud and thanksgiving; this I now promise.

The poor shall eat and be satisfied; those who seek him shall praise the Lord. May your hearts live forever! All the ends of the earth shall remember and turn to the Lord; and all the families of the nations shall worship before him. For dominion belongs to the Lord, and he rules over the nations. To him, indeed, shall all who sleep in the earth bow down; before him shall bow all who go down to the dust.[476]

If you, my most merciful God, are willing to listen to my humble prayers and save such an unworthy person such as I, all the other sinners spread throughout the world will be moved at the sight of so much mercy poured out on the worst one of all and will look back in sorrow on their sins and detest them with their whole heart; then, filled with hope they will break

---

[474] *Ibid.* 22:25 [DR 21:24–25].

[475] *Ibid.* 22:25 [DR 21:26].

[476] *Ibid.* 22:26–29 [DR 21:27–30].

out in songs of praise for your infinite mercy. All of them will recognize with respect and with affection your role as Lord and Master of all created things and of grace in this life and glory in the next.

I shall live for him. Posterity will serve him.[477]

I will live with you, of you and for you through all eternity. By my example, I hope that all who follow me trust you and serve you wholeheartedly. For the purpose, I offer my death together with the death of my Redeemer, Jesus, who was the salvation of the whole world.

Future generations will be told about the Lord, and proclaim his deliverance to a people yet unborn, saying that he has done it.[478]

This death of mine in your grace which, after such an unworthy life, is solely the result of your highest mercy will be published to all Christians who are your beloved people reborn of you to a life of grace. All will be filled with hope and love for you so that after serving and loving you on earth, they will also be made worthy to glorify you in heaven.

O Lord, do not rebuke me in your anger, or discipline me in your wrath.[479]

My God and my Lord, who have given me existence in order to save me and surely not to condemn me, who created me for heaven and not for hell, I beg you to act on your desire to see me saved. So do not condemn me to the pains of hell. I must soon present myself before your tribunal, do not impose the sentence of eternal death on me.

Be gracious to me, O Lord, for I am languishing; O Lord, heal me, for my bones are shaking with terror.[480]

I deserve every evil and every punishment in this life and in the next; please, O my God, have mercy on me. Give enough strength to my body so that it does not drag down my spirit and impede me from conversing with you, and give my spirit enough grace so it can suffer with patience every pain and leave this world in your grace.

---

[477] *Ibid.* 22:29–30 [*DR* 21:31].
[478] *Ibid.* 22:30–31 [*DR* 21:31–32].
[479] *Ibid.* 6:1.
[480] *Ibid.* 6:2.

My soul also is struck with terror, while you, O Lord—how long?[481]

I am full of anguish and horror at the thought of how much evil I have done; and the worst is that, because of weakness of mind and strength, I do not know if I can wholeheartedly and with deep fervor implore your pity and beg your pardon. Therefore, please have mercy on me! Do not delay, O Lord, pour out on me your mercy during this agony of death.

Turn, O Lord, save my life; deliver me for the sake of your steadfast love.[482]

Why do you hesitate, O Lord, to look upon me with the tender eyes of your pity? One holy glance of yours will restore me and free me from all these pressures. Do this, O Lord, and heal me, not because of my own merits of which there are none, but solely out of your mercy.

For in death there is no remembrance of you; in Sheol who can give you praise?[483]

If I die both in body and soul, I will not be able to praise you forever. Then, O Lord, save me so that I can glorify you and love you forever.

I am weary with my moaning; every night I flood my bed with tears; I drench my couch with my weeping.[484]

I would like, O my Beloved God, to dig out of the depths of my heart enough sighs and shed from my eyes enough tears that they would flood the bed on which I lie in order to move your most sweet heart to have pity on me!

My eyes waste away because of grief; they grow weak because of all my foes.[485]

I see myself attacked by three powerful adversaries in a way that my heart finds no relief but instead becomes more desperate because of them: your justice that terrifies me, my sins that rage within me, the tempting demons that make war on me. If you do not help me with your pity, I am on the verge of desperation.

---

[481] *Ibid.* 6:3 [DR 6:4].

[482] *Ibid.* 6:4 [DR 6:5].

[483] *Ibid.* 6:5 [DR 6:6].

[484] *Ibid.* 6:6 [DR 6:7].

[485] *Ibid.* 6:7 [DR 6:8].

Depart from me, all you workers of evil, for the Lord has heard the sound of my weeping.[486]

In the name of the Father, of the Son and of the Holy Spirit, depart from me, you damned insidious stalkers of my soul. You do not have any power over me; the omnipotent Lord has robbed you of all such power, he who has stooped down to listen to the cries of his servant and heard his prayers.

The Lord has heard my supplication; the Lord accepts my prayer.[487]

The one consubstantial Trinity has agreed to my cries in my favor: the Father by the merits of his only begotten One, the Son out of love for his Father and the Holy Spirit for the sake of the glory and display of his mercy.

All my enemies shall be ashamed and struck with terror; they shall turn back, and in a moment be put to shame.[488]

Imprison yourselves in the darkest abyss filled with distress and shame, you infernal demons: you do not have any more hope of conquering me when the Almighty One, for his glory, has fortified my weakness, raised me up out of my misery and made me formidable to you.

Be gracious to me, O Lord. See what I suffer from those who hate me.[489]

O Most Sweet Lord, have pity on me, look at me crestfallen before my enemies and assist me with your grace.

O Very Just Judge, dismay my enemies, beat back the multitude that makes war on me. Rise in my defense, O Great Omnipotent Warrior, because your enemies confront me in defiance of you. So defend your cause rather than my own. Say to my poor soul: "I am your salvation, your Savior" and I will laugh in the face of all my enemies both in life and in death.

---

[486] *Ibid. 6:8 [DR 6:9].*
[487] *Ibid. 6:9 [DR 6:10].*
[488] *Ibid. 6:10 [DR 6:11].*
[489] *Ibid. 9:13 [DR 9:14].*

O Lord of hosts, God of Israel, who are enthroned above the cherubim, you are God, you alone, of all the kingdoms of the earth...you alone are the Lord.[490]

Lord of Hosts, who have the seraphim and cherubim for a footstool before your throne and who is the God of all and supreme Master of all the kingdoms of the universe, wipe out the horrible blasphemies of your hellish enemy, who mocks me in order to inflict insult on you, to weaken your providence and show you as a God so weak he cannot save me, as a cruel God wishing to damn me. Free me from his hands, save this poor person who has no other help than what you give, but who has everything in you. Make yourself known as a God so powerful, so good, so merciful (as you indeed are) by conquering through my weakness an enemy who is so powerful and so proud and by saving a sinner deserving of hell for all the reasons they raise.

Band together, you peoples, and be dismayed...for God is with us.[491]

Gather together for counsel, arm yourselves for the final battle, O demons, do what you will: I fear nothing because I have God on my side. Rather, armed with God as my shield, with the cross of my Redeemer as my sword, with my most powerful Mother as my standard, I challenge in battle all of hell and I laugh at you. Dare much, but you can do nothing; armed by my God I will break the horn of all your pride and my God will rejoice in triumph over you through me who is weakness personified.

By this I know that you are pleased with me; because my enemy has not triumphed over me.[492]

I have feared for my salvation because of my sins and for having so many times in my life given in to hell in the face of very little temptation. But now that I see how much I am confirmed by your grace in such great temptations, my heart rejoices, my spirit has conceived such secure hope that I will be saved that I rejoice in sight of my conquering those who so often conquered me.

---

[490] Isaiah 37:16, 18 [*DR* 37:16–18, 20].

[491] *Ibid.* 9, 10 [*DR* 8:9–10].

[492] Psalm 41:11 [*DR* 40:12].

Hear my prayer, O Lord; give ear to my supplications in your faithfulness; answer me in your righteousness.[493]

Listen, Lord, to my prayers; do not hold back from lowering yourself to give a kind audience to my requests. Even if I do not deserve even to be heard, my petitions deserve pity (though they are totally worthless in themselves) because the truth of your promises remains firm by which you have committed your word, an infallible word because it is divine, and obliged yourself simply on the basis of your goodness to attend to the requests of whoever comes to you humbly and confidently. If my prayer is not of this kind, make it so in order than it may deserve to be listened to. The prayer that I raise to you is this: make me live and die in your grace.

Answer me quickly, O Lord; my spirit fails.[494]

O Lord, do not delay pouring out your graces on my spirit since so little life is left for me and if you do not help with your grace, I will trip and fall.

Do not hide your face from me, or I shall be like those who go down to the Pit.[495]

I am always weak, so much so that there is nothing evil that I can ever avoid doing, especially at this point because of my bodily weakness, my sluggishness of spirit and the violence of temptation. Therefore, with all my heart I beg you not to turn your very kind face away from me or I shall be among the number of those condemned to eternal death. Do not permit this, O my God, my merciful one.

Teach me the way I should go, for to you I lift up my soul.[496]

Show me, Lord, the right path I should follow: the one, my God, that you foresee I need in order to be saved. I am totally blind without your light, illumine me, direct me, stop me if I were to veer from the right path. Only you know the path of my salvation and perfection; see that I take it, even though I may find it disgusting because it is loaded with

---

[493] *Ibid.* 143:1 [DR 142:1].
[494] *Ibid.* 143:7 [DR 142:7].
[495] *Ibid.*
[496] *Ibid.* 143:8 [DR 142:7].

obstacles, troubles, temptations, pains and nothing I care for; this is what I want. If I beg to do otherwise, do not listen to me. This is entirely my sincere wish that is, I hope, final and irrevocable.

Show your strength, O God, as you have done for us before.[497]

I glance back on my life and recognize a marvel of contradictions because I see myself a mix of your graces and my thanklessness. You have always favored me with graces, lights and impulses but I was always rebellious against your illuminations. O God, do not pay attention to my lack of gratefulness that justly deserves your total abandonment of me. Instead, look back at those graces that should not be lost because they were your gift and the fruit of the blood of my Redeemer God. So as not to lose them, I ask you to add grace to grace and join even greater mercies to both the old and the new ones. Command your light to illumine me and your grace to assist me all the more so that such great lights and graces do not go to waste. This way I will be grateful forever.

My God in his steadfast love will meet me.[498]
Surely goodness and mercy shall follow me all the days of my life.[499]

My most merciful God, surround me and gird me with your mercy. Go before me to direct me, stand above me to defend me and surround me to protect me from every assault of the enemy; follow me to smash every attack of hell; stay within me to disperse all the miseries that fill me. Above all else I beg, my God, that you assist me with your merciful grace so that I respond rightly to each grace and do whatever you wish of me and not transgress in any way. What use are your graces if, by my own fault, I did not respond to them? What good is your mercy if I abuse it? Continually illuminate this blind mind; speak always to this hard heart in a way that it will always follow your light and obey your call. If you foresee that I will be thankless and recalcitrant to your enlightenment, give my mind an even brighter light to which you foresee I will generously respond and a stronger push to my heart by which you foresee I will obey. Give me the lights and impulses, O my God, on which you foresee my eternal salvation depends, and not the ones to which you see I will not correspond by my own fault and

---

[497] *Ibid.* 68:28 [*DR* 67:29].
[498] *Ibid.* 59:10 [*DR* 58:11].
[499] *Ibid.* 23:6 [*DR* 22:6].

so lose your friendship. O my most merciful God, my Most Holy and beloved Lord, this is the one grace I ask of you above all others, with my every desire, breath and groan of my heart. This is the grace that is the first, principal and only object of pious prayers, the ultimate goal of many vows. Any other grace I asked you for is completely directed to this one.

Indeed, I know that you on your part wish my eternal wellbeing and that this depends on those lights and impulses by which you have very often spoken to my heart and mind. Always speak to me more, O Father, whenever I cannot do things more congenial to your heart or whenever in speaking to me *[I prevent]* you from engendering your word in me spiritually. Speak out of love and due to the merits of your Word who became flesh and died for me. You, O Beloved Word, breathe into my heart your effective and all-powerful love so that it accomplishes what you inspire in me; breathe into me your Spirit for your glory and for the love of your Most Sweet Mother. And you as well, O Most Lovable Holy Spirit, instill in me your grace and your gifts for the glory of your name, for the merits of the blood the God-Made-Man shed for me and through the intercession of your handmaid, daughter, spouse and my protector, Mary the Most Holy Mother, so that I, responding to your graces, am saved in order to glorify my God and my mother eternally.

O Lord, all my longing is known to you; my sighing is not hidden from you.[500]

My Lord, to whom all the hidden recesses of the heart are open and clear, you know all my desires and you hear all the cries and sighs of my afflicted heart. I cannot speak to you with my tongue, but I speak to you in the intimacy of my heart; I cannot speak to you in words, but I speak to you in groans; even though I am not worthy to be yours during life, I do not request anything else of you than to be entirely yours in death, and then forever to your eternal glory.

Yet it was you who took me from the womb...On you I was cast from my birth, and since my mother bore me you have been my God. Do not be far from me.[501]

---

[500] *Ibid.* 38:9 [DR 37:10].
[501] *Ibid.* 22:9–11 [DR 21:10–12].

My God, my entire hope, because of you I drank the milk of my mother's breast, and that of my Mother the holy Church as well as of the most merciful Mother Mary ever since I placed all my hope in you. From when I was spiritually conceived in her womb, I have always recognized, adored and confessed you as my God because that is what you are. You are such by nature and therefore my God, the God of all people and of all things. You are my Father under many titles: I was created by you, adopted by you and generated to the life of grace in the virginal womb of your spouse and my mother, the holy Church, of which you are the Father, Spouse and Head; my brother because adopted by the heavenly Father in your likeness, his only begotten and firstborn Son, because you became human, [*sharing*] in my nature and with my blood, Son of one mother of our race. By these many titles you are mine and I am entirely yours. Now do you have the heart to abandon me at this point, abandon me forever? You cannot do so as my God because all my hope, joy, and your highest glory as God is to save a guilty person from a thousand hells. You cannot do so as my Father because, although I have many times ceased to be your son, you have never stopped being my Father and as a father you must save me in order to reach the goal for which you created me. You must do so for the sake of your honor so that a son adopted by a father who is God will not be a slave of his greatest enemy; you must do it in order not to lose the price of your suffering and death with which you bore me into the life of your grace and as a brother you have taken on the obligation of saving me; this was the reason you became human and my brother, my guarantor, my savior.

I know very well that you do not fail me; all the failure is on my part; but you make up for all this failure because of the kind of God you are, because of the fatherly richness of your mercy, because of the love of the blood you have shed. Recall that we have dwelled within the same motherly body, we were born of the same maternal womb, we have drunk from the same breast, you physically, me spiritually. Thus, out of love of this breast, this milk, this mother whom in an excess of goodness you have given me as a mother, do not abandon me, do not condemn me to hell so that your enemies may not have the glory of treading down your son, your brother that you adopted out of so great a love.

O Lord, I am your servant...the child of your serving girl.[502]

My Lord and my God, remember that I am your servant; if because I am a servant who is useless, ungrateful and treacherous I deserve punishment and not pity, recall that I am the son of your mother, who was exalted to the infinite dignity of being your mother, who considered and called herself your servant. Whatever grace you confer on me, you are also conferring on my mother, because that loving mother appreciates as her own all gifts made to her children. For love and glory, for the merits and intercession of this mother of mine I request paradise of which she is the Lady. Hers is paradise, as an inheritance given by the Eternal Father, as a dowry presented by her Spouse, the Holy Spirit. It is her kingdom because you conquered it and gave it to her as her Son so that she would reign as Queen in your kingdom and hers. Now it is my right as her son to enter into possession of the inheritance of his mother, the heir of her dowry, and to enjoy her kingdom. I am, it is true, unworthy, ungrateful, and deserving of being disinherited. But if she, the Mother of All Mercies, chooses to recognize as her son someone so completely pitiful, then, through the grace of my mother, I beg for paradise. If it is your right as Father of all the just to give it to your children, it is her right as mother of sinners to give it to her sinful children who weep out of contrition at your feet and invoke the immense richness of the mercy of their very own mother.

Turn again, O God of hosts; look down from heaven, and see; have regard for this vine, the stock that your right hand planted.[503]

Look down from highest heaven with eyes of pity on this vine that I am, planted by your hand, O Father, watered by your blood, O Son, warmed by your ardor, O Holy Spirit. Defend it from the enemy by your power, O Father; cultivate it by your cross, O Son; enrich it with your fruit, O Holy Spirit, so that it can produce the grapes of eternal life.

Now I have put my words in your mouth.[504]

Teach me how to pray to the Father, O Divine Son. I do not know how to pray, nor do I know what I ought to ask for or what is expedient for

---

[502] *Ibid.* 116:16 [*DR* 115:16].

[503] *Ibid.* 80:14–15 [*DR* 79:15–16].

[504] Jeremiah 1:9.

my salvation. Direct me. What can you deny me, O Father, if whatever I ask for is also requested with me by your only begotten Son and my Redeemer and Advocate, Jesus? He has pledged your divine word that you would listen to any prayer made in his name. I present my request to you: that you stoop to give me this grace of salvation because when you give it to me, I will receive it as done to him by reason and on the basis of his blood. Do you have the heart, O Father, to deny such a grace to a Son who is so loved and so loving? You cannot consider only my sins when the merits of my Redeemer are so infinitely greater than my sins. He begs you for me, no, he prays for himself because he, the Head, prays for the members of his Body and every grace bestowed on the members he considers as given to himself, the Head. Look at me, O Father, united to the Head by means of Faith, of Hope, and make me live always united to him by love and grace in this life so I can live united with him in the glory of heaven. Just as I pray to the Father in your name, by your merits, so I pray also to you, only begotten Son, in the name for the merits of your mother. That son, very unworthy indeed, of such a mother begs you to save me and choose to reward in me the merits of my mother, of your mother, and so grant me paradise in response to the humanity that you received from this mother. In this way, you glorify the Father in yourself and glorify yourself in your mother forever.

Let my prayer be counted as incense before you, and the lifting up of my hands as an evening sacrifice.[505]

See to it, O Lord, that my prayers do not stumble but reach your throne as pleasingly as sacred incense. Therefore I unite my prayers with those of all the saints and angels, of the Most Holy Mary and of your Divine Son through the sacrifice which he made of himself to you on the cross in the evening hours. With your crucified Son and with his Most Sorrowful Mother I unite my thoughts, affections, sufferings, prayers, sighs and death, my Beloved Father. Out of love for your Son and for the prayers of such a mother, accept the sacrifice of my life and save me.

Turn away the disgrace that I dread, for your ordinances are good.[506]

My thoughts torture me too much. All the demons whisper to me that I am condemned to eternal disaster. Encourage me because your spirit is

---

[505] Psalm 141:2 [*DR* 140:2].

[506] *Ibid.* 119:38 [*DR* 118:39].

sweet, your judgments are amiable and your nature is to do good to all and to save all.

Deal with them…for my groans are many and my heart is faint.[507]

If the Lord drives me away as I deserve, I turn to you. I beg before the tribunal of your great pity, Mother of Mercies. You cannot drive me away precisely because I am full of misery and sin since this was the reason that God made you the Mother of All Mercies and Mother of Sinners. No one who has recourse to you with a true heart is condemned. Will I be the only one who is unfortunate? This is who you are, Mother of God, and I believe it; you are this for all sinners. Have pity on me by reason of the infinite obligations you owe to the Most Holy Trinity that has exalted you so loftily and honored and enriched you! Have mercy for the sake of glorifying the most pure blood of your Son drawn from your own body! Take pity on me by reason of the glory due your name and in order to show your mercy! The devils berate me saying that God has abandoned me and that I cannot escape their hands. Make them end up shamed and confused. Help me, defend me. If I have you, I have everything.

If the Lord had not been my help, my soul would soon have lived in the land of silence.[508]

How long would I have been burning in hell as a victim of Divine Justice if your intercession had not preserved me, O Mother! It would be useless for me to have been preserved up to the present if you do not preserve me forever. Ask for these great graces for me out of your mercy. Ask because of what you owe your Most Loving Holy Trinity; for the sake of the gift your Son's blood has given you; for the sake of all the zeal you have for your Son's honor and as well as your own, do not allow that so much blood be lost on account of my sins; do not permit that the death of a God become my greatest punishment in hell.

For my name's sake I defer my anger, for the sake of my praise I restrain it for you, so that I may not cut you off. For my own sake, for my own sake, I do it, for why should my name be profaned? My glory I will not give to another.[509]

---

[507] Lamentations 1:22 [*DR* 1:19].

[508] Psalm 94:17.

[509] Isaiah 48:9, 11.

O Mary, be my Mary! To me you are everything good, all hope, all strength, all comfort, all solace at this fatal moment of my death, because you carry all that is good in the very powerful and sweet name of Mary. In your name, Mary, you bear what it means to be Mother of God, and to be the Lady and Star of the Sea. As Mother of God, calm the anger of your Son against me; as Lady, block and fight the schemes of the demons; as Star guide me in this stormy sea and under your guidance I am sure of reaching the port of blessed happiness. Out of love, then, and for the glory of your name, as well as out of zeal for your Son's honor, bind me with the gentle bonds of your praise so that, from now on, I do not cease to give you praise and never cease doing so for all eternity. You, who bound a God with indissoluble bindings to our human flesh, tie my will with eternal bonds to your feet so that I may never again leave you. Plant in my mind, on my tongue and in my heart the names of Jesus and Mary for with these names of life I can never die.

How could you allow, O Mother, that in hell I would blaspheme your most holy name that is worthy of all honor and all blessing? How could you permit that the devils would have me to insult and thereby cover your name with abuse by ridiculing me as one who is damned after having placed all his hope in you, the Mother of the Almighty, who could have requested paradise for me? Is it not you, the Mother of the Wisdom of the Father, who is charged with my salvation? You who know how to act and win the cause of even the most enormous sinner when from his heart he invoked you, the Mother of Mercy? If I am damned, then your mercy will not be glorified for there is no room for that in hell. So with all my heart I beg, O Mother, to act so that forever your mercy will be glorified by my unworthy self; the more unworthy I am, so much the greater will be the glory that results for your name, for your mercy. Do not grant to your enemies the glory of having as their slave a servant of the Queen of Heaven, a son of the Mother of God.

Be my Lady and I will be your servant. Because you are the Mother of the Creator of the World, both visible and invisible, your reign and sovereignty extends wherever your only begotten Son rules, for he is by nature the Lord and Master of the Universe. Your Son has so desired to exalt you. I wish to serve you for all eternity not out of force but with all my heart and all my will. I cannot be such a servant in hell, but only in heaven because the glory of the reign granted you by the Most High God is like the divine reign of the Most High. Request for me, then, the grandeur of being your servant who glorifies you with the whole heavenly court. I wish to be thus from this moment on. I esteem the glory of serving the Queen of Heaven as a humble slave more than that of being a ruler over all earthly thrones.

Be a Mother to me and I will be your son. This request seems too rash: that an unworthy and filthy slave, the vilest in the entire universe, would ask to be adopted as a son of the Queen of Heaven, of the very Mother of God. It is indeed so! I would not dare to ask you for so much if I were not aware that your kindness is equal to your greatness, your pity equal to your dignity. You are a Mother who is all the more glorious in proportion to your greater mercy. Rather, you consider your greatest glory to be in caring for the needy, in comforting the most miserable. You are a queen who is all the more sublime in dignity the more you are merciful and humble. You consider it your honor to lower yourself for us and in this way you reveal yourself worthy to be the Mother of that God who abased himself from the heights of glory to the lowest level of vileness to become our Brother and Redeemer. This Son of God who became your son and our brother has given you as our Mother. To make you such, he enriched you with all humility, charity, kindness and mercy for such a mission. Out of love for such a son, for the glory of your humility and mercy, as a demonstration of your immense charity, be my Mother; do not refuse me this great grace. I am indeed too unworthy of this, but I beg you for it through Jesus, for the infinite obligation that you have to such a Son. I am unworthy, but Jesus Christ is worthy of it.

You cannot deny it to Jesus, and for Jesus' sake you cannot deny it to me, because I ask for nothing other than that your only begotten Son be born in me by means of your intercession. I beg of you a grace that is as glorious for you as was that of bearing a Divine Son; so acceptable to your Son who rejoiced to become your Son and to be given birth by you; so pleasing to the Eternal Father that he rejoices in seeing his only begotten regenerated in others and for this reason he gave him to you and he made him all yours so that the Father's real and natural Son is also your real and natural Son; and so glorious for the Holy Spirit who will rejoice in generating the God-Made-Man spiritually in me just as he generated him bodily in the virginal womb. So be my Mother! I know that out of your immense piety you desire it. I am totally unworthy of it; make me worthy so that I truly live and die as your son, your devoted son, obedient, like you in character and in virtue. Deny me every other grace, but not this one. If I have this, I have everything, because if you are my Mother, I have the most powerful Protector against all my enemies; the wisest of Advocates who wins all my causes; a very sweet Consoler in all my afflictions; a secure Hope in all my needs including the greatest need of all, [*your presence*] at the point of my death. I want to hand over my spirit into your hands so that you would deign to present it to your Son and in your grace save me.

Unite to yourself, O my Mother, my spirit and my heart in a union so close that I will never be parted from you. If this prayer is too audacious, chain me to your feet so that I live as your faithful servant at your feet on earth and in heaven, and by your goodness, one from whom you can receive glory because he is a servant always committed to serve you and love you in time and in eternity.

For Saturday: Acts of Hope

I will both lie down and sleep in peace[510]

My God and my Father, as your son I rest secure in your fatherly bosom and here I wish to give my whole self so that from this bosom of my Father God (where I hope to remain always by means of grace), I hope to pass into eternal rest in the same bosom to his glory. This hope alone sweetens my bitterness and cheers me in my sufferings, encourages me in my fears. Thus, I sleep in my Father God's loving arms, and although my sins may be countless and innumerable, I am encouraged by thinking that your mercy is infinitely greater. In this great ocean all my sins are washed

---

[510] Psalm 4:8 [*DR* 4:9].

away. It is true that I have too often abused so many mercies but it is even more true that all my excesses have not reached the bottom of your mercy; for my Redeemer makes up for all of my abuses by his own blood, and in this sea all my sins are dissolved. And although I have been so ungrateful to my Redeemer, indeed, he has supplied even for such ingratitude. If all these sins impede the power of this divine blood from being applied to me, I hope that such graces will come from Mary Most Holy, the Mother of Mercy. This mother enjoys showing that she is the Mother of Mercies where misery is the greatest. I cannot imagine another person being more pitiful than I am and so it is in this person that the magnificence of the mercy of my Divine Father will shine, the efficacy of the blood of my Redeemer and the power of my most merciful Mother, the Immaculate Spouse of the Holy Spirit. On these three unmovable rocks I land the small skiff of myself, tossed by such great storms, by so many whirlwinds, by so many pirates, namely, my sins, my fears of being lost and the persecutions of the demons. On these three very firm foundations, I am secure: 1) on the *infinite mercy of God my Father* who desires to save me and is able to and who has given me his word that he will save me; 2) on the *infinite merits of my redeemer Father* who has taken on himself the responsibility of saving me when he died for my salvation and has totally committed himself to save me, to make effective in me his passion and death, and to receive from the Father the reward for the blood he shed; 3) on the *most powerful patronage of my Mother Mary,* who as Mother of the Almighty One can do so, because as Mother of Mercy she wished to do so and because as Mother of God for sinners, is completely obliged to defend my cause and save me. With my hope resting on this foundation, it cannot be wrong.

A hope founded on my own deserts, even if I had those of all the saints, would prove fruitless; but what cannot fail is my hope based on God, on my Redeemer, and on my Mother. Everything points to the fact that all my hope stands true and sincere. Still, this hope is your gift; give it to me, O my God, for your glory, for the merits of my Redeemer, for the intercession of Mary, my Mother. With this sure hope I am as certain of being saved, my God, as much as it is certain that you, on your part, wish all to be saved. It is as certain as the infallibility of your word; as certain as it is that my Jesus has died for the salvation of all, and as Mary is the universal Advocate for all.

Therefore my heart is glad, and my soul rejoices; my body also rests secure.[511]

My heart leaps in such bounds of joy that it forces my tongue to sing hymns of praise and happiness, so much so, that my body and all my senses are filled and all rejoice in you, O my God, my only hope. This grace in the midst of all my agonies provides me with such jubilee and canticles that I do not stop repeating to your glory and my comfort: "*O my God, my hope.*" No one knows or imagines your beautiful heart and your loving spirit, if they do not hope in you, if they do not abandon to you everything that they are. I declare that I not only hope but I "superhope," aware of your spirit of kindness, charity, goodness and mercy, incompressible by any mind and unspeakable by any tongue. This spirit you rejoice showing toward the most miserable and needy persons because they trust in you. I indeed have even greater hope with you and in you, my God, than even a daughter in her mother, a son in his father, a friend in his or her friend, spouses in one another; none have greater faith that my trust in you, my Almighty God, my most loving Mother, my most faithful Friend, my most merciful Spouse. No one ever had faith in you, my God, and ended up lost.

Has anyone trusted in the Lord and been disappointed?[512]

It is impossible for someone who trusts in you to remain confused, just as it is impossible for you not to be a God true to who you are, one whose nature is goodness itself and who, on his own part, has infinite joy in using his mercy with everyone and in saving all. Must I be the only one so unlucky? Am I the only one with whom your most sweet heart would wish to be severe? In my case alone would you change your spirit and nature? Ah no! I want to entrust myself to you, my God, and not give up trusting until I obtain what I hope for, that is, to praise you forever.

But for me it is good to be near God; I have made the Lord God my refuge.[513]

Let me leave behind anyone who wishes to place their happiness in friends, riches or earthly greatness for I, on my part, find all my joy in

---

[511] *Ibid.* 16:9 [*DR* 15:9].

[512] Sirach 2:10.

[513] Psalm 73:28 [*DR* 72:28].

you, O my God, Three in One. Indeed, I have all things because I have placed all my hope in you. In you I have every good, every dignity, every happiness in this life together with hope of the beatific vision in the next life. Although right now I am the refuse of the world, disgusting to everyone as the lowest kind of filth, I have everything because I have every hope in you and thus all good things.

In him my heart trusts; so I am helped.[514]

I hope, and do so with a certainty resting on you, that I will have the pleasure of your company for all eternity in heaven. Then, Most Holy Trinity, I will be able forever to contemplate your unveiled face! I will always be able to contemplate a Father producing a Son who is consubstantial and coeternal with him! A Son begotten amid infinite splendors of the entire holiness of all glory! A Holy Spirit coming forth as the fruit of this mutual love of Father and Son, but uncreated, infinite, eternal, incomprehensible! I will for all eternity admire a Father, who is God begetting a God who is Son and who rests in his Son's arms as upon a throne; an only begotten Son who is always being born of the Father and rests in the bosom of the Father as upon a throne; a Spirit, the personal Love of the Father and Son, breathed forth from the bosom of both and who properly takes repose in the same bosom! Then from all eternity, it will be my call to bless you, Father of a divine Son by nature and my Father as well by means of a perfect adoption because it leads to glory; I am to praise you, consubstantial Word of the Father and my Brother in life and glory; I will have the task of loving you, Holy Spirit, Love of the Father and Son, and my Love also because I am loved and transformed by you and will remain in and of you through fruitful and blessed love!

For all eternity I will be all yours without fear of being lost. We will be one by means of love! O my wonderful fate! O my enviable happiness! God will be mine and I will be my God's! God will be all mine and I will be entirely my God's! I will become like a ray of the beauty of God, richly springing from God's treasuries; I will be powerful and wise because I share in the greatness, power, nobility, and wisdom of God! I will be, by participation, what God is by his essence! I will sit with God at his table: my food and drink will be God.

---

[514] *Ibid.* 28:7 [DR 27:7].

I will be in God, with God and of God! My God will be my rest, my life, my food, my joy, my every good!

When, O my God, will I no longer be that miserable subject of so many evils that I now find myself to be? When will these eyes become two fonts of light in your gaze? When will this mind reach the point of never ceasing to contemplate you, this tongue of praising you, this heart of loving you? This will be my entire joy: loving and praising you without end and without interruption. This is why I desire, hope, and beg for paradise, not for my own glory, but to glorify you; not simply for my joy but to give you joy and to give to the saints a reason to admire and thank your infinite mercy for having saved my unworthy person, guilty of a thousand hells. When, O my most loving Trinity, will you receive the sacrifice of my life, the holocaust of my heart, so I can thank you and be happy with you in your virginal fruitfulness, your incomprehensible glory, happiness, and greatness? When will I be able to be sure that I can no longer offend you and never separate myself from you?

He reached down from on high, he took me; he drew me out of mighty waters.[515]

O my heart, why do you hesitate before your God, even after he has given you so many promises of his infinite love? He has given me my entire reality, and he did so in order for me to enjoy him for eternity. This is the reality I deformed by my own fault, and he has reformed it with his own blood, poured out in immense pain to prevent my loss of divine life. No architect wants to lose a masterpiece he has created and labored over with so much love; would God want to fail in his? He wants to save me no matter the cost. No father wishes evil on his child; could a father of infinite love and mercy want to do so? No one wishes to fail in his task; would God want to lose it? He has only one goal and can have no other: that his own glory be known and loved on earth and then in heaven, so he would cease to be God if he did not have his glory as the object of his actions; likewise, he would stop being divine if, on his part, he did not wish me to be saved and to be blessed forever.

O Lord, could you then have the heart to lose someone that cost you all of your blood that cost you a divine life offered amid a sea of

---

[515] *Ibid.* 18:17 [DR 17:17].

pain and contempt? Oh, no! Whoever would doubt this, O my God, would do you the greatest insult. How, O my God, will I not trust you if you have already freed me from all evils, and supported me with a patience worthy only of you, since I could not bear sufferings myself and you not only support me but pity me? You have freed me from hell as many times as I have sinned; you have awaited my repentance with such patience and called me with so much love when I moved far from you, when I turned my back upon you as you strove to call me and I responded with defiance; you kept after me and I fled you and pushed you away from me.

Would it be possible that you, a God who is so good, so loving, and so committed to saving me, that you would abandon me now that I want with all my heart to follow and love you? O Lord, I do not do so out of fear of the death that draws near but only from the desire to serve you. If you see that my will is not true, give me a serious, sincere and effective one because, without a doubt, that is the kind of will that would save me. This is what I pray and I hope for from you, my Father, who has created me for paradise. I ask this and hope for it through the merits of your only begotten. This I ask of you and trust in you, O my Redeemer who died to save me; I ask it of you for the glory of your Father, who sent you into the world and condemned you to the death of the cross to free me from eternal death. This I ask of you and trust in you, O my sanctifying Spirit who has adopted me with your grace in holy baptism in order to prepare me for the perfect adoption in heaven. I ask you this for the glory of the Father and on the merits of your Son, through the intercession of my Mother as well as so I can glorify you in heaven with the Father and the Son and give the Three of you every honor and every glory through all the ages. Amen.

He will call upon me and I will give an answer. My fortune shall be with him.[516]

Now, O my beloved Lord, is the time to fulfill your promises by hearing my poor, humble prayers. If there were many times when I was not worthy of being heard because of my sins and to test my trust, now I ask you with all my heart in this my greatest need and I hope for this grace

---

[516] *Ibid.* 90:15 [Vulgate; *translation from Italian*].

with certainty. My hope is all the greater when my reasons for hope are less. In this way, the hope is more worthy of you because you are saving an unworthy soul and you save him solely because he hopes for eternal salvation from you.

Protect me, O God, for in you I take refuge.[517]

I give you no other motive, my God, than that you show the greatest mercy to the greatest sinner for his eternal salvation, if I but beg you to save me because I hope in you. I have nothing deserving of paradise, rather all I deserve is hell, but indeed I hope for paradise from you and I beg for such a grace and I will desire it only because I hope in you. This is the greatest difference between your spirit and that of humans. No one receives something good from another just because he or she hopes for it; but for you the greatest merit for obtaining some gift is to hope for it from you.

I will protect those who know my name.[518]

This is what you declare for all, and I, urged on by your promise, although loaded down with demerits and ingratitude, I ask that I be saved simply because I hope in you.

And those who know your name put their trust in you.[519]

Why despair? For my part, I will declare that I hope and I will always hope in you, O my God. I have done you much disrespect; however, I will never commit the most enormous disrespect against your goodness, the one most insulting to your kindness, the most painful to your desires, the most piercing to your most loving heart, namely, to distrust you. Whoever distrusts you does not know you, does not appreciate your pity, does not know the immensity of your mercy. I, though blind, indeed know by means of your light that you are a God who does not crave anything more than revealing your goodness, mercy, and infinite love toward poor sinners in order to save them. I therefore confess, my God and my Father, that you can save me because you are omnipotent; that you wish to save me after so many sins though you detest them from your heart, because you are a God of incomprehensible mercy; and

---

[517] *Ibid.* 16:1 [*DR* 15:1].

[518] *Ibid.* 91:14 [*DR* 90:14].

[519] *Ibid.* 9:10 [*DR* 9:11].

because you are totally committed to save me because you are a God of fidelity whose word is infallible. Therefore you command me strongly that I, the greatest of sinners, trust in you. What does it cost you to save me? Your omnipotence is your will.

You are obliged to save me due to the merits of my Redeemer. How can I not desire to entrust myself to you, my God, when Faith teaches me that you are uniquely a spirit of love and unspeakable is your goodness? I will not be able to fall when I am supported by your power and charity, O Father; I will not be able to lose the life of heaven if I follow you, O Son, who in order to save me you have paved the way to salvation with your wisdom and truth; I will not be able to be lost if I have abandoned myself entirely to your guidance, O Holy Spirit, God of infinite goodness and mercy.

But I will hope continually, and will praise you yet more and more.[520]

How much my wavering is heartened when my trust reinforces the thought that the more I trust you, O my God, the more I honor your name, I praise your goodness and I give glory to your mercy. My heart urges me to entrust myself to you to reflect that the more I am burdened by sins and worthy of hell, all the more does trusting in you bring you honor and praise, because if it is your glory to save a just person whose merits have gained him or her heaven, it is to your greater glory to save a sinner. Because thus you show all the more your mercy; you manifest more gloriously your most sweet heart. I trust in you, my God, and so I can praise and honor you all the more, glorify you all the more, increase my hope in you. Strengthen it in a way that I do not lose hope if I do not obtain as much as I hope for. In this way, you give the saints in heaven a motive for exalting your infinite mercy in having saved a guilty person simply because of his hope in you.

But those who wait for the Lord shall renew their strength, they shall mount up with wings like eagles, they shall run and not be weary, they shall walk and not faint.[521]

O God, grant me the gift of hope in you so that I am no longer that weak and miserable person I have been until now; because with

---

[520] *Ibid.* 71:14 [*DR* 70:14].

[521] Isaiah 40:31.

hope in you I will be stripped of my weakness and misery, and I will be invested with a share in your power and your treasures. This way, as I am transformed by grace in you, I will no longer fear and I will rush firmly toward the enjoyment of you face to face unveiled in heaven without being hindered by the weight of my sins which you have pardoned, nor by the efforts of hell which you have destroyed, nor by the rigor of your justice that you have already satisfied for me by your goodness.

But the Lord takes pleasure in those who fear him, in those who hope in his steadfast love.[522]

If you, O my God, are a God of salvation rather than of perdition, your spirit is to save and not to damn. If you find you happiness in the one who fears to give you insult and who trusts in you, I beg, my Beloved Lord, give my heart a strong fear of offending you and a lively hope of being saved so I am an object of your pleasure and a son according to your heart. O Lord, with a compassionate heart, grant that I may be an eternal object of your love!

Although he should kill me, I will trust in him: And he shall be my savior.[523]

I have such great hope in you, my God, that even if you would show me in a revelation that I am among the number of the lost, I declare that I would still trust you and would hope for paradise from you because such a revelation would be a test of my hope and not a decree of my condemnation so I will be able to cry out forever: My God is my Savior, I will love him forever.

Will you frighten a windblown leaf and pursue dry chaff?[524]

Who am I, O Lord, and who are you? You are Lord of all powers, God the Creator of all, and I am nothing; do you wish to fight against a nothing? Is it against a nothing that you wish to show your omnipotence? What glory is there for an omnipotent God to break a small branch, or stomp on the tiniest worm? This is something for a slight breeze or a little boy with tender feet. But to transform a worm into a prince on a

[522] Psalm 147:11 [*DR* 146:11].
[523] Job 13:15 [*DR*]
[524] *Ibid.* 13:25.

throne, a hell-bound criminal into an heir to the heavenly kingdom: this is the glory of a God. Anyone can break in pieces a clay pot, but to put it back together and make it into a vessel of gold worthy of heaven, this is the work of an omnipotent God. If you wish to act as a God and seek your glory, your greatest glory, work as a God by saving me. Out of love of your greater glory, then, save me.

Turn, O Lord, save my life; deliver me for the sake of your steadfast love. For in death there is no remembrance of you; in Sheol who can give you praise?[525]

Turn your very kind face toward me, O Lord; free me from slavery to sin and hell; save me simply out of your mercy. If you save me, you can manifest your attributes; your omnipotence that breaks the chains of my sins; your mercy that heals me from all my misery; your goodness by enriching such an unworthy person with gifts; your love in pardoning an enemy and making him your son, heir to your glory; your justice that is superabundantly satisfied by the merits of my Redeemer; and I will glorify all of these forever. On the other hand, according to my merits I will go to hell and not be able to glorify you, nor laud you, nor love you. For your glory, for the glory of your attributes, save me so I can glorify you for all eternity. It is true that your justice is glorified in hell, but it is a forced glory and against your character; it is a glory that you wring from your enemies, not a glory that they willingly give you, while in heaven you, along with all your attributes, receive it from your saints who offer it wholeheartedly. May your glory be great that your justice pries from the damned, never to be satisfied. Infinitely greater is the glory that your justice receives in heaven, satisfied infinitely by my Redeemer. Thus, for the greater glory of your justice, save me, O my God, save me!

Is your steadfast love declared in the grave, or your faithfulness in Abaddon? Are your wonders known in the darkness, or your saving help in the land of forgetfulness?[526]

To the extent, O Beloved God, that you are responsible to see your mercy glorified, along with the truth of your promises, the infallibility of your word, to the extent you are obligated to be named just and holy

---

[525] Psalm 6:4–5 [DR 6:6].

[526] *Ibid.* 88:11–12 [DR 87:12–13]. *Abaddon is the deepest area in Sheol, the abode of the dead.*

in all your actions and to make known your stupendous marvels, save me. In hell, amid those horrors of darkness no one praises you, no one honors you, no one glorifies you; rather you are the object of the hate and the blasphemy of the damned. To not allow, O my God, that I must hate my ultimate highest and beloved good, or to curse the single object of my praise and blessing. I would not worry about hell if I could love and bless you; indeed, I would willingly throw myself into that devouring flame if I could change it into an angelic flame. But if that is not possible, save me just so I can love, praise and bless your Most Holy name through eternity.

He delivered me, because he delighted in me.[527]

I have no other motive, nor could I have one, O my God, than to hope in you if I did not know that your joy is to wish all people to be saved. I hope that I would be numbered among that happy throng of the elect solely through you goodness because thus your infinite mercy is pleased. What other good could there ever be for me if I am worthy of such a grace? None. Only your goodness and mercy become the single motive for you to save me and for me to hope for paradise. In myself, I find all the reasons for desperation because I have nothing but my sins. In you, however, I have greater motives for hope, all the greater in light of how much your goodness outdistances my malice.

In you, O Lord, I take refuge; let me never be put to shame. In your righteousness deliver me and rescue me.[528]

My God, it seems I am presumptuous, but it is true confidence; if I appear presumptuous, forgive me. With all my heart, I trust in you and I beg you to give me a place in your eternal kingdom; if you do not wish to give it to me out of mercy, I demand it in justice. My prayers are bold, but my Redeemer makes me bold. He has bought me paradise at the price of his blood; on the basis of justice it is owed me. You cannot deny it to me because you cannot deny your only begotten. It was an excess of mercy to give me such a great Redeemer; but taking this gift into account, he is all mine along with his merits; these I offer you for paradise. He obliged himself to suffer and die for your glory and for our wellbeing; and you are obliged to give paradise to those who are true

---

[527] *Ibid.* 18:19 [DR 17:20].

[528] *Ibid.* 71:1–2 [DR 70:1–2].

believers and lovers of your Jesus. He has satisfied the obligation; you must reward his merits through me. I realize very well that this does not, and could not, depend on you; it depends only on me if I do not apply my Redeemer's merits to myself. This application is your grace merited for me by Jesus; so I ask and hope for this grace from you so I can be sure of paradise. How can you, O Father, deny me this little thing after giving me much more? It has cost you too much to give me your Son; it costs you nothing to give me heaven; rather, paradise is already mine since all has been given me with Jesus. Grant that you may always be mine through faith and grace on earth and thus I will be all yours by the glory of heaven.

Do not become a terror to me; you are my refuge in the day of disaster.[529]

Since a God with his justice worries me, encourage me with your sweet pity, O my Mother, my Hope. If God casts me out, I turn to you; but if you drive me away on the day of my death, to whom will I turn? For the sake of your mercy, do not do this, O Mother.

Guard me as the apple of the eye; hide me in the shadow of your wings, from the wicked who despoil me.[530]

How hard the devils work to take my hope in you out of my heart! If I lose this, I lose all. Defend me, then, O Mother, as the apple of your eyes; shelter me under the mantel of your care and so, protected by you, I will not fear all hell together.

For you have been my help, and in the shadow of your wings I sing for joy. My soul clings to you; …But those who seek to destroy my life shall go down into the depths of the earth[531]

At that fatal moment of my death I will not fear, sheltered under the wings of your protection. With you as my defense, I do not fear either the horror of death or the fury of the demons. I rejoice as I hold your hand like a child does his mother…In you, Mother, I have all because I have a most powerful protector against all my troubles. If I rest under your mantel I put hell in flight.

---

[529] Jeremiah 17:17.

[530] Psalm 16:8–9 [DR 17:8–9].

[531] Ibid. 62:8–9.

For you alone, O Lord, make me lie down in safety.[532]

I know and confess that I lack every good and am full of evil; still, I am happy in such misery because you have asked for such hope in you. This is the only hope I have and with it I have everything because I hope to obtain everything through you.

You are my servant, I have chosen you and not cast you off; do not fear, for I am with you.[533]

This one grace I ask of you, O Mother, and with it come all graces. Say to this very vile creature, to this monster: *"You are my servant, I have chosen you for my own, and I will not abandon you; do not fear, because I am with you to help you in all your needs."*

But whoever takes refuge in me shall possess the land and inherit my holy mountain.[534]

Let me listen to the words of your most merciful Mother. Whoever trusts in her is sure to enter into possession of paradise, of which she is the Queen. As Queen, she has received from her Son the power to allow entrance to enter whomever she wishes. I wish, therefore, to entrust myself in everything to you, my most Sweet Mother, my most powerful advocate and medium of mercy.

Before I cried out, you heard me; while I speak you hear me.[535]

Who would not wish to trust in you, who would not want to put all their hope in you, O Mother, who is so open to listen to my prayer, why would I not pour them out to you? Rather, Mother Most Loving, you anticipate the prayers of your servants with your graces. Mother of All Mercies, you feel pity at the mere sight of our miseries. Have mercy on the most miserable creature on earth in his extreme need; so the he can glorify your mercies forever and be among the number of the saved simply through your intercession and his trust in you. How can I be damned if the Mother of God, through her goodness, has adopted

---

[532] *Ibid.* 14:8 [*DR* 14:9].

[533] Isaiah 41:9–10.

[534] *Ibid.* 57:13 [*DR* 57:13].

[535] *Citation not given*

me as her son? The Son of God will not deny the inheritance to his brother, the son of the same mother.

See, the Lord's hand is not too short to save, nor his ear too dull to hear.[536]

How can I hesitate before you, O my most pure Mother, when you have begged the pardon and eternal well-being for so many sinners? How many reign above, reign through you, and throw down their crowns at your feet, recognizing that their blessedness comes through your protection. Indeed, your goodness is not lessened, your mercy is not diminished so that you cannot or do not wish to hear me when I beg for my eternal salvation. Through you I hope for paradise. I will be saved also through your intercession and I will glorify your immense pity along with the blessed in heaven.

Be a rock of refuge for me, a strong fortress to save me.[537]

O Mother, be my advocate in the presence of your Son; defend me from his justice; defend my cause because a single word from you is enough to implore all graces and save me. Remember that you are my hope because you are the special hope of the greatest sinners and I have no other means for being saved if I do not make recourse to you.

Cast your burden on the Lord, and he will sustain you.[538]

In you, O my Lady and Mother, I rest all my hope; I entrust all my concerns to you, O loving Mother, sure that you will nourish me with the milk of your pity to the point of begging blessed glory for me.

---

[536] *Ibid.* 59:1.
[537] Psalm 30:2 [*DR* 30:3].
[538] *Ibid.* 55:22 [*DR* 54:27].

FOR SUNDAY: ACTS OF LOVE

I love you, O Lord, my strength. The Lord is my rock, my fortress, and my deliverer.[539]

I glance back at my past life and realize, O my God, that I have every reason to love you. I see myself completely surrounded by the flames of your love, ringed by so many blessings, all the effects of your infinite love toward this most miserable and most cared for (yet most ungrateful) creature. So I feel called upon to love you above all things. I must and wish to love you as my Almighty One, by which you have called me out of nothingness and have conserved my life in every danger of losing it over many years; I must and wish to love you as my Light, by which you have enlightened me with the glow of the true Faith, and have kept me safe in an age so blind and evil; as my Wisdom, by which you have overseen me and drawn me to yourself with such lights to my mind and impulses to my heart, even though it is so very hard and ungrateful; as my Strength by which in so many temptations have empowered me to prevent my falling and have received me after so many falls with pity and mercy; as my Patience by which you have supported me when you had every reason to cut off my life many years earlier and push me into hell. I must and wish to love you as my Creator, who has given me my being; as my Conserver who has kept me alive; as my Benefactor since there were more of your graces than moments of my life; as my Liberator who has delivered and preserved me from the many dangers of soul and body; as my Lord, my God, my treasure, my mercy, all my glory, dignity and greatness and as my one good. What do you say, O my God, shall I love you eternally? If I look at myself, I am totally unworthy since I am a piece of coal from hell, unworthy of your love.

But if I do not deserve to love you, you still deserve to be loved. My God, on behalf of how much you deserve and are worthy of being loved, on behalf of the love due to your infinite loveliness, on behalf of how you are bound by your honor, on behalf of the love that you have for who you are, I beg you to grant me the grace of being able

---

[539] Psalm 22: 1 [*DR* 17:1].

to love you forever. You have loved me with an eternal love without beginning: I desire and am bound to respond to such a love, and I cannot do it in any other way than by loving you with an eternal love, without end. If I could love you in hell, I would willingly throw myself into those flames to change them all into seraphic fires; but since I cannot love you there, I ask you to make it possible that I love you forever. Thus, from this moment for the rest of my life that remains and for all eternity I proclaim that I want to love you at every moment with all my mind and heart and soul and life and forces; with all the I am I intend to love you as much as you choose to make up for my shortcomings and for those of all the world and to love you with all the minds and hearts of all creatures because you deserve all love, and I unite my weak affections with those of all the just and the blessed in heaven, with the Most Holy Mary, with the humanity of my Redeemer and with the love of your own divinity.

O God, you are my God, I seek you.[540]

O God, my God, this heart sighs for you and would wish to watch for you always so it can always love you.

My soul thirsts for you; my flesh faints for you.[541]

My God and my every good, my poor and totally needy spirit desires you. It is for you that this heart gasps as its love and the center of its affections; this mind as for its light and the object of all its thoughts; this tongue as for the goal of all its praises. Father, as a son, I sigh for you; Master, as a disciple, I seek you; Guardian, I long for you as a little child; God of Love, as a loveless one, I await you.

"Come," my heart says, "seek his face!" Your face, Lord, do I seek. Do not hide your face from me.[542]

My heart speaks to you, my God, and asks you for nothing other than your love, to love your divine loveliness, your divine beauty that provides all the happiness of heaven. Will it be unworthy of loving you? By my deficiencies I am not worthy of these; up to now, I have not loved you. May it never be true that you can fill the hearts of the blessed, but you

---

[540] *Ibid.* 63:1 [DR 62:1].
[541] *Ibid.*
[542] *Ibid.* 27:8 [DR 26:8].

cannot draw out my heart! That you are the very happiness of heaven and yet are not able to content my heart!...Do not permit such an affront to your beauty that you are worthy of such love and yet I do not love you. Take this cruel and ungrateful heart from me and give me a heart full of love.

Your name is perfume poured out;...Draw me after you, let us make haste.[543]

O my God, how could I ever aspire to such a dignity as to be able to love you? If you had not commanded me to love you, I should have bought the power to love you with my blood and life if I could do so. I have felt in my heart an inclination to love you because it was made uniquely your own, even though I have not loved you. In my malice I have defeated the natural inclination given me to love you.

You loved me from all eternity without interruption, you have enticed me with so many blessings and still I did not love you. I did not love you because my heart is contaminated by other loves. Purify it, fill it totally with your love for I cannot love you without your love.

Tell me, you whom my soul loves, where you pasture your flock, where you make it lie down at noon.[544]

How much I would undergo to have the good luck of finding you and loving you, O my Love! You have every reason to draw away from me since I have all my life stayed far from you. You have every reason to hate my heart! I rejoice that you are loved by so many. I offer you their love and I ask you to give me a glimmer of a true and sincere love for you.

Let me see your face, let me hear your voice; for your voice is sweet, and your face is lovely.[545]

My God, my beauty and sweetness, when will you show me the loveliness of your face? When will you speak to this heart so that it detaches itself from all that is created and resolves to love you? Oh, me! You have spoken to me often, you have told me of your loveliness, and I still have not loved you. The demons themselves have mocked my hardness of heart in looking at a God who loves me so, who so desires my love; and I have not

---

[543] Song of Solomon 1:3–4 [*DR* 1:4].

[544] *Ibid.* 1:7.

[545] *Ibid.* 2:14.

loved you. I confess myself to be worse than all the devils in hell, who do not love you because they cannot love you and, all the worse, their greatest misfortune is that they cannot love you. I, instead, can and should love for every reason because you are infinitely lovable, because you have shown me your love in so many ways, you have strongly commanded me to love, and you have searched for my love in so many different ways, and I have not loved you, nor do I.

I have poured out my love on creatures and have not loved my Creator in whom alone I can discover how I may learn the way to love, the power to do so and duty I have to love. What a shame is mine, O God, not to be worthy of loving you! I wish at least to die content, I wish to die for your love, or to love you so much more for what remains of my life and then for all eternity.

I will remove the heart of stone from their flesh and give them a heart of flesh.[546]

What a barbarous heart I have! Totally bound and fenced in by the fire of your love, and yet not feel even a touch of it. All creatures love you in their own way, my God, all call me to love and I do not do so. Divine Love, Conqueror of the Almighty, can you not conquer a little piece of clay! Dig out of this breast this heart of rock and give me one totally inclined to love you.

My flesh and my heart may fail, but God is the strength of my heart and my portion forever.[547]

O Love, you go in search of the one who flees you and do you flee from me who want you so much? I do not desire anything but to love my God and I force myself to love you all the more when you scold me, O God, for not knowing how to love you. My heart shrinks from love. If I do not know how to love, teach me what I must do to love you. I love you with all I am. I desire that all the little pieces of me would break into searing flames of your love. I want as many hearts to be enflamed as there are seraphim, as there are stars in heaven, as there are grains of sand on the seashore, as there are drops of water in the sea, as there are atoms in the air, as there are flowers in the field, as there are thoughts of the angels. I want as many hearts as the universe can contain to be

[546] Ezekiel 11:19.
[547] Psalm 73:26 [DR 72:26].

341

full of immense love. I desire to love you as much as the saints and the blessed have loved you, still love you and could ever desire to love you. I consume myself in desires, yet I still do not love you. You, God of my Heart, love yourself in my place for all other loves are less than you deserve.

Let him kiss me with the kisses of his mouth![548]

O Most Divine Spirit, the loving kiss of the Father for his Word, come into my heart, teach me how I should love my God. Tell me that the way to love him is to love him without ways, without measure. Then, O triune God, most noble and lovable, I want to love you with the love of all the saints. This is so little. With the love of the angelic hearts, it is still too little. With the love of all hearts, and if all hearts could form one heart, it would still be not enough. An infinite lovableness requires an infinite love. I am happy that you are infinitely more worthy of being loved than all the love that you could receive from all possible creatures. But when you lower yourself to love me with your infinite love, this love becomes mine, and I return it to you who deserve it so that it is not lost in me, this vile and worthless creature.

From on high he sent fire; it went deep into my bones.[549]

May my God be praised, who has chosen to content my heart by giving me his love, his heart, his Holy Spirit. This Spirit God who is love, having pity on my ignorance and powerlessness, has taught me to love my God above all treasures, all pleasure, all creatures. He loves himself with the Father and the Son through me and in me and with me. By God's grace, may the Spirit always be the Spirit of my soul and the Heart of my breast and the Love of my body through grace on earth and the glory I give in heaven.

The glory that you have given me I have given them, so that they may be one, as we are one, I in them and you in me, that they may become completely one.[550]

My beloved Jesus, you are in me and I am in you until we become one in love. I seek too much, but when I see you this way I burn to beg you to

---

[548] Song of Solomon 1:1.

[549] Lamentations 1:13.

[550] John 17:22–23.

make me all one with you by love and grace as you are with the Father and the Spirit by nature. Trusting in how great is your condescension, I love the Father with you, and with your Holy Spirit, with your Most Holy Mother and with all your faithful people; I also love you with your own heart because you are all mine and so I am all yours. Yours is the love of the Father, of the Holy Spirit, of Mary with all the blessed but all this I return to you; with these I unite my love on earth so that I can unite myself with them in heaven always, as I hope.

Turn away your eyes from me, for they overwhelm me![551]

As much as I force myself to love you, I realize, O my God, that I do not know how to love you. If I could love you as much as I desire, I would beg you for mercy because I have not loved you at all during all the time that I have lived. I would now make up for past failings; I make of this poorest of all hearts a burnt offering to you. Stoop down to accept it simply out of your goodness so I can love you forever.

The love of Christ urges us on.[552]

O Love of my Crucified Love, you belong to a God-Made-Man. You have given him in his human nature every kind of pain and suffering; you have covered him in wounds and contempt; you made him die for me. Give me the grace to bind myself with your bonds to the foot of the cross of my Jesus so that neither hell with all its plots, nor the flesh with all its allurements, nor the world, nor any other creature with its deceits could in the least draw me away from my one and highest good. I want to live and die at the feet of Jesus, with Jesus, and for Jesus so I can love him forever.

Let anyone be accursed who has no love for the Lord.[553]

No one deserves more than I to suffer the punishments of being banned from all society since I have not loved such a good Lord. I do not deserve to have courage since I have spent myself on everything but him. I detest my ingratitude.

---

[551] Song of Solomon 6:5.

[552] 2 Corinthians 5:14.

[553] 1 Corinthians 16:22.

My beloved is mine and I am his.[554]

I am all yours, O my God, I am totally for you. You are all mine, all for me. I am no longer I, but it is my Jesus who lives in me and I in him. His love has brought me out of myself to live and die with Jesus and for Jesus.

In your majesty ride on victoriously for the cause of truth and to defend the right.[555]

Most Beautiful Flower, give me this grace: guard my heart so that you reign with absolute power over me and I may be allowed to reign with you.

I will be a father to him, and he shall be a son to me.[556]

O my God, be my Father, and as the loving Father that you are assist me in this time of my greatest need and give me the grace that I will love you as your true son in time and in eternity.

And now, O Lord, what do I wait for? My hope is in you.[557]

You, my love, are the only object of my desires, of my love. I want nothing else, O my Most Holy Trinity, than to see you face to face and to love you forever.

My Lord and my God![558]

I find solace, my one and triune God, in the fact that you are the being beyond all being, font of all that is, Omnipotent One, uncreated and eternal, infinite in every perfection and virtue, without beginning and without end. You are completely undivided in your being, such that all creatures with their reverence could add nothing to your well-being because you possess all goods in your being, and not even your enemies with their contempt can take away any good. You are a God so great and so powerful that you draw glory as much from the reverence of your servants as from the contempt of your enemies. I am pleased that your mercy will be glorified in heaven and your justice in hell. I

---

[554] Song of Solomon 2:16.

[555] Psalm 45:4 [DR 44:5].

[556] 2 Samuel 7:14.

[557] Psalm 39:8 [DR 38:8].

[558] John 20:28.

appreciate the fact that if I have been bold in offending you, you have a strong arm to punish me; I beg you, however, to see to it that I glorify your mercy in heaven, not your justice in hell, because then your glory is more pleasing, for it is voluntary.

Great is the glory, without equal, that the blessed give you, as well as the glory that your justice forces from the damned. But since it will be to your greater glory, save me so that I can rejoice in you and with you. From now on, I unite my meager pleasure to that in which you rejoice together, O my Most Holy Trinity, Father, Son, and Holy Spirit, to whom be every honor, glory, and power for all ages upon ages. Amen.

My delights were to be with the children of men.[559]

O sweet, kind, merciful, and most beloved Mother of mine, Most Holy Mary, you have a heart filled with kindness and totally turned into love by God's love. Even if your many perfections and virtues demonstrate that you are the one most similar and closest to God, it is, above all, the love that you have for us that reveals you as such. Therefore, you are the one worthy to be the Mother of a God who, out of love, came down to earth to become your own true Son and to ransom the world. This is why he changed you completely into love, tenderness, and compassion toward us miserable little creatures. Moreover, as a reflection of your Son you declare it is your joy and delight to care for our needs, comfort our sorrows, and share your goods with us. With all my heart, tongue, mind, power, and life, in the name of all creatures, I love you and rejoice in your dignity and prerogatives more that if they would be my own. Indeed, [I enjoy] them better than mine because they are those of my Mother whom I love immensely more than I love myself. I unite my weak happiness with the infinite joy of the Most Holy and most beloved Trinity, with all the heavenly court, with all the just and all creatures. Grant, O great Mother, that I can rejoice over you, with you, and through you forever!

---

[559] Proverbs 8:31 [DR]

CHAPTER SEVEN
MEDITATIONS ON THE HOLY EUCHARIST

FIRST PART [560]
TREATISE ONE

On the great sacrifice of the Mass: on its marvelous value
—on its effects and mysteries
—with advice for attending it with great results

LESSON I

THE GREAT BENEFIT OF THE HOLY MASS

I. Our most beloved Redeemer was not content to leave the Holy Eucharist solely as a sacrament, but he wanted to also bestow it as a sacrifice. As a sacrament, it endures as long as the sacramental form *[of bread]* remains and so can only be enjoyed by a person who receives it *[in communion]*. As a sacrifice, however, it is shared in not only by the celebrant but, in addition, through the one who offers it, the Eucharist is shared by the one who assists at it as well as by all Christians.

---

[560] Originally published as part of Sarnelli's work, *Il mondo riformato*, in the section entitled: *Trattato sopra il gran sacrificio della Santa Messa—del suo mirabile valore, de' suoi effetti, misteri e ceremonie—con pratiche per ascoltarla con gran frutto.* The Redemptorists in Ciorani republished it as *Gesù Redentore vivente nell'Eucaristia—nella meditazione di S. Alfonso M. De Liguori e del Beato Gennaro M. Sarnelli*, Materdomini: Valsele Tipografica, 1997. This translation is based on the text of the 1888 edition of the *Opera Omnia* (Naples), Volume III containing *Il mondo riformato…*, Part I, pp. 177–197; 206–210.

The Council of Trent teaches that Jesus Christ instituted this divine mystery so that as a sacrament it would be our spirits' nourishment for eternal life, while as a sacrifice the Church would have constant sacrifices to offer the Most High God to remember and thank the Infinite Majesty, to repair the evil of sin, as a remedy for our daily needs, and as a relief for human misery.

Right from the beginning of the world, at least after the first sin, there was always some kind of sacrifice to honor the true God, but they were all imperfect, all symbols, figures, images of our great sacrament the one, true sacrifice, completed and perfected by divine wisdom. It is the one sacrifice that surpassingly includes all the perfection of the ancient offerings. As St. Leo says, this sacrifice contains the Body and Blood of Jesus Christ, the immaculate Lamb of God who takes away the sins of the world. If God accepted those earlier sacrifices, it was because they signified that the Savior of the world would one day come to offer himself in an oblation to the Most High God. When he came, all the sacrifices of the Old Law would disappear, just as, at the rising of the sun, the stars disappear.

See what the Mass is! After the consecration, found upon the altar is the body of Jesus Christ with all its gifts: his most holy soul clad in all its virtues, enriched with all its richness, merits and sanctity. He comes with his divinity inseparably united to his humanity, intimately united to the Word, identified with the nature of the Father and the Holy Spirit. This comes with such effect that if, in some impossible way, the Holy Trinity, although omnipresent, were to cease being everywhere, it would still be found in the consecrated host, intimately present to the most holy humanity of the divine Son, whose person keeps the same unity. Who could believe this truth of faith and not become ecstatic over the grandness of the gift? Saint Francis de Sales has reason to say that the most holy and sovereign sacrifice of the Mass is the center of the Christian religion, the heart of devotion, the soul of piety, the unspeakable mystery that embraces the depths of divine love by which God seeks to truly communicate the magnificence of his grace and favor to us. O my heart, what you owe your God who has given you birth in the heart of the holy Church, where at every moment you can possess and rejoice in filling yourself with this infinite treasure! Give thanks to God.

II. The holy Mass is that divine testament marked with seven seals, namely, the testimony of the ancient Scripture, of the New Law, of the Church, of the holy Fathers, of miracles, of the demon that has tried to destroy it with all his might and of heretics who have fought so strongly against it. The holy Mass is that precious tree beneath the shadow of which the holy Spouse has hurried to recline, that dear Redeemer sacrificed on Calvary and then transplanted into the perpetual sacrifice in the Church so that the faithful might be kept far from the true death of sin and damnation. "In the hour of holy Mass," writes St. Lawrence Justinian, the heavens are opened, the spirits of the just stand spellbound." There is no offering to the Creator that is greater, nobler and more pleasing than the Mass. This is so because in this sacrifice honor is given to God, joy brought to the angels, paradise opened to the exiles, worship provided for the Church, debt paid to justice, guidance given to holiness, obedience submitted to law, faith offered to the Gentiles, joy poured out on the world, consolation provided for believer, unity bestowed on the people, an end put to the old sacrifices, a beginning established for grace, strength infused into virtue, peace rained upon the human race, hope opened for the troubled, light shown on the erring, a path laid for the pilgrim and glad glory to the universe.

The holy Fathers called the holy Mass the inexhaustible mine of merit, the tree of life, the manna of paradise, the comfort of the afflicted, the ransom of the sinner, the antidote to temptation, the terror of enemies, the shield against human persecutions, and the living memory of the Passion of Christ in which are hidden all the treasures of God's knowledge and wisdom. In giving us the holy Mass, Jesus Christ intended that we live no longer in great poverty but that we have at our disposal all the richness and gifts of paradise. The Mass is a treasure, but one that is indeed hidden: although truly offered to all, few however are those who recognize its magnificence and who wish to profit from it. O sacrifice beyond words! Who could not love you! O precious inheritance that encapsulates a paradise! Who would not wish to possess you? You are that precious pearl! To possess you it would be worthwhile to sell all other goods and possessions! O humans, why do you not assist at holy Mass every morning? Why do you not attend every holy Mass you can? Why do you not participate in it with love, reverence, and thanksgiving? Oh my! What great good is lost by little attention at

Mass? God desires that you do not get to the point of losing your soul for which you care so little that you consider it less important than some vulgar gain or trivial pleasure!

PRACTICE: This great sacrifice is called the *Mystery of Faith* because it is the principal mystery and main support of our religious life. With this sacrifice we testify that God is our beginning, our end, and supreme rule of all things, while we offer it to God as a profession and sign of our service and as a reminder of the Lord's absolute and independent sovereignty. For this reason, we offer numerous acts of faith, hope, charity, and worship. By the holy Mass, we are taught about the debt we owe to believe in Jesus our Redeemer and Mediator, who revives and enkindles in us a response of gratitude and love for great blessing. Rupert writes in this manner: "By such a warm and moving memory as this, love grows firm and builds its edifice upon the foundation of faith." Therefore, make an effort to assist at a many Masses as you can, and do so with devotion. This is the devotion above all other devotions, one that is not subject to illusion because it is taught by faith; cling to it as the matter on which all our happiness depends. Participation in the Mass is a prize containing infinite consequences of the greatest value, while attending it without devotion and irreverently is an evil from which come a thousand other woes. The greater number of Christians attend Mass out of habit, without grasping the mystery, and so they gain little fruit from it. Many people spend all their time with certain capricious little private devotions and then miss this one that is the acme of all devotions. Rather, offer your entire heart in the worship found in the Mass. To do so with greater fervor, study its marvelous greatness and attentively consider its value.

LESSON II

THE SACRIFICE OF THE HOLY MASS
IS THE SAME AS THE SACRIFICE OF THE CROSS

I. This not just a memorial or stage play representing the sacrifice in which Jesus Christ offered himself on the cross for the sins of the world, but is the very same sacrifice that was offered and so it is of infinite value. Not only is the sacrifice the same but also the one who offers it is the same as the one who offered the sacrifice of the cross. On Calvary, Jesus was both priest and sacrifice; in the Mass the same Redeemer is not only the sacrifice but also the priest and pontiff who every day offers himself to the eternal Father through the ministry of priests who in their offering of the Mass represent the person of Christ and offer the sacrifice in his name: "The one who now does the offering through priestly ministry is the one who offered himself on the cross."[561] This is the reason that in the consecration the priest does not say "This is the Body of Christ, this is the Blood of Christ"; rather, he says "This is my Body, this is my Blood." What great fortune of the Christian Law, what a great privilege to have God as its priest! *Tu es sacerdos in aeternum.*[562] The Mass is so identified with the sacrifice of Calvary that both have the same infinite value, both are equal. Both are the same sacrifice, but with only this one difference: the sacrifice on Calvary was with blood; the sacrifice of the altar is without the shedding of blood. Just as a great king who sheds his blood in a glorious battle is not a different person from himself when he wears day-to-day clothing or conceals himself in an inn.

What has been said is not just a romantic way of speaking but is a truth of faith, taught by the Council of Trent: "One and the same is the sacrifice; it is simply offered in a different way." Thus, the Church sings that the offering made to the Holy Trinity in a single Mass has the same worth as the death of Jesus on the wood of the cross. Similarly, each time Mass is celebrated, the mystery of human redemption is reenacted: "As often as the commemoration of this sacrifice is celebrated, the work of our redemption takes place." So it is that Rupert puts it

---

[561] Council of Trent, Session 22, Chapter 2.

[562] Psalm 110:4.

well when he says that participating in the holy Mass is like finding one's self present at the execution of the Redeemer and sharing in it. O world always so inimical to Jesus Christ! How do you assist at the death and funeral of your Redeemer, dead for love of you in order to give you eternal life! And, you my heart, participating at the holy Mass, imagine yourself on Calvary at the foot of the cross together with those disciples and holy women; lovingly accompany the Mother of Sorrows and your suffering and dying Redeemer.

II. Jesus' love for us was so great that, as he hung for three hours on the cross, he willed to remain in this way up to the end of the world, continually begging, through the voice of his tears and his blood, for us to have every grace and all the means needed to become holy. Because, however, the plan of divine providence did not include this permanence as necessary nor as fitting, our dear Redeemer chose to satisfy his loving desire by this inexpressible invention for remaining always with us as a peaceful sacrifice so as to honor, appease, satisfy, and thank his divine Father and to obtain for us a fully gracious hearing, obliging himself as an eternal priest to carry our prayer by imploring an ever more kindly response. So whenever the holy Mass is celebrated, the highest and most sublime work of our religion is renewed: it has the same great value as if Jesus had, instead of choosing to shed his blood and give up his life, offered just one Mass in satisfaction to the divine Justice, this Mass alone would have been completely sufficient to satisfy for all the sins of the world, even for an infinite number of worlds, and to save the entire human race. Everything Jesus merited by his Passion is all applied through the holy Mass. Look at what a great thing it is to celebrate or participate in the holy Mass. It is an event in which that Lord who died for all almost returns to die for each one, applying to each who devoutly participates the merits and efficaciousness of his Passion and death.

So the disciple would say that just one Mass is as valuable as the death of Jesus Christ: The celebration of Mass has the same worth as the death of Christ on the cross. Saint Thomas [*Aquinas*] teaches in every Mass one finds all the results and all the worth that Jesus provided in suffering and dying. What Jesus accomplished on Calvary's cross is now celebrated in the holy Mass. O my heart, when you share in the holy Mass, renew your faith and think of your dear Redeemer covered with blood, fixed by nails, crowned with thorns, raising his voice to heaven from those sacred altars, just as he did on Calvary and with tears and sighs beg the divine Father for your salvation and that of the whole human race: *Jesus offered up prayers and supplications, with loud cries and tears,…and he was heard because of his reverent submission.*[563] Notice, O Christian, the great love of Jesus who was not content to redeem you once, but as many times as there are Masses celebrated anywhere in the world, by means of which he returns mysteriously to sacrifice himself, empty himself and die for you. Oh dear, how many divine initiatives from our loving God are missed because of our neglect! In the Mass we have all the treasures of heaven, yet we want to remain poor and in misery! Do we believe in this divine mystery or not? If we do believe, how can we put so little value on holy Mass? O Faith, O Hope, O Charity, O Most Holy Piety, where are you?

PRACTICE: The sacrifice of the Mass is so great that it can only be offered to God. Indeed, the Church does offer the Mass to honor saints; this is done in thanks to the Almighty for the graces he has provided to the saints. In these Masses, we are only commemorating the saints whom we ask to pray for us.[564]

When participating in the Mass, give thought to the mysteries of the divine Passion. This devotion is not invented by humans but by Jesus, who says: "When you celebrate or participate in the Mass, remember my Passion, recall my suffering": *Do this in remembrance of me.*[565] There is no other act of devotion that is more pleasing than obeying the Redeemer who teaches us to consider his Passion and death in the Mass. Blessed Susone's mother attended Mass every day for thirty-three years, and meditating during them she sensed the most thrilling and devout emotions and frequently broke into tears. A holy priest saw Jesus standing beside two devout young girls who kept their thoughts on his holy Passion as they participated in the Mass. He saw Jesus in the moments of that mysterious suffering on which each of the girls was meditating and at the same time he saw the demon dancing around an old lady who was attending the Mass but was turning her thoughts to foolish little worldly vanities.

---

[563] *Hebrews 5:7.*
[564] Council of Trent, Session XXII, Chapter 3.
[565] Luke 22:19.

Lesson III

The Important Prayers of the Mass

I. In order to produce higher esteem for this great sacrifice, consider how, in the holy Mass, many important circumstances are reflected that are not found in the sacrifice of the cross by means of which we can always use to spur us on to hope in the rich graces of heaven. 1) On Calvary, Christ was sacrificed only once, and that offering lasted only three hours; in the Mass he is sacrificed on many altars at all hours. 2) On Calvary, the executioners committed a deicide; in the Mass, the priest and the Church participate in a unique offering. 3) Those who were present at the crucifixion were mainly enemies who blasphemed against the highest Good; in the Mass the majority of the faithful weep for their sins while loving and glorifying Jesus Christ. 4) On Calvary, Jesus found himself drenched in a sea of blood, of insults and suffering, with his Mother weeping, his disciples sorrowing, the holy women afflicted and wailing; now, however, we see him triumphant and in his glorified flesh.

Moreover, the divine flesh of Christ is now immortal, endowed with all the qualities of a glorified body. Thus it seems that his present humility gives all the greater honor and glory to the Trinity. Therefore, the holy Mass is both the original and the copy, like an eternal trophy, planted by the Redeemer at the point of the defeat of death, of the devil and of sin. Properly then, the offering of the holy sacrifice horrifies hell as it is forced to remember its loss while the angels proclaim Jesus' triumph. Jesus himself, who often spoke of his Passion, now marvels constantly at the glory that surrounds him and rejoices contentedly over the great benefit that we have received. See what humans must do for this great benefit that has been given them in this great sacrifice of salvation! O Infinite goodness, St. Gregory exclaims, the Lord who, raised from death and never to die again, with a loving and divine ingenuity chose to sacrifice himself anew, to offer and give himself up as a victim to the divine Father, as well as to offer for us in every Mass all his holy merits and his precious blood! Cry out, then, my heart with the holy Church: "O sacred banquet, in which Christ welcomes us, recalls the memory of his Passion, and fills us with grace while we receive in it a noble pledge of our future glory."

II. Ask yourself this, O Christian: if this sacrifice were celebrated in only one place, by one priest, how reverently would you assist at it, how much desire would you bring there, how much veneration would you have for that one priest, how thankful would you be to God? If the Redeemer was found today in the world, what would you not do, what suffering would you not be willing to endure in order to go and embrace him, to receive his blessing, to ask for some grace, and how grateful would you be to have the good fortune to reach him? We would certainly give up our life, and go to the ends of the earth to enjoy something like this. Yet, O God, is it not the same Jesus who came into the world and who now rests among us on the altar! Oh dear, instead, what an abundance of divine grace by which to reach greater heights of thanks and the most fervent kind of love do we waste by being tepid and negligent!

Tell me: if you found yourself on Calvary at the foot of the cross, able to see all those precious drops of blood spread everywhere, pouring out of the pierced body of Jesus, what faith would you not manifest, what hope, what love, what gratitude, what reverence, what tenderness, what thanksgiving, what prayers, what adoration, what sighs, what tears! Do you perhaps not believe that the sacrifice of the cross and that of the Mass are the same and that both have the same effects, the same purposes, the same power and effect? The Angelic Doctor responds: "Whatever is the effect of the Passion of the Son is the effect of this sacrifice: they both contain the dying Christ." Does this not, then, make you an enemy of yourself by voluntarily depriving yourself of such benefits by your lack of faith and of reverence in assisting in the Mass? What an ingrate! O foolish world, how can you not desire to understand such great divine mysteries! And if you do understand, why are you not always in church to participate with immense humility, so to speak, in as many Masses as are celebrated? O holy Faith, if you reigned in the brightest light in the minds of the faithful, they would clearly know that going to Mass is to ascend Calvary to receive in their hearts the blood of the Redeemer and understand how the priest is turned into Jesus Christ, and all heaven stands enraptured in an ecstasy of wonder! Let us then approach the sacrifice of the Mass with a lively faith, and let us receive in spirit and truth the overflow of divine graces together with the drops of precious blood which is spiritually sprinkled on the altar for the sake of the souls who devoutly participate.

PRACTICE: St. Bonaventure writes that it was no less a blessing that Jesus gives each morning in the Mass than when he became incarnate. The Mass is a living memorial of all Jesus' love and is like a synopsis of all his major blessings because in it is represented and renewed the memory of the Redeemer's Incarnation, life, passion, death and glorification, and consequently of our redemption and justification. The entire life of Christ on earth was like a continuous solemn Mass in which he was the temple, altar, priest, and victim. Therefore, to be devout in the holy Mass is to encounter all the genius of Christ, to be grateful for all his greatest blessings. Thomas More, that famous supporter of the Catholic faith in perverted England, assisted at Mass every morning. One day, while at the sacrifice, he was called three times hurriedly in the name of the king, but he did not leave the sacred altar until the Mass was finished; he said that he was then at the service of a king who on all altars was to be given the first and greatest attendance. Likewise, on a similar occasion, the saintly Bishop Ludgero responded to Emperor Charlemagne the same way.

Lesson IV

The Mass Maintains the Church

I. The Mass is so powerful that through it the Church remains alive, as well as does its divine worship and Christianity itself. St. Epiphanius calls it the principal support of Christians: *The Principal Sustainer of Christians*. Saint Bonaventure says that if this sacrifice would be taken away from the Church, the whole world would become unbelieving, drowned in countless errors, the Christian people would become a pack of beasts seeking idolatry as other nations now do: *It is by this sacrifice that the Church stands, and Christian belief lives and grows, as well as does divine worship.* Rupert writes that if the Mass were taken from the world, faith would die, hope would fail, love would grow cold, and the universe would fall into ruin because it would no longer obey the dear words of the innocent Lamb who calms the divine justice. In fact, the demons appeared to Luther and, after talking with him for a several hours, finally persuaded him that in order to make the Catholic Faith crumble, there was no near-at-hand plot available than to abolish this tremendous sacrifice, the great support of Christianity, and then, indeed, he would be able to create countless disasters. It is with good reason that Rupert exclaims: Woe! Woe to the world if there were no holy Mass! Woe to those centuries and to those countries in which the use of this great treasure has been abolished! Woe to those faithful who have this great treasure but do not wish to profit from it! And ever greater woe to those who with endless chatter, vanity and irreverence disturb and profane it. Pay attention, O Christian, to keeping your eyes open, pray to Jesus that he pardon your past negligence and no longer wish to stay among the unhappy number of the blind who, amid some many beautiful opportunities to be saved, wish to live without virtue and to rot in vice.

II. To be devout at Mass and to attend it every morning as you should is a good sign of one's predestination. The Mass is an infinite treasure in which the participant is reconciled to God, obtains effective enlightenment for conversion, acquires anew grace and virtue, grows in merits and perseveres in goodness. *It is an unfailing treasure for mortals; those who get it obtain friendship with God.*[566] This is so because, with such devotion, at the same time that one is honoring one's creator with the most pleasing reverence, one is also begging through a prayer that brings grace, perseverance and holiness of life. The Eternal Father who has created everything through his divine Word and who, by means of this Word embedded in human flesh, has brought about the redemption of the world, has given all the predestined to his beloved Son: *Ask of me, and I will make the nations your heritage.*[567] To be respectful, devout, and loving toward this great sacrifice that is a living memorial and, indeed, is the greatest work of the Redeemer, gives the great hope of being a member of the chosen flock of Jesus Christ destined to eternal joys. Look at the predestined, says the apostle, who are called by God and who are in the close friendship of Jesus Christ who, being all-powerful, can save them because he passionately loves them and wishes to save them: *He is able for all time to save those who approach God through him,*

---

[566] Wisdom 7:14.

[567] Psalm 2:8.

since he always lives to make intercession for them.[568] All the more so, Father Vega says that with this sacrifice, one glorifies Jesus Christ greatly, since by means of it one restores the honor that was taken from him in his life and Passion. At that time the innocent Jesus was accused and condemned as a criminal; but by offering Jesus Christ to the Father and treating him with profound reverence, we come to render him the honor what his enemies stole from him. By offering him in satisfaction for our sins and for preservation from future sins, we come to confess and expose our guilt, our misery, together with his innocence, his virtue, and holiness. Moreover, Jesus remains then most highly pleased with devotion to the holy Mass because we esteem the greatest and most loving of all his works that his goodness has ever known how to create. This is why St. Brigid during the time of Mass saw fire fall from heaven on the altar showing that the Redeemer came to inflame with his holy love those faithful hearts. During the elevation of the host, she saw Jesus in the form of a very charming young man, who said: "I bless all of you who believe and devoutly participate in the Mass, and I will be the judge of those we do not believe." All this is absolutely true, if we, while assisting at this tremendous sacrifice, compensate Jesus for the honor refused by the Jews and do not increase the dishonor and affronts of vanity and irreverence. Oh my God, never allow that!

PRACTICE: Try to instill in others, especially those under your care, these truths about such a great mystery, now reduced to such little thought and purpose among the greater part of the faithful with so great dishonor to the Almighty, with such detriment to the Church, with such real prejudice that such great disorder should be wept over with tears of blood. Try to provide effective remedy at all costs. The great Council of Trent, which knew this all too well by the divine light, very specifically left us the task of making good use of the Mass and commanded preachers and pastors of people to declare actively and with effort the immense treasure that is found in this sacrifice and the great gain that can be achieved by devoutly participating in the holy Mass. It commanded that we give the attention that is due, not only to sanctifying ourselves, but also to sanctifying others by praying during it for sinners and for the advance of the holy Church.

---

[568] Hebrews 7:25.

LESSON V

THE MASS HONORS THE MOST HOLY TRINITY

I. We owe God our Creator a great deal, and we have many debts to the Greatest Good. St. Thomas reduces these to four: honor God's majesty, fulfill God's justice, thank God's generosity, and beg God's kindness. We can fulfill these obligations extensively by means of the holy Mass. Thus, we must honor God, our source and our goal, who merits honor and infinite praise suited to the immensity of God's greatness: *Praise him according to his surpassing greatness!*[569] But how can a lowly creature glorify a God in the way that matches this greatness? If you were to honor an emperor, what gift would be suitable to his stature? How could a mere nothing honor the Creator of the universe, in whose view all creatures fade like a puff of smoke! God possesses infinite perfections, each of which is infinite and deserves infinite recognition. Imagine every kind of created being; you still would never find an offering worthy of God. An offering fit for such a God could only be the same God. But by means of the sacrifice of the Mass, you can honor God in the way he deserves to be honored and glorified, since that same God who sits upon his throne of majesty descends to become the victim on the altar in an act of unexplainable submission at the hands of a priest, prepared to lose the sacramental being acquired by the consecration and to lose it in protestation to the sovereignty of God and to the dependence that all created things have on God. This is what Jesus does every time Mass is celebrated because, with an infinite value that is his Body and Blood and the offering of an infinite excellence in which he himself consists, he renders to the Most High God infinite glory. Therefore, God cannot be honored with any greater offering than that which is given in the holy Mass in which an infinite God honors the Most Holy Trinity as much as it is adorable, and he humbles himself before him, even to the point of a little bread. There is no tongue that can sufficiently explain nor a created mind sufficiently comprehend how much this sacrifice of divine praise honors God: *Those who bring thanksgiving as their sacrifice honor me.*[570] Only that God grasps the immensity of his being, he alone knows how much he is honored by the sacrifice of the altar.

---

[569] Psalm 150:2.
[570] Psalm 50:23 *[DR 49:23]*.

II. It is certain that even one Mass gives more honor to the Almighty than that given by all the patriarchs with their faith, all the prophets with their zeal, all the martyrs with their blood, all the popes with their vigilance, all the doctors with their wisdom, all the confessors with their virtues, all the virgins with their purity, all the hermits with their penances, all taken together. Moreover, one Mass alone gives more glory to God than all the ministry, obedience and love of the angels, archangels, thrones, dominations, principalities, powers, virtues, cherubim and seraphim. Finally, it gives more than the incomparable honor and glory that the Most Holy Mary gives with all her immense merits and sanctity. Indeed, in one minute the Mass gives more pleasure to the Host Holy Trinity that all the angelic and human creatures, created and possible, united together [This is true even if the Almighty were to create an infinite number of beings as holy as the Archangel Michael and the great *[John the]* Baptist. It is with reason that enlightened souls consider as nothing all the glory and worship given to the Almighty in heaven and earth when one considers the honor that is given to him by the Mass. Here is the reason. All the honor that angels and humans give to God is the worship of creatures, and thus finite and limited. But the honor that the Creator receives through the holy Mass is an infinite honor because it is a God equal to the Father who humbles himself before his altar to glorify that divine majesty. Therefore, the greater honor which one holy Mass raises to the Most Holy Trinity is greater than all the honor of all created things, which are infinitely distant from him. So all created glory evaporates in comparison to the uncreated and infinite glory. As the Eternal Father contemplates his Most Holy Dear Son, it seems that not the tiniest thing is missing: *This is my Son, the Beloved, with whom I am well pleased.*[571] This is the reason that St. Ignatius comes to call the Mass "The glory of God" since this the greatest possible sign in which the extrinsic glory of God could be expressed.

Your path is a joyful one, you who love God: you do not have to bemoan the fact that you do not know how, you cannot even glorify your Creator as you should and he deserves. Consider yourself a large field to harvest and fill your loveless heart. Go to church, attend the holy Mass and when you see Jesus on the altar, offer him to the Most Holy Trinity

---

[571] Matthew 3:17.

and intend, by means of the holy Mass to give God all the glory God deserves and which creatures ought to offer. Desire to supply for all the worship and honor that the ingratitude of sinners take away, as well as that of unbelievers, of Jews, of schismatics, of atheists. Intend to supply for all dishonor that you owe to that infinite Master and have omitted, all that fervor which is lacking in the tepid and unloving faithful. Realize that in doing this you are giving to God more honor than all the world would give if it were holy and perfect, and that the Lord with such an offering is so pleased by such an offering that he no longer remains grieved and angered by the sins of all. One reads of a holy person who was zealous for the honor of God and so blurted out his desire saying: O my Father and my God, I want a thousand tongues to proclaim your greatness; I want a heart that was as large as a thousand hearts to glorify and worship you. Oh, if all creatures in the world were under my power I would desire all of them to burn with your holy love! Would that every tongue, every nation, every people, every person recognize the love of their Creator. I would want to give you more glory all by myself than is given to you by heaven and earth. Then this person heard a voice speaking: "My dear child, be consoled, because one Mass gives me more glory that what you desire for me." Most holy Trinity, if my offerings are not pleasing to you because they come from an ungrateful heart, you cannot but enjoy Jesus Christ through whom I draw every breath of life and through all the moments of eternity. I intend to honor you, glorify you, please you as you deserve. I intend to make up for all my ingratitude and for those of the whole human race. Accept, O Divine Father, these humble sentiments that I present to you in union with those of your Son. Out of love for him, I pray you to pardon me, hear me, and sanctify me along with the whole world.

PRACTICE: In offering the holy Mass to God, you make an offering more pleasing than if you practiced all the virtues and suffered all the martyrdoms possible. Urban VIII wrote that if the citizens of paradise were capable of envy, they would envy our great good fortune: that by this great sacrifice we can gain so much and so glorify the Most Holy Trinity. Therefore, we must be most devout to profit from it and we must hold it in the highest reverence. Jesus Christ does not wish to pay this worship to the Most Holy Trinity alone; he wants us to accompany him. Therefore, he has provided that the holy Mass be a community sacrifice in which all the faithful take part and join together with the priest and all who offer it. Moreover, you unite your adoration to that of the whole court of heaven, and especially with all the seraphim who stand around the altar. Intend with every breath you take to honor, adore, and glorify the Most Holy Trinity through Jesus Christ along with all his infinite perfections and particularly his adorable providence that is so injured, muted and spurned by the words and actions of the thankless faithful. Unite your voices with the prayers the spirit of the Church and pray often the divine words of the holy Mass: *Through him, and with him and in him, O God Almighty Father, in unity with the Holy Spirit, all glory and honor is yours.* Unite all you do in word, action, or suffering to the offering that Jesus makes of himself to the eternal Father, so that, as St. Peter teaches, in every action, and in every moment the Most High may be glorified through Jesus: *May God be glorified in all things through Jesus Christ.*[572]

Lesson VI

The Mass Appeases God's Justice

I. It is our inescapable duty to appease God, but instead of doing so, we do nothing but offend God. Appeasing the divine justice is a task so difficult that no creature could accomplish it. So the Lord, grown angry with his lying people, speaks thus: *Though Moses and Samuel stood before me, yet my heart would not turn toward this people. Send them out of my sight!*[573] Indeed, in the centuries of old, the flaming sword of God's anger laid low cities, armies, peoples and kingdoms: *Cut down old men, young men and young women, little children and women...And begin at my sanctuary.*[574] Because of an adultery, the divine justice had 25,000 persons of the tribe of Benjamin killed; and this was done when the marriage contract was simply signed. For one blasphemy by Sennacherib, God had an angel put to death 85,000 soldiers and then had the impious

---

[572] 1 Peter 4:11.
[573] Jeremiah 15:1.
[574] Ezekiel 9:5.

emperor killed at the hands of his own sons.[575] Because of the Achan's theft of *[spoils of battle]*, God brought great ruin on the Israelite army.[576] Due to David's pride, God sent the plague that in three days slew 70,000 persons. Based on the murmuring of the Jews, God created fiery serpents to devour them.[577] God ordered the world destroyed by the flood.[578] God saw to it that the Pentopolis burned,[579] Nineveh was destroyed[580] and thousands of people and kingdoms were destroyed: *The Lord has demolished without pity.*[581] Still today, countless adulteries, blasphemies, thefts, pride, irreligiosity, sacrileges exist, and God has not torn down homes, cities and kingdoms for such crimes! Sin has not lost its evil, not become less grave, rather, has increased its gravity since God, to destroy it, died on a cross. The reason for such mercy today is the holy Mass by which the dear human Son's self-offering to the eternal.

Father has calmed his justice and the voice of his innocent blood begs pity for the human race, for whom Jesus makes himself our advocate so we may escape the lightening of God's anger: He is the atoning sacrifice for our sins, and not for ours only but also for the sins of the whole world.[582] Knowing this, the ancient patriarchs and prophets, with tears and sighs, continually called upon the divine mercy to quickly send that immaculate angel who would appease his justice: *O my Lord, please send someone else.*[583] This is the victim that has obtained mercy for sinners. What might have happened to us if the admirable Redeemer would not have appeased the divine heart, inflamed to the point of letting the whole universe run on into perdition due to the divine justice and still continuing to sin, were it not for the fact that in the Church a sacrifice to mitigate the reignited insult to God from new sins? Certainly at this time the world, under the weight of its iniquity, should already have collapsed as unable to bear the load of so

[575] 2 Kings 19:35–37.
[576] Joshua 7:1–5.
[577] Numbers 21:6.
[578] Genesis 6:17.
[579] Wisdom 10:6.
[580] Nahum 1ff.
[581] Lamentations 2:17.
[582] 1 John 2:2.
[583] Exodus 4:13.

many faults. But the holy Mass is what keeps it standing: *[Christ] gave himself up for us, a fragrant offering and sacrifice to God.*[584]

The Council of Trent teaches that no sinner has committed so great a sin or becomes so lost that he cannot receive the grace and gift of repentance with pardon of his great sinfulness through the sacrifice of the Mass: ... *appeased by this sacrifice, the Lord grants the grace and gift of penitence and pardons even the gravest crimes and sins.*[585] St. Thomas explains this, saying that this is the case, not because the Mass in itself cancels the sins just as the repentance does, but it cancels them through imploring the helps necessary for repentance and by offering satisfaction to God, and through erasing the punishment the penitent deserves. Jesus, as the priest in the name of the penitent adores the eternal Father and, as the victim humbling himself with the offering of his death, puts himself in place of the guilty person who is not worthy to continue to live because of his crimes. This infinite submission of the dear divine Son compensates with infinite return the wrong done God by our transgressions. Thus God is again honored and appeased for our wrongs that negated the very abundant and efficacious helps *[offered us]*. By looking into the face of Jesus, sacrificed for our love, God lays aside all his anger and grants us every blessing.. It is therefore correct for St. Cyril to call the Mass the Appeasing Victim, and Eusebius to name it the Remedy for the Well-being of the World, the Offering for the Souls of all the Faithful, the Sacrifice to Destroy All Sin. St. Jerome *[names it the]* Saving Offering, Pure Victim, Price canceling the warrant that decrees our sentence of ruin, the Rainbow of Peace that reconciles the world to God, the Ark of the Covenant that enriches with blessings wherever it resides. Oh, if it were not for the holy Mass, how could we escape a punishment proportionate to our excesses if this heavenly rainbow did not remind God of his pity? What would become of us if, instead of appeasing the divine Justice through the holy Mass, we were to continue to irritate it with scandal and irreverence? Note here how blind are those Christians who go in search of the shortest Masses, the least devout ones. Attend to the words that the holy Church in the sacrifice raises to the Almighty to obtain mercy for the whole human

---

[584] Ephesians 5:2. In the Latin Vulgate, the text appears as Ephesians 5:1; also Sarnelli misquotes the Latin text as "...gave himself up for our sins."

[585] Council of Trent, Session XXII, "Doctrine Concerning the Sacrifice of the Mass," Chapter II.

race: We offer You, O Lord, the chalice of salvation…for our salvation and for that of the whole world.[586] The Most Holy Trinity will not punish us as we deserve for our sins, will not bring down this ungrateful world: it turns its eye on this work of unspeakable charity.

O God, look at Jesus, who places himself between you and us, between his justice and my sins and stands to appease you: receive with a serene face and smile the offering of infinite value; let Jesus be our protector that you have given us for our Redeemer. Remain pleased for the sake of Jesus Christ, O Eternal God, and through love of Jesus Christ illumine all who come into this world so that they may know and love you, the highest truth and Jesus Christ whom you have sent to redeem it and to save it: and thus to have eternal life.

PRACTICE: The Angelic Doctor says that the Mass has the power to obtain enlightenment and grace for the person and benefit for the deceased. By means of the holy Mass, one can obtain from God the gift of faith for heretics, schismatics, Jews, pagans. There is no one so lost who cannot be brought to penitence through the holy Mass. A great servant of God said that when the Lord punishes with public or private punishments, the best manner to assuage him is to have many Masses said and to participate in a large number. In every breath you take, make the intention to offer Jesus to the eternal Father for the salvation of the world and often renew this intention. This way you give a great help to the Church and infinite joy to the Host Holy Trinity who has decided to reconcile the world to itself through Jesus Christ: *Through him God was pleased to reconcile to himself all things.*[587] Especially renew this precious offering during times of harvest, gathering, carnival, and other worldly celebrations when more often than not the people let loose and surrender to every kind of dissolute activity, and like drunkards run to every kind of pleasure. Also pray to the Lord that he not punish the world with the worst chastisement by allowing every kind of sin to create more scandals and abuses. Punishment, to the extent that it is not known and felt, becomes all the more horrible and universal. May the Most Holy Trinity free us from all this through Jesus Christ.

---

[586] Offertory Prayer for chalice in Tridentine Latin Mass
[587] Colossians 1:20.

Lesson IX

The Efficacy of the Mass

I. Christian Faith requires us to have recourse to the Creator and to hope for help and graces from his generous hands. No other action honors the Most High and what he does better than prayer. Therefore the Lord has determined to grant efficacious grace by means of prayer, and so it is necessary to pray in order to live as Christians and be saved. We have a continuous need to turn to God to obtain the proper needs for our incessant troubles. But this exchange, established between God and humans by means of prayer, is always interrupted by our sins. Thus, the Lord can justifiably deny us grace. Woe to us if it were not for the holy Mass, since the more our necessity for overcoming sin increases, the more we make ourselves unworthy of help! So, may our dear Redeemer be blessed a hundred thousand times for having been pleased to leave behind for us this sacrifice of infinite effectiveness by which both the just and the sinner can pour out with the greatest confidence their request and bring back grace in abundance. Theologians teach with St. Thomas that the holy Mass has infinite value, and so simply by being what it is, it can obtain all graces. So as much as we can ask, it is always tiny in comparison to the greatness which we offer the Most Holy Trinity in offering Jesus Christ himself. Whoever desires to be saved and become a saint must put all their efforts into making their prayer effective. During holy Mass, prayer becomes most effective in bringing down grace in ways that might not happen at other times. It is certain that if you do not participate in it devoutly each morning, there will occur vices from which you cannot free yourself, virtues you cannot develop, graces that will go unreceived, and blessings you will not enjoy. O people, O people, how little it takes to find salvation.

Although the Lord has promised to listen to whoever begs at any season, in any place, at any hour, it is nevertheless in a church as a home specially consecrated to him that God keeps his loving eyes open wider, his generous ears more intent to hear the prayers of his faithful who pray there. So our prayer during Mass is much more effective and we are able to rejoice more along with the prophet who received the abundance of

God's mercy in his Temple.[588] Moreover, the Lord has promised that he treats more graciously and in a special way those who gather in his name. In the holy Mass, we find ourselves united with a large number of the faithful in prayer, and so our prayer has to become more powerful and effective. Above all, the prayer of a person participating in the holy Mass unite in prayer with the priest who, in this rite more that ever, is like the head of a family or a public ambassador and universal advocate, a mediator between God and the people gathered around the altar, as if in a divine audience chamber to deal with the most important business of the human race: *He acts as ambassador for the whole earthly planet, an intercessor before God.* Because the priest represents Jesus Christ and is delegated to that role by the holy Church, his beloved bride, his official actions and prayers become very appealing to the divine Father who sees in the priest the image of his dear beloved Son, as Suarez says, and so very graciously accepts this purest of offerings so very pleasing to him and so gladly listens to their prayers. Every priest (in addition to the particular prayer he is obliged to make for whom the Mass is being said) is bound in a special way to pray in the name of all who are present. That is why the Prayer over the Gifts reads *Blessed be God for...the Bread (the Wine) we offer; it will become for us the Bread of Life (Spiritual Drink).* And the Response says:...*May the Lord accept this sacrifice...for our good....* Thus, our prayer united with that of the public minister arises all the more dearly to God and becomes all the more effective. Thus the visible priest is not only like a public ambassador of the whole Church but also of each of the faithful participating in particular, becoming mediator for each of us in the presence of the invisible priest, who is Jesus Christ offering himself to the Father *as the great price of human redemption. The whole Church itself becomes present* with the merits of all the just and of all the saints, along with all its immense faith and confidence that cannot deceive. She confides as much as she can in this sacrifice that she offers for the salvation of the whole world. The priest, relying on the efficacy of the Church's faith, speaks to the Lord in complete confidence: *Do not look upon our sins but upon the faith of your Church....* Certain persons who seek the consolation of participating in the Mass attend them in a hurry. But they would do better to increase their loving worship and realize that a fewer number

---

[588] Psalm 18:6.

of Masses devoutly attended is more pleasing to the Lord than a large number of Masses assisted in tepidly.

II. The holy Mass is not offered only by the priest but also by all of the faithful who participate. In this great sacrifice, the primary celebrant is Jesus Christ; the secondary celebrants in order are the Church, the priest, and those who participate. Thus all the faithful can unite themselves to that sacrifice and act in their own way as a priest and offer it to the Almighty. It is all the faithful that St. Peter spoke of when he said: *You are a chosen race, a royal priesthood, a holy nation.*[589] The dear Son of God was so in love with us that he communicated to us, not only his blessings, but also a great part of his own authority, wishing us to be cooperators in the great unfolding of divine glory and the salvation of the chosen ones. Thus he granted to all Christians this great title of priest, consecrating them for this with his own blood in holy baptism. For this great benefit the saints thank him in heaven: *You have made us to be a kingdom and priests serving our God.*[590] It is not only the visible priest, says Guarrico, who offers Jesus Christ to the Most Holy Trinity, but with him all those who join in to offer him in sacrifice. The Mass is not a private treasure but is public and communal to all the faithful who join in to participate; one reads, one offers, but all share in the offering and in the ritual; and the Prince receives the gift from all. Indeed, the priest in celebrating the Mass always prays in the plural: *Let us pray*, to be sure that all who participate remember to join and offer their prayer with his. He calls this sacrifice not only *his* but that of all who stand around the altar: *Pray, my sisters and brothers, that your sacrifice and mine may be made acceptable.* And during Eucharistic Prayer I, he states *this sacrifice which we offer for ourselves and for whom we pray….*Just as the priest who is celebrating the Mass can offer it for himself and for others, so each of the participants can offer it together with the priest for themselves and for others. Look at how many reasons you have to hope for every grace if you devoutly participate in the holy Mass. Truly, if we assist with a lively faith, we can make heaven come down to earth and the earth rise up to heaven. Poor us for our weak faith!

[589] 1 Peter 2:9.
[590] Revelation 5:10. The text actually reads: "you have made them…"

PRACTICE: In attending the holy Mass, pray for the advance of the holy Church and for all the living and the dead as the Apostle teaches us: First of all, then, I urge that supplications, prayers, intercessions, and thanksgivings be made for everyone…This is right and is acceptable in the sight of God our Savior. The Lord said to St. Catherine: I ask you affectionately, daughter, to recommend to me always the salvation of sinners: toil, weep, pray so that I may use the mercy I desire for them. To make up for the lack of the human race, honor, offer, thank, beg the Most Holy Trinity through the holy Mass. St. Francis de Sales says: Make every effort to attend Mass every day to offer your Redeemer to God his Father with the priest for yourself and for the whole Church. The angels are always present, St. John Chrysostom tells us to honor this Most Holy Mystery and as we find ourselves among them with the same intention, we can receive many helpful influences through their company. The hearts of the Church Triumphant and Militant come to unite themselves to Jesus in this divine action in order to snatch, with him, in him and for him, the heart of God the Father and to make his mercy entirely ours. What happiness of soul, to be able to contribute your efforts for such a precious and desirable good.

THIRD PART [591]
TREATISE THREE

Instructive Lessons on the Most Blessed Sacrament of the Eucharist [592]

LESSON I

JESUS' LOVE IN THE MOST BLESSED SACRAMENT

I. The most lovable Redeemer, after passing thirty-three years among human beings, *knew that his hour had come to depart from this world and go to the Father,*[593] but his heart would not allow him to go far from us and to leave us alone in this valley of tears, even though he would bear us to heaven engraved on his heart and before long would see us again in his glory. So what did his infinite love do? It invented a marvelous way to remain always with us on earth, while still ascending into heaven. He instituted the Most Blessed Sacrament of the Eucharist, where he would leave his whole self—body, soul and divinity—formed in such a way that his real presence could be found on many altars, in many churches, all over the world. Thus, so he could console all his own while he entered triumphantly into heaven, he insured that he would never be parted from them or from us: *Remember, I am with you always, to the end of the age.*[594] Rather, the love of Jesus for us was so great *that the night when he was betrayed, he took a loaf of bread.*[595] As he thought more than ever about how he might do good to humans, they were planning stronger than ever how to put him to torture and death. The flame of his great love never shown more bravely than when he kept it burning even in the midst of injury and punishment. O Lord, bring about what you said to us when you changed yourself out of love to remain with

---

[591] This translation is based on the text of the 1888 edition (Naples) Volume III and IV containing *Il mondo riformato...*, Vol. Two, Part III, pp. 172–236.

[592] Title continues with note: "Which can also serve as an entire novena before the great feast of the Body of Christ and for its entire octave."

[593] John 13:1.

[594] Matthew 28:20.

[595] 1 Corinthians 11:23.

us on earth after you have been thrown out with the most merciless and shameful death! O Infinite goodness! Oh my heart, are *you perhaps among the number of those ungrateful ones* who amid such excesses of love do not burn with love *for a God full of love and kindness toward you?*

II. Unspeakable is the ardent desire Jesus has to institute this sacrament, although he would have known that with the coming of this moment also comes the hour of his bitter passion and death: *I have eagerly desired to eat this Passover with you before I suffer.*[596] It is as if he were saying: I know that at the time I institute this Most Blessed Sacrament, I must fall victim to my enemies who will inflict every kind of torture; but still the love that I bear for souls is so great that I do not care that my hour of suffering and death comes because I leave you this pledge of my infinite love. I will suffer, and my pains will gain for you the glory; I die, and my death will be your life. O unspeakable, infinite blessing! It was not enough for you, O loving Jesus, to be born and to die for us, if you would not remain with us in this sacrament! My dear Redeemer, what can I give you for this great love if I do not thank you for having created me and redeemed me? But what monstrous ingratitude would be mine if, instead of thanks and love, I mistreated you and offended you; instead of remembering my great benefactor, I have thought totally the opposite, other than God! Ah, how I would weep over such an evil with endless tears! How I would wash away the stains with my own blood! O my heart, at least begin to love Jesus from now on and to offer him love in return for love. O my sacramental Lord, you are a book of paradise where I read in large print the love that you bear me. Your divine presence is not only the fire of charity to inflame my heart but also the light to teach truth and faith. Now I come to you, O my God, so that you might enlighten me with the splendor of your light and warm my affections so much that my heart does not push you away any more and that it does not forget again the loving Lord who wished to remain as a prisoner enclosed in the tabernacle for me: *I will place my dwelling in your midst...and I will walk among you, and will be your God.*[597]

---

[596] Luke 22:15.
[597] Leviticus 26:11.

PRACTICE: Be thankful for such a great blessing. Gratitude charms God's heart and draws new favors and great blessings. Ungrateful persons sadden the sweet heart of God and dry up the fountains of divine grace to their great disadvantage. St. Lawrence Justinian writes that as many as there are blessings contained in the Most Blessed Sacrament, so many should be our thanksgivings, that is, countless and infinite. St. Catherine of Siena was accustomed to say every one of the faithful should be full of love for the eternal God having giving us Jesus in the Sacrament. St. Francis Borgia thanked the eternal Father every evening for having given us Jesus in the sacrament; once he forgot to do so and then it came to mind after he went to bed. He wanted to get up but the Lord appeared to him and said: "Listen, your thanksgiving pleases my Father so much that I made it for you." Intend to thank the Most Holy Trinity to the glory of God through Jesus Christ many times a day for having given us his Son and for having left him with us in the sacrament. Along with St. Bernard, ask Jesus Christ "What will I return for yourself?" My dear Redeemer, what can I give you for having given me yourself? May I always thank you and bless you and all my people do so.

Lesson II

What Great Benefits Are Brought Through the Institution of the Most Blessed Sacrament

I. It is impossible to find a work that offers more glory to the Most Holy Trinity than the institution of the Most Blessed Sacrament. Through it the eternal Father shows his omnipotence by renewing and gathering together the greatest miracles that he ever worked. The dear Son of God celebrates the most marvelous inventions of his wisdom, remaining always in heaven and as well on earth, rejoicing at the right hand of the Father while conversing with us sacramentally. The Holy Spirit celebrates her intense love, manifesting by means of this sacrament the dearest and most distinguished tenderness of this love. In a word, all created things in heaven and earth are almost a frolic of the divine power *playing on the surface of his earth.*[598] The institution of the Sacrament is the greatest effort of the omnipotence, wisdom and charity of God, something St. Thomas calls the Greatest of Miracles: *The greatest of the miracles worked by Christ.* Thus it is that Scotus asserts that the Holy Eucharist was the final sign toward which all the Church's devotion looks. Sacred churches, altars, priests, ceremonies, feasts, and all the other sacraments seem like so many minor planets, organized with remarkable harmony around this divine sun of the Sacrament of the Altar. St. Thomas teaches that in this sacrament is collected all that is sacred and holy in the Church: *Almost all the sacraments are summed up in the Eucharist.* Moreover all the ordinances of the Old Testament (which deserve great reverence and veneration), the arc, the manna, *[Aaron's]* staff, the temple, the Holy of Holies, the sacrifices, the holocausts, the victims, and all the other ceremonies are nothing other than a figure, a symbol, an image of the Most Blessed Sacrament. O Most Wise God, who raised your only begotten Son out of love for us and returned him to us forever in the Sacrament after so many miracles in this so marvelous affair; it belongs to your glory to perform a miracle of goodness to overcome the hardness of my heart that does not burn with love amid such a fire of love. Oh, come here, you who have a desire to glorify God, come and announce to the whole world the loving invention of the Redeemer.

There is no other work that gives more joy to us than the Most Blessed Sacrament. For it is through the sacramental Jesus that the justice of God is kept appeased and pardon is given to the world for its well deserved punishments. By it, God maintains his ungrateful people alive. Through it, he accepts our repentance for sin. Through it, he gives compunction to hearts and pardon to the guilt of grave faults. Through it, he gives strength and victory against temptations. Through it, he illumines and fills souls with his favors, he fills them with heavenly consolation and draws them to his love. St. Cyprian writes, Oh me, when I stand in the presence of the Most Blessed Sacrament, you have no need to shed many tears to be forgiven; as soon as you approach sighing, you are enlightened, made repentant and pardoned. Blessed Sassone says that prayer made before the sacramental Lord are more easily heard and in this presence one obtains those graces which perhaps otherwise would not have been gained. This

---

[598] Proverbs 8:31.

.

is due to the merits of his passion actually represented here and offered to the Father by means of the liberality and gratitude of this venerable sacrament. Indeed, devout souls experience joy and great confidence before the Sacrament that pours into them that great Good that rests on the altar to communicate lights, graces and favors in abundance. David, gazing at a distance in spirit at the Most Blessed Sacrament prefigured in the Ark of the Covenant began to exult before it, to rejoice and dance. It is very certain, says the Disciple, that in the presence of the Most Blessed Sacrament grace is found most abundantly. Blessed Paula da Foligno, as she passed through great anxieties and spiritual afflictions, had recourse to the Most Blessed Sacrament and there after long prayer saw Jesus as leaving the tabernacle to console her and to free her forever from those disturbances, leaving her full of heavenly sweetness. Woe to the world if it were not for the Most Blessed Sacrament! Woe to those peoples and those souls who do not wish to profit from these gifts and even greater woe to those who profane it with irreverence and sacrileges. Most holy God, I who am a sinner flee from the threat of your anger and throw myself into the arms of your mercy. Enlighten me, pardon me, welcome me, save me through Jesus Christ.

II. It is with reason then that Father Granata speaks about this great Sacrament in this way: All the marvels of nature turn silent here. All the prodigies of grace turn silent because this work is unique among all graces. O Most Blessed Sacrament, you are the life of our souls, the medicine of our wounds, the consolation of our worries, the memorial of the divine passion, the testament of infinite love, dear companion of our pilgrimage, the joy of our exile, the pledge of our happiness. This was the great and rich bond that at the end of his life our most lovable Redeemer wished to leave to show his ardent love, as a living pledge of those promises that he had made and of all that he had to give us. When the prophet Elijah was about to depart this world, since he had nothing else to leave his disciple Elisha, he gave him his mantle; but our Savior as he rose to heaven wished to leave us his Most sacred Body and all of his Self. By means of that mantle, Elisha walked dry-shod through the waters of the Jordon River. We, by means of this Sacrament, pass through the waters of troubles without being drowned in the waves of impatience and desperation. My dear Redeemer, who from this tabernacle of love are casting out rays of light to illumine and sanctify souls, enlighten me, sanctify me. O Holy

Light, Most Divine Light, who knows my needs and the darkness of this miserable heart, clear it out of me and fill me with your grace. O True Love, from which come all other loves, Oh why do I not burn in this sacred fire? O Lord, change me, convert me, renew me, turn me completely into love and fervor toward you, complete mortification toward myself, total love toward my neighbor. Do this for the sake of the blood you have shed for me, do it for your glory, do it for the great love of your eternal Father.

PRACTICE: While visiting the Most Blessed Sacrament, revive your faith by reflection on the fact that here you find yourself in the presence of an infinite God made human out of love for you. When you enter into a church, imagine you are entering into heaven; yes, into heaven. Think of the seraphim encircling the sacred altar. Imagine the saints, that is, all devout souls venerating and loving the Lord. Behold the Father and the Holy Spirit who are with Jesus in the Blessed Sacrament by their divine union with the Son. Behold the entire Most Holy Trinity. Faith, O Christian heart, faith! Imagine vividly that Jesus is standing loving listening to you and looking at you from that altar, and by uniting his prayer to yours he is offering you to the Eternal Father and praying to him for you. In every breath of your life intend to offer to the Most Holy Trinity the sacramental Jesus for your salvation and that of your neighbor; renew this intention often. This is what the Lord said to St. Mary Magdalene de'Pazzi: *Continually offer to the Father my passion, myself and my creatures: everything that now will serve to form a preparation for receiving me in Holy Communion.*

Lesson III

Jesus Dispenses Graces in the Most Blessed Sacrament

I. Consider the great good fortune of having the Most Blessed Sacrament with you, at the feet of which you can pour out your heart, show your misery, receive consolation in trials, help in needs and make requests face to face with your Lord. Jesus in this sacrament grants gracious audience all the time and in every hour of the day, to all kinds of people. Father Avila says: why do you think this Jesus wished to remain with us so hidden in tabernacles if not so that all may come, all may enjoy it, everyone may gain what they can. The Lord calls himself the very flower of the field, the lily of the valley: *I am a rose of Sharon, a lily of the valleys.*[599] He says this to make you understand that just as the flowers of the field and the lilies of the valley do not remain closed in by hedges, nor surrounded by walls like those of gardens, but are open to the public, to anyone who wishes to enjoy them, so this blessed Jesus is always available for the benefit of everyone who approaches him with love to ask for graces. Cardinal Hugo puts it in these words: *I show myself to all so I may be found like a flower of the field.* St. John sees the Redeemer with breasts full of milk bound up by a golden belt: *Girt about the paps with a golden girdle.*[600] This is meant to signify that just as a mother whose breasts are filled with milk goes about seeking babies to reduce their weight, so Jesus filled with grace and blessings, totally lovable and generous, with this heart full of love and with hands full of gifts, desires and waits for any who come to beg him, to visit him in the Sacrament, so he may enrich them with the fullness of his dearest blessings: *As a mother comforts her child, so I will comfort you.*[601] There is a story about St. Catherine of Siena that she would yearn for the Most Blessed Sacrament just as a child who runs to the breast of its dear mother: *Like an infant at its mother's breast, so did she long for the Eucharist.* O my icy heart, what about you?

II. St. Teresa says that Jesus did not choose to remain among us in his majesty, but clothed himself in the poor appearances of bread, and kept himself thus humbled on the altars to make himself friendly toward all, sweet and easy to deal with, so that all would come to him with childlike intimacy and love, and so willingly approach his infinite goodness. Thus he calls to and invites to himself his loved ones: *Arise, my love, my fair one, and come away.*[602] He wants them to treat him as a friend, a father, a spouse, with love and confidence.

You do not have to go around like the spouse of the Song of Songs, sighing and crying in order to find your beloved: *I will rise now and go*

---

[599] Song of Songs 2:1.
[600] Revelation 1:13 [*DR*].
[601] Isaiah 66:13.
[602] Song of Songs 2:10.

about the city, in the streets and in the squares; I will seek him whom my soul loves. I sought him, but found him not.[603] You do not need to search out where he resides, where he rests: *Tell me, you whom my soul loves, where you pasture your flock, where you make it lie down at noon.*[604] Wherever you go, you may find your God in the Sacrament. Oh, what happy fortune if we would only profit from it! Father Avila speaks divinely when he says, "The Lord has willed to stay with us in the Sacrament so that at every simply cry, at every small 'Oh, my' he can hear us and watch over us like a caring mother with her sick little child; she never leaves its side, never goes away, but listens to its murmurs just as if she were sick herself." O Sweetest Physician, O Most Loving Father, O Mother whose love goes beyond words, how much we owe you for the love you bear us! No trail can come near us that you are not willing to help with. We cannot open our mouths without you hearing. Oh, how dear is your presence, my sacramental love! Oh, how heavenly it is to converse with you! Thank your God who has created you in this era of grace during which you can always enjoy being face-to-face with that great good that was so longed for and desired by the patriarchs and prophets of old. On your journey, make use of the great treasure, like parched deer draw near to that divine fountain and drink of that living water which leads you to eternal life: *Everyone who thirsts, come to the waters;...come.*[605]

PRACTICE: Visit the Most Blessed Sacrament as often as you can with love and reverence. Imitate St. Francis Borgia who did not let a day pass without visiting it seven times. During trips, when you arrive at a hotel, go immediately to find a church where you can spend a long time lightening your heart at the feet of the Most Blessed Sacrament. When you arrive at your residence, take the room nearest the church whether it is a suite or a hovel, and there, as if you had the sacramental Jesus present, turn toward the church so that whether you are meditating or studying or whatever you are doing, your heart is always fixed on the Most Blessed Sacrament; always act as if you were continuously in the sweet and dear presence of your sacramental Lord.

---

[603] *Ibid.* 3:2.

[604] *Ibid.* 1:6.

[605] Isaiah 60:1.

TREATISE TWO
Instructive Lessons on Holy Communion

Lesson V

Jesus Gives His Entire Self in Holy Communion

I. Our dear Redeemer was not content to remain with us in the Sacrament. Out of his infinite love for us, he gave us his entire self in Holy Communion so that we could eat of his divine flesh under the appearance of bread and unite us intimately heart-to-heart with him. He found this new way of intimacy and union in order to enter into our very being and make us participants in his treasures. See how in the Last Supper he consecrated the bread and the wine substantially changing them into his body and blood. Then, turning lovingly to his disciples and in their person to all of us, he seemed to say: "Rejoice my own dear ones who until now have seen me and have spoken with me, but later you will be able to eat of my body and drink of my blood, fill yourselves and unite with me in a way of inexpressible charity and ever more intimately than you are now. Therefore, take, my beloved: *This is my Body*, take what I give you, eat it and comfort yourselves. Do not open the gift only once but forever": *Take, eat: This is my Body.*[606] Indeed, from the moment the Eternal Word became human, he desired to give us his flesh as food. Listen to the expressions of love with which he spoke one day to St. Matilda: "You will not find a bee throwing itself more recklessly into flowers to draw out the honey than I, with greater urgency, enter into your heart to find my delight in it." Oh, what a magnificent reason St. Teresa had to cry out completely in awe-filled love for Jesus: "O King of Heaven and Earth, what do these words of yours mean: my delight is to be with the children of mortals? What do you lack in your happiness, O my Good, that you should go searching for such a vile worm as I?" The voice that was heard at the Jordan River, telling that your heavenly Father is pleased in you, must extend over all of us unworthy beings since you make us your equals. Learn from this great love of Jesus and by the ardent desire which moved him to give us this sacrament, draw near to Jesus with desire and love.

---

[606] Matthew 26:26.

II. What a great gift Jesus Christ has made to us by giving us Holy Communion! The infinite goodness of God, says the Angelic Doctor, willed that this great action give everything in its entirety: In the Eucharist, God the Father gives us all that he is and all that he has with the Son and Holy Spirit. All of Christ's riches are divided into three kinds: goods of his holy humanity, those of his divinity and those of his divine personhood united to our humanity. In Holy Communion, Jesus gives a share in all these treasures and their joy. He gives you his body and blood, he gives you his grace, he gives you his divinity, and he gives you moreover his merits, his satisfactions, his virtues; in short, he sanctifies you with all his sanctity. The Lord, by giving us Holy Communion, pours out on us such an abundance of his treasures that there is nothing left to give. He arranges in our hearts all those riches that the divine Father has placed in his hands: The glory that you have given me I have given them.[607] St. John Chrysostom says: In offering the Eucharist, the whole treasury of God's kindness is opened. No matter how many gifts our God has given us, there is none equal to this one. He gave existence to creation and supports it at every moment; the grace of baptism, and those of the sacrament of reconciliation. He gave all his treasures but he was still not content for he had not yet given himself. Is there anything more God could give you? No, says St. Augustine, even though God is omnipotent, after giving you Christ, there is nothing left for him to give you; even though he is the All-Wise One, he can think of nothing more to give you. Although he is the richest of all, he has nothing further left. By means of Holy Communion, we humans are wholly in possession of God: They are so rich they [*possess*] all God is. He adds: O Overabundance of Love! O Flood of Love, which not only waters our hearts but makes them bloom with joy! O Blessing Without Equal! Oh, how can anyone be aware of these loving actions and not be inflamed with a sacred divine fire and fail to exclaim full of awe and happiness: Why me, dear God, why are you so good to me?

III. The Lord, by leaving us Holy Communion, intends to have us remember him always. Thus, immediately after instituting this sacrament, he says to his own: Think of me forever: *Do this in remembrance of me.*[608] He has given so many treasures to us, dispensed so many graces, imparted so many gifts to win our hearts. By leaving us so many created things to

---

[607] John 17:22. The 1888 text gives the citation as John 18:22.
[608] Luke 22:19.

serve the human race and remind us of the Creator of all, he excites in us love for the giver. The Lord forgives all that does not support his plans when we ungrateful mortals, instead of making use of all these creatures to recognize and love the Creator more, abuse them by falling in love with them and forgetting God. So in order to bind humans with more bonds to make them always recall their God and to love him alone, this infinite goodness invented this unspeakable way of remaining always with us in the sacrament and completely giving us himself in Holy Communion in order thus to steal our hearts with the violence of gentleness. And so always keeping him near us in thought as well as often within the depths of our being, we should recall his love and respond without ever forgetting him. Love is insatiable, desiring always to live in the memory of the loved one. The Lord, in order to excite in us this memory, made sure there was not just some mild agreement between us, but rather he himself would serve as the pledge. O clever miracle, exclaims William the Parisian, that amid such fires of charity, such delicacy of love, such excesses of good will, there could arise so much coldness on our part as to have a totally closed heart that would not burn with love for such a loving God! How right to say with the Apostle, *Let anyone be accursed who has no love for the Lord.*[609]

PRACTICE: Prepare yourself by purity, humility, mortification and love to receive the favors that Jesus imparted to [*Maria*] Vela [*y Cueto*], the Cistercian nun, in her fervent communions. After receiving the host one morning, she was enraptured in spirit and it seemed to her that Jesus took her heart and placed it [*next to his own*] within his own chest; he pressed the two together, forming one heart so that her affections and desires were conformed to his in seeking always the greatest glory of God. At another time, after preparing for communion with special devotion, it seemed to her that the Savior showed her the wound in his most sacred side and said: "Come away, my beloved spouse, from every earthly affection, enter here and let yourself rest in my heart." Then she felt as if every bit of her self-love was extinguished and all of the divine love escaping from the breast of Christ inflamed her as all its thrilling ardor beat within her. From this she learned that in the Sacrament is all the fire of charity needed to burn up all earthly affections. And from that moment, it seemed to her that all the altars where the Blessed Sacrament was kept became like fiery furnaces.[610]

---

[609] 1 Corinthians 16:22.

[610] Maria Vela y Cueta, *Libro de las Mercedes*, September 22.

LESSON IX

THE HUMILITY OF JESUS IN HOLY COMMUNION

I. St. Bernard, meditating on the great love that Jesus has for us and his profound humility in leaving us Holy Communion, exclaims: Oh, the force of holy love, you have made Jesus forget his infinite dignity! The Apostle says that the dear Son of God emptied himself to become incarnate because, though he was equal to the Father, by taking on our nature as a human being, he would become less than the Father. Moreover, by remaining present in the sacrament, Jesus can not only say, "I am less than the Father," but indeed "I am less than human in appearance, and even less that any other living thing, since I present myself in the semblance of inanimate food under the appearance of a little bread, I who am Life Itself." St. Thomas says, *On the cross he gave up only his divinity; here he leaves behind also his humanity.* This is not simply a repeat of the abasement of the Incarnation but it even outdoes that with an excess of humility and love. What more? An infinite God, eternal, immense is found truly hidden in each little fragment. He obeys the voice of whatever priest calls him through the words of consecration. Then he keeps himself humble and hidden in the tabernacle, ready, indeed desirous, to come to communicate his whole self to anyone who desires to receive him for the right reasons. O Love, O Love, what have you done? You have done everything a god could do to humble and empty yourself so that you could exalt and divinize your creature. *Thus he has given us...his precious and very great promises, so that through them you...may become participants of the divine nature.*[611] "Come, love God," says St. Augustine, "that God who in this sacrament of humble love knows how to raise you up; combine the warmth of his eternal light with the clay of your mortality."

II. Jesus, before instituting this sacrament, wanted to leave us an admirable example of humility, and so he set aside his garments and put on an apron. Then, kneeling at the feet of his disciples, he washed them, kissed them,

---

[611] 2 Peter 1:4.

dried them, pressed them lovingly to his breast and even demeaned himself thus at the feet of Judas. He said, "Do you know what I intended to do by this action? I have given you an example, so that just as I have done for you, so you would do for each other, and be humble toward each other, charitable and respectful: *I have set you an example that you also should do as I have done to you.*[612] But, O my Jesus, how far Christians stray from your example and teachings! What monstrous disorder! A God humbles himself, and humans grow proud! A God hides himself, and humans want to stand out! A God abases himself and humans exalt themselves! Infinite Majesty annihilates itself and a worm inflates itself! O, what intolerable human pride! O Holy Humility, so loved and practiced by Jesus Christ, so exalted and glorified in the holy Gospel, who will not love you? Whoever despises you will be despised by God; whoever embraces you will be embraced by God. Learn from your Redeemer to be humble; submit to your superiors, to your inferiors, to everyone for God's sake. Seek to appear as little as possible before humans; flee boasting and vain complacency, self-esteem and human respect. Remember what you truly are, not what you think you are, nor how you appear to others; rather, how you stand before God and nothing more.

III. St. John Chrysostom says: Pay attention, O Christian, how much your God has exalted you; ponder well the food upon which you feed; the food which the angels themselves do not dare to look at freely because of its splendor but which that Infinite Majesty hands to you. You feed upon a God and a God unites himself with you! *Here he pastures us, thence he unites with us!* St. Jerome was once ready to receive communion and considering God and himself, exclaimed: "O Lord, why do you humble yourself so much that you can come to visit a publican, a sinner like me? And then you not only want to eat with such a one, but also to be that which is eaten? The greatest saints considered themselves impure when they thought of the sanctity that should be possessed to receive Holy Communion:

> *What a wonder!*
> *The poor, humble servant*
> *Consumes the Lord.*[613]

---

[612] John 13:15.

[613] *O res mirabilis, manducat Dominum pauper, servus et humilis.* Hymn: *Panis Angelicus.*

O God, God, who are you; who am I? O Divine Word, who abides in the bosom of the Father, why do you come to live in the heart of a little human being? O King of Glory, Creator of All, heaven is your throne, earth is your footstool; and I see your grandeur bow and descend into this vile world to come to enter under the roof of my smelly and muddy heart! O God, how will I repay such an honor! Your charity is the cause of your great humiliation in order to exalt me and move me to love you. I thank you and offer endless praise, O my most magnanimous Redeemer. Oh, if only I would respond to your love! Oh, if I would only humble myself as you have done for me! I have recourse to you to remedy my lack of love and my pride. You can change my affections and heart; do so, Dear Jesus, love yourself as much as you deserve to be loved by us.

PRACTICE: Jesus finds no greater joy in creatures than when he finds a truly humble heart. The more you judge yourself unworthy to receive Jesus, that much closer you draw to the truth; and the more you are disposing yourself to receive him with an abundance of grace. Be humble; love humility and humiliation greatly if you wish to be just before the Divinity. Before receiving Communion, let one of your most frequent considerations be this: "Who is God? Who am I?" Reflect seriously, recharging your faith. As you draw near the altar, when the priest says, "Behold the Lamb of God," form this thought: In this consecrated host, under this appearance of bread, is the fullness of God, the Creator of heaven and earth, an omnipotent God, eternal, immense, infinite, become human for me! Afterward, move on to consider who you are, you who receives this God! Pray to the Lord that he enlightens you to be able to penetrate *[the mystery of]* who you are and who God is. Say often the beautiful words of St. Augustine: my God, may I know you, may I know myself: who you are, who I am: *I will know you; I will know myself.*

Lesson XIX

How Worthwhile is Spiritual Communion

I. Spiritual communion is an exercise of devout acts, as St. Thomas teaches, that allows us to share in the fruits of the Sacrament without receiving it [*physically*] in Communion; by it the person embraces Jesus Christ and unites his or herself to him in spirit. This type of communion consists in an ardent desire to receive Jesus and to unite with him in a vivid faith produced by love. The holy Fathers speak of such communion in great and glowing terms. The Council of Trent warmly commends it and urges the faithful to practice it frequently. Father Taulero, after he has enumerated the effects of sacramental Communion, adds: These precious fruits are also shared by those who, with eager and devout spirit, make an act of desire to communicate. Such a practice is so pleasing to God that Blessed Joanna della Croce used to say that she received no fewer or less important favors in spiritual communion than she did in actually going to communion. So extensive is God's goodness that he accepts good desires as equal to the action itself when we cannot carry it out. Dear Jesus, I want to love you; I promise you to communicate by desire very often and to always yearn for your blessed love.

II. The holy effects of spiritual communion are countless and St. Thomas orders them into three categories; he says that by means of this activity, Jesus 1) pours out his charity in forgiving sins, 2) reins in passions and 3) allows the person to share in his merits by an anointing with his precious blood. Rosetto, referring to the teachings of the Angelic Doctor, asserts that the value gained by the person through spiritual communion is sometimes greater than that received by sacramental Communion. His reasoning is supported by the Council of Trent, which says that this [*spiritual*] communion can be more effective and profitable than the sacramental Communion because it can be repeated whenever we wish, even at every moment, and so, by the multiplying the acts with devout and fervent affections, one can attain more merit and virtue than in one sacramental Communion. Oh, how much is missed by those who overlook this devout practice. If they only knew the great treasures of which they are depriving themselves, they would weep tears of blood over their negligence. Apply yourself with fervor to this divine practice because that is the way to quickly find yourself (and with so little difficulty that you would hardly notice it) far advanced in the ways of God with an immense treasure of merit and virtue. Imagine the Lord telling you what he once said to his beloved St. Gertrude when she was making an acts of spiritual communion: "O Daughter, drink now from my heart the power and abundance of my most gentle divinity.

III. The Disciple says that there are those who ought to make special use of this practice: 1) The sick who cannot receive communion sacramentally. 2) Those on the brink of death who do not have sacramental Communion available to them. 3) Those who have been denied sacramental Communion by their confessor...All those who serve God with a pure heart and desire to unite themselves in spirit with the Lord. This is the way to receive communion whenever you wish, even at every moment. Neither illness, nor business, nor relatives, nor weather, nor location, nor time can delay your union with your Jesus. Therefore, do not get impatient, sad or upset if you cannot receive sacramental Communion as frequently as you want. Instead, with true humility and fervent love increase daily your spiritual communions, just as St. Francis de Sales recommends: "When you cannot actually go to Communion, do so in heart and spirit. Unite yourself through an ardent desire to the living flesh of the Savior. Rejoice, then, you who are devout, and be happy that nothing can separate you from your Jesus."

O Divine Bread, how much I desire you! O Life of my Life, I sigh for you! O heavenly Treasure, how lovable you are! O Love above All Other Loves, how much you are worthy of being glorified! O Inexhaustible Fountain of all Good Things, renew my faith in me, increase my hope, expand my love, inflame my desires, make me worthy of receiving your dear promises. O my King, O my God, my sweetest Savior, I believe you are present in this Sacrament, I adore you, I bless you, I thank you who have never hesitated to give so many divine ways that are mild and efficacious for always living in your presence, united to you. How much I owe you, my most generous Lord, how much I owe you! May your infinite kindness be forever known, blessed and loved. Give me, O Lord, such understanding that I may receive you, every moment through desire, and, as often as I am able, sacramentally. In death, may I expire embraced by you, and after death, enter very quickly to praise you, thank you, love you, and enjoy you face to face along with the Most Holy Mary, the angels and saints in paradise.

PRACTICE: Do not avoid frequenting sacramental Communion by putting all your confidence in spiritual communion; rather, add the one to the other as often as you can. Make spiritual communion at least three times a day, in the morning, during the day when you pay a visit to the Blessed Sacrament and in the evening after your examination of conscience. It is an error to believe that one can make spiritual communion only if one is fasting. Would that every one of our breaths were a desire to be united to Jesus. As long as it is licit to love God, so long is it licit to communicate spiritually. Venerable Agatha della Croce, knowing the great usefulness that she received from such a holy practice, made communion by desire two hundred times during the day and night. Prepare for spiritual communion with the same reflections, devotions and acts that you use to receive sacramental Communion: especially practice making acts of love; these are the most excellent and fruitful means for people to unite themselves to Christ; this is precisely what you are seeking in such communions. This is the very activity of the blessed: to love God. Sometimes imagine being at the foot of the holy altar upon which you pretend to see a very beautiful pyx filled with sacred hosts; there adore the Lord in spirit and in truth. Long, like a thirsty deer, for the fount of living water; hunger for the food of heaven. And then imagine having received the sacred host and embrace, adore, love, thank and beg Jesus whom you have spiritually in your heart. Hold tightly to this amorous divine embrace as long as you can after your spiritual communion.

CHAPTER EIGHT
UNION WITH GOD

The Christian Led Along the Road of Devotion[614]

RULE ONE

HOW TO UNDERTAKE THE SPIRITUAL JOURNEY

Many persons are vividly moved in the course of a retreat or a mission and develop a spirit of repentance and great fervor. They then desire to move further into God's service. But very often they lack a wise director to take charge of counseling and guiding them. Since they are inexperienced and of a practical bent, they sometimes blunder badly. They get off the right path by indiscreetly trying various practices without any order to them and so they find themselves in very risky situations where they are completely at a loss and imperfectly prepared. So they waver and get nowhere. In this case, besides suffering a loss of energy and instead of gaining any advance, either present or possible, they are put in danger of falling into serious error or of losing heart. Therefore, to offer some first-aid to these people, I propose some brief instructions, trying to be very clear so that every type of person can understand the rules well and can act with a great certainty founded on the wisdom of saints and proven by the centuries-old experience of spiritual direction.

Do not think that the way of perfection is founded on those exercises of devotion that are based on your ideas and that you find

---

[614] This translation is based on the text of the 1888 edition (Naples) Volume VII containing *Il Cristiano illuminato…*, Vol. Two, Part II, pp. 83–88, 204–209, containing the pamphlet titled *Il Cristiano diretto nel cammino della divozione.*

pleasing, even though in themselves they may truly be virtuous. The spiritual life does not consist in fasts, nor hair shirts, nor bodily penance and mortification. It is not found in the recitation of a great number of private or vocal prayers, or in the spread of charitable donations and works of mercy. It does not come from long hours of discussion with spiritual persons, or from daily Holy Communion. It does not consist in expressions and tender acts of affection, in heartfelt sorrow, in copious tears and frequent sighs. It does not lie in the enjoyment of sweet thoughts about the Lord.

Rather, it is founded on the true devotion of a living faith and a sublime hope, on substantial love and perfect conformity to the will of God, on solid virtue acquired by interior mortification and denial of your own will. It flows from profound meditation on the almighty mysteries of the Redeemer and on imitation of him, along with knowledge and understanding of the divine immensity that prepares the way for the heart to throw itself on the bosom of the Highest Good, by entering into the Lord's power and uniting one's own heart with the heart of God. Those other penitential and devout actions are not perfection; they are not the goal of devotion; they are merely means that help along the road for acquiring true devotion and shortcuts for arriving at the holy mountain of perfection.

Recognize this mistake in order to avoid allowing self-confidence to become attached to these exterior activities while you have not even begun or understood the first lesson of the school of the science of the saints. They teach their followers that to acquire it, they must first rid their own heart of all its own being and drown their own will and self-love in the adorable sea of God's will that is made known to us by means of holy obedience. This urgent and disquieting inclination to this or that spiritual activity seen as an end in itself is an attachment to one's own will and is greatly prejudicial to one's spirit. Instead, a person must be indifferent and willing to deprive oneself of anything if it is the Lord's will, without becoming disturbed and upset. What is much worse is if a person becomes obsessed with such activities and regards them as ends in themselves when they are nothing more than means (and often very weak ones) for arriving at the Great Goal. *True devotion*, says St. Teresa, *consists in not offending God and in being resolute in doing every good thing.*

You should ponder the great blessing that the Lord presents to you by calling you to the spiritual life. What a great gift he gives you in removing from the vanity of this world so he can admit you into the garden of [the Song of Songs] to serve your heavenly Spouse perfectly and to fix your heart on the wonderful love of the greatest Good, to the point of living in full obedience to such goodness, thankful, loving, faithful, and united to such a great benefactor. You must also develop a sense and esteem for spiritual things and for excellence in this sovereign journey so that you brace yourself with strength and courage to enter into this grand undertaking with a generous and resolute spirit. Many people, because they have not grasped the grandeur of this blessing, walk it feebly and timidly. They put off a solid resolve and, at any little difficulty that comes their way, hesitate to walk further. They do not recognize by the light of faith their great good fortune and the grand and glorious advantages that are more desirable and more worthwhile than possessing the universe. Others think of doing great things *for God* when, in fact, it is God who is doing great things for them; the only thing they deserve on their own is to be buried, humbled, and confused.

For those who take the right road, the spiritual journey is easy, sweet, full of contentment and of the joy of the Holy Spirit, rich in the dear peace of God. Many people, however, through their own fault, want to make it bitter, rough, and difficult. They let themselves be overpowered by their own fears and allow themselves to be conquered by the demon who invents difficulties and dire consequences, and paints a picture of bitterness and contradictions, fabricating depression and sadness. Consequently, a person who is not trained and who is poorly formed in virtue does not know how to overcome human weakness or how to find comfort by mean of trust in the goodness and protection of the Lord. So he or she is dismayed, dejected, loses heart, and fears to resolve to take a step into this blessed journey. O God! How can you judge such a life to be hard and distressing when you have not even tried it and experienced it? No, it is not bitter, not rough, not depressing or sad to give oneself entirely to the service of God and to walk along the road of perfection. Although at first sight and viewed from afar the spiritual life may seem so to someone who has not tried it for they see it as consisting in exercises of mortification and self-abnegation. But in truth, it is a matter of peace and tranquility. When a person sets out on the journey, accompanied by the anointing of the loving grace of God and invigorated by the strong and sweet love of the Lord, it is found to be sweet and very pleasing. One finds so much joy and holy pleasure that one would never want to see it end and does not know of an adequate way to bless and thank God who has offered the invitation to such good fortune and happiness. If you do not believe this, try it. Enter generously in the name of God on this way of paradise and you will discover how good, how lovable and how pleasant it is to see the Lord to whom you are giving all your service with a resolute and sincere heart; open your whole being to this blessed divine love that fulfills and contents our hearts. St. Teresa says it well when she remarks: *Lord, you act as your prophet stated: you pretend to make your law difficult, while I do not view or find the path that leads to you to be narrow. I have experienced many times how much it helps if someone resolves at the beginning to get something done, difficult as it may be; if they do it to make God happy, there is nothing to fear. The devil has a great fear of resolute persons because no matter how much he tries to damage them, it is turned to their advantage.*

To enjoy such a good thing, though, you must not withdraw your affections and share your heart with earthly creatures. You must keep a very close eye on it, keep it away from created things and open it only to the desire of eternal goods, to the love of your Creator. The Lord is a jealous spouse who does not put up with division and withdrawal, does not accept alien affections in your heart. He wants all for himself, entirely open to his love to fill it with his sweet grace, to pour down on it his soft light, to draw it all to himself and to unite it to his divine heart in perfect charity and in close friendship. If you divide your heart and attempt to serve both God and the world, to please both creatures and the Creator, to follow both your worldly will and the divine will, you are fooling yourself. You will not enjoy a peace and serenity, spiritual joy and tenderness that the Lord imparts to hearts that are detached from created things and are totally intent on pleasing and loving the Highest Good.

Ungrateful and unresponsive hearts will not be visited by that sweet and penetrating love which he gives to bring joy to those who love God alone with all their affections. God wants this divided and dissipated heart of yours to stop resisting and spreading itself so much on creatures and vanities that it actually destroys itself and loses the grace and friendship of God, ending up drinking the deadly poison of sin. That is just what has happened to many, many spiritual persons who, by dividing their hearts and turning their affections little by little from the love of the Creator, have gone on to eternal ruin. Do you believe that you can find fulfillment and contentment in created things and earthly goods? It is impossible! God alone has created your heart and created it solely for himself and for his love; only God can fulfill you. Take care then, and save your heart for God. Since God is enough for your little heart, be content not to search for any other love than God's. Quit dividing your affections among creatures, but bring them back into yourself in order to sacrifice them in an eternal burnt sacrifice to your loving and lovable Lord.

Be careful not to allow yourself to be surprised by the emotions of sadness and depression that your natural gloom arouses. The demon incites and inflates them under that dark cloud to hold you in check and to keep you from advancing on your spiritual journey. This is the birthplace of inquietude, impatience, diffidence, tedium, avoidance, and aversion for devout practices. These emotions turn into an impossible burden for you by rendering your heart stale, stupid, drowsy, oppressed, and unable to know how to relieve your mind with filial confidence in God and so they separate you from divine love. Do not excuse and defend yourself due to this threat of sadness saying you do not know how to serve God, how to pray, how to advance along the way of the spirit. Your sadness and disquiet will obscure the little good that you accomplish and perhaps even make you lose what you have; they will not now allow you to acquire the virtues you need. Why, if you wish to remedy this evil, do you apply something that will increase the illness? To learn how to serve God, to pray, and to advance in perfection, the means are a resolute and generous heart, an open and willing soul, a firm and steady confidence that will not collapse and become dismayed in the face of difficulties but has faith in God, makes continual recourse to God, puts up with bitter reactions through cheerful resignation, overcomes difficulties and delays with lively faith in the immense mercy of God. And to do this without depression, sadness, diffidence, disquiet, and complaints. O child of God, do not let yourself be conquered by your domineering passions but take yourself in hand and smother them in the wide bosom of the confidence and love of your God.

RULE THIRTEEN

ON THE UNION OF THE PERSON WITH GOD

There are three stages or ways for the person on the road of perfection. 1) The Purgative Way is that into which a person enters after conversion, when he or she guards against sinning always more seriously, destroys bad habits, and removes the perverse remains of sin by contrition through prayer and penance. 2) The Illuminative Way is that in which the person, cleansed by the fire of contrition, washed by the tears of repentance, humbled and refined in the press of penance, comes to be illuminated by the Lord to walk the ways of perfection by the exercise of solid virtue in the spirit of prayer, by denying one's own will through interior mortification and the devout and profound consideration of the holy mysteries of the life, passion, and death of our Lord Jesus Christ. 3) The Unitive Way is the one into which the cleansed and enlightened person, who is strengthened and perfected in the exercise of virtue, enters to be united in an ardent and perfected love of the Creator by means of the contemplation of his attributes and greatness; then the person is raised up, snatched away by a unique gift to the Creator, and swept up in the power of the Lord in the following manner:

Our Lord God, by showing persons the heart of his divine love, draws them out of themselves and removes their own powers in order to envelop them in a sea of his unspeakable sweetness, to embrace them, and unite them to his love, allowing them to taste the heavenly delights of his blessed knowledge and infinite love. At this stage, they are fed by those sovereign favors. They not only offer and surrender themselves promptly to the sacred union which is made with God, but cooperate with all their power, forcing themselves to unite with and embrace the divine goodness more strongly in a way that allows them to recognize how this ineffable union and mighty bond of love with the divine heart depends on the Lord's work without which they would be unable to make the least effort to reach this point.

This divine union happens often without the person cooperating except by a simple consent, allowing their self to be united without resistance to the goodness and love of the great and highest good. Sometimes persons cooperate when they feel drawn by divine love to run headlong in following the lead of the sweet call of divine love that pulls and embraces it. At other times this union happens almost insensibly when the person does not feel or notice the divine action in them nor is aware of one's cooperation.

Thus, the goal and completion of perfection of a person consists in this union with God, and all the person's acts and practices ought to lead and look to this end. This happy possession is to be desired and hoped for. To arrive there, nothing opposed, nothing painful, nothing mortifying or bitter should be avoided as one runs courageously and steadily along the Purgative Way and Illuminative Way until one arrives at the Unitive Way.

There are various ways in which a person should proceed to arrive at union with God. It is true that a perfectly burning love would be enough for it is the chain that binds the person closely to the Creator. The more a person is renewed, matures, burns, is rekindled and perfected and consumed in holy love, to that extent and in proportion to it does that person know God, run to God, come closer to God, is comforted by God, is embraced by God and is united with God. One does not arrive at this very lofty love in a single moment, but by steps and paces. For it to be reached, one must keep a balance in lowering and surrendering oneself on the one hand to be able to be freed, to exalt, to be consoled and embraced by God on the other. Thus, I propose three principal means for arriving at this exalted love and divine union, granted that there are other means that must go along with them but are not as central.

Mortification is indispensably necessary, both interior and exterior mortification, of the senses and of one's powers; that is, a perfect self-abnegation of one's own will and of self-love to purge one's own heart so all disordered affections are cleared out to make room for the love of God in order for it to take complete possession of the person and remove all there is of self. The more that one destroys this human heart, the more that one annuls and mortifies one's own will against self love, so much more does one become capable of God's love and the more one is exalted by God, consoled, united, and embraced.

Conformity to the will of the Lord in all events and coincidences of daily life, the sacrifice of one's own will in honor of the will of God, submerging one's own desires in the admirable sea of the divine pleasure to wish nothing but what God wills, to want only what makes God happy, in the way it pleases God and because it pleases God. Thus, the will of the human and God's will no longer appear as two wills, but one, with no way to distinguish what is your will and what is God's so that the result is like one single will, one single purpose, one single work, one single desire, one single heart. This practice is a great help in uniting the person with God; we might be tempted to say that when this practice reaches perfection it unites the person with God. Then the person, who finds himself or herself fixed in this blessed union, perfectly possesses this uniformity of will with the will of the Lord. "What a great power this gift of our will to God has," says St. Teresa, "because God uses it to unite himself with our nothingness. The truest union is the union of our will with God."

The activity of meditative prayer is what continues to accompany the person to console and inserts the person into the bosom of that infinite love and into union with God. Moreover, such prayer reinvigorates the spirit, helps and urges it to mortification and self-abnegation, and permits it to ascend the steps of divine conformity. Therefore, one must attend profoundly to this activity if one desires to arrive at the perfection of holy love and to the heights of divine union.

Be careful, however, that since this high level of perfection and holy union is offered you, you learn all the elements of the spiritual journey. Do not think that you have arrived at this state, or be tempted to think that you can arrive before you have been cleansed, enlightened, and well-taught in understanding and in the exercise of the holy virtues; nor can you arrive before the Lord calls you to it and freely brings you to himself. I advise you to fully accept the confusion and humiliation of recognizing your lowliness and how you are unworthy of even walking this earth and of living in the world. Accept bitter tears and a true spirit of sorrow over your sins, your ingratitude and unresponsiveness, your defects and deficiencies, and have a resolute spirit of repentance. Have an ardent desire to arrive at a high degree of perfection, not just to please yourself and to find enjoyment or to bask in the delights of heaven here on earth and live a carefree life. Rather, desire it to please and bring happiness to your God, your Creator, your Redeemer and the Spouse of your soul who plans for you outstanding virtue, the most fervent love and total perfection in piety. So I leave you with the warning of St. Teresa: *What greater conquest can there be than to make God happy? While alive, conquest does not consist in pleasing God more, but in doing his will.* Remember that all you have and all you hope for is a gift of God. If you trust in yourself, be careful that there not fall on you the awful verdict of the Redeemer who proclaimed that these unspeakable truths are hidden from the hearts of the smart and the prudent, but are imparted to the humble. It is indeed true that those rich in themselves die in poverty of spirit, while the hungry and thirsty are fulfilled.

CHAPTER NINE

LESSONS ON PRAYER

PART THREE [615]

On the necessity and efficacy of prayer together with the rules and requirements for its fruitfulness and efficacy.

CHAPTER ONE

THE NECESSITY OF PRAYER

Prayer [616] is defined by the Fathers of the Church: *the request of proper things from God.* Prayer is divinely commanded and is absolutely necessary for the salvation of anyone who has reached the use of reason. Thus, the divine Teacher makes it known to the whole world that prayer is not just proper or useful for salvation but that it is necessary to pray always and not to set it aside: *Jesus told them a parable about their need to pray always and not to lose heart.* [617] The apostle repeats this precept when he commands us never to stop praying: *Pray without ceasing.* [618] This responsibility to pray

---

[615] This translation is based on the text of the 1888 edition (Naples), Volume I, containing *Il mondo santificato…,* Part III, pp. 191–223.

[616] Translator's Note: "Prayer" in this chapter is the translation of the Italian word *"preghiera,"* that can have two different meanings: 1) "prayer" may be used as a general term for any form of speaking and listening to God (e.g., asking God for help, praising God, thanking God, meditation, mental prayer, etc.) 2) It can also be used to refer to one specific type of prayer, that of *asking God for help* (as different from other ways of conversing with God); this is the type of prayer more exactly called "prayer of petition." In this chapter, "prayer" is used primarily in this second sense: prayer of petition. As the text goes on, Sarnelli relates prayer of petition to the wider meaning of prayer.

[617] Luke 18:1.

[618] 1 Thessalonians 5:17.

is imposed by the virtue of religion by which we are bound to testify with our prayer and petition that God is the author of every good thing that we wish to obtain, that we wish to depend on his providence, and that we hope for help and grace from his hands: *In what day so ever I shall call upon thee, behold I know thou art my God.*[619]

Indeed, the holy doctors agree with each other in teaching that prayer is necessary for adults with a necessity of means [*that is, it is a* sine qua non] without which one cannot reach eternal salvation. Therefore it is a matter of faith that in the ordinary course of divine providence efficacious grace is not given except by means of prayer, so whoever does not pray does not receive it and is not saved. This is why St. Augustine writes: *We believe that no one comes to salvation unless God invites them; no one invited reaches their salvation except by the help of God; no one deserves help who does not pray.* He also, when writing against the Pelagians, and St. Jerome in writing to Ctesiphon, expressly say that prayer is no less necessary for salvation than grace; moreover, that salvation is inseparably attached to final perseverance, which one does not attain except by means of prayer. It is true, continues St. Augustine, that the first grace presented to the will by God is given without the person requesting it, but the second is not so granted because the person is enlightened and can help himself or herself by means of the first grace by praying to receive more: God gives the first to us even before we ask as the beginning of our faith; but later ones, such as perseverance *[are only given]* if prayer prepares the way.

St. Thomas explains the passage in the Gospel of Luke where we read that the heavens were seen to be opening with the Holy Spirit hovering over the Redeemer in the form of a dove, when he was in prayer after his baptism: *when Jesus also had been baptized and was praying, the heaven was opened.*[620] He says that the Lord wishes to teach us that prayer is necessary for everyone to be able to receive graces after baptism and be saved: *Namely, because prayer after baptism is necessary for the faithful.* Therefore, although in baptism all faults are canceled, the inclinations that dispose us to sin remain alive and these we must rein in, dominate, and overcome through the helps we obtain from prayer.

---

[619] Psalm 55:10 [*DR*]; *NRSV*: "This I know, that God is for me. In God, whose word I praise, in the LORD, whose word I praise, in God I trust; I am not afraid" (Psalm 56:10).
[620] Luke 3:21.

There is a story found in the lives of the ancient Fathers that a young man named Paccone, who withdrew into the Scythian desert to do penance, after many years was so fiercely assaulted by foul temptations that he became desperate to the point of wanting to kill himself. So he went to the mouth of a cave inhabited by two ravenous hyenas so they would devour him. At the smell of human flesh, the beasts rushed out, but instead of tearing him to pieces, they laid down like two little puppies at his feet, licking them. This quieted the hermit and he returned in triumph to his little grotto. But then what? After a few days the demon came back to torment him with the most hateful fantasies and he again fell into desperation. He ran throughout the desert seeking death, and seeing a serpent in the sand, he grabbed it, held it to his chest and manhandled it, but it did not bite him. But the temptation continued in the poor deluded man, who turned against heaven and wailed because he could not find a way to die, when he heard a voice from on high that said: "You poor fool, how did you think you could overcome the temptation by your own power? Call upon God and when you have realized your own powerlessness and placed all your confidence in God, then you will conquer." Enlightened in this way, the hermit clearly understood that to conquer temptations there is no other way but through prayer. So he turned to prayer to the Lord and his passions subsided. He found himself a victor over hell. He understood by reflecting on it that the Lord could have immediately freed his troubled spirit but did not wish to do so; instead he preferred to work three miracles in preserving him from the hyenas, saving him from the snake and speaking to him from heaven, instead of the one of freeing him from temptations without fervent and continuous prayer and not otherwise.

How many Christians find themselves in hell! They ended there simply because they did not pray and so would have overcome temptations, conquered passions, avoided sin if only they had repented, made a good confession and been saved. This is their greatest despair: knowing that they have lost heaven and merited hell for not having spoken from their hearts: *O God, save me!* What desperation, what pain, what worm that gnaws and does not die! Thus they will reach their extreme despair on the day of judgment when they are asked to give an account to the divine justice because they have not prayed and have nothing else to answer as an excuse except that they were insensitive in heart and tongue, desiring and asking for earthly goods and temporal pleasures while not wishing to beg God for his grace, for virtue, for the kingdom of heaven. Their evil will clamp their jaws, pierce them with pain, and cover them with shame.

On the other hand, even infidels, Mohammadens, heretics, if by the help of sufficient grace, they sincerely would beg the light from God and an awareness of the truth, even these will be saved. The just and faithful Almighty One will grant them the efficacious grace to know the true faith and the way to embrace it. Just as among many others, there is the case of the centurion Cornelius, who is greatly praised in the Scriptures for the continual prayer he offered to the true God.

It is a great chastisement of God when he allows people to become so stupid and blinded by the darkness of their sin that they no longer pray for salvation since these unhappy ones through their own fault and well-deserved punishment remain deprived of the only way left for them to be able to escape from their evil and to save themselves! These are the very unhappy ones who rush toward final impenitence and draw close to final ruin. O God, God of all mercy and Father of lights, free all from such a punishment! Blessed the pure, who instead of staying attached to the earth, pay attention to God and in this stormy sea do not turn their eyes from heaven and from the words of the Creator: instead of a pool of iniquity, they want to be a sanctuary; not a barn filled with useless straw, but a granary filled with a choice harvest.

Christians, always recall what happened to the great Apostle Peter, who went so far as to deny his own dear master because, instead of praying that night, cowardly went to warm himself among the enemies of Christ. The Lord, foreseeing the danger, had shortly beforehand warned the disciples to be vigilant and pray so they would not fall into temptation: *Pray that you may not come into the time of trial.*[621] O God! Who of us can be so sure? Who will not flee the occasions and not always pray, if even the greatest pillars of the holy Church fell for having missed just one chance to pray?

---

[621] Luke 22:40.

CHAPTER TWO

THE EFFICACY OF PRAYER

Not only is prayer necessary for salvation, it is moreover efficacious for obtaining all that is worthwhile. What wonderful things sacred Scripture and the saintly Fathers have to say about the power of prayer: matters very gratifying and glorious about the Lord as well as joyful and gracious for us; things that when considered are enough to make even a heart of stone desirous of always praying. Prayer is what can free us from all vices, can make us acquire all virtue, and then obtain for us all graces. Note the infallible promises of Jesus Christ who assures us this way: whoever asks, obtains; whoever seeks, finds; and whoever knocks will have the door opened: *Everyone who asks receives, and everyone who searches finds, and for everyone who knocks, the door will be opened.*[622] Elsewhere the Redeemer promises us that the heavenly Father will give the blessed spirit to whoever asks for it, that is, all the gifts of the Holy Spirit, every heavenly grace and perfect sanctity: *how much more will your Father from heaven give the good Spirit to them that ask him?*[623]

Indeed, the most lovable and generous Lord adds that he will give all blessings, even temporal ones, provided these are not hurtful to the person: how much more will your Father in heaven give good things to those who ask him![624] And the infinite Goodness, in order to encourage the faithful to ask always and to confide in him, says this: If a son asks for bread from his father, might he give his son a rock instead? And if he asks for a fish, would he by chance give him a serpent? And if he wants an egg will he give him a scorpion? Surely not. But the father will give his son what he desires and rightly requests: *Is there anyone among you who, if your child asks for a fish, will give a snake instead of a fish? Or if the child asks for an egg, will give a scorpion?*[625] Therefore, the Lord then adds: if you miserable humans, grasping, miserly, little advanced in doing good and very inclined to do evil, know how to give your children the good things they ask for, how much more will your heavenly Father, who is infinitely

---

[622]Matthew 7:8.

[623]Luke 11:13 [DR].

[624] Matthew 7:11.

[625] Luke 11:11–12.

good, generous and inclined to dispense grace, who loves his creatures infinitely and to whom it costs nothing to give, not give every good, every favor, every grace, every good thing to the one who asks him? *If you then, who are evil, know how to give good gifts to your children, how much more will the heavenly Father give the Holy Spirit to those who ask him!*[626]

In summary, there is nothing good that cannot be obtained by means of prayer when it is filled with faith: *So I tell you, whatever you ask for in prayer, believe that you have received it, and it will be yours.*[627]

And there is more! Our most loving Lord of all is not content to dissolve all shadow of hesitation and diffidence and to fill our hearts with faith so that we would always seek the greatest graces and expect them without hesitation. He goes so far as to swear many times in the most holy Gospel, by that God of infallible truth that he is, to concede all graces to the one who asks him properly: *If you ask me for anything, I will do it.*[628] *Very truly, I tell you, if you ask anything of the Father in my name, he will give it to you.*[629] If someone prays with a lively faith, it is powerful enough to move mountains and to throw them into the sea when the glory of God and the good of humans require it: Jesus answered them, *Have faith in God. Truly I tell you, if you say to this mountain, 'Be taken up and thrown into the sea'...it will be done for you.*[630] Holy prayer!

The infinite goodness cannot abide the listlessness of humans that causes him to complain that they do not ask. So he urges them, invites them and, one could even say, forces them and begs them to ask and hope. He promises the fullness of his grace and peace in answer to their prayers, a sea of contentment and joy and an all-powerful efficacy: *Until now you have not asked for anything in my name. Ask and you will receive, so that your joy may be complete.*[631] As the Redeemer said: You do not ask; is it because you do not believe you will be heard? Oh no, try it! Ask and see that the effects will fully correspond to my promises and to your hopes. I swear to

---

[626] Luke 11:13.
[627] Mark 11:34.
[628] John 14:14.
[629] John 16:23.
[630] Mark 11:23.
[631] John 16:24.

you and I assure you by whom I am that it will not fail and it will never go empty, not even by a word, not even by a syllable, not even by a comma of my infallible eternal words: *For truly I tell you, until heaven and earth pass away, not one letter, not one stroke of a letter, will pass from the law until all is accomplished.*[632] Notice that this is God speaking! In truth, to doubt the efficacy of prayer and to fear being repelled is a doubt of faith and a doubt of the Gospel and a doubt of God himself!

II. In fact, the greatest and outstanding graces that the Lord grants come either during prayer or because of it. Moses raised his hands to heaven and his heart to God in prayer and was made to achieve for his people the marvelous victory against the Amalekites: *Whenever Moses held up his hand, Israel prevailed.*[633] And it appears that he was also able, by means of prayer, to assuage the anger of the Almighty who wished to destroy that lying people by saying: *Now let me alone, so that my wrath may burn hot against them and I may consume them.*[634] At these words, St. Jerome was struck with awe at the power of prayer: *The prayers of his servant blocked the power of God.* It was prayer that was able to stop the sun in its course at the command of Joshua: *the Lord heeded a human voice.*[635] Jonah, swallowed by the whale, was spewed out on the shore because he prayed: *I called to the Lord out of my distress, and he answered me.*[636] By his prayers, Daniel was preserved in the lions' den and was saved from death. He was also marvelously consoled by the Lord while praying and received revelations of divine mysteries: *while I was speaking in prayer, the man Gabriel...said to me...At the beginning of your supplications a word went out.*[637] Solomon was filled with a marvelous wisdom because he knew how to ask it of the Lord: *Because this was in your heart, and you...have asked for wisdom and knowledge... wisdom and knowledge are granted to you.*[638] Moreover, the Lord also granted him riches, glory, and victory: *I will give you also what you have not asked, both riches and honor all your life.*[639]

---

[632] Matthew 5:18.
[633] Exodus 17:11.
[634] *Ibid.* 32:10.
[635] Joshua 10:14.
[636] Jonah 2:2.
[637] Daniel 9:21–23.
[638] 2 Chronicles 1:11–12.
[639] 1 Kings 3:13.

It was by prayer and blessing the Lord that the young men in Babylon conquered their enemies and turned the flames of fire lit to devour them into fresh roses: *They walked around in the midst of the flames, singing hymns to God and blessing the Lord.*[640]

King Hezekiah obtained many marvelous graces by his prayers. When he became sick, he was told by the prophet Isaiah, speaking for God, that he was near death: *Set your house in order, for you shall die; you shall not recover.*[641] The prince wept at the news and begged the Lord for his life: *Then Hezekiah turned his face to the wall and prayed to the Lord:*[642] He had hardly finished his prayer when the Lord ordered the prophet to return to Hezekiah and tell him that he had seen his tears and heard his prayer; he would not only free him from death but even add fifteen years to his life, and moreover, would give him victory over the Assyrians and protect his city: *Turn back, and say to Hezekiah, prince of my people,…I have heard your prayer, I have seen your tears; indeed, I will heal you;…I will add fifteen years to your life. I will deliver you and this city out of the hand of the king of Assyria.*[643]

The great Judas Maccabeus, as often as he called out to the God of Hosts, conquered enemies; but twice he was conquered by Antiochus and Bacchides;[644] and in those cases one does not read that he had prayed.

What more? There is the famous case of Anna who was sterile, yet had the good fortune to become the mother of Samuel as a reward for her prayers: *She continued praying before the Lord.*[645] Judith scored her great victory over Holophernes' army and killed that tyrant by means of her prayers and those of others on her behalf: *Till I bring you word, let nothing else be done but to pray for me to the Lord our God.*[646]

---

[640] Daniel 3:24.

[641] 2 Kings 20:1.

[642] *Ibid.* 20:2.

[643] *Ibid.* 20:5–6.

[644] 1 Maccabees 6:47; 9:18.

[645] 1 Samuel 1:12.

[646] Judith 8:33 [DR].

Likewise, Esther freed her people from death by means of prayer: *Go, gather all the Jews to be found in Susa and hold a fast on my behalf.*[647]

Sarah was freed from her trials and the curse as well as blessed by God and prospered as a reward for prayer: *Continuing in prayer with tears [she] besought God.*[648] Thus it came about that an archangel came to console her at the same time as Tobias' family was praying: *At that very moment, the prayers of both of them were heard in the glorious presence of God. So Raphael was sent to heal both of them.*[649]

The chaste Susanna was freed from the lies of the evil old men by means of her prayer: *Through her tears she looked up toward heaven, for her heart trusted in the Lord...The Lord heard her cry.*[650]

O God, why do we not feel affection with our whole heart for holy prayer? Why do we not pray at every moment with every breath we take? No indeed, prayer is not tedious and difficult; it is not hard to attain. Let us raise our hearts to God, call on his infinite goodness and we shall be completely heard, comforted and consoled: *Lift up your face to God. You will pray to him, and he will hear you.*[651]

Furthermore, the Holy Spirit came into the upper room to ignite the hearts of the disciples with heavenly fire while they were are prayer: *All these were constantly devoting themselves to prayer.*[652] As these new disciples were praying, they were filled with the Holy Spirit. *When they had prayed...they were all filled with the Holy Spirit.*[653] There is also the famous centurion Cornelius who was directed by an angel to embrace the faith in Jesus Christ as reward for his prayers as he offered them at that moment: *Cornelius prayed constantly to God..."Your prayers and your alms have ascended as a memorial before God."*[654] Furthermore, the

---

[647] Esther 4:16.

[648] Tobit 3:11 *[DR]*.

[649] Tobit 3:16.

[650] Daniel 13:35, 44.

[651] Job 22:26–27.

[652] Acts 1:14.

[653] *Ibid.* 4:31.

[654] *Ibid.* 10:1, 4.

Lord acted to order for Ananias to restore sight to the eyes and health to the soul of Paul, now converted, while he was in prayer; the prayer of Saul was the symbol of those whom the divine goodness wishes to enrich with grace: *Look for a man of Tarsus named Saul. At this moment he is praying.*[655]

What more is there for me to say when the divine Scriptures, the Holy Gospels, the books of the saintly Fathers, the annals of the Church and the examples of all ages are full of the effectiveness of prayer and of the countless graces God has bestowed on the world in answer to prayer? St. Bonaventure says it well in stating we should love and appreciate prayer above all else because it delivers us from all evil and brings every blessing: *In this is understood that prayer is to be greatly loved because through it we receive the obtaining of every good and the removal of every evil.* Theodoret also has good reason to call prayer "*omnipotent*": *While prayer is only one thing, it can be everything.*

So it would please the Almighty if all churchmen would preach constantly to the people and persuade penitents to always pray and not stop! They must do so because it is precisely their apostolic ministry to follow as closely as possible the teaching and example of the divine Teacher who in all the four Gospels preached not once but hundreds and thousands of times on the necessity and effectiveness of prayer. It is no mystery that our Redeemer so vividly and frequently taught, explained, charged, counseled and commanded nothing so much as to pray often and well. From this we clearly grasp: the necessity and efficacy and value of prayer in relation to the world; the glory, the pleasure and the honor that result for the Creator; the great obligation all of us priests have to persuade everyone with zeal and fervor to take up the activity of holy prayer, and to instruct people in the manner and practices for praying well. Yet, how often this great good is bypassed. What a sad and dangerous omission!

---

[655] *Ibid.* 9:11.

CHAPTER THREE

ONE MUST PRAY WITH ATTENTION AND AFFECTION

WHY SOME PRAYERS ARE NOT HEARD

If, however, prayer is so effective in obtaining things and the faithful say so many prayers, and if no one is so lost that they have no devotion, why do they all remain the same: poor in spirit, lacking in virtue, loaded down with vice, in misery, weak, and inclined to every temptation?

We say so many Our Fathers, the prayer taught by Jesus Christ himself, which contains a summary of the paradise of graces the request for which exactly matches what the Lord wants to grant; and yet most do not obtain these wonderful graces for which they beg by means of such prayers. So many Hail Marys are said, the prayer composed by St. Gabriel, St. Elizabeth and the Church (or rather, by the Holy Spirit), in which are contained the most apt praises of the Mother of God to her greatest pleasure. Nevertheless, we are not able to reach the point of gaining the protection and love of Mary who is accustomed to lavish grace and heavenly blessing on her devotees. We say so many Glory Bes that give great honor to the Most Holy Trinity and they obtain nothing. We say the Creed so many times, the prayer composed by the twelve apostles, that contains the principle articles of our most holy religion and, nevertheless, countless Christians are very ignorant of the doctrines of our faith and very weak in its holy works. We repeat acts of divine faith, hope and charity through which the heart draws ever more closely to God, by which it is illuminated in its awareness of heavenly truths, expanded in the hope for eternal goods, enkindled in holy love and united to our Creator. Still, how many not only do not reach such precious favors and even do not grasp these great truths? We recite so many offices, psalms, rosaries and chaplets with their mysteries through which the Lord reformed and sanctified the world, but today for the most part there is so little fruit harvested. And the same is true for other prayers and petitions.

But why indeed is there such little efficacy in prayers of such strength, that they were able to stop the sun in its course, raise the dead, move mountains from dry land and throw them into the sea? This is why: you are praying with your mouth but not your heart; because you repeat prayers but do not enter into prayer; you "say prayers" but you do not "pray"! *You ask and do not receive, because you ask wrongly.*[656] You say Paters, Aves, Creeds, rosaries, litanies and many offices, acts and protestations; you read many pamphlets and litanies but without consideration, without reflection, without attention, and therefore without affection, without fervor, without devotion and without results. These prayers are said by rote, by the mouth but not the heart, by the tongue but without the mind, with the lips but without understanding. You have no idea what you are saying. *You do not know what you are asking.*[657] How can you wish God to hear you when you do not even know what you are saying and do not mean it yourself? *God does not listen*, says St. Gregory, *to the prayer of the person who does not mean what he or she is saying.* Clearly neither the Scriptures nor the Church taught you pray this way. Your imagination, your lack of devotion, your ignorance were the teachers of it. Likewise, you cause great damage if this is the same way you attend Mass or pray before or after Communion; it is even worse if this is the way you prepare to approach the Sacrament of Reconciliation. What a mess! Oh, what disaster for souls does hell work in this way! The life of a person like this turns into a gab session. Two religious were reciting their prayers without devotion and they had a vision of the devil who stank to high heaven and who said to them: *This is the kind of incense that rises from the way you pray.* O dear, at how many, many Christians can the same insult be hurled!

This is what some do to gain a bit of satisfaction thinking that they are doing something for God and so they flatter themselves to have satisfied sufficiently the great and rigorous obligations that they have to think about the Creator and their own souls. Some persons, to complete their list of prayers to honor various mysteries, and a lot of saints, content themselves by hurtling through their prayers headlong so they can finish them all without caring how they pray or why they do so. These dissipated persons are like people who cast a glimpse at their face in a mirror but do not stop to consider their features and instead glance and run and right away forget who they are: *for they look at themselves and, on going away, immediately forget what they were like.*[658] How many are lost because of such ignorance! This is a common

---

[656] James 4:3.

[657] Mark 10:38.

[658] James 1:24.

temptation for persons who are not people of prayer; they do not understand where the force and effectiveness of prayer lies. Therefore, how important it is to urge the use of mental prayer from which great benefits come. When one knows how to meditate, one knows how to pray; the one who knows how to pray, knows how to obtain; the one who obtains is saved. This is why St. Thomas speaks correctly when he says meditation is the first milk of true devotion.

St. John Damascene says that prayer is the raising of the mind to God: *It is the elevation of the mind to God*, or as St. Augustine puts it, it is speaking with God, asking him for graces of the heart: *It is speaking to God*, or as St. John Climacus says: *Prayer is the friendly conversation and a person's embrace with God.* When attention is missing in prayer, it lacks its essence, its substance, its whole being; one cannot then call it prayer but a shadow, a ghost, an appearance of prayer. True prayer, says St. Gregory, does not consist in words or thoughts but in considering and asking with reflection and with the heart: *Real petition is not in words but in the thoughts of the heart.* For what purpose are a multitude of words? The devil, who cannot remove prayer from the world with his illusions, has reduced it to such a bad end that for innumerable Christians this great weapon has been rendered useless instead of all-powerful and valuable to combat all of hell, as well as bring about an infinite number of victories.

May it please you, O my God, that the whole world would learn such an important truth: they would not groan weighed down under the burden of so many vices, and so many would not be lost! What a great thing! Yet so many prayers are recited and people do not know how to raise their mind to the Creator even a little bit; they do not know how to recollect themselves and conceive an act of love, of hope, a devout affection! Would that the faithful might enjoy a touch of paradise in their prayers, might acquire infinite merits, might obtain every grace! Rather, they desire to lose such great good practically for nothing.

ON THE VARIOUS WAYS TO PRAY

In order to have better understanding and clarity in such an important matter, we should distinguish four types of vocal prayer. The first is the kind made with teary eyes, one's heart in one's throat and consists more of feelings than words; these inspire sorrow and love. Prayer of this kind does not differ from mental prayer because it is both vocal and mental just as prayer ought to be and has great merit and grand effect as well as being pleasing to the Lord. The second is when one is paying attention to the meaning of the words of the prayer, but they do not penetrate the heart very much, are not internalized and so produce little fruit. The third, which is less fruitful than the preceding occurs when one recites the prayers and pays attention to the words but with passing attention and just in a general way, such as do those who recite memorized devotions by heart and routinely, and those others who are illiterate, yet recite the Latin prayers but have no idea what they are saying. Instead, to make such prayer very fruitful (although one does not understand the words), they think of God while saying the prayers and raise their minds to God by reflecting on some mystery of the Faith. The fourth kind is the type is the situation where one prays with voluntary distractions; this manner of prayer is defective and is worse than in speaking rudely to God. Who speaks with God in saying prayers, who is asking for grace, who is really praying? Come on, don't you know?

It follows then that to be perfect, there must be something made up of both thoughtfulness and prayer. The person who thinks without praying produces flowers without fruit. The one who prays without thought produces fruit but with no meat in it, because it makes prayer tepid, not up to par, ineffective. This is why St. Bonaventure says that to pray well requires meditating well so that the thoughts enlighten the one who prays and becomes the life that fulfills and gives the very essence to prayer: *Meditation produces and informs the meaning of prayer.* Besides, Bishop Hugo adds that consideration is so necessary for prayer that it is never possible to succeed perfectly if it is not preceded and attended by meditation: *Meditation is necessary for prayer.*

St. Bernard speaks in a heavenly way when he said that we must walk the way of heaven with two feet, that is, with consideration and with prayer: consideration teaches us what we lack and prayer obtains it. Consideration shows us the way and prayer makes us continue on it; by consideration we notice the dangers that loom and by prayer we surmount them: *Let us go up as with two feet, mediation and prayer; the former teaches what is missing and the latter obtains what is lacking; the former shows the way, the latter leads us; the first illumines us to recognize the dangers, the latter makes us evade them.*

SOME WAYS TO MAKE PRAYER EFFECTIVE

In order to make your prayers, acts, offices, rosaries, protestations and chaplets, etc., effective, and to excite sorrow, devotion, love and fervor (thus gaining what you ask and desire), when at prayer or during mental prayer, recite and consider, read and meditate, speak and reflect. As you go along speaking the words, you should stop and meditate. Let there be more affection of the heart than words; where you find recollection, affection, and sorrow, stop there without moving on. Precisely in this way did the Apostle pray, and so he teaches us that we should do so as well: *I will pray with the spirit, but I will pray with the mind also.*[659] The prophet also wishes to intimate this when he says: *Sing ye wisely.*[660] Notice how the order of things should run, says St. Augustine. You should mediate, because meditation gives birth to knowledge and the awareness of truth; knowledge begets sorrow; sorrow produces devotion, and devotion makes sure that prayer is perfect: *Meditation gives birth to knowledge, knowledge to compunction, compunction to devotion and devotion makes prayer perfect.*

The fact that when you recite your prayers in this way you do not finish all of them as you are accustomed to is not important; recite a few of them, let the rest go. Be sure that none of the saints will feel the least bit dishonored by this pious omission. Instead, it is very clear that more honor is given to the Most Holy Trinity, the Most Holy Mary, the angels and the saints, and that greater solace comes to those in purgatory from one Our Father said the way St. Francis prayed, I mean with affection and consideration, than hundreds and thousands said routinely and distractedly.

Father Lessio teaches that it is much more worthwhile to say a few prayers with attention and recollection than a great number in haste and dissipation. He also preferred for the faithful not to burden themselves with a lot of prayers but to say a few prayers devoutly every day. That is what the Lord said to St. Brigid: *A person who carefully reads a few lines with faith and devotion gives me more joy than the one who reads numerous verses inattentively.* The Most Holy Mary told Blessed Eulalia the Cistercian: *My daughter, if you want to give me more pleasure and yourself more interior joy, when you recite the Hail Mary, don't rush*

---

[659] 1 Corinthians 14:15.
[660] Psalm 46:8 *[DR]*.

through it. Father Nierembergh reasons this way: To say the rosary and the Hail Mary with affection and tenderness is one of the sweetest devotions, blessed by countless miracles. A few Hail Marys with love and devotion are more valuable than many said without affection. The Most Holy Virgin alerted a person devoted to her who said the entire rosary every day by telling him that it was much better to say five decades with attention and love than to say fifteen in a rush with little devotion. When vocal prayer is said with the greatest respect and not in a negligent and distracted way, we should realize that the heart can say four times what the tongue can only say once. Therefore, this lack of reverence becomes displeasing to God and pushes him away from responding because it affronts him. The souls of some monks appeared to a Cistercian religious and complained about the little devotion with which the members of the monastery recited their prayers of petition. They told him they were stuck in purgatory because these distractions in reciting the prayers made the prayers weak and ineffective for helping them and others. The Divine Master wishes that our worship, adoration and prayer to the Divine Majesty be in spirit and truth, and tells us that such is the desire of our heavenly Father: *the true worshipers will worship the Father in spirit and truth, for the Father seeks such as these to worship him. God is spirit, and those who worship him must worship in spirit and truth.*[661] So now what is left for those to argue, who are accustomed to adore the Most High and say their prayers without recollection and devotion, yet wish to defend such prayers and make them pass for good? What Jesus Christ has to say and command is perfectly clear.

---

[661] John 4:23.

412

CHAPTER FOUR

OTHER REQUIREMENTS FOR MAKING PRAYER EFFECTIVE

In addition to what we have already mentioned for making our prayers effective and dear to God are the following.

I. Keep in God's grace or at least desire to return to God. Whoever is in the state of mortal sin and seeks temporal graces from the Lord will not be heard while he or she remains a sinner, not only because such a person is God's enemy, but because he or she shows no concern about remaining in that situation. If you live as my friends and in my grace, says the Lord, everything you ask of me I will give you. *If you abide in me, and my words abide in you, ask for whatever you wish, and it will be done for you.*[662] The prophet says your sins have caused a total separation between you and God; your faults are planted in between you and God like a dark cloud that does not allow your prayer to arrive in God's presence: *You have wrapped yourself with a cloud so that no prayer can pass through.*[663] *Rather, your iniquities have been barriers between you and your God, and your sins have hidden his face from you so that he does not hear.*[664]

II. We must ask for things that are proper, ones that are not contrary to the honor of God or hurtful to ourselves. We can licitly ask for temporal goods from God but only conditionally: if such are for the glory of God and helpful to our spiritual lives. Otherwise, to be heard would be a punishment. Jesus Christ taught us to ask for his grace and the kingdom of heaven; he then assures us that all the rest will be given along with it, even without asking: *But seek first the kingdom (of God) and his righteousness, and all these things will be given you besides.*[665] Solomon while still young asked the Lord for wisdom and nothing else, and his prayer was so pleasing to God that the Lord not only gave him marvelous wisdom (as

---

[662] John 15:7.
[663] Lamentations 3:44.
[664] Isaiah 59:2.
[665] Matthew 6:33 *[New American Bible]*.

everyone knows) but at the same time enriched him with every sort of blessing, even temporal ones. People want to believe that they are asking for something good, but in God's eyes this is not so: their intention is not as completely pure and holy at it seems to appear. The mother of James and John thought that she was asking heavenly things from the Divine Master when she asked that her two sons might sit next to him in heaven. Yet she was corrected by the Lord as being an improper petitioner.

III. It is necessary to have a lively faith and not hesitate: a grain of this blessed trust is enough to obtain a paradise of graces. You will obtain the favors of heaven according to the measure of your confidence: *According to your faith let it be done to you.*[666] Diffidence should never enter your heart, not over past sins that have already been confessed, nor over your daily defects which you desire to amend. This is because, as the Angelic Doctor teaches, the obtaining of graces is founded on the mercy of God, on his promises, on the merits of Jesus Christ and on the intercession of the Church, not on our own merits. These form the basis which no one can ever lack, even the worst [*sinner*]. The Divine Goodness is so great that it grants graces to those who have faith in the divine promises, even if they do not deserve them: *Let us even ask in prayer for those things which we do not deserve.* Then the saint continues, this happens because to obtain justice, merit is necessary; but to receive graces, it is enough to pray: *Merit is based on justice, but request is based on grace.* Still the very request that we make to God transforms us into being his friends and disposes us to merit the graces: *The very prayer which is made to God makes us friends of God.* How pleasing to God and how many graces were obtained by the woman who for twelve years suffered from her incurable illness, but who, with true and lively faith, confidently drew near to touch the robe of the Redeemer to be healed! *If I only touch his cloak, I will be made well.*[667] And Jesus Christ praised such a faith and heard her in an instant: *Take heart, daughter; your faith has made you well.*[668] It was thus for the famous centurion who was highly praised by the Lord and to whom he granted all blessings: *A centurion came to him, appealing to him...And he said to him, "I will come and cure him."..."Truly I tell you, in no one in Israel have I found*

---

[666] *Ibid.* 9:29.
[667] Matthew 9:21.
[668] *Ibid.* 9:22.

such faith.[669] Similarly, that leader of the synagogue begged the Redeemer to come and heal his little girl who was dying: *Come and lay your hands on her, so that she may be made well, and live.*[670] And then, when news arrived that she had already died, he said to them: Have faith and you will receive the grace: *Do not fear, only believe.*[671] They then did believe and her life was restored.

The Divine Master responded this way to that father who begged him to free his possessed son: *If thou canst believe, all things are possible to him that believeth.*[672] The good father, full of humility and confidence, with tears and sighs began to exclaim: *I do believe, Lord: help my unbelief.*[673] And thus he got what he asked. Oh, holy Faith, to the extent you trust, to that extent you obtain! *Let your steadfast love, O Lord, be upon us, even as we hope in you.*[674] Blessed are those who possess [*trust*]; they can say with the prophet: *I will enter into the powers of the Lord.*[675]

IV. Those who wish to receive God's mercy must show mercy to their neighbors; it is fitting to excuse them, be compassionate to them, help them, pardon them and pray for them: "As you deal with your neighbor, I will deal with you," says Jesus Christ, "Do not wish to judge and you will not be judged; do not wish to condemn and you will not be condemned; give and it will be given to you; be generous with your neighbor and I will be generous with you." Moreover, he calls the merciful "blessed" and as a reward promises them the fullness of his mercy: *Blessed are the merciful, for they will receive mercy.*[676] This holy love excites a sea of filial confidence in one's heart, a small grain that is sufficient to obtain every good thing. The great benefactor Tobias spoke beautifully when he said: *Alms shall be a great confidence before the most high God, to all them that give it.*[677] And on the other hand, severity, harshness with one's neighbor makes us little acceptable to

---

[669] *Ibid.* 8:5.

[670] Mark 5:23.

[671] *Ibid.* 5:36.

[672] *Ibid.* 9:22 [*DR*].

[673] *Ibid.* 9:23 [*DR*].

[674] Psalm 33:22.

[675] Psalm 70:16 [*DR*].

[676] Matthew 5:7.

[677] Tobias 4:12 [*DR*].

the God who is all love and kindness; thus in their prayer such people sense a heart of stone, they find a hard and cold soul that has no way of knowing how to recover a sense of confidence in God. *Judgment will be without mercy to anyone who has shown no mercy.*[678] Therefore, your confidence in God should the same as your compassion for your neighbor. Try it if you do not believe me, and you will see how valuable in the eyes of God fraternal charity is.

V. The humility of the faithful is, one could say, the arbiter of the divine will. It is impossible, says the prophet, for God to despise and not attend to a humble and contrite heart: *A broken and contrite heart, O God, you will not despise.*[679] Moreover, the Lord declares that the prayers of humble and gentle hearts always please his divine heart and always will. Thus they have no fear that their petition will be refused and so become almost almighty before God. *The prayer of the humble and the meek hath always pleased thee.*[680] Therefore, be humble not just on the tongue but also in the heart; love humility, accept with patience bad situations for the love of God: *The prayer of the humble pierces the clouds, and it will not rest until it reaches its goal; it will not desist until the Most High responds.*[681] And then there is St. Lawrence Justinian who says very well that humility and charity are like two wings of the seraphim by means of which we enter securely and confidently into the adored bosom of the divine goodness, and obtain all that we could ever ask for and as much as we would know how to desire: *Spiritual humility and charity are the wings of prayer; by their strokes we fly even into the inner being where the Word, residing in the fatherly bosom, is generated by his eternal power.*

VI. Thus it is worthwhile to persevere in prayer, since the power and efficacy of prayer rests on perseverance: *Obtaining comes solely from the continuation of prayers*, says St. Hillary. Some who are trapped in vices pray to God to free them; but not seeing themselves heard right away, experience boredom and stop praying. Others, who are stimulated by

---

[678] James 2:13.

[679] Psalm 51:17.

[680] Judith 9:16 [*DR*].

[681] Proverbs 35:21.

grace to practice some noticeable good or to undertake a new state of perfection, begin to pray to the Lord to give them the efficacious grace to follow those holy inspirations, but then they grow weak and give up on prayer and so lose the good desires and the grace of that vocation.

The Lord infallibly promises to listen but does not promise that he will immediately grant the grace that we request, although there are times when he immediately hears our prayer. So as in many other cases, it happened to Tobit whose prayers were quickly presented to the divine view and were very acceptable to God and marked with a divine response, but the fulfillment of the grace did not arrive until almost four years later: *So now when you and Sarah prayed, it was I who brought and read the record of your prayer before the glory of the Lord... God sent me to heal you and Sarah your daughter-in-law.*[682]

CHAPTER FIVE

WHY THE LORD DELAYS AT TIMES TO GRANT US GRACES

When our requests will have their hoped-for results is not for us to know; it is for us to adore the divine judgments and to conform ourselves to the adorable decisions of divine providence that arranges things according to his purposes and so not always according to our timetable and desires no matter how good. Nevertheless we are certain that we will be heard when it is most expedient for us. The apostle says: *At an acceptable time I have listened to you, and on a day of salvation I have helped you.*[683]

Sometimes the Lord delays answering the blessing if it is for his greater glory or for our greater good; here are some reasons for such divine workings.

I. In order to see us persevere in entreating at his feet, humble and contrite, dependent on his goodness and asking for it; this is very pleasing and gives glory to the Lord.

---

[682] Tobit 12, 14.

[683] 2 Corinthians 6:2.

II. For the honor and propriety of his Majesty that grants us graces so that we notice his gifts and we appreciate them. What can be easily acquired, can be easily squandered. We should highly prize heavenly favors as coming from the hands of God.

III. To test our faith, our hope and our love of him; to exercise us in patience, humility, and in conformity to his desires.

IV. To make us more deserving by repeated devout acts of the theological and moral virtues, which are the religious principles at work in prayer.

V. To get us to engage in the holy virtues, works of mercy, acts of charity to our neighbor, and so prepare a happier paradise for us. To induce us to purify our hearts more thoroughly and to remove those obstacles which often oppose the greater flow of divine graces, to mortify ourselves in those passions that would otherwise become eternally rooted in us and which, consequently, we would never effectively cast out of our self-centered hearts.

VI. Because divine justice wishes some recompense and satisfaction for the offenses it has receive from us, especially for that ingratitude we show when the Infinite Goodness has called us again and again to his love but we, who in our weakness seek to follow our passions, make ourselves deaf to the divine inspirations. By delaying the execution of our desired graces and by pretending not to hear us, his justice is repaid and satisfied and all of the disorder of our fault is corrected by such a punishment.

VII. Because the Lord wants to concede major graces to us, graces worthy of him, way beyond what we are asking for, and therefore wishes to dispose us to receive the abundance of his favors which far outrun our devout acts and anything we may deserve.

VIII. To excite and deepen our prayer; by putting [*the answer*] off, that apparent refusal ignites in us more and more holy desires, rekindles our faith, expands our hope and excites our holy love. Our spirit gasps for the Greatest Good, pulled by the force of sighs and tears over the desired graces.

IX. To conform us to the image of Jesus crucified by bearing along with him the weight of the passions, weaknesses and temptations which torment us.

Finally, it is true that it is always proper for us to pray. When we raise our prayers to God they return to us carrying divine blessings, although we do not always obtain what we ask. O Holy Faith! Thus the prophet chose to say: *My prayer shall be turned into my bosom.*[684] Holy prayer, soul of my soul, life of my life, heart of my heart, never will I desert you, lessen you or cease to beg my God, even though I find myself surrounded by an army of troubles, or in the middle of an ocean of aridity, of darkness, of desolation, of trials, of sufferings or of pains: *With me, a prayer to the God of my life.*[685]

CHAPTER SIX

WHY IT IS NOT BEST FOR OUR PRAYERS TO BE HEARD IMMEDIATELY

If we were always heard immediately, it would diminish the blessed interaction between God and the world. Conversation with the Most High is very precious, very honorable to religion, highly beneficial for us. I am talking about the helps and graces that lie in asking and hoping in divine providence. *Call on me in the day of trouble; I will deliver you, and you shall glorify me.*[686]

Besides, this earth would no longer be a vale of tears but a worldly paradise, because if we were immediately freed from temptations, defects and problems, if we would instantly obtain virtues and perfections, if in a second we would conquer passions, we would live in perpetual peace and tranquility without suffering. But this is not something that could belong to the world from the moment that sin entered the scene. Even less is it proper now for Christians who have to conform themselves to their Head, Lord and Master Jesus who came to earth, not for pleasure, but to battle, to suffer, to endure and to die amid insults and sufferings for

---

[684] Psalm 34:13 [DR].

[685] Psalm 42:9.

[686] Psalm 50:15.

our example, comfort and love: *we suffer with him so that we may also be glorified with him.*[687]

If we were to enjoy here on earth only peace and happiness, how could we insure that we would not become even more attached to earth and that the desire for earthly life would not be so ignited in our weak and disordered hearts that [*we would want*] to remain eternally at home in this exile and pilgrimage and become totally forgetful of the Creator and our true homeland? That is what would happen because even now we live entranced with earthly life despite its being filled with stings, sown with thorns and full of bitterness. Who does not understand that this kind of endless peace is not for us who are wayfarers, mortals and sinners but for the blessed who have achieved it? It is for us to enjoy God's peace, but only in our heavenly homeland if we live faithful to God in this world of exiles. Whoever legitimately enters combat and conquers will be crowned; don't you grasp that?

Although when troubles are pressing, when temptation is strong and you run the risk of falling, the Lord will then quickly run to help. Even before the person forms a prayer, the proper help is already at hand: *I call upon the Lord, who is worthy to be praised, and I am saved from my enemies.*[688] When does that Infinite Good ever avoid helping someone who calls on him? He will never allow that we be aggravated and molested beyond our powers, but will always administer help to enable us to suffer trails with patience, until he concedes us the grace that we hope for: *No testing has overtaken you that is not common to everyone. God is faithful, and he will not let you be tested beyond your strength, but with the testing he will also provide the way out so that you may be able to endure it.*[689] Your ignorance, your weakness of faith, your impatience is what leads you into complaints and quarrels unworthy of a Christian.

Because God's infinite wisdom has determined and disposed this to be the case, it is a sign that this is best; if something else were more expedient, the Great Good would have made a different disposition. If the Lord did not wish to listen to us, he would not have hundreds of thousands of times recommended, commanded, counseled and almost begged us to ask for his graces. St. Augustine says: *He would not have exhorted us to ask unless he wanted to give.*

---

[687] Romans 8:17.

[688] 2 Samuel 22:4.

[689] 1 Corinthians 10:13.

Therefore we live secure that in his own good time we will be fully heard by that Lord whose goodness is so inclined to what is beneficial, whose word cannot lack truth, whose generosity is so desirous to spread itself, whose power can do all things, and for whom it costs nothing to give us every blessing. All the divine attributes, even his justice (for we have his word that he wishes to listen to us), assures us that no one's prayers can be repulsed, no supplication not be heard if we pray as we should. If that infinite goodness, says St. John Chrysostom, pours out so many graces even for the good of those who do not call on him, how much more will he enrich with all blessings the holy person who does not hesitate to ask and beg? *You open your hand, satisfying the desire of every living thing.*[690] Blessed are we if we thirst for holy virtues and spiritual perfections. No day will pass without our devout desires being fulfilled! *Blessed are those who hunger and thirst for righteousness, for they will be filled.*[691]

Speak with such security and filial confidence to the Lord that you would weep at his feet until you are heard; do not stop praying because you do not see yourself possessing all the holiness you desire. Repeat with trust and love: *I will not let you go, unless you bless me,*[692] speaking just as Jacob did to the angel, and was greatly praised by the Holy Scriptures for having won over the heart of God by his holy impertinence and loving violence: *I will not let you go, unless you bless me.*[693]

The Redeemer wishes to suggest this to us by that famous parable in which he presents the friend who received a guest in his house late at night and went to his acquaintance to ask him for three loaves of bread to feed his guest. The friend, however, refused him and scolded him for coming at so late an hour to ask for food. But he did not cower but rather was pushed by his need to beat on the door and continue to beg. Thus his friend could no longer stand the disturbance that was going on to make him get up, so he gave him as much bread as he wanted so he would go away: *I tell you, even though he will not get up and give him anything because he is his friend, at least because of his persistence he will get up and give him whatever he needs.*[694] That is what I want you to do to me, Jesus is here suggesting: ask me for graces with loving and humble pestering and with

---

[690] Psalm 145:13.
[691] Matthew 5:6.
[692] Genesis 32:26.
[693] *Ibid.* 32:28.
[694] Luke 11:8.

filial confidence and do not doubt that in good time you will be fully heard: So I say to you, *Ask, and it will be given you.*[695] It seems that these three loaves were meant to symbolize for us faith, hope and charity, for which we ought to fervently pray to God incessantly. Or better, to desire and request that every breath of our lives be addressed to the greater glory of God, that we be made holy with ever greater perfection, and that by our prayers, penances and good works we cooperate in the salvation of the human race.

And there is more. The most kindly Redeemer, in order to encourage us to pray always and not fail, told the parable of the unjust judge who, in order to stop being bothered by the continuous insistence of the widow, executed justice and granted her request: *Then Jesus told them a parable about their need to pray always and not to lose heart.*[696]

The Lord wished to leave us the marvelous example of this very important truth in the person of the Canaanite woman of the Gospel. This very noble woman with a little girl possessed by a devil desired to see her freed and left her own country to rush to the Redeemer to ask for this grace: *Just then a Canaanite woman from that region came out and started shouting, "Have mercy on me, Lord, Son of David; my daughter is tormented by a demon."*[697] She came back to beg, to yell. Christ did not even deign to give her a glance and spoke not a word to her: *But he did not answer her at all.* The disciples moved by compassion intervened to ask in her name: *And his disciples came and urged him, saying, "Send her away, for she keeps shouting after us.* The Lord protested that he did not want to answer her now: *He answered, "I was sent only to the lost sheep of the house of Israel."* Nevertheless the generous woman got in front of Jesus Christ, adored him and again began to beg: *But she came and knelt before him, saying, "Lord, help me."*

What did Jesus Christ do! He pretends not to have compassion on her, upbraids her in front of the whole crowd, mortifies her, finally treats her like a dog because she was a Canaanite and he declares her unworthy of his children's bread: *It is not fair to take the children's food and throw it to the dogs.* But then what? This grand person of heroic virtue does not resent this, does not take offense, does not waver in her faith, does not lose hope, does not weaken in love. Instead, more than ever constant and generous, she backs up her request, repeats her insistence in complete

---

[695] *Ibid.* 11:9.

[696] Luke 18:1.

[697] Matthew 15:22–28. For all citations in this paragraph and the following one.

humility and full of confidence: "Lord," she says, "it is true that I am unworthy of your favors, I do not deserve the blessings of God for my little girl. I confess before heaven and earth my lowliness, but I remind your Holiness that the dogs eat the scraps that fall from the table of their owners: *"Yes, Lord, yet even the dogs eat the crumbs that fall from their masters' table."*Then the Redeemer, unable to keep the consequences of his infinite charity suspended and hidden from this great soul, stops and, as in an act of admiration for such virtue in the foreign woman, praises her, proclaims her, exalts her and does so in the presence of that crowd before which he had just humiliated her: How wonderful, woman, is your faith, your constancy, your perseverance, receive what you desire. I give you more than you seek from me. May your daughter be freed from the demon, may she be safe, may she be holy: *"Woman, great is your faith! Let it be done for you as you wish. And her daughter was healed instantly.* What marvelous power prayer has!

In the prayer of this great woman, notice, O Christian, all the conditions which should accompany your prayer to make it effective before the Almighty.

1) The Canaanite prays with her whole heart, with feeling and fervor. 2) She desires to love Jesus Christ and begins to do so. 3) She asks for just and salutary things. 4) She acts out of love for another in desiring to see her daughter freed from the tyranny of the devil. 5) She has great faith; despite being refused many times, she hopes and trusts deeply in the Lord. 6) She shows great humility. While very noble in family, she puts human respect underfoot, along with human gossip and the ridicule of the dissolute. She is not ashamed to run through the public square to reach Christ, and call out for mercy and pity amid a vulgar crowd, notwithstanding the rejections and repulses. Finally, her famous prayer is crowned with unconquered perseverance in praying and crying out. She does not stop until she sees herself heard, despite all the suggestions of common sense, the devil and the whole world. May it be pleasing to you, O my Lord, to deal in this way with the prayers of your faithful people! May your infinite goodness be thanked eternally, that in the person of this blessed woman you wished to admonish, instruct and console us, and to give our hearts faith and confidence, so we do not become dejected and pray less because of a delay in the graces requested and because of the apparent (but loving) refusal.

As for you, O Christian, you are an elder in Faith after so many years of knowing the true God, after being born and created in the holy Church, enlightened by so much truth, instructed in the Gospel teachings, urged on by so many good examples, confirmed by so many sacraments, moved by so many miracles. How can you, as soon as you feel pressured and tempted, if you do not immediately obtain what you want and seek, fall into depression and hesitancy? You languish, you murmur, you cry in desperation that you have poor luck with heaven and you fill the world with moans and lamentation? What a shame! Where is your Faith? Where is your Hope? Where is your Love? What a disgrace you are, O Christian Elder! You could be knocked over by an old lady! Instead of exclaiming with Job: *Although he should kill me, I will trust in him.*[698] You dare to call out with the wicked: *God has forgotten, he has hidden his face, he will never see it.*[699] You ingrate!

Rise, you faithful, let us pray in order to honor the Creator, and to give a sign of our dependence on his sovereignty. Let us pray to overcome temptations, dangers and distractions. Let us pray that we do not succumb in bad circumstances. Let us pray to obtain all the graces from heaven for us and for our neighbor. Blessed will we be if our prayer is faithful and preserving: there will be no evil from which we will not be liberated and preserved; there will be no good that we do not attain. No, our prayers cannot fail. Whether in private or public, whether naturally or superhumanly, whether now or later, we will certainly be fully heard.

If the grace is slow in coming, do not be one who despairs, but with humility and resignation faithfully continue to pray and wait with a lively and infallible faith for what you asked or something even better. St. Bernard reasons with divine hope in this way: You, whoever you are, do not make light of holy prayer. I assure you that the Infinite Good, to whom we address our prayer, takes great interest in it and as soon as it flies from our hearts to his lovable Majesty, he writes it in the book of his wisdom with eternal letters: be sure (notice that beautiful word: *sure*) that we will obtain one of two things: what we request or something more useful for us and more joyous: *No one should underestimate their prayer; I tell you that he to whom we pray does not underestimate it. As soon as it comes*

---

[698] Job 13:15 [*DR*].

[699] Psalm 10:11.

out of our mouth, he writes it in his book and we can hope without any doubt for one of two things: either he will give what we ask or what he knows will be more helpful.

O Lord, for love of Jesus Christ, enlighten us to make us understand these great truths and to get us to practice them faithfully! Do this, O most noble Trinity, for the honor that results for your Holy Name, for the honor that results for the Holy Gospel, for that joy that Jesus Christ receives, for the advancement that is reached by the Church, for the great good that comes to the whole human race. Grant that by loving you, the Great Good, we have affection for holy prayer and that we follow your commands exactly: *So that we may deserve to reach what you promise, make us love what you command. Through Christ, etc.*

My Dear God, God of All Mercy, Father of All Consolation, you are always very lovable, always generous, always doing good, always respectful; either hear us quickly or grant the grace slowly, either give what we ask or pretend to ignore it; grant us audience or seem to cast us away from you. Yes, always be the great God that you are: infinite goodness, infinite charity, infinite generosity, infinite mercy. That is what we believe, what we confess and what we adore. I know very well your lovable and admirable providence and I also know quite well that when you least show compassion for us in our troubles, that is when you are most lovingly helping us, listening to us. Pretend not to care about our ills, not to listen to our cries, to sleep through our storms; but this is not real. Meanwhile, more often than not, you are going to great lengths to prepare the immortal crown of our predestination and secretly hearing us, testing our faith, our hope, our charity, our humility and our virtue: Yes, O my Lord, it is enough for me to call on you to know that you are my God, my greatest benefactor. If you do not listen to my prayer, you are always listening to my wellbeing, for your greater glory and for my greater benefit: *On the day I called, you answered me, you increased my strength of soul.*[700] O Infinite Wisdom! O marvelous Providence! O lovable judgments of my God that are totally hidden! May that Great Good be ever blessed for not voiding my prayer or his mercy. And forever blessed be my Creator who will never withdraw his infinite mercy from me as long as I do not withdraw my prayer from the throne of his goodness.

---

[700] Psalm 138:3.

CONCLUSION

Look, O Christian, at the easy and secure way to Paradise that appears before your eyes by means of the consideration of the eternal maxims and of holy prayer. St. Teresa speaks divinely when she says: *Prayer is the royal way to heaven, through which you gain great treasures. No matter how much you use it and suffer to do so, may it never seem too much; there will come a time when you will understand that nothing is too much to give for such a great prize.* Everything depends on your wish to profit from it, on throwing yourself resolutely into this journey and in practicing what we have proposed to you. You already know that the Almighty God, who created you without your effort, will not save you without your effort. Heaven is a kingdom to be conquered, and to be conquered by faithful adherence to God's lights and at the cost of any fatigue. But do not fear that the divine grace you request will be unable to make every apparent roughness easy, sweet and loving by his divine anointing. When hell, in order to impede your eternal salvation, causes you weariness, regret, weakness and difficulty in your holy acts, lift your spirit and eyes to heaven and recall that there is your home, your county, where you will have joy without end. Courageously tell yourself what the Blessed Mother said to St. Symphorian when he was being led to martyrdom: "My son, my son, remember your eternal life: look to heaven, how beautiful it is: see your Creator there to invite you into those unspeakable and infinite joys": *Son, son, remember eternal life, look up to heaven; and there see the Ruler.*

CHAPTER TEN

SOME ASPECTS OF PRIESTLY MINISTRY

TREATISE THREE [701]

The exercise of sacred preaching with its rules, practice and instructions

SECTION ONE

THE NECESSITY AND EFFICACY OF SACRED PREACHING

There is no doubt that in the plan of divine Providence the usual way to draw the human race to an awareness and love of its Creator is by means of sacred preaching: *How are they to hear without someone to proclaim him?* [702] The Father of Lights has conferred a sovereign power, a marvelous force, an almighty efficacy on his word when spoken with wisdom and zeal. Using this means, it instructs the intellect and removes the ignorance about the eternal mysteries. It recalls and illuminates the mind in the knowledge and desire of eternal things. It moves the human will to rein in passions, to overcome oneself and to become a disciple of the divine Master, a faithful imitator of his example and a ready enactor of his holy wishes.

By means of sacred preaching, the Almighty's wisdom, through the breath of the Holy Spirit, brings to the consciousness of what is eternal and true. By means of it, sinners are converted and brought

---

[701] This translation is based on the text of the 1888 edition (Naples), Volume XI containing *L'Ecclesiastico santificato…*, Part II, pp. 112–123;130–139.

[702] Romans 10:14.

to his grace. Moreover, it perfects the upright and moves them to rise to a higher level of holiness. In short, by means of it, the faithful are gathered into the Church Militant and the elect are led into the Church Triumphant. *Indeed, the word of God is living and active, sharper than any two-edged sword, piercing until it divides soul from spirit.*[703] There is no mind so blind and darkened that it cannot be enlightened and illuminated by the splendor and light of heavenly doctrine. There is no heart so hard and fractured that it cannot be penetrated and its trust healed by the divine word. There is no soul so careless about eternal goods, so stunned by its dangers, so alienated from what pertains to spiritual wellbeing, so attached to earthly things that it cannot enter into itself and, at the sound of the heavenly voice, make sense of the explanation of the eternal truths. The whole world confesses this. The records of all the ages attest to this. The work and experience of all zealous ministers of sacred preaching reveal and confirm this.

There are two hands that push the unhappy person to draw away from the Creator and from a good life and so fall into the abyss of vice. There are two chains that restrain the person so as not to shake loose from their lies and escape their miserable slavery; I am talking about ignorance and an evil inclination to pleasure: *Therefore my people go into exile without knowledge.*[704] But the divine word knows how to arrest these two infernal hands and break these two hellish chains. It is by instruction that ignorance, the mother of vices, is remedied and the uninstructed intellect is enlightened as it teeters on the brink of the precipice like one blinded by darkness. By reflecting on the great evils amid which the person runs and the infinite goods which are being lost, the will is persuaded to control its evil inclinations, conquer its passions, battle itself, and so live and act virtuously: *he sent out his word and healed them, and delivered them from destruction.*[705]

Thus it is that the opportunity for holy and fervent preaching instructs, illuminates, converts and sanctifies people. On the other hand, its absence ruins the spirit and causes the death of souls. This is the tremendous famine and destructive starvation that an offended God spreads through the earth when he chooses to punish severely the

---

[703] Hebrews 4:12.

[704] Isaiah 5:13.

[705] Psalm 107:20 [*DR* 106:20].

ingratitude and corruption of its inhabitants. This is the punishment that all Christian people should fear above all others: *The time is surely coming, says the Lord God, when I will send a famine on the land; not a famine of bread, or a thirst for water, but of hearing the words of the Lord.*[706] This starvation gradually makes the spirit faint, causes virtue to vanish, weakens the will and ultimately kills that purity and honesty of lifestyle with its justice and piety which should be the inseparable companion of all the faithful: *In that day the beautiful young women and the young men shall faint for thirst.*[707] St. Jerome, commenting on this passage, explains the meaning the Lord gives to this starvation and then enumerates its pernicious results: *From this we understand, by losing customary modesty and purity, all the virtues die.* May the divine goodness guard all nations and people from this horrible punishment. Pray God, O priests, that you do not find yourself in the hands of an angry God for being an instrument of such a disaster: the eternal ruin of your people.

In fact, in those areas in which priests either do not want, or do not know, how to preach the divine word with the power, example and zeal that ought to accompany it, one finds a large part of the unfortunate people with a listless and drab faith, a timid hope, a depressed charity and a chaotic religious life: virtue is impeded, the power of Christian discipline is dissipated and all the vices, all the abuses triumph. Who among wise pastors does not recognize this and look for a remedy? Who among those zealous for divine honor and the salvation of their neighbor does not weep over such ruin?

On the other hand, when by great good fortune some fervent missionaries happen upon this scene, or when those areas are provided and fortified with virtuous priests and zealous ministers of holy preaching, watch! The Christian spirit, first battered, scattered and humbled, begins to pull itself together. Those poor little people begin to breathe again in the plentiful light of divine grace and feel themselves effectively moved to change their lives for the better. Faith revives, hopes are lifted in confidence, love grows warm and depressed religious life becomes revitalized and grows better; the places gain back their former religious practice with reverence and veneration. Thus Christian discipline and cult flourish again. Indeed, as happens to plants that are poorly rooted

---

[706] Amos 8:11.

[707] *Ibid.* 8:13.

and left without proper feeding, they lose their strength, they droop, lose color, gradually drop the greenery that graces them. But if it happens that a wise and careful farmer arrives there, who begins to water and cultivate them regularly, they immediately begin to straighten up, regain their vigor, consolidate their forces and begin to send out leaves and flowers and an abundance of fruit, mature and ripe. How sad the persons who lack the proper and opportune watering of the divine word! But happy are those who are watered with this heavenly dew and the course of whose lives are accompanied by this divine light up to the gates of their eternity: *Your word is a lamp to my feet and a light to my path.*[708]

Experience teaches and confirms the marvels of this grand truth. One finds throughout the world entire countries and peoples, or the greater part of their inhabitants, so well taught, en lightened, upright, virtuous and temperate that the land seems a paradise, fertile in virtue and flourishing in elect. Among them is visible the discipline that filled the early Christians. It seems that such virtue is passed on by heredity to such fortunate generations. The origin of such good comes, as these people themselves testify, from what happened to them once (or still is going on): namely, [*the arrival of*] zealous pastors and priests who purposely attended to all the aspects of their office and faithfully and perseveringly practiced the exercise of their ministry. On the other hand, there are peoples so undisciplined and ignorant, so irreverent and irreligious, so blind and vicious, so stupid and insensible to all that pertains to eternal salvation that they bring shame to the holy name of Christian they bear and to the holy religion they profess. But this is the result of the negligence of their pastors and priests who do not pay any attention, or pay little, to instruction, enlightenment, care and direction of those people along the way of eternal salvation with the proper presentation of the divine word along with frequent and attentive administration of the sacrament of reconciliation.

We cannot deny that there are some people with a hard nature of little docility; but they are rare. However, it is true that there is no nation so wild and opposed to good that it cannot be led to a Christian way of life and along a path of duty when all the priests of that land, joined together in commitment and will, attend to their holy ministry with virtue and zeal.

---

[708] Psalm 119:105 [*DR* 118:105].

SECTION TWO

THE DUTY OF PREACHING, NEGLECTED BY MANY PRIESTS

It is truly a bitter spectacle, worth crying over inconsolably, to see such a large number of clerics among whom it is rare to find one who knows how to open his mouth, even to serve the people as a part-time and simple teacher of the divine law and the obligations of Christian faith. Those unfortunate people, like Tantalus in the middle of the lake, are dying of thirst and lacking food amid a crowd of priests who, if they were attentive and zealous, could be teaching and sanctifying not only the areas where they live but entire dioceses and provinces. Those people have reason to complain about the shortcomings of such priests and to mourn the fact that the ministers of their eternal salvation are plentiful but the people find themselves in extreme want and in great peril of failing to gain the kingdom of heaven: *Thou hast multiplied the nation, and hast not increased the joy.*[709] A shame to be wept over in eternal grief!

Priests want to believe that here we are speaking only of those who in justice are bound to the office of preaching and of pastors who ought to feed the sheep assigned to their care with the suitable and abundant opportune sustenance of the divine word and with vigilant and frequent administration of the holy sacraments. It is true that pastors of souls are bound to this obligation by a triple chain: natural reason, divine precept and the laws of the sacred canons demand it of these offices without exception. But it is no less certain that every priest is set apart from others by divine providence and taken from the secular world to be placed in the Church hierarchy for no other reason than to exercise the profession of helping and of healing others for the glory of God: *Every high priest chosen from among mortals is put in charge of things pertaining to God on their behalf.*[710]

The very title you bear, O priest, shows and intimates your obligations. Priest means *sacred Leader, Teacher of the Holy, Giver of the Consecrated.*[711] How can you call yourself a sacred leader if you do not

---

[709] Isaiah 9:3 [DR].

[710] Hebrews 5:1.

[711] *Sacer dux, sacra docens, sacra dans.*

at least join the soldiers of Christ under the standard of the Crucified to conquer the kingdom of heaven? How are you the teacher of divine mysteries if you do not commit yourself to instructing the people in an awareness of the great God and not train them in the sacred laws? How can you be a careful administer of sacred things if you do not attend to acquiring the knowledge that makes you capable of administering the great sacrament of reconciliation, something so useful and necessary for the salvation of the people that need it? Or if you will not watch over and charitably care for the poor dying people? You are a priest in name only, not in fact. You have the character of a priest, but do not fulfill the office. Your work does not appear full and perfect in the eyes of God and you become unworthy of that eternal glory that the Lord promised to those priests who perfectly fulfill the whole of his status: *you have been weighed on the scales and found wanting.*[712]

The tremendous disgrace will befall such a priest as fell on that negligent servant who did not put to use the talent given him by his master. He was declared bad and lacking simply because he was lazy: *You wicked and lazy slave!*[713] For being a useless servant he was condemned to death by his master, sentenced to the eternal darkness: *Throw him into the outer darkness, where there will be weeping and gnashing of teeth.*[714]

Perhaps a priest who is not charged as pastor of souls under strict obligation in justice would not be condemned to hell because he did not attend to the wellbeing of others and did not have zeal for the his neighbor. But surely, by this omission, the offended God will withdraw from this ungrateful man the abundance of his graces, his special assistance, his effective helps, and the other gratuitous gifts that the Divine goodness shares with his faithful servants who respond gratefully. He will also withdraw that final perseverance which opens the gates of paradise: *For judgment will be without mercy to anyone who has shown no mercy.*[715] Oh dear, if only all of us priests had the right to exclaim with the Apostle that we deeply fear for our eternal wellbeing if we do not attend to teaching the people and to run with them along the way to heaven: *An obligation is laid on me, and woe to me*

---

[712] Daniel 5:27.

[713] Matthew 25:26.

[714] *Ibid.* 25:30.

[715] James 2:13.

if I do not proclaim the gospel! [716] This obligation is due either in justice or out of one's vocation; it is an obligation of response, of gratitude owed to our sovereign Lord and greatest benefactor. If you wanted, O priests, to belong to the secular world, to your earthly home, to yourselves, why did you dare to enter into the ranks of the ecclesiastical hierarchy? Why are you, a sterile and fruitless plant, occupying the land and the places in which others might have been placed instead of you, who would have administered those fruits of holy zeal which you are not producing? Do you twist those opportunities, that life, those fruits, not to fit them into the plan of the heavenly farmer who planted you and tended your place in his field but to fatten your family purse and to eat them up in feeding yourselves and spend all your time in laziness and licentiousness: *he came looking for fruit on it and found none. So he said "Cut it down! Why should it be wasting the soil?"* [717]

What are you going to do, then, you priests of God's Church; what are you going to do? What do you think? What consumes your divinely graced life? *Why are you standing here idle all day?* [718] Every other activity, every other care, every business that is not truly for God's sake and for the salvation of souls is a trifle, laziness, a waste of time, and detour from your status and your goal. You who are the angels of the Church Militant, the leaders of the people to the kingdom of heaven, the ministers of eternal salvation should not rest except for the glory of God: the *priesthood shall be theirs by a perpetual ordinance.* [719] Wake up, you leaders of the people, teachers of the world, ministers of the divine word, shake off at once the lethargy of your deadly laziness, and firmly conquer the stupor of your useless life. Raise your eyes of faith, look at the many regions, the numerous people, the countless persons who are famished for the eternal harvest and are already disposed to receive the liveliest movements of grace by means of your apostolic ministry: *Look around you, and see how the fields are ripe for harvesting.* [720] Get up quickly and go again into the vineyard of your heavenly Patron to work: cooperate with his other vigilant workers who night and day are

---

[716] 1 Corinthians 9:16.

[717] Luke 13: 6–7.

[718] Matthew 20:6.

[719] Exodus 29:9.

[720] John 4:35.

at labor: *You also go into the vineyard.*[721] Go and collect the sheaves of elect who are ripe for the heavenly granary. Hurry, at least at this eleventh hour of your day, accompany all the others who are ceaselessly laboring, and you will still receive from your good Patron the payment for the entire day. Better late than never. Who knows, today may be the eleventh hour of your life for you! Who knows if this may not be your final invitation! Who knows if this may not be the ultimate occasion the Divine goodness will offer you for fulfilling part of your priestly ministry after your negligent past and for you to render worthy service for your Church and meritorious actions for eternal life? Amid such great danger for yourself and with such great prejudice to the people, do not flatter yourself, O priests, in the face of every human and divine reason, that this is not the case. It can easily be so, and for many of you, it will indeed be so.

Do not let yourself be fooled by the temptation of undecidedness and diffidence. Do not draw back from the effort due to fear of your inability and insufficiency. There are different offices in the Church of God and many ministers for the wellbeing of his people. Some are possessors of five talents, others of two, for others one is enough. Do what you know how to do; charge yourself and make use of the talent which God has given you and ask God for what you lack. This is the way to fulfill your obligation and to receive abundant help from the goodness of God who is so pleased by persons of good will that he assists at the works undertaken for this glory and honor: *The decrees of the Lord are sure, making wise the simple.*[722] We are only instruments in the hands of God and so we do by ourselves as much as we can; yet, by cooperating with the help of grace we make our ministry efficacious and far more fruitful than the work of those priests who boast of many talents and think that they do everything by their own intelligence and virtue.

It is a fact that many priests who have little confidence in themselves produce fervent and effective work while others, who presume too much on their wisdom, accomplish a ministry that is of little use and profit. The effectiveness of the divine word and its effect on a person's conversion do not depend on the loftiness of ideas, the lilt of sentences, the profundity of the doctrine or the industry and feelings of human beings but rather on

---

[721] Matthew 20:7.

[722] Psalm 19:7 [*DR* 18:8].

the force of divine grace that accompanies sincere and fervent preaching and on the living and simple presentation of the heavenly mysteries: *My speech and my proclamation were not with plausible words of wisdom, but with a demonstration of the Spirit and of power.*[723] This is why St. Gregory asserts that no priest should excuse himself from the exercise of his ministry because he does not know how, he is unable or he does not have the power to perform it. Let each one do what he can and the Lord will supply the rest.

As often as not, this fear is merely illusory and a much too common cloud for priests who have not yet begun to try and they have an overwhelming dread of speaking in public. But in truth, this is a baseless worry; they can do it. How many priests who did not believe they could even open their mouths, shook off this passing fear and overcame their early repugnance to become by divine grace optimal ministers of the divine word. The beginning of new jobs always seems difficult but with practice they quickly become, not just an easy, but rather an enjoyable ministry. If you still do not believe me, in the name of God, give it a try.

Moreover, if some priest were not capable, he can make himself useful. If he is not fit, he can make himself so by applying himself and practicing. Today there are many opportunities for learning and exercise.

SECTION FIVE

SPIRITUAL GUIDELINES FOR CERTAIN SUCCESS IN THE MINISTRY OF HOLY PREACHING

Before going into a discussion of the parts and rules of the profession of preaching in order to instruct churchmen and to organize their ministry of preaching, I think it not only opportune but necessary to take the time to offer a very brief explanation of the spiritual elements needed to assure the work of divine ministry and to reach the wonderful goal of the conversion and sanctification of people. These rules and spiritual advice are so connected to and ingrained in the practice of this holy ministry

---

[723] 1 Corinthians 2:4.

that this art of instruction, without the accompaniment of the science of the saints, will go nowhere. The soul of preaching is the spirit of the one who preaches, a spirit of good example and prayer, a spirit of virtue and perfection, a spirit of zeal and upright intention. Otherwise the divine word will not result in the effective and powerful kind of liveliness and force that will allow it to overcome what is merely human.

We already know by divine faith that preaching has a marvelous force and sovereign effectiveness in so far as it is accompanied by the grace of heaven, which alone can penetrate hearts and move them, soften them, illuminate them, convert them and make them hasten along the way of the holy commandments. Is it not true that the preacher's voice strikes the ear but does not touch the heart unless it comes armed and reinforced with heavenly help? Only the Lord, says the prophet, can give to the one who preaches the Kingdom of God the graces and virtue, the force and efficacy which breaks open the heart and converts the soul: *The Lord shall give the word to them that preach good tidings with great power.*[724] And so it is the case that every priest who exercises this divine ministry ought to be invested with this kind of faith and hope to direct the course of his preaching toward the glory of God and the salvation of others and never place trust in himself, in his talents, in his knowledge, in his artistry of speech. Only by turning to God and confiding in that omnipotent Lord do we obtain our effectiveness and the help to our work; without this help we are only dust and ashes, we are but insects, a mere nothing. All this is divinely expressed when that great Preacher to the Gentiles writes: *Such is the confidence that we have through Christ toward God. Not that we are competent of ourselves to claim anything as coming from us; our competence is from God.*[725]

For this purpose we go on to propose the following spiritual hints without which priests will eat themselves up with fatigue and load their listeners down with burdens; neither will the priests make themselves fit and worthy ministers of the divine word nor will the people be truly converted to God: *Who has made us competent to be ministers of a new covenant, not of letter but of spirit; for the letter kills, but the Spirit gives life.*[726]

---

[724] Psalm 67:12 [DR].

[725] 2 Corinthians 3:4–5.

[726] *Ibid.* 3:6.

Therefore, armed with this faith and strengthened by this trust, priests who accompany their preaching with the activity of holy prayer and implore continuously the effective helps of the Great Father of Lights so that he assists them and directs them in their words, will illumine and convert the people by means of their ministry. St. Augustine requires this attitude in all evangelic preaching in order to render the work fruitful: *That his work may succeed, prayer is a more effective than speaking; therefore, he prays before he preaches.* Prayer is the key to heaven that opens and reopens the doors of the treasures of divine grace that causes our work to turn out upright and properly ordered, strong and effective, most acceptable in the sight of God and full of heavenly fruit in the salvation of the faithful.

Regarding this truth, we have received the writings and example of all those fervent workers who were charged with this apostolic ministry and have drawn an infinite number of persons to God. The Divine Majesty has given us great teachings on this, not the least of which is his going into the desert for forty days before beginning to spread the seeds of his heavenly doctrine by means of the words in his sacred preaching. He retired for prayer onto the mountain or into the desert and in the temple, in order to give us an example and remembrance: *he spent the night in prayer to God.*[727] Priests, therefore, as ministers of preaching, must hold themselves to daily acts of holy prayer, must precede their preaching with prayer, accompany their preaching with prayer and follow their preaching with prayer and thanksgiving to the Giver of All Good Things. To sum up, the preacher must animate all his words with the spirit of holy prayer and must be a man of prayer. In this way his preaching will sanctify his own soul and will save those to whom it is directed: *The virtue of prayer,* says St. Lawrence Justinian, *illumines a person, for prayer solves doubts better than research and more quickly uncovers secrets than study does.*

Even prayer is not enough to enliven sacred preaching unless it is matched by virtuous and holy example, namely: detachment, abstinence, refraining from foolish talk, modesty, humility, patience and acts of charity. The greatest obstacle that gets in the way of people's hearts and prevents them from drawing profit from the divine word is the absence of the practice of these virtues in the preacher and a feeling that he presents little good example. When they ask to see the outcome of his ministry, they

---

[727] Luke 6:12.

become suspicious and, receiving no proof they no longer regard him as a man sent from God for their eternal salvation, but rather an intruder who is seeking his own ends and profit. The majority of the people are moved more by what appears before their eyes than by the intrinsic truth of the topic. They remain persuaded more by example than by words and they respond more willingly to the sight of virtue than to the force of reason. Therefore, what extremely wonderful effects come from preaching accompanied by the holy example of the preacher; on the other hand, how weak and insufficient without this exemplarity of conduct Those holy preachers have won a world for God, converted souls and even unbelievers more by their heroic example than by awesome miracles. In places where many do not consider conversion, not even at the sight of prodigies, they still cannot resist the force of virtue practiced by those who invite them to the awareness and love of the Creator. There is nothing, says the Council of Trent,[728] that better moves the faithful to devotion and excites piety than the upright life, holy conversation, honesty and exemplarity of the priests. Their example is minutely observed and scrutinized by the people and they make a marvelous impression in their hearts, drawing them to imitate them and to receive their instruction with reverence as the voice of God.

Moreover, it happens that the people gain much less from the divine word administered by their local priests because among them one rarely finds a priest living among the people who is held in veneration and is regarded as a man of God, a true minister at the holy altar. The people always notice many of their priests who are proud, irascible, vindictive, wheeler-dealers, litigators, self-interested, unmortified, useless, lazy. They hang around with everybody, in the plazas, or shops or houses and listen to gossip and worldly discussions. Stop this! Preach the word of God and convert people! These priests cannot be distinguished anymore; they are no different than a man of the world, one of the mob; they are, all the same, admired by the worldly, scandalous to the weak. Yesterday with the guys, tomorrow at the altar; yesterday the jokester, today the preacher; yesterday in the market, today in the confessional; yesterday with the gossipers, today in the sanctuary; then they preach and screech but, O God, to what effect? The laity laugh at them in their hearts, turn their backs, think the opposite, or worse, they start to whisper during the

---

[728] Session 22: On reform.

sermon itself and say: if these maxims that our priests preach are true, why don't they practice them? If we are to live in this way, why don't they live it? If they are persuading us to rein in our passions, why are the priests not mortified themselves? If what they preach is worthwhile, why are they not the first to put it into action since they know these things better than we do? And so their preaching not only goes up in smoke but only causes shock, contradiction and murmuring among their people. At the same time that they are correcting the bad actions of others, they are shamefully condemning themselves, says St. John Chrysostom: *Words without action condemn the teacher.* Saintly example, Christian virtues, works of eternal life are what are sought more than words, says St. Thomas, otherwise we are imitating the Pharisees, so often rebuked by the Redeemer because they do not act upon what they preach to others: *they do not practice what they teach.*[729] Learn, O priests, says Salvian, to match your works to your words, and thus, in the ears and in the eyes of your people, your doctrines and teachings will become a harmonious chorus matched to a good life and worthwhile interaction. First bear the noble burden that you want to place on your people and then they will willingly accept it as a desirable means and sweet promise of their eternal salvation: *Let your works fit your words, and yes, your words match the works; and take care to do before you teach. The most beautiful order is this: let the burden that you want to impose first be carried by you.* This is the same as what the Divine Master wished to teach by coming into the world to care for his people, no less by his admirable life than by his preaching the heavenly doctrine: he preceded his teaching with a period of thirty years filled with the holiest interaction during which he did not preach with his voice but preached nevertheless, and very effectively, by his holy example: *I wrote about all that Jesus did and taught from the beginning.*[730]

Recall the advice that the Apostle gave never to offend with the shadow of bad conduct the mind of another so that your holy ministry does not fall into derision: *we are putting no obstacle in anyone's way, so that no fault may be found with our ministry.*[731] Instead, let others experience you as true ministers of the Most High God in every action you take, in your exercise of every type of virtue: *we have commended ourselves in every*

---

[729] Matthew 23:3.

[730] Acts 1:1.

[731] 2 Corinthians 6:3.

way: through great endurance, etc.[732] Take to heart the honor of God, the honor of the Church, the honor of your status. Thus your lives, O priests, accompanied by those three noble endowments and properties described by St. Bernard as characteristics of every minister of the holy altar, namely, the fervor of holy preaching, the aroma of holy prayer, and the example of virtuous interaction, will make you pleasing in the sight of God, precious to the salvation of the people, profitable to yourselves and worthy of the sanctity of your status: *The example of life, the word of preaching, the fruit of prayer.*

It is true that the above-mentioned virtues cannot be separated from the exercise of self-mortification which truly enlivens the spirit, purifies it, and centers it ever more on God. The more persons mortify their exterior, the more is their interior comforted and revived, and the more lively and fervently do its expressions well up out of the heart. These then produce marvelous effects in converting others by means of that divine grace which triumphs all the better and is communicated to those hearts that it finds more mortified and more emptied of self-love. With these weapons holy people have won and overcome hell, have conquered hearts and have made their ministry full and perfect. That is what the Divine Majesty wishes to get us to understand in that great lesson that he left us in the Holy Gospel: *Very truly, I tell you, unless a grain of wheat falls into the earth and dies, it remains just a single grain; but if it dies, it bears much fruit.*[733]

Still, these are not the only qualities that should adorn a minister of holy preaching, for even the one who possesses them must still not lack the following ones. He must administer the divine word with fervor and zeal, solely for the increase of the glory of God and with a lively desire to convert and save others. These efforts will then give birth in the preacher to those vivacious and penetrating feelings, those burning and fervent expressions, those ardent and heavenly affections which create a loving violence in his listeners and convert them to God with marvelous effectiveness. Those cannot fail in their preaching to people of the eternal mysteries and the wonders of the next world in this way if they have an awareness of the greatness and goodness of their God, if they recognize the preciousness and beauty of an immortal soul

---

[732] *Ibid.* 6:4.

[733] John 12:24.

made in the image of its Creator, and redeemed by the blood and death of a God-made-man, if they love the salvation of their neighbor, if they have heartfelt compassion for the blindness and ignorance of those poor little ones who do not realize their eternal dangers and are running along the path of perdition.

Moreover, it is proper that the preaching be substantial and solid, full of the eternal truths, supported in the sacred Scriptures and the holy Gospel. Those great maxims must be explained with exactness and sincerity and with the proper expressions and ceremonies that the sacredness of the doctrine deserves, in imitation of our Divine Lord and Master and according to the examples of the holy Fathers and of those zealous preachers who speak of nothing other than Jesus crucified. This demands preaching without frills, without affectation, without human conceits, without shadow or dirt of self-love and self-esteem. Not in studied formality, not with strange terminology, not with wandering erudition, but with God in their hearts and with their hearts on their lips. Otherwise, the preacher's voice makes noise in the ear, but does not reach within; it feeds the mind but really does not move the will to detest sin, to rise from vices, to embrace virtue and to love their Creator, the Highest Good.

Pay attention to the strange difference which always exists from one preacher to the next. A learned man speaks after having spent many months at his books to form and learn his preaching; it is possible he will speak it plausibly but it will be without the slightest fruit of eternal life, without awakening one good act, one devout affection, one Christian resolution from his large audience. All his fine oratory has gone up in smoke; you cannot recognize whether he has proclaimed his own talents or the eternal truths; he has preached himself rather than Jesus Christ. Perhaps, it could better be said we realize that he has proclaimed his own doctrine and sought to gain applause and fame, but he did not think about glorifying his Lord and converting his neighbor. Whoever does not wish to believe this in theory must believe it in the effects it produces in those who listen to the preaching.

On the other hand, when a true minister of the holy altar preaches, he is informed by the spirit of God; he possesses the science of the saints; he approaches his office solely for the glory of the Lord and for the salvation of souls; he shows a manner of simple and sincere feelings; he presents divine truth, honestly and plainly with ordinary language but fervently and animatedly, as well as with apostolic words [*Such a preacher*] reaches, converts, and draws to God not just one person or one people, but the entire world. Here is the reason for the great difference: the famous preacher speaks to his audience as a man, in a way pleasing to human genius, based on human wisdom. The zealous preacher also speaks as a man to his listeners, but only about the glory of God, in order to draw souls to God, trusting in God, or to put it better, God preaches through the instrument of a man of holy and upright intention, invested with the spirit of God. This was all well known to the most illustrious and learned Cardinal Bona who wrote: *A sermon the arises from natural instincts, even though it contains many good things in itself, is devoid of fruit, like a noisy wind and clashing cymbal. But the words filled with the Spirit of God, even if unimpressive and very simple in themselves, bear abundant fruit.*[734]

The venerable teacher Avila, an apostolic preacher, was asked what he thought about a learned sermon given that morning by the young Father Louis Granada. He frankly responded in the presence of the preacher himself that to his mind such discourses simply had no appeal when he did not often hear the name of Jesus and St. Paul. The wise young priest took advantage of this remark, thought about it himself and changed his style. From that time on, he preached Jesus Crucified from his heart and in this way produced marvelous results in countless persons as is well known. This is the purpose and the result of the [*priestly*] vocation and preaching: instruction, conversion and sanctification of others to draw them to the possession of eternal life: *I appointed you to go and bear fruit, fruit that will last.*[735] When we arrive to the point of profoundly understanding with the Apostle that we are nothing but dust and ashes, that all the good we do and say is God's grace and mercy (*by the grace of God I am what I am*),[736] we can then praise ourselves along with him, by glorifying God that his divine grace did not issue fruitlessly from our ministry, but rather abundantly and superabundantly for the sanctification of ourselves and for the salvation of the world: *his grace toward me has not been in vain.*[737]

---

[734] De discret. Sp. Chapter 14.

[735] John 15:16.

[736] 1 Corinthians 15:10.

[737] *Ibid.*

The only thing left to say is to remind you ministers of sacred preaching that after having yourselves practiced personally all the rules and all the arts of the science of preaching and of the spirit of preaching, you must never choose to regard yourself as deserving and worthy of converting people to God and of carrying out your ministry excellently. Think of yourselves always as useless servants who have only fulfilled some portion of your obligations toward your supreme Lord: *When you have done all that you were ordered to do, say, "We are worthless slaves; we have done only what we ought to have done!"*[738]

---

[738] Luke 17:10.

BIBLIOGRAPHY OF MAJOR WRITINGS
OF GENNARO MARIA SARNELLI

[The years of publication in this bibliography are based on those given by Maurice de Meulemeester, CSsR, for the first edition of the works that were included in his Bibliografie générale des écrivains rédemptoristes, II, 1935, 373–377. *Titles of Sarnelli's works have slight variations in different editions of the writings; the most complete title in the English editor's opinion is given below. The edition used by the translator, unless noted differently in a footnote, was the edition published in Naples: Tipografia e Liberia di A. E. S. Festa, 1888. 14 volumes.*

To the editor's knowledge, none of these works, or even extended sections of them, have been translated into English. Sarnelli published at least ten additional short works on spiritual subjects beginning in 1732; seven unfinished manuscripts were found after his death.

The booklet **Massime Eterne (Eternal Maxims)** *is not included because it is generally attributed to St. Alphonsus Liguori (1732 edition) although Sarnelli published the work first, in 1728(?). In the early years of publication, the two men closely shared their writings so such coincidences of the early writings are not fully explained.]* [739]

1733

La via facile e sicura del Paradiso [Volume I] *Opera divisa in due tomi utilissima a secolari, ecclesiastici, e religiosi, per facilitare a ciascun anima l'esercizio della vita divo ta, e per introdurla in commune nelle parrochie comu nità e famiglie. Che contieni la necessità, la facilità, e l'efficacia*

---

[739] See Fabriciano Ferrero's article in Chapter Three of this volume, Section VIII, on the early Redemptorist apostolate of the pen.

dell'orazione mentale, col metodo, e co'suoi atti pratici, con varj trattati meditativi, colle pratiche so pra le massime eterne, e varie conzonicine divote. Naples, 1933. (The Easy and Sure Way to Paradise. A Very Useful Work Divided into Two Volumes for the Laity, Church men and Religious to Help Each Status of Person Live a Devout Life, and to Introduce it into Parishes, Communities, and Families in Common. Which Contains the Necessity, Ease and Effectiveness of Mental Prayer, with a Method and with its Practical Activities Along with Some Topics for Meditation, as Well as with Practices About the Eternal Truths and Some Devout Little Hymns.)

La via facile e sicura del Paradiso. Tomo secondo, che contiene la quinta parte dell'opera, cioè vari avvertimenti, atti, e considerazioni, per preparazione, e ringraziamento alla confessione, e communione, un lungo esame per la confessione generale, quindeci considerazioni istruttive sopra il SS. Sagramento dell'Eucaristia e sua visita. Con molti discorsetti e colle pratiche sopra la santa Messa; la preghiera; la divozione alla gran Tinità, a Maria Santissima e sue novene, agli angioli, a' santi, ed alle anime del Purgatorio. Con le regole e cogli atti per la matina, e per la sera, e con altre divozioni, ed esercizi, per ben regolare la vita, e morire santamente. Naples, 1733. (The Easy and Sure Way to Paradise, Second Volume, which Contains the Fifth Part of the Work, Namely, Some Advice, Acts and Considerations for Preparation and Thanksgiving at Confession and Communion, a Long Examination of Conscience for a General Confession, Fifteen Instructive Considerations About the Blessed Sacrament and Visits. With Many Points and Practices for holy Mass; Prayer, Devotions to the Great Trinity and the Most Holy Mary and her Novenas, to the Angels and Saints and for the Souls in Purgatory. With the Rules and Exercises for Morning and Evening, Along with Other Devotions and Activities for a Well Regulated Life and a Holy Death.)

1736

Ragioni legali, cattoliche, e politiche in difesa delle republiche rovinate dall'insolentito meretricio. Naples, 1736. (Legal, Catholic and Political Reasons in Defense of Republics Ruined by Blatant Prostitution.)

Divozioni pratiche per onorare la SS. Trinità e Maria SS. Operetta nuova, impressa ad istanza d'un'idegno secolare.

1738

Naples, 1736. (Practical Devotions to Honor the Most Holy Trinity and the Most Holy Mary. A New Short Work, Published at the Request of a Worthy Layman.)

Il quatro maggio 1738 in Napoli, a futura memoria dei posteri e per esempio di ogni cattolica nazione, Napoli 1738 (The 4th of May 1738 in Naples, a Future Memorandum for Posterity and as an Example for All Catholic Nations.)

Il mondo santificato [Volume I] *dove si tratta della meditazione e della preghiera. Opera istruttiva ed illuminativa utilissima ai secolari, ecclesiastici, e religiosi, per facilitare a ciascuno stato di anime l'esercizio della vita divota, e per introdurre nella Chiesa Comunitá e famiglie l'uso dell'orazione in commune.* Naples, 1738. (The World Sanctified Which Treats of Meditation and Prayer. An Instructive and Illuminative Work Very Useful for Laity, Churchmen and Religious to Facilitate in Each State of Life the Practice of The Devout Life and to Introduce into the Catholic Community and Families the Use of Common Prayer.)

Il mondo santificato [Volume II] *Opera utilissima per ogni stato di anime che contiene nella prima parte le pratiche per l'oratione in particolare ed in comune. Nella seconda parte: meditazioni sopra le massime eterne per la vita purgativa.* Naples, 1738. (The World Sanctified. A Very Useful Work for Every State of Life That Contains in the First Part Activities for Both Individual and Common Prayer. In the Second Part Meditations on the Eternal Truths and the Purgative Life.)

Il mondo riformato nell'istituzione, ed educazione de' fanciulli. Opera utilissima per gli ecclesiastici, e per li padri di famiglia. Dove si dimostra l'obbligo grande, ch'essi anno d'allevar cristianamente la gioventù. Colle maniere pratiche per la buona educazione. Naples, 1738. (The World Reformed through the Instruction and Education of Children. A Most Useful Work for Churchmen and for Parents of Families. In Which Is Demonstrated the Great

1739

Obligation They Have to Raise Children in a Christian Manner. With Practical Ways for Good Education.)

Le sagre congregazioni ad onor di Maria SS., utilissime al cristianesimo, colle regole facili, e brievi da osservarsi da'congregati. Colle maniere da introdurre le congregazioni di spirito, che chiamansi segrete, e sue regole. Naples, 1739. (The Holy Confraternities in Honor of the Most Holy Mary, Very Useful for Christianity, with Short and Easy Rules to be Followed by Members. With the Manner for Starting Spiritual Confraternities, Called "Private," and Their Rules.)

Il Cristiano santificato. Opera utilissima per ogni stato di anime, che contiene le meditazioni per la vita purgativa, ed illuminativa, con varie regole, atti, ed esercizi per vivere cristianamente. Colle novene per le feste di Maria Santissima, e sue pratiche. Naples, 1739. (The Christian Sanctified. A Very Useful Work for Every State of Life that Contains Meditations for the Purgative Life, as Well as for the Illuminative, with Some Rules, Acts and Activities in Order to Live in a Christian Manner. With Novenas for the Feasts of Mary Most Holy and Their Practices.)

Considerazioni sulle glorie, e grandezze della Divina Madre per prepararsi colle novene alle sue feste, e solennità, e per introdurre, e facilitare nelle chiese, communità, e famiglie l'esercizio in comune delle Sante novene. Naples, 1739. (Considerations on the Glory and Greatnesses of the Mother of God for Preparing Oneself by Novenas for Her Feasts and Solemnities, and for Introducing and Conducting the Community Activities of the Holy Novena in Churches, Communities and Families.) *[This work was republished as an appendix to Il Cristiano santificato in the 1740 edition.]*

Il mondo riformato. Opera utilissima per ogni stato di anime, che contiene vari trattati istruttivi e illuminativi sopra le principali obbligazioni del Cristiano. Naples, 1739. (The World Reformed. A Very Useful Work for Every State of Life that Contains Several Instructive and Enlightening Treatments on the Principal Obligations of a Christian.)

Il mondo riformato. Sagre lezioni contro agli abusi. Opera utilissima, che istruisce, e illumina il Cristiano negli obbligi di sua religione. Colle regole, e cogli atti per un santo tenor di vita. Naples, 1739. (The World Reformed. Sacred Lessons Against Abuses. With Rules and Acts for a Holy Standard of Life.)

All'ecclesiastica gerarchia, a' baroni, ed a' magistrati, per frenare gli abusi della bestemmia, e disonestà. Naples, 1739. (To The Ecclesiastical Hierarchy, to Barons, and Magistrates, in Order to End the Abuses of Blasphemy and Prostitution.)

Breve Notizia per introdurre exercizio dell'orazione. Si tratta della necessità e dell'efficacia della preghiera colle regole, e maniere da renderla fruttuosa, ed efficace, colle pratiche, e cogli atti, per far l'orazione in comune nelle chiese, comunità, e famiglie. Si propone la visita as SS. Sacramento ed all Divina Madre, l'esercizio per ascoltare con gran frutto la S. Messa, gli atti prima, e dopo la confessione, e comunione, con varie di pratiche, ed esercizi Cristiani. Naples, 1739. (A Brief Note for Introducing the Exercise of Prayer. Treatment of the Necessity and Efficacy of Prayer with Rules and Ways to Make it Fruitful and Efficacious, with Practices and Acts for Making Prayer in Common in Churches, Communities and Families. The Visits to the Blessed Sacrament and the Mother of God are Proposed as Well as Exercises for Attending Mass with Great Fruitfulness, as well as Activities Before and After Confession and Communion with Various Practices and Christian Activities.)

Aggiunta delle maniere particolari da racchiudere, e rattener perpetuamente a freno le meretrici, da ricapitare le ravvedute, da conservar le fanciulle pericolanti, e manetener sempre purgata la repubblica dalle dissolutezze carnali.

Colle risposte alle opposizioni. Naples, 1739. (Further Thoughts on the Particular Ways of Separating and Permanently Maintaining a Brake on Prostitution. On Rehabilitating the Repentant. On Protecting Young Girls in Danger. On Keeping the State Forever Free from Carnal Dissolution. With Responses to Objections.)

Ragioni cattoliche, legali, e politiche in difesa delle republiche rovinate dall'insolentito meretricio. Coll'aggiunta delle maniere da restringere, e frenare le meretrici, da conservare le fanciulle pericolanti, e mantenere le contrade purgate dalle carnali dissolutezze. E si risponde alle opposizioni. Naples, 1739. (Catholic, Legal and Political Reasons in defense of the State ruined by Blatant Prostitution. Further Thoughts on the Particular Ways of Lessening and Permanently Maintaining a Break on Prostitution; On Rehabilitating the Repentant; On Saving Young Girls in Danger; On Keeping the State Forever Free From Carnal Dissolution; With a Response to the Opposition.) *[A combined edition of the original 1936* Ragioni *and the 1939* Aggiunta.*]*

Ristretto delle ragioni cattoliche e legali e politiche in difesa delle republiche rovinate dall'insolentito meretricio..., Napoli 1739 *[A synopsis of the prior work.]*

1740

L'anima desolata, confortata a patir cristianamente, colla considerazione delle massime eterne. Operetta istruttiva, ed illuminativa, utilissima per le persone tribolate, che attendono all'esercizio dell'orazione, ed al cammino della perfezione. Naples, 1740. (The Desolate Soul, Comforted to Suffer in a Christian Way with Consideration of the Eternal Truths. An Instructive and Illuminative Booklet, Very Useful for Troubled Persons Who Pay Attention of the Exercise of Prayer and the Road of Perfection.)[740]

L'anima illuminata, nella considerazione de'beneficii di Dio, generali, e particolar, nell'ordine della natura, e della grazia. Con varii tratti illuminativi, utilissimi, ed acconci ad ogni stato di anime, per accendersi nell'amore del sommo Benefattore. Naples, 1740. (The Illumined Soul, in Considering the Blessings of God in General and in Particular, in the Order of Nature and of Grace. With Some Illuminating, Very Useful Treatments, Suitable for Every State of Life in Order to Stir Oneself to the Love of the Great Benefactor.)

---

[740] Regarding the importance of this work for later generations: This work was republished six times in the 18th Century and on into the 19th. See M. de Meulemeester, *Bibliographie*, Il, 373–377. Its structure is as follows: Part 1. The blessings of God amid trials, desolation, sickness and crosses (p 7).The marvelous effects of suffering are shown, both in the regard to the good of the person who suffers, as well as in the glory it gives God (p. 62).Part 2. The wiles of the devil by which he tries to disturb the desolate soul are uncovered. Responses to their difficulties and scruples (p. 141), Part 3. Some lives of saintly persons who were troubled and desolate, their virtuous suffering (p. 193). Meditations on the dolors of Mary at the foot of the cross (p. 274). A service for the Feast of Mary Desolate with a description of the Risen One and ending with the singing of the Regina Coeli (p. 303–304).Devout Hymns. Canzoncine divote (p. 305–308). The Alphabet of Perfection (p. 309). (See Ferrero, *El Beato Janero Mᵃ Sarnelli...*, p. 20).

Il Cristiano illuminato nei pensieri di vita eterna per la via purgativa and nei sentimenti per la via illuminata. Diretto nella via della divozione colle regole e pratiche per avanzarsi nella perfezione. Ammaestrato nei misteri della religione e negli obblighi di sua professione. Santificato contenente le meditazioni per la vita purgativa ed illuminativa, e varie regole, atti ed esercizi per vivere cristianamente e salvarsi. Opera utilissima ad ogni stato di persone. Naples, 1740 (The Christian Illuminated in Thoughts of Eternal Life Through the Purgative Way and in Sentiments for the Illuminative Way. Directed Along the Way of Devotion with Rules and Practices for Advancing in Perfection. Trained in the Mysteries of Religion and in the Obligations of Perfection. Sanctified with Meditations for the Purgative and Illuminative Life and Various Rules, Acts and Exercises for Living in a Christian Manner and for Salvation. A Very Useful Work for Every Status of Person.)

Opera contro all'abuso della bestemmia. Tomo unico, diviso in tre libri. A'principi, a' baroni, a' magistrati, a' sagri prelati della Chiesa, a' parrochi, a' predicatori, a' confessori. Colle regole, maniere e pratiche, ordinate, per frenare quel delitto. Naples, 1740. (A Work Opposing the Abuse of Blasphemy. A Single Volume, Divided into Three Books. To the Princes, Barons, Magistrates and Holy Prelates of the Church, to Parish Priests, Preachers and Confessors. With the Rule, Manner and Actions Directed to Restrain this Crime.)

Maniere efficacissime, proposte a' sagri pastori e vescovi della Chiesa per bandire l'esecrando abuso della bestemmia, giusta gli ordini e le regole de' sommi pontefici, de'concilii, ed a tenor delle pratiche de' santi prelati. Naples, 1740 (Very Effective Procedures Proposed to the Sacred Pastors and Bishops of the Church for Blocking the Disgraceful Abuse of Blasphemy, Properly According to the Orders and Rules of the Supreme Pontiff, the Councils and According to the Practice of Holy Prelates.)

Ragionamenti istruttivi, ed illuminativi contra il vizio della bestemmia a' parrochi, ed a' predicatori. Coll'istruzione pratica, e co' casi morali a' confessori per ascoltar le confessioni de' bestemmiatori, e renderli emendati. E colle maniere da far opportunamente la fraterna correzione a quie' viziosi. Naples, 1740. (An Instructive and Illuminative Rationale Against the Vice of Blasphemy for Pastors and Preachers. With

Practical Instruction and Moral Cases for Confessors Who Hear the Confessions of Blasphemers and for Getting them to Amend. With the Way to make Fraternal Correction for These Vicious Acts.)

1741

Della discrezione degli spiriti. Operetta instruttive, iluminativa e direttiva per regola e cautela delle anime che attendono all'esercizio della orazione ed al cammino della perfezione, e loro Direttori. Naples, 1741. (On the Discernment of Spirits. An Instructive, Illuminating and Directive Little Work for the Regulation and Warnings for Souls Who Attend to the Exercise of Prayer and to the Road Toward Perfection, and for their Directors.)

1742

L'ecclesiastico santificato nelle istruzioni del suo ministero. Opera utilissima, dove si tratta della frequenza della S. Communione, del gran sagrificio della Messa, de'suoi misterj, e cerimonie. Colle pratiche per ascoltarla, e celebrarla con gran frutto, e della riverenza alle Chiese. Naples, 1942. (The Priest Sanctified in the Carrying Out of his Ministry. A Very Useful Work in Which is Treated the Frequency of Communion, of the Great Sacrifice of the Mass, of its Mysteries and Ceremonies. With Practices for Attending and Celebrating it Very Fruitfully, and of Reverence for the Church.)

1743

Il Cristiano diretto nel cammino della devozione. Istruzione spirituale, che contiene in compendio le Regole, gli Avvertimenti, le Pratiche, per guida, e profitto dell'Anime, che desiderano introdursi, ed avvanzarsi nella Via della Perfezione. The second part treats of *Il Cristiano illuminato, ammaestrato, e diretto ne'Pensieri di Vita Eterna, negli obblighi pnncipali di sua Religione, nel Cammino della Vita spirituale.* Naples, 1743. (The Christian Directed Along the Path of Devotion. Spiritual Instruction, which Contains in Brief the Rules, the Events, the Practice, for the Guidance and Profit of Souls that Desire to Be Introduced and to Advance in the Road of Perfection. The Second Part Treats of the Christian Illuminated, Taught and Directed in

Thoughts of Eternal Life, in the Principle Obligations of Religion, in the Path of the Spiritual Life.)

Pie pratiche di devozione alla Santissima Trinità e a Maria Santissima per la preparazione ad una buona morte da farsi una volta ogni mese. Naples, 1743. (Pious Practice of Devotion to the Most Holy Trinity and to Mary Most Holy to Be Made Once Every Month as a Preparation for a Good Death.)

CPSIA information can be obtained at www.ICGtesting.com
Printed in the USA
LVOW10s0221041215

464902LV00002B/2/P

9 780764 825484